THE
ROOTS
OF AFRICAN CONFLICTS

Edited by
ALFRED NHEMA & PAUL TIYAMBE ZELEZA

The Roots of African Conflicts

The Resolution of African Conflicts

THE
ROOTS
OF AFRICAN CONFLICTS

The Causes & Costs

Edited by
ALFRED NHEMA
Executive Secretary, The Organization for Social Science Research
in Eastern & Southern Africa (OSSREA) Addis Ababa
&
PAUL TIYAMBE ZELEZA
University of Illinois at Chicago

Published
in association with
OSSREA
Addis Ababa

JAMES CURREY
Oxford

OHIO UNIVERSITY PRESS
Athens

UNISA PRESS
Pretoria

OSSREA in association with

James Currey Ltd
73 Botley Road
Oxford OX2 OBS
www.jamescurrey.co.uk

Ohio University Press
19 Circle Drive
The Ridges
Athens, Ohio 45701
www.ohioedu/oupress
www.ohioswallow.com

Unisa Press
P.O. Box 392
Unisa
Muckleneuk 0003
www.unisa.ac.za/press

1 2 3 4 5 12 11 10 09 08 08

ISBN   978-1-84701-300-2 (James Currey paper)
ISBN 10: 0-8214-1809-2 (Ohio University Press paper)
ISBN 13: 978-0-8214-1809-3 (Ohio University Press paper)
ISBN 13: 978-1-86888-492-6 (Unisa Press paper)

British Library Cataloguing in Publication Data
The roots of African conflicts : the causes & costs
1. Political violence - Africa 2. Low-intensity conflicts
(Military science) - Africa 3. Africa - Politics and
government - 1960-
I. Nhema, Alfred G. II. Zeleza, Tiyambe, 1955-
355'.0218'096

Library of Congress Cataloging-in-Publication Data
available on request

Typeset in 10/11 pt Photina
with Castellar display
by Long House, Cumbria
Printed and bound in Malaysia

Contents

List of Tables & Figures

Tables

Figures

Acknowledgements

This book is the outcome of the OSSREA's Research Programme on *African Conflicts* that sponsored an international conference titled 'African Conflicts: Management, Resolution, Post-conflict Recovery and Development' which was held at the United Nations Conference Centre (UNCC) in Addis Ababa, Ethiopia, from 29 November to 1 December 2004. The conference's major objective was to provide a platform by means of which various stakeholders could present their findings on various themes focusing on conflict management and resolution as well as post-conflict recovery and development. The conference also provided a forum through which participants could share experiences learnt in the area of conflict management and recovery.

Over 180 participants attended the conference which was officially opened by His Excellency, Ato Girma Woldegiorgis, the President of the

Federal Democratic Republic of Ethiopia. International participants included academics, researchers, members of the diplomatic corps, members of Parliament, representatives of regional and international organizations, operatives of non-governmental organizations, policy-makers and donors.

A total of 62 papers were presented at the conference under the following nine themes:

- Conflict Prevention, Management and Resolution
- Economic Policies and Poverty Reduction
- Elections, Political Parties and Sustainable Development
- Elections, Political Parties and Democratic Consolidation
- Ethnic Conflict, Policies and Development
- Democracy Consolidation and Development
- Peace-building, Post-conflict Rehabilitation and Development
- Religion, Health and Society
- Human Rights, Gender and Human Security

The papers in this volume and its companion volume, Nhema & Zeleza (eds), *The Resolution of African Conflicts: The Management of Conflict Resolution & Post-Conflict Reconstruction*, review several strategies intended to ensure conflict resolution and post-conflict recovery in Africa. The ranges of interventions which are examined in the various chapters include, *inter alia*: negotiation frameworks within the extant economic, social, political and cultural configurations; the role of international actors and regional organizations like the African Union and the International Criminal Court, and sub-regional organizations; the utilization of continental early warning systems; and finally a discussion on the role of democratic constitutional governance as a panacea for conflict resolution in Africa.

OSSREA acknowledges the financial support of the Swedish International Development Cooperation Agency (Sida/Sarec), the Norwegian Agency for Development Cooperation (NORAD), and the Netherlands Ministry of Foreign Affairs for this initiative and other OSSREA research activities. We also appreciate the input of the OSSREA Secretariat who in many ways have contributed to the success of this project.

The original versions of the chapters by Errol A. Henderson and Thandika Mkandawire were published in *Studies in Comparative International Development* 35 (2) (2000) and *The Journal of Modern African Studies* 40 (2) (2002) respectively and we would like to thank the two journals for their permission to republish them here.

Alfred Gwarega Nhema
Executive Secretary
The Organization for Social Science Research
in Eastern and Southern Africa (OSSREA)
Addis Ababa

Paul Tiyambe Zeleza
Professor and Head
Department of African American Studies
University of Illinois at Chicago

Notes on Contributors

Abdel Ghaffar M. Ahmed is Professor of Social Anthropology, University of Khartoum, Sudan and Professor II University of Bergen, Norway. He is also former Executive Secretary of OSSREA (1992–2002). His recent publications include: *Anthropology in the Sudan: Reflection by a Sudanese anthropologist* (2003), *African Pastoralism: Conflict, Institutions and Government* (2001), *Africa in Transformation: Political and Economic Transformation and Socio-Economic Development Responses in Africa*, 2 volumes (2000), and *Environment and Sustainable Development in Eastern and Southern Africa: Some Critical Issues* (1998).

John Akokpari has taught at Dalhousie University, Canada and the University of Lesotho, and is currently a Senior Lecturer in the Department of Political Studies at the University of Cape Town. His recent publications include, 'The AU, NEPAD and the Promotion of Good Governance in Africa', *Nordic Journal of African Studies* (2004), 'Ghana: Economic Dependence and Marginalised Foreign Policy-Making' in *Diplomacy and Developing Nations: Post-Cold War Foreign Policy-Making Structures and Processes* (2005), and 'Citizenship and the Immigration Debate in Lesotho', *Development Southern Africa* 22 (1), 2005.

Errol A. Henderson is Associate Professor of Political Science at Pennsylvania State University. His specializations include international relations theory, analysis of war and peace, culture and world politics, African politics and African-American political ideology. His major publications include *Afrocentrism and World Politics: Towards a New Paradigm* (1995) and *Democracy and War: The End of an Illusion?* (2002), and he has published numerous articles in such journals as *International Studies Quarterly, Journal of Conflict Resolution, Journal of Peace Research, Journal of Politics, Peace & Change, World Affairs, Studies in Comparative International Development,* and *International Interactions.*

Cephas Lumina is Senior Lecturer, Faculty of Law, University of KwaZulu-Natal, South Africa. He is the co-author of *Forms of Business Enterprise: Theory, Structure and Operation* (2004), and *Dare to Call it Treason: Outlines of a Counter-Coup Strategy in Law* (2005), as well as book chapters and monographs, such as 'Political Conditionality and its Implications for Human Rights: The Case of Zambia' in *The Quest for Peace in Africa: Transformations, Democracy and Public Policy* (2004), *Administrative Law* (2002) and *Constitutional Law* (2002).

Sandra J. MacLean is an Associate Professor of Political Science at Simon Fraser University, British Columbia, Canada. Her research mostly focuses on

Southern Africa and is concerned with governance and globalization, related to issues of health, human security and development. Among her most recent publications are co-edited volumes, *Advancing African Security and Development* (2002) and *Crises of Governance in Asia and Africa* (2001), and articles in *Third World Quarterly, Global Networks, Canadian Foreign Policy, Canadian Journal of Development Studies, New Political Economy* and *Journal of Contemporary African Studies,* and as chapters in a number of edited volumes.

Ali A. Mazrui is the Albert Schweitzer Professor in the Humanities and Director, Institute of Global Cultural Studies at Binghamton University, State University of New York, Binghamton, NY. He is author or co-author of more than twenty books, including *The Power of Babel: Language and Governance in the African Experience* (1998), *Black Reparations in the Era of Globalization* (2002), and *The African Predicament and the American Experience: A Tale of Two Edens* (2004) as well as numerous articles in scholarly journals and the public media. In addition to his written work, he is also creator of the BBC television series *The Africans: A Triple Heritage* (1986).

Pamela Mbabazi is a Development Planner by training and is currently Dean of the Faculty of Development Studies at Mbarara University of Science and Technology, Uganda. Her research interests include governance issues, the impact of globalization on third world countries and peace-building issues. Recent publications include *Supply Chain and Liberalisation of the Milk Industry in Uganda* (2005) and *The Potentiality of African Developmental States; Uganda and Botswana Compared* (2005), and articles including 'Ethnicities in Crises of Governance in Africa: The Case of Uganda in the Great Lakes Region' (2001) and 'Governance for Reconstruction in Africa: Challenges for Policy Communities and Coalitions' (2002).

Thandika Mkandawire is Director of the United Nations Research Institute for Social Development (UNRISD) and former Executive Secretary of the Council for the Development of Social Science Research in Africa (CODESRIA). He is a member of the editorial boards of *Africa Development, Africa Review of Books, Development and Change, Global Governance, Journal of Development Studies, Journal of Human Development* and *Oxford Development Studies,* and has recently served on the executive committees of various international organizations. Author of numerous essays, his recent books include *African Intellectuals: Rethinking Politics, Language, Gender and Development* (2005); *Social Policy in a Development Context* (2004); and *Our Continent our Future: African Perspectives on Structural Adjustment* (2 volumes) (1999).

Timothy M. Shaw is Professor of Human Security and Peacebuilding at Royal Roads University, British Columbia, Canada and was most recently Professor of Commonwealth Governance and Development and Director of the Institute of Commonwealth Studies, University of London. He has taught at Dalhousie University in Nova Scotia for thirty years and been a visiting faculty member at the Universities of Ife, Zambia and Zimbabwe, and continues as Visiting Professor at Mbarara University in Uganda and Stellenbosch University in South Africa. Recent publications include contributions to Hawkesworth and Kogan, *Routledge Encyclopedia of Government and Politics* (2004), Hocking and McGuire, *Trade Politics* (2004), and Stubbs and Underhill, *Political Economy & the Changing Global Order* (2005).

Fondo Sikod is Associate Professor of Economics at the University of Yaounde ll in Cameroon. He is the author or co-author of several articles, including most recently, 'Evolution of Poverty in Rural Cameroon in the Era of Globalization' (2003), 'Challenges of Reconciling Informal and Formal Land and Resource Access Tenure: Evidence from WWF-supported Conservation Sites in Cameroon. In the Proceedings' (2003), 'Prospects for Sub-Sahara Africa to Grow in an Era Dominated by the Knowledge and Information Technology' (2002), 'Macroeconomic Effects of External Debt Servicing in Cameroon' (2002), and 'Constraints to Managing Urban Poverty in Cameroon' (2001).

Aaronette M. White is an Assistant Professor of Women's Studies and African and American Studies at Pennsylvania State University. She has taught and conducted research at Harvard University, the University of Amsterdam, the University of Suriname, and the University of the Western Cape in South Africa. Her most recent publications include 'Racial and Gender Attitudes as Predictors of Feminist Activism among Self-identified African American Feminists,' *Journal of Black Psychology*, 'African American Feminist Fathers' Narratives of Parenting,' *Journal of Black Psychology*, 'Psychology Meets Women's Studies greets Black Studies, treats Queer Studies: Teaching diversity and sexuality across disciplines,' *Feminist Teacher*, 'Talking Feminist, Talking Black: Micromobilization Factors in a Collective Protest against Rape,' *Gender & Society*, and 'Teaching Community Psychology in Postapartheid South Africa,' *Teaching of Psychology*.

Paul Tiyambe Zeleza, is Professor and Head, Department of African American Studies at the University of Illinois at Chicago, and formerly Director of the Center for African Studies at the University of Illinois at Urbana-Champaign. He is also Adjunct Professor of History and African and African-American Studies at Pennsylvania State University and Honorary Professor at the University of Cape Town. He has published scores of essays and has authored or edited nearly twenty books, including most recently *The Study of Africa* (2 volumes), *Rethinking Africas Globalization* (2003), the *Routledge Encyclopedia of Twentieth Century African History*, *Leisure in Urban Africa* (2003), *Science and Technology in Africa* (2003) and *African Universities in the Twentieth Century* (2 volumes) (2004). He is the winner of the 1994 Noma Award for his book *A Modern Economic History of Africa* (1993) and the 1998 Special Commendation of the Noma Award for *Manufacturing African Studies and Crises* (1997). He has also published works of fiction.

List of Acronyms

ACCORD	African Centre for the Cooperative Resolution of Disputes	MJP	Movement for Justice and Peace
ADB	African Development Bank	MNCs	Multinational Corporations
AGOA	African Growth Opportunities Act	MPCI	Patriotic Movement of Ivory Coast
ANC	African National Congress	MPIGO	Popular Movement of Ivory Coast's Far West
AOF	Afrique Occidentale Française	MTN	Mobile Telephone Network
AU	African Union	NDPP	National Director of Public Prosecutions
CBOs	Community-based Organizations	NEPAD	New Partnership for Africa's Development
ECA	Economic Commission for Africa	NGOs	Non-Governmental Organizations
FPI	Ivorian Popular Front	NRM	National Resistance Movement
GLR	Great Lakes Region		
HDI	Human Development Index	OAS	Organization of American States
HDR	Human Development Report	OAU	Organization of African Unity
HIPC	Highly Indebted Poor Countries	PAIGC	African Party for the Independence of Guinea-Bissau and Cape Verde
HPI	Human Poverty Index		
HURIPEC	Human Rights and Peace Centre	PDCI	Democratic Party of Ivory Coast
ICC	International Criminal Court	PIT	Ivorian Worker's Party
ICISS	International Commission on Intervention and State Sovereignty	PRSP	Poverty Reduction Strategy Papers
		RDR	Rally of the Republicans
IDPs	Internally Displaced People	SADC	Southern African Development Community
IGAD	Inter-Governmental Authority on Development		
IGD	Institute for Global Dialogue	UDN	Uganda Debt Network
		UHT	Ultra Heated Treated
INGOs	International Non-Governmental Organizations	UN	United Nations
		UNCTC	United Nations Counter-Terrorism Committee
IT	information technology	UNDP	United Nations Development Programme
LRA	Lord's Resistance Army	UPE	Universal Primary Education
MDGs	Millennium Development Goals		

Introduction
The Causes & Costs of War in Africa
From Liberation Struggles to the 'War on Terror'

PAUL TIYAMBE ZELEZA

Violent conflicts of one type or another have afflicted Africa and exacted a heavy toll on the continent's societies, polities and economies, robbing them of their developmental potential and democratic possibilities. The causes of the conflicts are as complex as the challenges of resolving them are difficult. But their costs cannot be in doubt, nor the need, indeed the urgency, to resolve them, if the continent is to navigate the twenty-first century more successfully than it did the twentieth, a century that was marked by the depredations of colonialism and its debilitating legacies and destructive post-colonial disruptions. The magnitude and impact of these conflicts are often lost between hysteria and apathy – the panic expressed among Africa's friends and the indifference exhibited by its foes – for a continent mired in, and supposedly dying from, an endless spiral of self-destruction.[1] The distortions that mar discussions and depictions of African conflicts are rooted in the long-standing tendency to treat African social phenomena as peculiar and pathological, beyond the pale of humanity, let alone rational explanation. Yet, from a historical and global perspective, Africa has been no more prone to violent conflicts than other regions. Indeed, Africa's share of the more than 180 million people who died from conflicts and atrocities during the twentieth century is relatively modest: in the sheer scale of casualties there is no equivalent in African history to Europe's First and Second World Wars, or even the civil wars and atrocities in revolutionary Russia and China. The worst bloodletting in twentieth-century Africa occurred during the colonial period in King Leopold's Congo Free State (White 2003).

This is not to underestimate the immense impact of violent conflicts on Africa. It is merely to emphasize the need for more balanced debate and commentary, to put African conflicts in both global and historical perspectives. Not only are African conflicts inseparable from the conflicts of the twentieth century – the most violent century in world history; many postcolonial conflicts are rooted in colonial conflicts. There is hardly any zone of conflict in contemporary Africa that cannot trace its sordid violence to colonial history and even the late nineteenth century. 'For instance', to quote Niels Kastfelt (2005:2), 'the region from the southern Sudan through northern Uganda to Rwanda, Burundi, and Congo – now the scene of brutal civil wars and genocide – has a long history of colonial violence in the form of slave trading, slave labor, plantation labor, plantation terror and a violent gun culture which all have to be taken into account when explaining the contemporary situation.' Thus, it cannot be overemphasized that African conflicts are remarkably unexceptional: they have complex histories; they exhibit multiple and multidimensional causes, courses and consequences.

The papers in this two-volume collection seek to advance our understanding of African conflicts by going beyond the conventional and fashionable analyses of Africanist scholarship, often inflected with, if not infected by, Afropessimism, or the simplistic stereotypes conveyed in the Western media that are infused with Afrophobia. The first volume examines the causes and costs of violent conflicts in Africa, and the second focuses on the challenges of conflict resolution and post-conflict reconstruction. Combining sophisticated theoretical insights and rich empirical details, the authors, collectively, illuminate the forces and factors that generate violent conflicts and the effects that these conflicts have on socioeconomic development, political stability, democratic freedoms, human rights, cultural progress, and even environmental sustainability. There can be no singular explanation for or solution to Africa's conflicts. At best, one can only say that these conflicts are rooted in the complex constructions and conjunctures of Africa's political economies, social identities, and cultural ecologies as configured out of specific local, national, and regional historical experiences and patterns of insertion into, and engagement with, an ever-changing world system. In so far as the causes of the conflicts are multiple in their dynamics – internal and external, local and transnational, economic and political, social and cultural, historical and contemporary, objective and subjective, material and ideological, concrete and emotive, real and rhetorical – the strategies for managing and resolving them can only be multidimensional. This collection of essays is as strong in unraveling the sources of violent conflict in postcolonial Africa as it is in unveiling the various conflict resolution mechanisms that have been tried across the continent, and in showcasing the successes and failures of several post-conflict reconstruction efforts. Its strength lies in the sobriety and seriousness of its analysis and the solutions proffered that transcend the facile observations often encountered in the academic literature and popular media.

This Introduction is divided into three parts. First, I provide a broad historiographical survey of the typologies of wars in Africa in which I distinguish between five types, namely, what I call imperial wars, anti-colonial wars, intra-state wars, inter-state wars, and international wars. Second, I look at the current US 'war on terror', its causes, its connections with Africa's other wars, and its unfolding consequences for the continent. Third, I examine the political economy and cultural ecology of war, singling out the political and structural dynamics of African wars, their economic and social dimensions, gender inflections and implications, their transnational and imperial contexts, and their costs and consequences, subjects on which the chapters in this volume concentrate. In the conclusion, I briefly explore other critical aspects of African wars, especially the generational, religious and diasporic dimensions of these wars.

Typologies of War in Twentieth-Century Africa

During the twentieth century Africa was ravaged by wars of one type or another. Some of them, especially the liberation wars, were part of the momentous mission to remake African societies, to regain Africa's historical agency so cruelly seized by Europe through colonialism. At the dawn of the twenty-first century Africa, is faced with a new form of war even as it desperately seeks to quench the wars of the last century. This is the US-led 'war on terror', a crusade that knows no spatial or temporal bounds, spares no expense, leaves a trail of wanton destruction, and wreaks havoc on the infrastructures of global order, development and democracy. To date, two governments have been toppled, the Taliban in Afghanistan and Saddam Hussein's regime in Iraq, by savage wars of conquest reminiscent of the wars of colonization of a bygone era.

Africa's wars since the late nineteenth century can be differentiated in terms of their causal factors and dynamics, spatial scales and locations, temporal scope and duration, composition of perpetrators and combatants, military equipment and engagements deployed, impacts on military and civilian populations, and consequences on politics, the economy, society, the environment, and even on cultural structures and mental states as mediated and filtered, as all social processes and practices are, through the enduring and hierarchical inscriptions of gender, class, age, ethnicity, and sometimes race and religion. Each of these dimensions could be singled out for analytical and classificatory purposes. In this essay, I distinguish between five types of wars, basing the distinction primarily on their political thrust and ideological tendencies: imperial wars, anti-colonial wars, intra-state wars, inter-state wars, and international wars.[2] It cannot be over-emphasized, however, that in reality there are close and complex interconnections between these wars. Nevertheless, the classification does have heuristic value. According to this schema, the 'war on terror' is not new; it exhibits various characteristics of four of the five typologies, especially imperial and international wars.

For each of these typologies further subdivisions can be made. Three main forms of imperial wars can be identified in twentieth-century African history. The first two, the First and Second World Wars, were fought when much of Africa was still under colonial rule. African involvement in the two wars consisted, first, of providing troops, second, of serving as a theatre of war, and third, of the mobilization of production for the war effort. Hundreds of thousands of people from the colonies were conscripted into colonial armies or incorporated into metropolitan armies to fight on behalf of their imperial power against the other European powers, and, in the case of the Second World War, against imperial Japan as well. During the First World War parts of East and West Africa served as important theaters of war, while North Africa was a crucial combat zone during both wars. Colonial production, extraverted and coercive as it already was, was ruthlessly reorganized to produce record amounts of primary agricultural and mineral commodities for the imperial armies and economies. All in all, Africa made massive contributions to the two world wars at the expense of its own development, although the wars created the conditions and contradictions that galvanized anti-colonial nationalism (Page 1987, 2000; Miller 1974; Osuntokun 1979; Kerslake 1997; Killingray and Rathbone 1986; UNESCO 1985; Sainsbury 1979; Oberst 1991; Akurang-Parry 2002a, 2002b).

The Cold War constituted the third imperial war of the twentieth century in which Africa was implicated directly and indirectly, ideologically and militarily, politically and economically. It started when most African countries were still under colonial rule, but heated up during decolonization and after independence. This may have been a Cold War for the superpowers and their key allies in NATO and the Warsaw Pact, but it generated hot proxy-wars in many parts of the global South, especially in a postcolonial Africa desperately trying to forge nation-states out of the cartographic contraptions of colonialism and to rid itself of the last vestiges of colonialism in the settler laagers of Southern Africa. From the Congo to the Horn of Africa to Southern Africa, the Cold War fomented or facilitated destructive wars and conflicts (Kalb 1982; Issa-Salwe 2000; Percox 2004; Noer 1985; Borstelmann 1993; Harbeson and Rothchild 1995; Munene et al. 1995; Akinrinade and Sesay 1999; Oyebade and Alao 1998; Gordon et al. 1998).

In fact, Mahmood Mamdani (2004) claims, it was in Africa that the US strategy of proxy-war to 'roll back', not simply 'contain', radical states, was first concocted with the formation of what he calls Africa's first terrorist organization, RENAMO in Mozambique, which was bankrolled by racist Rhodesia and later apartheid South Africa and received American political support. Soon, the RENAMO model was exported to Nicaragua where the Contras were set up. It all culminated in the attempted 'rollback' of the Soviet empire itself in Afghanistan. It was then that the process began of ideologizing war as religious and privatizing it through the creation of a global network of Islamic fighters who would later come to haunt the US. Thus, while the Cold War may have created auspicious conditions for, and even accelerated, decolonization and enabled African states to gain international influence by manipulating superpower rivalries, the developmental, democratic and humanitarian costs of the wars it engendered or aggravated were extremely high, and persisted even after the collapse of the Soviet Union in 1991. Indeed, it could be argued that the current US 'war on terror' is a direct outcome of the late Cold War.

Anti-colonial wars can be subdivided into two groups. To begin with, there were wars waged *against* the colonial conquest itself, that were later followed by wars of liberation *from* colonial rule. The first set of wars involved both conventional and guerrilla wars against invading imperial armies that often contained African troops from other territories or communities within the territory already brought to colonial heel. On the whole, strong centralized states tended to wage conventional wars and after their defeat embark on guerrilla war, while smaller and weaker states or acephalous societies resorted to guerrilla warfare from the beginning. Examples of this abound across the continent and are well illustrated in the case of West Africa and Southern Africa where colonial conquest lasted for decades (Crowder 1978; Ranger 1967; Isaacman 1976; Boahen 1990). As is well known, only Ethiopia managed to win decisively against the

European invaders to retain its independence, although in 1935 Mussolini's fascist Italy returned to avenge the defeat of 1896 and redeem its lost imperial glory, and brutally occupied the country for six years (Dilebo 1996; Milkias 2005). The wars of conquest – pacification they were called in the self-serving and sanitized rhetoric of empire – exacted a heavy demographic price, which, when combined with the predations of primitive colonial accumulation, most graphically and grimly illustrated in King Leopold's genocidal 'red rubber' tyranny in the Congo that slaughtered 10 million people (Hochschild 1998), led to the deaths of many millions of people and spawned such vast dislocations that some medical historians have called the years between 1890 and 1930 'the unhealthiest period in all African history' (Patterson and Hartwig 1978: 4).

The wars of liberation, often triggered by the obduracy of settler minority regimes supported by the Western powers in defence of global wealth and whiteness, against appeals of common sense and decades of peaceful protests by the colonized, also exacted horrendous costs. The brutal story and statistics from Algeria are well known – more than a million dead (Horne 1978; Talbott 1980; Shepard 2006; Alexander et al. 2002; Maran 1989). Angola and Mozambique have their own tragic tales to tell of horrendous liberation wars and atrocities perpetrated by fascist Portugal aided by NATO (Marcum 1969–78; Harsch and Thomas 1976; Davidson 1972; Birmingham 1992; Cann 1997). So do Zimbabwe where a protracted guerrilla war was fought under the delusionary obstinacy of Ian Smith's regime (Ranger 1985; Lan 1985; Kriger 1992; Ellert 1993; Bhebe and Ranger 1995, 1996), and Namibia under the illegal usurpation of apartheid South Africa (Herbstein and Evenson 1989; Leys and Saul 1995; Namhila 1997; Emmett 1999). And that beloved country itself, South Africa, trapped longer than any in murderous racial fantasies, was rendered increasingly ungovernable by civil unrest and guerrilla attacks that led to the demise of apartheid in 1994.[3] Even Kenya's war of national liberation – dubbed Mau Mau by the colonialists – that was once seen as less ferocious than the liberation wars of Southern Africa, now appears to have been waged with a staggering level of imperial viciousness; some 1.5 million people were detained, a far cry from the official figure of 80,000 (Elkins 2005).

The anti-colonial wars were protracted and brutal; in some cases hardly a generation passed before wars against colonization turned into wars from colonialism. These were defensive, unavoidable wars, waged at enormous cost in African lives and livelihoods, driven by the desire to maintain or regain political autonomy, the precondition for establishing the social contract of democracy, the political culture of human rights, and the economic possibilities of development. While these struggles liberated African societies from colonialism, in many cases they left a lasting legacy of conflict that, sooner or later, festered and erupted into vicious post-colonial conflicts, as happened in Algeria in the 1990s (Martinez 2000; Volpi 2003) and in postcolonial Angola and Mozambique where UNITA and RENAMO served as 'apartheid's contras', as William Minter (1994) calls them (also see Ciment 1997; Ekwe-Ekwe 1990; Dinerman 2006). Indeed, the unfinished business of liberation is at the heart of the current crisis and conflict in Zimbabwe (Hammar et al. 2003; Carmody 2001; Campbell

2003), not to mention other countries in the region, including South Africa where high levels of violence persist and struggles are raging for the future of the country and the soul of the ruling ANC (Melber 2003; Gumede 2005; Gordon 2006). It is also important to remember that Africa's anti-colonial wars, which helped to bring to an end the 'age of empire' transformed European and world history. For example, the crisis engendered by the Algerian war ushered in the Fifth Republic in France and decolonization in Mozambique and Angola liberated Portugal itself from four decades of fascism. Thus, by dismantling the colonial empires and undermining the architecture of imperial racism, Africa's liberation wars encouraged Europe to 're-humanize itself', in Ali Mazrui's (2003: 21) memorable phrase

Unfortunately, independence brought little respite from the ravages of war for people in many countries. The instabilities and insecurities of postcolonial Africa are rooted in the political and cultural economies of both colonialism and the post-independence order itself that are latched on to the shifting configurations and conjunctures of the international division of labor, especially the legacies and challenges of state-making and nation-building, on the one hand, and the struggles over underdevelopment, dependency, and sustainable development, on the other; how to establish modern societies that are politically, economically and technologically viable in a highly competitive, unequal and exploitative world. The diversities of Africa's nation-states, the fact that they are almost invariably multi-ethnic, multi-religious, multi-lingual, and multi-cultural in the midst of relatively high levels of material poverty and uneven spatial and social development, and have until recently been dominated by authoritarian and corrupt governments, created a combustible mix that periodically erupted into open conflict and warfare. At the heart of all these conflicts and wars are struggles over power and resources; power cohered around the state and its governance structures, developmental capacities, delegative practices and distributional propensities, and resources in terms of their availability, control and access. Resources may be abundant or scarce, and either condition can be a source of conflict, depending on the organization and patterns of control and access. Control can be articulated in binding legal or flexible customary terms, embodied in community, corporate or state entities, and it might imply exclusionary or open access. The mediations of access include the trinity of contemporary analytical discourse – class, gender, and ethnicity (race in the global white North) – to which we have to add, at least in the African context, the constructions and identities of religion, region and generation. The regimes of access are further characterized and affected by gradations or scales of limitation.

It is obviously not possible in an introduction to give an extended account of Africa's postcolonial wars, except to point out that they have taken two major forms, intra-state and inter-state wars. Each in turn can be further subdivided. In terms of their objectives, we could distinguish six types of intra-state wars: secessionist wars, irredentist wars, wars of devolution, wars of regime change, wars of social banditry, and armed inter-communal insurrections. By secessionist wars I refer to wars fomented by groups or regions that seek to secede from the postcolonial polity and establish an independent nation-state. The most famous example is that of the secession of the Igbo-dominated provinces in south-eastern Nigeria that proclaimed an independent republic of Biafra, which triggered the civil war that cost Nigeria dearly in terms of the numbers of people who died – up to a million – not to mention the destruction of material resources and the social and political capital of inter-ethnic and inter-religious relations, national cohesion, and democratic governance (Harneit-Sievers et al. 1997; Okocha 1994; Oyeweso 1992).

Irredentist wars are generated when a group in one country seeks to be united or reunited with the country to which it is ethnically or historically related. Struggles by Somalis in Kenya and Ethiopia wishing for unification with Somalia constitute the best known cases of irredentist conflicts and wars (Carment 2006; Laitin and Samatar 1987; Schraeder 2006; Mburu 2005). The Somali government often supported Somali rebels in the neighboring countries, thereby turning irredentist claims and conflicts into inter-state wars, as was the case during the Somali-Ethiopian wars over the Somali-populated Ogaden region of Ethiopia in 1964-67 and 1977-78 (Dougherty 1982; Gorman 1981; Selassie 1980).

Wars of devolution are spawned by attempts by marginalized ethnic, religious and regional groups to renegotiate the terms of incorporation into the state and the national political space and their objective is decentralization rather than outright secession (Veney 2006). The long-running civil war in the Sudan, rooted in the history of colonial divisions, uneven development, exploitation and marginalization between the North and the South, was reignited in 1983 following the introduction of *Sharia* – Islamic law – by the Numeiri regime and disputes over sharing oil riches, and it persisted until the signing of a peace agreement in early January 2005 by which time more than 4 million people had been displaced and many more killed (Iyob and Khadiagala 2006; Johnson 2003; Khalid 2003; Kebbede 1999). But in the meantime, another regional conflict, also based on the effects of marginalization and resource disputes, had erupted in the Dar Fur region (Ardenne-van der Hoeven et al. 2006; Flint and de Waal 2005; Totten and Markusen 2006).

Wars of regime change are those often engineered by self-described revolutionary movements that seek to overthrow the existing government and establish a new socio-economic dispensation, including conditions and content of citizenship. An important example is the National Resistance Movement-Army (NRM-A) of Yoweri Museveni, which captured power in Uganda in 1986, the second guerrilla organization in an African country – after Chad – to succeed in doing so (Amaza 1998; Kasozi 1994; Mamdani 1995; Kabwegyere 2000). Since then, wars of regime change have been waged in various countries from Liberia to Sierra Leone to Ivory Coast (Adebajo 2002; Moran 2006; Marshall-Fratani 2006), and from Somalia to Ethiopia to the two Congos, often with disastrous results that have often led, not to state reconstruction as in Uganda and Ethiopia, but rather to state retrenchment or even collapse, as in Somalia (Kusow 2004; Lyons and Samatar 1995). Some of the movements waging these wars are best considered, like RENAMO, as 'terrorist' in their unwillingness to distinguish between military and civilian targets; indeed, they thrive on perpetrating systematic violence against civilians to demonstrate the incapacity of the state to protect them.

By wars of social banditry I mean widespread acts of violence that are socially organized against the state and other social institutions, with the objective not of capturing state power as such but of creating chaotic conditions that are conducive to predatory accumulation. There is a rich historical literature that distinguishes between criminal banditry and constructive banditry that is redressive, redistributive and protective in nature (Isaacman 1976; Crummey 1986). While mindful of such distinctions and of the role of social banditry in traditions of anti-colonial resistance and protest, in this context I use the notion less in its heroic conception and context and more in terms of its corrosive effects on state institutions, its propensity, indeed purpose, to destroy organized collective political life, to dissipate it in fiercely competitive and combative enclaves of power and accumulation led by warlords (Reno 1998; Thomas et al. 2005; Alao et al. 1999; Lezhne 2005). To be sure, warlords and 'terrorists' became interchangeable in some parts of Sierra Leone, Liberia and the Democratic Republic of Congo (DRC), but the inability of some of these groups to capture and restructure state power might be an indication of their very banditry, of their *lack of interest* in exercising state power. Post-Siad Barre Somalia presents the quintessential manifestation of social banditry in postcolonial Africa.

For their part, armed inter-communal insurrections are often episodic eruptions of violence, sparked by specific incidents that stoke long simmering antagonisms, anxieties and aggressions. They can lead to great loss of life and if unchecked can mutate into prolonged warfare between ethnic and regional militias, which in turn can develop into guerrilla armies that threaten the viability of the nation-state. The periodic explosions of genocidal violence in Rwanda and Burundi, demonstrated most horrifically in the Rwandan genocide of 1994, show the potential destructiveness of inter-communal conflicts abetted by the state and reinforced by the devastations of economic stagnation, as well as the politicization and manipulation of ethnic differences by a cynical and bankrupt political class.[4] Militant or militarized ethnicity is evident in many other countries currently undergoing democratization, as the tensions and twists arising from the competitive politics of democracy often find articulation in the entrenched identities, idioms and institutions of ethnic solidarity. In Nigeria, for example, democratization has led to the resurgence of ethnic identities and the proliferation of regional and local struggles over the entitlements of citizenship expressed in the language of 'indigenes' and 'settlers'. These struggles have increasingly spilled into the formation of ethnic militias that have wrought havoc on Nigeria's civil society, unleashing periodic convulsions of inter-communal violence (Vickers 2000; Agbu 2004; Osaghae 1996).

Postcolonial Africa has experienced inter-state wars, although on a far lesser scale than other regions and in comparison with the prevalence of intra-state conflicts. This is perhaps a lingering tribute to the inviolability of national borders in the collective African political imaginary that was sanctified by the charter of the Organization of African Unity (OAU), the predecessor of the African Union inaugurated in 2001. One can distinguish, in terms of the combatants involved, between bilateral wars and multilateral wars. Bilateral include the Somali-Ethiopian war of 1978–9, the Tanzania-Uganda war of 1978–9, and the Eritrea-Ethiopian war of 1998-2000, and the multilateral wars are illustrated by the multinational war over the DRC that started in 1998 and was still going on by the end of 2004. The war between Tanzania and Uganda was prompted by Uganda's invasion of northern Tanzania, and Tanzania was only too keen to rid the region of the detested Idi Amin regime (Avirgan and Honey 1982; Kiwanuka 1979). The rather senseless war between the two impoverished neighbors and erstwhile allies, Ethiopia and Eritrea, was provoked by border, currency and trade disputes and characterized by mass deportations and mobilization, and trench warfare reminiscent of the First World War (Negash and Tronvoll 2000; Fessehatzion 2002; Jacquin-Berdal and Plaut 2005). The DRC war, bred and superimposed on an already ferocious civil war, was fueled by a mad scramble for the country's vast mineral, forestry and agricultural resources, and involved Angola, Namibia and Zimbabwe on the side of the DRC government and Rwanda and Uganda on the side of the rebels (Khadiagala 2006; Nest 2006; Adelman and Rao 2004; Clark 2002). The destructiveness of these wars was incalculable in the loss of human life and damage to material infrastructure and environmental resources. By the end of 2004, according to several estimates, the war in the DRC alone had claimed a staggering 3 to 4 million lives (Institute for Peace and Justice 2005; *Care News* 2005; Fonseca 2004; Hawkins 2004)

International wars, fought either outside the continent's borders in which African troops are involved or against foreign countries, constitute the fifth major form of wars in which postcolonial Africa has been involved. Here we can identify four major types of international wars: first, the use of African troops in international peace-keeping operations, mostly under the auspices of the United Nations; second, the Arab-Israeli war; third, the recruitment of African combatants or mercenaries in international theaters of war; and fourth, African participation in the American-led 'war on terror'. Since the end of the Cold War the developed countries have become increasingly reluctant to deploy peace-keeping troops in conflicts in the global South, including those in Africa. While it is widely known that thousands of foreign troops, often under UN auspices, as well as African troops under regional organizations such as ECOWAS and the AU, are deployed in peace-keeping missions in regions and countries plagued by conflict across the continent, it is little appreciated that African peace-keeping troops are deployed in foreign conflicts (Bellamy and Williams 2005; Singer 2001; Rotberg et al. 2000; Adebajo and Sriram 2001; Francis 2005). For example, in 2003, 21 African countries reportedly contributed 10,191 troops – or 23 per cent – out of 43,007 troops deployed worldwide, with contributions ranging from four from Côte d'Ivoire to 3,340 from Nigeria (Sura and Hagen 2005).

Several African countries, principally in North Africa led by Egypt, have been directly involved in four of the six Arab-Israeli wars: the first in 1948–9 following the establishment of the Israeli state; the second in October-November 1956, after Egypt nationalized the Suez Canal, in which Israel was supported by Britain and France; the third in June 1967 in which Israel captured more Arab lands and Egypt's Sinai peninsula; the fourth in October 1973 in which Egypt and its allies scored some early

victories and after which the OAU called for African states to break
diplomatic relations with Israel and all but three did; the fifth in 1982–4
involving the Israeli invasion of Lebanon, by which time Egypt had signed
a peace treaty with Israel; and the sixth in July-August 2006 when Israel
invaded Lebanon again, this time to fight the Lebanese movement,
Hezbollah (Gawrych 2000; Laskier 2004; Kokole 1993; Peters 1992; Ojo
1988; Oded 1987).

The conflicts in Western Asia – the Middle East of imperial cartography
– became a magnet for recruits from several African countries. In the
1980s Afghanistan became the epicenter of the last gasps of the Cold War.
The US was determined to turn the Soviet occupation of Afghanistan into
the Soviet Vietnam, and it was only too happy to recruit, train and support
the *mujahadeen* (Mamdani 2004). Among the militant Muslims who flocked
to Afghanistan were thousands from Algeria, Egypt, the Sudan and other
African countries who would later return and form the backbone of radical
Islamist movements – what the Western media call Islamic fundamentalism
– that launched campaigns of terror against discredited secular states and
institutions and individuals associated with Western modernity. Algeria
found itself caught in this bloody maelstrom following the aborted elections
of 1992 in which the Islamic Salvation Front was poised to win. In the
ensuing civil war multitudes were killed, up to an estimated 150,000 by
2000. The case of the Algerian civil war brings into sharp relief the
intricate connections in some of Africa's contemporary wars between
domestic and international factors, reformist and reactionary motivations,
secular and religious movements. This war and many others represent the
clash of modernisms – modern political Islam and the modernizing
neocolonial state (Volpi 2003; Bonora-Waisman 2003).

Africa & the Current 'War on Terror'

The US-led 'war on terror' that Africa and other parts of the world are
increasingly being expected to fight is clearly not new. It has elements of
the imperial wars, inter-state wars, intra-state wars and international wars
described above. Fundamentally lacking in many of these wars and the
'war on terror' is the liberatory logic of anti-colonial wars. The 'war on
terror' is an imperial war in so far as it seeks to advance the agenda of the
world's pre-eminent imperial power, the United States. It obviously involves
intense conflicts between and within states, and is international in its scope.
While wars against terror are not new, the current US-led war is occurring
in new contexts characterized by four key developments in the world
system.[5] The first is globalization, both as a historical process and as an
ideological project. Interconnectedness among the world's continents,
countries and cultures, in temporal and spatial terms, has intensified
through new communication and transport technologies that have
accelerated the flows of capital and commodities, ideas and individuals, and
values and viruses, and facilitated the growth of transnational movements
and reflexivities. At the same time, the world political economy is becoming
more regionalized as blocs emerge or are consolidated to fulfill long-

standing dreams of pan-territorial or racial solidarities and to mediate the corrosive and competitive pressures of contemporary globalization.

It is also a conjuncture characterized by democratization as marked by an increase in the number of states following and abiding by features of democratic governance, minimally characterized by elections and multi-party politics, the pluralization of associational life and the expansion of political space thanks to the unrelenting struggles of social movements, and the emergence of a global rhetoric of democracy – the so-called 'third wave'. Most of these developments coincided, or became more visible, with the end of the Cold War. The US emerged as the single superpower, which in its triumphalism sought to impose a new order on a world that was less amenable to superpower management and manipulation because it was becoming more globalized, regionalized and democratized. This is at the heart of the conundrum of US global policy and standing, a hyperpower whose hysterical unilateralism finds few adherents even among its European allies. Faced with diminishing global economic power and little political and moral capital, the US increasingly relies on naked military force to enforce its will, now in the name of an amorphous 'terrorism'. And the rest of the world is expected to embrace the 'war on terror' as its own.

In discussing the 'war on terror', we need to pay attention to the analytical problems it poses, namely, its conceptions, causes, constructions, consequences and challenges, that is, how it is defined, generated, waged, and the effects it leaves behind and the political and policy issues it presents. Needless to say, there is considerable controversy on how the terms 'terrorism' and 'war' are defined. Africans remember only too well how their liberation movements and leaders used to be called 'terrorists' by the imperialists. There is also the problem of the identity of 'terrorists' as state and non-state actors. The tendency is to depict 'terrorists' as non-state actors and to talk of states in terms of 'state-sponsors of terrorism' when in fact historically states have perpetrated some of the worst acts of terrorism. After years of much deliberation and disagreement, the United Nations finally in December 2004 issued a report that recognized that the perpetrators of terrorism can be both state and non-state actors and placed emphasis on attacks on civilians and non-combatants, noting that terrorism flourishes in conditions of poverty, inequality, oppression, humiliation, conflict and occupation (United Nations 2004).

No less problematic is the description of the 'war on terror' as 'war'. What sort of war is it? Who are the combatants and enemies in this war? What are its spatial and temporal boundaries? If it is a 'war', then surely it must be subject to international conventions of war, yet the US treats the prisoners of its 'war on terror' outside any acceptable legal standards at the 'legal black hole' of Guantánamo Bay in Cuba where abducted suspects from around the world, including children, have been subjected to incommunicado interrogations and indefinite detentions without trial. The scandal of Abu Ghraib in Baghdad, with its pornographic images of torture, primal degradation and gratuitous humiliation of Iraq prisoners, which unleashed a wave of worldwide dismay, contempt and anger against the United States, shows that the US believes that this 'war' can be waged without civilized constraints (Hoffman 2004).

The causes of the 'war on terror' are no less difficult to decipher. Some find an explanation in official US rhetoric about the historic effects of September 11, or doctrinal shifts in foreign policy to pre-emptive strikes and spreading democracy as the new overriding goal. Others find greater explanatory power in the structural forces of the needs of a permanent war economy and efforts to manage the opportunities and problems of globalization that reinforce US tendencies toward exceptionalism and unilateralism, or they stress the imperatives of US Western Asia policy anchored in the political economy of oil and the uncompromising defense of Israel, all of which entail and buttress what I call the republicanization of America (Zeleza 2004b).[6]

It could be argued that terrorism has become for the US a convenient substitute for communism, a new enemy essential for a permanent war economy and necessary to produce nationalism and promote patriotism in this new era of 'globalization'. For a country that spends nearly half of the world's military expenditures – there have been huge increases in US military spending since 2002 – enemies are essential, and the more ubiquitous they are the better. Terrorism fits the bill. The prefix 'Islamic' as in 'Islamic terrorism' allows for the substitution of the political language of policies and interests by the cultural language of religion and civilization. In short, it makes it possible for the US to wrap itself in self-righteousness and to demonize others for their wickedness. Nationalists and other militants in the Muslim world have inherited the appellation of 'evil' once used to describe the Soviet Union and to mobilize support against it, most importantly, and somewhat ironically, among militant Muslims themselves, and as a civilization Islam can be tarred with the atavisms of premodernity. Both discourses are based on, and seek to ignite, deep-seated anti-Islamic memories in Western culture. Religion and civilization make a potent mix in the clash of US imperialism and political Islam that the US itself turned from an ideological tendency into a political organization during the anti-Soviet crusade in Afghanistan in the 1980s.

All this serves to particularize and primordialize global terrorism, depicting it as an upsurge of religious fanaticism and civilizational envy in the Muslim world that has nothing to do with the policies of successive US governments, including those of the current Bush administration. The litany of the policy abominations as seen from the region is a long one indeed.[7] The wide and wild application of the term 'terrorists', and occasionally 'insurgents', to apply to all opponents of US imperial policies seeks to delegitimize what is, at heart, nationalist resistance against imperialism. It is a familiar story in the annals of empire – spreading democracy and freedom as an alibi for a country – the US – that has difficulty running its own elections and has historically not respected the democratic rights and civil liberties of its own minorities.

It could be argued that the 'war on terror' represents an attempt by the US to recenter global hegemony around military prowess in which US power remains uncontested, although the quagmire in Iraq has dented it. It is a weapon of global domination, a declaration and demonstration of US global supremacy. The unilateralism of the 'war on terror' – waged illegally against all wise counsel from the United Nations and other international organizations as well as most of the US's European allies – reflects not only imperial hubris, the arrogance of hyperpower, but also a sense of exceptionalism, a mystical belief in the country's manifest destiny that is so deeply rooted in its national imagination. Also, the economic prosperity enjoyed by the United States during the Second World War, which ended the Great Depression, left a deep impression regarding the positive effects of high military expenditures that has not been questioned by any administration since then.

The costs of the 'war on terror' have been high. As far as the US itself is concerned, the war is being fought on two fronts. First, there are the hot wars abroad, beginning with the invasion of Afghanistan in 2001 and followed by Iraq in 2003, and there are thinly veiled threats against other 'rogue states', principally Iran and North Korea. Second, there is the cold war at home enacted through the imposition of a stringent homeland security regime, which threatens the civil liberties of US citizens and the rights of immigrants in which Muslims and their institutions and people of 'Middle Eastern' appearance have been targeted for racist attacks. By mid-November 2006, the war had directly cost a staggering $345 billion and was still rising.[8]

For people in the 'war zone' within Afghanistan and Iraq and for the surrounding countries, the war is as real as it is vicious: rampant deaths and destruction accompanied by social dislocation reflected in skyrocketing crime, rape and kidnapping, as well as economic devastation manifested in rising unemployment, destruction of the oil infrastructure, and corporate war profiteering, not to mention the social, environmental and political damage done to these countries' health, education, environments and sovereignty. According to an article in the British medical journal, *The Lancet*, the Iraq war led to the deaths of an estimated 654,965 between March 2003 and July 2006 (Burnham et al. 2006).[9] The figure included those who died from gunfire and direct combat as well as from increased lawlessness and the indiscriminate destruction of the country's infrastructure that left behind shortages of medical facilities, clean drinking water, and adequate incomes and jobs. In the US invasion of Afghanistan in 2001 an estimated 25,000 perished. And we are only in the early days of the war.

For the rest of the world the US-led 'war on terror' undermines international law, the United Nations, and global security and disarmament by galvanizing terrorist groups, diverts much-needed resources for development, and promotes human rights abuses by providing governments throughout the world with a new licence for torture and mistreatment of prisoners and opponents.[10] Many people around the world now regard the US, to use the words of the Council on Foreign Relations (2002), as 'arrogant, hypocritical, self-absorbed, self-indulgent, and contemptuous of others'. In a recent report, Human Rights Watch (2005: 500) singled out the US as a major factor in eroding the global human rights system.

Africa's geopolitical stock for Euro-America has risen in the post-2001 world, bolstered by US concerns about militant Islam, the alleged vulnerability of fragile states as sanctuaries of global terrorist networks, and the need for 'safe' energy resources outside the volatile Middle East.[11] For Africa itself, this renewed attention has not brought any tangible benefits, whether in increased investment or in support for its fundamental interests of development and democratization. On the contrary, the war threatens human rights in Africa and reinforces old conflicts and foments new ones. As several human rights organizations including Amnesty International (2001a: 5) have warned, draconian actions and the subversion of international humanitarian law undermine the counter-terrorism measures by invoking the very instrumentalities of terrorism in their disregard for human rights, in ostensibly pursuing security at the expense of respect for human dignity. The backlash against human rights in the US-led 'war on terror' has bred widespread resentment and even hatred that have swelled the ranks of the 'insurgents' fighting against the US in Afghanistan and Iraq and terrorists bent on attacking American interests elsewhere, and fuelled divisions between the US and many of its allies in Europe and across the world. It has also provided alibis for governments, including many in Africa, as well as international agencies, to violate or vitiate their human rights commitments and to tighten asylum laws and policies.[12] In the meantime, military transfers to countries with poor human rights records have increased which portends ill for human rights.

Many African governments have rushed to pass broadly, badly or cynically worded anti-terrorism laws and other draconian procedural measures, and to set up special courts or allow special rules of evidence that violate fair trial rights, which they use to limit civil rights and freedoms, and to harass, intimidate, and imprison and crackdown on political opponents.[13] This is helping to strengthen or restore a culture of impunity among the security services in many countries. Amnesty International (2003, 2004) has issued reports critical of new draft anti-terrorism laws in a number of countries from Kenya to Tunisia that threaten to undermine international human rights standards.[14] African friends and foes of the United States have been basking in the new climate of intolerance and impudence. For example, Morocco, an archaic Western-friendly monarchy, used anti-terrorism laws to detain 5,000 people following the May 2003 bombings in the country. In Zimbabwe, a self-declared anti-imperialist enclave of tattered radical credentials, there was a sharp escalation of state-sponsored intimidation, torture, arbitrary arrests and political killings, and orchestrated attacks on the independence of the media and the judiciary (Amnesty International 2001b: 28–34).

In addition to the restrictions on political and civil rights and the subordination of human rights concerns to anti-terrorism priorities, the 'war on terror' is inflicting other collateral damage on Africa. As a report by Human Rights Watch (2003: 3) noted

> pre-existing political tensions between Muslim and Christian populations in a number of African countries threatened to become inflamed, and increasingly violent. Côte d'Ivoire, Ethiopia, Kenya, Nigeria, South Africa, and Tanzania all faced the possibility of worsening communal tensions. Bloody riots between Muslims and Christians in Kano, northern Nigeria, following demonstrations against the US bombing of Afghanistan, had already left a high death toll. A pro-Taliban demonstration was also reported in Kenya's predominantly Muslim coastal city, Mombasa.

Western anti-travel advisories undermined the economies of countries dependent on tourism, while increased security and defense expenditures threatened to reduce humanitarian and development assistance. In the Horn of Africa, the war on terror provides a new stimulus for age-old rivalries and conflicts and cover for discredited authoritarian regimes, as evident in attempts by the Ethiopian government to insinuate itself with the US and bolster its dented international reputation following the botched elections of 2005 by threatening to attack the movement – the Union of Islamic Courts – that seized control of much of Somalia from the warlords and the nominal government; the Islamists were accused of having links with al-Qaeda (BBC 2006; Clayton 2006).

The Political Economy & Cultural Ecology of War

Given the range and diversity of Africa's wars, it stands to reason that their causes are as varied and complex as their courses and consequences. Some attribute these wars to the lingering legacies of colonialism, but for many, especially in the Western popular and academic media, singular ahistorical and internalist explanations tend to be offered, assigning the wars to either Africa's primordial afflictions of 'tribalism', or the depredations of the continent's proverbial poverty and inequalities, or authoritarianism and poor governance.[15] The 'ancient ethnic hatreds' thesis is sometimes overlaid by the 'new barbarism' thesis that depicts African wars as irrational and pathological. To be sure, these wars are often provoked and sustained by ethnic rivalries and polarizations, economic underdevelopment and inequalities, poor governance and elite political instability and manipulations, but these factors, individually or collectively, have a history rooted in the political economy of colonialism, postcolonialism, and neo-liberal globalization; they are as much internal in their causation and scale as they are regional and transnational, involving national, regional and international actors and networks that are simultaneously economic, political, military and social.

Much of the current literature focuses on Africa's intra-state wars and conflicts, and especially the so-called 'new wars' of the post-Cold War era. It cannot be overemphasized that there is little that is new about the wars of the 1990s and early 2000s. As several critics of the so-called 'new wars' paradigm have pointed out, these wars are an amalgam of 'old wars' – the age-old inter-state, extra-state, and intra-state wars.[16] Moreover, the 'new wars' can be explained using available analytical models and typologies, and there is no evidence that warfare has changed *fundamentally* in terms of types of participants, and patterns in the prosecution of wars, and their purposes (Henderson and Singer 2002). Analytical dichotomies tend to be drawn between the 'new' and 'old' wars in terms of their causes and motivations, levels of support, and violence. The 'new wars' are said to be driven by private greed rather than collective grievances like the 'old wars', and are depicted as criminal, depoliticized and predatory; they allegedly lack popular support, unlike the 'old wars' that enjoyed broad popular support; and they are executed through uncontrolled violence. These dichotomies are untenable on historical and empirical grounds: the characteristics of both old and new civil wars are indistinguishable.[17]

It stands to reason that Africa's wars and conflicts, including civil wars, are products of multiple causes and contexts, as would be evident from any study of a specific war informed by what I would call the political economy and cultural ecology of war, an approach that emphasizes and examines how political, economic, social and cultural factors cause and sustain war and conflict within and between states and societies. We need to incorporate in our analyses the interplay of historical and contemporary processes, the intersections of politics, economy and culture, the connections between local, regional and global systems, the role played by national and transnational formations, by the state, capital and civil society, and how material forces and popular discourses, institutional conditions and symbolic constructs structure and reproduce conflicts.

While this book largely focuses on intra-state or civil wars and conflicts, it examines many aspects of these wars including their political and structural dynamics, economic and social dimensions, gender inflections and implications, transnational and imperial contexts, and their costs and consequences. The collection opens with Ali Mazrui's wide-ranging paper, which offers intriguing paradoxes that characterize conflicts in Africa. He posits, controversially, that postcolonial wars have been more ruthless than anti-colonial wars; conflicts within borders more common and ferocious than across borders; ethnic conflicts tend to be preponderant in sub-Saharan Africa and religious conflicts in Arab North Africa; conflicts between blacks and whites have been more about the distribution of economic resources, while among blacks they have largely centered on the demarcation of cultural identities; conflicts have become more prevalent as African armies have become less disciplined but better equipped; and dual societies have been more prone to conflict than plural societies. The second part of Mazrui's paper discusses conflict resolution and anticipates many of the issues taken up in Volume II of this collection. He urges the need to cultivate toleration and foster constructive pluralization by promoting the development of multi-party systems, capitalism, federalism and more women's political representation, improving civil-military relations, and strengthening regional integration and building innovative Pan-African institutions and mechanisms of conflict prevention, intervention and resolution.

African civil wars are often characterized or dismissed simply as 'ethnic conflicts'. In a vigorous rebuttal of this view, Errol Henderson seeks to provide a systematic analysis of the extent to which civil wars in Africa are engendered by political, economic and cultural factors. He constructs several testable propositions related to a state's regime type, its level of economic development, and its cultural composition. With regard to the political factors, he examines the relative propensities of autocracies, democracies and semi-democracies in generating civil wars; for the economic factors, the relative contributions of levels of economic development and military expenditures to lowering or increasing the likelihood of civil war are assessed; and for the cultural factors, the presence of 'politicized ethnic groups' or 'ethno-political groups' is analyzed. Using regression analyses, the data reveal that there is little evidence that semi-democracies, which are often associated with the likelihood of civil war because they lack the institutional channels of dispute resolution available in democracies or the repressive capacities of autocracies, have been more prone to civil war in Africa than other regimes. Also insignificant are cultural factors, specifically the role of ethnic polarization. The economic factors are more salient: increased development is associated with a decreased likelihood of civil war, while increased military spending leads to increased likelihood of civil war. The most critical predictor of the likelihood of civil war lies in the destructive political legacies of colonialism, which left Africa with very weak and underdeveloped states, and the failure of Africa's leaders to effectively handle the dual challenges of state-building and nation-building.

The rest of the papers elaborate on more specific causes of violent conflicts in Africa. It is common to attribute civil conflicts to structural conditions, in which the social, economic and political organization of society, specifically the existence of structural inequalities and victimization among groups, is seen as the cause of conflicts. While objective realities or interests do indeed generate conflict, some writers contend that material conditions and inequalities are not sufficient by themselves to explain the intensity, ferocity and duration of conflicts; they often provide 'proximate causes', and psycho-cultural dispositions, or subjective factors, especially the psychology of victimhood and persecution, constitute the indispensable fuel. Conflicts erupt or persist when the memories of humiliation, oppression and marginaliza-tion, both real and mythologized, are triggered through new threats (Azar and Moon 1986; Deutsch 1991; Ross 1993; Brown 1993; Namwambah 2004). Clearly, wars and conflicts arise out of the combustible interplay of objective and subjective factors, the incendiary combination of material and sociocultural conditions and political and psychological dispositions.

The role of structural and subjective factors and history and mythology in generating protracted conflict can be seen in all its devastating manifes-tation in the Sudan. Analyses of the Sudanese conflict have tended to reproduce dichotomies, variously presenting it as a conflict between the North and the South, Muslims and Christians, Arabs and Africans, and oppressors and oppressed. Abdel Ghaffar Ahmed notes that, while there may be elements of all of these dichotomies, none of them explains the conflict. Often ignored are the rural-urban divide, and more importantly, the role of the country's opportunistic elite in fomenting ethnic and regional divisions that are at the root of the Sudanese conundrum. Ahmed insists on the multiple complexities of the Sudanese conflict, emphasizing the historical legacies of colonialism, which left behind underdevelopment and uneven development and acute socio-economic and political marginaliza-tion for groups in peripheral regions who have been fighting for inclusion since independence. He places primary responsibility on the elite, tracing the development of this class from the colonial period and the role it has played during various phases of violent conflict in postcolonial Sudan.

If the elites are critical in safeguarding a political community, citizenship is the bond that holds that community together. Rupturing the social contract of common citizenship is a certain recipe for conflict. The question of citizenship – who belongs and does not belong to the polity – remains at the heart of many conflicts in postcolonial Africa. The Ivory Coast is a particularly tragic example of this phenomenon. This is the subject of John Akokpari's illuminating paper. He argues that at the heart of the conflict in that country is the citizen-stranger dichotomy and its manipulation by the political elite. Thus it is not so much the artificiality of the African state, derived as it is from a colonial construct that embraced within its cartographic enclosures diverse ethnic groups, that causes conflicts *per se*; rather, conflicts erupt when the state fails to manage this diversity and to fulfill its social contract with citizens – to provide social services, security and equal opportunities. The denial of the badge of citizenship to certain groups, on whatever basis, almost invariably generates conflict as the aggrieved and excluded group or groups seek the redress of political inclusion or territorial secession.

This is what happened in the Ivory Coast as the once relatively peaceful and prosperous country was rocked by economic and political crises in the 1990s in the post-Houphouet Boigny era. Akokpari contends that under Boigny's reign ethnic diversity was managed and harmony maintained because on citizenship rights the individual was prioritized over the group, while his successors failed to do so. In fact, they sought to entrench their power in an economy reeling from the effects of economic recession and structural adjustment programs by manipulating ethnic divisions and attempting to exclude from the rights and privileges of citizenship migrant communities, some of whom had been in the country since long before independence and had helped fuel the export-led boom of earlier years, by using the divisive concept of Ivoirite – true Ivoriness. The irony is that exclusionary notions of citizenship were being advanced in countries like the Ivory Coast at the same time as globalization and liberalization were eroding the state's hegemony over citizenship.

In current discussions of conflicts the role of economic factors features prominently. This was not always so, and owes much to the work of the economist Paul Collier and his associates (Collier 1999, 2000; Collier and Hoeffler 1998, 1999), who advanced the influential and controversial typology of 'resource wars' according to which 'economic agendas' are at the heart of violent conflicts in Africa.[18] The argument is that the bulk of Africa's major conflicts since the mid-1960s have been driven by economic greed rather than political grievances, whether those related to economic inequalities, ethnic and religious cleavages, or political repression. While previously emphasis was placed on economic scarcity and inequality as a cause of war, this approach stresses the role played by resource abundance, the rise of self-financing rebel movements, and the emergence of civil war economies that are parasitic, illicit, and predatory, and dependent on external criminal financial and commodity networks. Its proponents seek to analyze not only the economic conditions, opportunities for, and rationality of organized violence; some try to construct quantitative models to predict the processes that lead to civil war, its severity, duration, and the remedial actions that can be taken. Often solution is sought in sanctions against the trafficking of products from conflict zones – the infamous 'conflict diamonds'; and vague appeals tend to be made for economic growth and diversification and political democratization (Seck 2004).

While few would dispute the fact that economic problems, struggles and inequalities constitute 'root causes' of many violent conflicts across the continent, *economistic* explanations such as those proposed by Collier and his colleagues have been vigorously contested on methodological, theoretical and policy grounds. Some have questioned their very definitions of 'civil war' and the quality of their data, the dichotomized notions of grievance and greed and the validity of the proxies used for them, the exclusive focus on rebels, and the occlusion of structural adjustment and neo-liberalism as the context that creates conditions for both conflict and predation through increased poverty and inequality and by weakening state capacity and strengthening regional and global markets and networks that rebel movements can access (Nafziger and Auvinen 2002; Pugh and Cooper 2004). Others have questioned the applicability of the thesis to many of Africa's wars and conflicts. Norman Mlambo (2004) mentions the wars of liberation primarily motivated by the desire for emancipation rather than the looting of resources, and land struggles in Southern Africa that seek the redistribution of scarce resources rooted in the inequities of settler colonialism. He is adamant that there is more to African conflicts than simple economic greed and that the sharp contrast drawn between economic and political motivations is unproductive analytically and in terms of devising effective conflict resolution policies.[19]

Many scholars sympathetic to the economic analysis of war have pointed out that even the 'economic agendas' of the recent wars in Sierra Leone, Angola, Mozambique, the Sudan and the Democratic Republic of Congo, the proverbial 'resource wars', can be questioned; these wars have been driven more by the struggle for political power than for the control of resources as such, or, to use the title of Arnson and Zartman's (2005) book, there is an intersection of 'need, creed, and greed'. Contributors to the study by Ballentine and Sherman (2003) find the greed or grievance dichotomy too limiting and stress the inseparability of political and economic factors, the complexity, diversity, and variability of the economic conditions and opportunity structures of war, the economic behaviors of the various actors from the rebels themselves to states and transnational organizations, and the contextual specificities and fluidities of conflict, and the role played by the processes of regionalization, privatization and globalization.[20] Michael Pugh and Neil Cooper (2004) are particularly critical of the tendency to ignore the negative impact of globalization and neo-liberal models of development sanctioned by the international financial institutions that have bankrolled many of the 'resource wars' studies,[21] and their misguided policy prescriptions on proscribing 'conflict goods' and imposing what they call simplistic 'liberal peace strategies' of post-conflict reconstruction.[22] They also question the 'national' focus of many of these studies and emphasize the regional dimensions of war economies – regional conflict complexes – noting the crucial mediations of regional economic, military, political and social networks in the global-local nexus in the geography of many so-called civil wars.[23]

In this volume, Thandika Mkandawire offers a compelling critique not only of Collier's thesis, but of much of the Africanist conflict literature. No perspective escapes his censure, not the apocalyptic view that depicts African conflicts as senseless madness, the culturalist view according to which conflicts are culturally encoded, or the neopatrimonial perspective that attributes conflicts to the self-destructive logic of prebendalism. He reserves his most scathing attack for the rational choice paradigm of economists, many of them affiliated with the World Bank or working for donor agencies, including Collier's 'looting model of rebellion', and their faulty methodological, theoretical and empirical premises and findings. He accuses these scholars of conflating political rebels with common criminals, enabling with causal factors, and individual with collective rationality. In the rest of his paper Mkandawire offers an illuminating alternative explanation of civil wars and rebel movements, arguing that these movements, which are composed largely of roving rather than stationary rebels, are urban in their origins and agendas and are produced by Africa's urban crisis, which has been exacerbated by structural adjustment programs. It is the urban roots of the rebel movements that account for their problematic and predatory relationship with the rural peasantry. He also suggests that rentier states have been more prone to rebellion than merchant states because of the higher levels of relative deprivation among the former.[24]

Most conventional studies of war, including those mentioned above, tend to ignore one fundamental aspect of war: the fact that wars are gendered in their causes, courses and consequences. As Joshua Goldstein (2001:1) puts it so poignantly, 'gender shapes war and war shapes gender.' The connections between gender and war are, of course, exceedingly complex and show enormous variations across time and space – between historical periods and among different cultures and societies – but there can be little doubt that war and gender reproduce each other in so far as they embody, exhibit and engender masculinity and femininity. Until quite recently the gender dynamics of war were largely ignored by male researchers, and when gender was brought in, usually by female scholars, much of the focus was on women and war. The latter is obviously a subject that deserves serious study in its own right, but it is also important to emphasize that the relationship between men and war is also a gendered one. Wars and militaries are critical mechanisms for the production and performance of masculinities. The varied involvements and impacts of wars for men and women are products of socially and culturally constructed gender roles. To feminist scholars the gendered nature of war is self-evident, even if they might explain the relations between the two quite differently. For example, the differentiated gendering of war for men and women is explained by liberal feminists largely in terms of sexist discrimination; radical feminists emphasize patriarchy, racism and imperialism; and postmodern feminists tend to focus on the contingency and fluidity of gender roles in war and the gendered discourses and representations of war (Reardon 1985; Ruddick 1989; Lorentzen and Turpin 1998; Peterson and Runyan 1999; De Pauw 1998; Turshen 1998; Mazurana et al. 2005; Dudink et al. 2004; Afshar and Eade 2004; Skjelsbæk and Smith 2001). In short, gender analyses of war examining the intersections between war and the constructions and reconstructions of both masculinity and femininity have enriched our understanding of both war and gender immensely.

The engagements and effects of contemporary wars on women are complex and contradictory. Women are both victims and agents, although their explicit involvement in waging war and influencing war outcomes remains relatively marginal compared to men. As the venues, actors and mechanisms of war have become more diffuse with the proliferation of intra-state wars, informal fighting forces, small arms, and terror tactics, the costs of war for women have risen. Although the number of combat deaths among men still outstrips that of women, women's direct war mortality rates have been rising worldwide – up to a quarter in 2000 (UNRISD 2005: 214).[25] Many more women have died from the indirect consequences of war including injuries, hunger, exhaustion, diseases, and the disruptions of flight, relocation and economic devastation. Widowhood and the growth of female-headed households impose severe strains, although they might also be empowering for some women. The physical and psychological devastation for women generated by pervasive and widely reported sexual violence including rape, sexual slavery, and forced marriages that often leave behind markedly increased rates of sexually transmitted infections including HIV/AIDS, not to mention unwanted pregnancies, is truly horrific. Women fall victim not only to different combatants but sometimes to peace-keeping forces as well, and wartime conditions generate increased demand for sexual services which leads to growth in prostitution and the trafficking of women. But women have also been active agents in wars as combatants, active supporters and provocateurs. The experiences and transformations wrought by war can also lead to changes in gender relations and sometimes be empowering for women, especially in contexts where women's groups emerge to assist those victimized by war and to fight for gendered peace and post-conflict reconstruction.

Aaronette White critically interrogates the question of the transformatory impact of war, specifically Africa's revolutionary wars of national liberation. She examines and reassesses Frantz Fanon's theory that the revolutionary violence of liberation wars was therapeutic and emancipatory for the colonized including women, that it was a humanizing force for both the colonized and the colonizer. White notes that women have been active participants in these wars, both as victims and agents, and it is possible to identify their empowering and disempowering effects. While national liberation and women's liberation movements are related, Fanon overstated the symbiosis between the two because he underestimated the resilience of the gendered, patriarchal underpinnings of African nationalisms, which were rooted in what White calls 'the androcentricization of inferiority', as contrasted with Fanon's 'epidermilization of inferiority'. For men, national liberation represented struggles over their own masculine identities. Thus armed struggles reinforced the masculinist propensities of nationalist movements and consciousness in so far as military forces as social institutions and military values valorize courage, virility, superiority and ideal masculinity. The intersections and interactions between militarism and masculinity that give rise to militarized patriarchal ideologies and practices are evident in the execution of the wars themselves, in the sexual division of labor between men and women in which women play largely subordinate roles often reminiscent of their domestic roles, not to mention their vulnerabilities to sexual violence and harassment, as well as in postwar realities in which women combatants and women's issues are often silenced and marginalized. For women, then, the psychological effects are more degenerative than regenerative. As for the empowerment effects, which are considerable, White notes that women combatants do not attribute them to the actual violence of war.

A full account of any of Africa's wars and conflicts would show the complex interplay of national and transnational forces, and that internal and external forces are deeply implicated with each other. As dependency theory has taught us, ever since the emergence of the modern world system the external is always already implicated in the local, although many dependency writers were wont to overemphasize external forces and underestimate local agency, and to depict the structural forces largely in materialist and economistic terms at the expense of their ideational, political and cultural dimensions. This underscores the difficulties of disaggregating the global-local nexus, and capturing the exact nature of external-internal connections and how they relate to each other. Ron Kassimir (2006) puts forward the concept of transboundary formations as an analytical device to transcend the external-internal divide and capture the dynamics created by the intersection of forces emanating from various spatial, social, structural and sectoral levels. It is a framework, he argues, that can yield useful hypotheses and provide insights in analyzing concrete events and processes in which different institutions operate and intersect, where networks of people form, and through which ideas and commodities are trafficked. For example, he shows that the case of conflict diamonds bears testimony to the critical role played by the global demand and markets for commodities, cross-border smuggling of commodities and arms, and recruitment of mercenary forces in engendering and sustaining many a civil war and regional conflict in Africa (also see Callaghy et al. 2001).

There can be little doubt that external contexts and actors have had a major impact in instigating, facilitating, aggravating or prolonging conflicts in Africa from the time of the Atlantic slave trade, through the colonial period, to the postcolonial era. Sandra J. MacLean's perceptive paper explores the intersections of local, national, regional and international factors in the political economy of conflicts. The transnational linkages and complexes that spawn, sustain or shape African conflicts are obviously multi-dimensional. Patterns of a country's or region's integration into the global capitalist system help structure its levels of underdevelopment, inequalities and the development of patrimonial relationships, all of which often contribute to the prevalence of civil strife and the outbreaks of violent conflict. It is certainly the case that many of Africa's dictatorial regimes, whose very existence was a source of conflict in so far as the closure of political space tended to channel opposition into armed revolts and rebel movements, were sponsored and supported by foreign powers and interests, especially during the Cold War. Both states and non-state actors, including the notorious warlords, often use or turn transnational formations into networks of plunder that nourish civil wars. In as much as the venal global networks of corruption, crime and violence are involved in generating conflicts, conflict resolution needs the mobilization of the more progressive global networks – from knowledge and policy networks to transnational advocacy coalitions – that can facilitate sustainable development, reconciliation and empowerment.

Since the end of the Cold War and the onset of the twenty-first century new forms of imperialism, often cloaked in the giddy rhetoric of globalization, are engendering new contexts and excuses for imperialist adventures that are stoking local and regional conflicts across the world. As noted above, the current US-led 'war on terror' is leaving a trail of wanton destruction, and wreaking havoc on the infrastructures of global order, development and democracy. Africa is being asked to participate in this new form of war, unleashed in the name of fighting 'terrorism' by an imperial power frantically seeking to maintain its eroding global hegemony, even as the continent desperately seeks to quench its old wars that continue to smolder and devastate large parts of the continent. The 'war on terror' has serious implications for democratization and human rights, as processes and projects, globally and for Africa. Clearly, many African countries are using the war and the language of anti-terrorism to roll back new and hard-won human rights and democratic freedoms (Mazrui 2006).

The legislative responses to terrorism are examined in considerable detail by Cephas Lumina who chronicles the anti-terrorism measures adopted post-September 11 in four selected African countries: Mauritius, Morocco, South Africa and Uganda. The paper places these measures in the context of the international legal framework on terrorism that includes the twelve universal conventions on specific aspects of terrorism and the regional conventions adopted by various organizations, and demonstrates, quite compellingly, that many of the new anti-terrorism laws undermine international human rights law, threaten the rights of refugees and asylum seekers, permit detention and torture, and curtail rights to a fair trial, freedom of association, expression and assembly, and privacy. The war on terror has given a new lease to racial discrimination and religious intolerance and even poses a threat to the rights of the child. The need to arrest and reverse this trend is incontrovertible if the continent is fully to achieve the historic and humanistic tasks of African nationalism – self-determination, development and democratization – and realize the age-old dreams of Pan-Africanism – regional integration and turning itself from a global pawn to a global player.

The costs and consequences of violent conflicts are immense. Except perhaps for the wars of liberation, violent conflicts have little redeeming value. They exact a heavy toll on society, the economy, and the environment, both directly and indirectly through deaths and injuries, sexual crimes and intimidation, population dislocations within and across national borders, and the damage and distortions they cause to societal networks and the fragile social capital of trust and interpersonal associations and intergroup interactions. Not to mention the devastation of the ecosystem, agricultural lands and wildlife, the destruction of society's material and mechanical infrastructures, the outflow of resources including 'capital flight' and 'brain drain', the proliferation of pathological and self-destructive behaviors, and the deterioration in the aesthetic quality of life.

The chapter by Fondo Sikod underscores the devastating implications of conflict for poverty and food security. His contention is that conflict is a cause of food insecurity and exacerbates poverty in Africa because it destroys or damages the human and physical capital that undermines production, leads to economic disruption and distortion of state expenditures, and encourages capital flight and diversion. More specifically, food security – the availability, access to and affordability of food – is severely affected in so far as violent conflict affects all key aspects of food production, distribution and consumption: rural labor supplies are disrupted as peasants are conscripted into armies, farms and agriculture-related infrastructure are destroyed, land is mined, and social cohesion is weakened as families and communities not only lose members but are also turned against one another. In some cases the destruction of physical capital and the resultant food shortages or even famines are not merely unfortunate byproducts of war, but are deliberately deployed as instruments of war. Food aid provided in times of conflict often contributes to conflict when it is used as a weapon by the warring factions, and threatens local production in the long term, thereby contributing to the perpetuation of poverty.

Violent conflict tends to reinforce both the underdevelopment of, and uneven development within, a country. This is clearly demonstrated in the case of Uganda, which is examined by Timothy Shaw and Pamela Mbabazi. Uganda's postcolonial turmoil has prevented the country from achieving the rate of development and social progress that was widely expected at independence. The protracted war in northern Uganda during the past two decades between government forces and the rebel Lord's Resistance Army has worsened the marginalization of the north, which fostered the war in the first place. In effect, Uganda has become two distinct nations, one in the relatively buoyant south that has, since the early 1990s, enjoyed economic recovery and reconstruction, peace and rapid economic growth, and the other in the stagnant north that continues to suffer from the devastating effects of warfare including an estimated 1.2 million internally displaced people. It is quite evident from Shaw and Mbabazi's paper that local, national, regional, continental and global forces are imbricated in complex and contradictory ways in Uganda's conundrum. Of particular concern are the implications of capitalist globalization and the regime of structural adjustment in fashioning new trajectories of developmentalism based on liberalization and privatization that foreclose the possibilities of constructing a truly democratic developmental state capable of pursuing policy options that might close the widening north-south gap and resolve the insurgency in the north.

Conclusion

This volume, and the collection as a whole, provides critical glimpses into the nature and dynamics of violent conflicts in Africa. Of course it is not, nor did it seek to be, comprehensive, in covering either Africa as a whole or all aspects of conflicts that have afflicted the continent since independence, let alone since time immemorial. In spatial terms, much of the focus is on eastern and southern Africa.[26] A comprehensive and comparative study of conflicts across the continent, covering all five regions, would yield important lessons and is long overdue. In temporal terms, the collection concentrates on recent conflicts; analyses over a much longer period, including the colonial era and perhaps even slices of the precolonial era, would deepen our understanding of the history of conflicts in Africa. Thematically, one could point to a range of topics that have not been given the emphasis they deserve, such as the generational, religious and diasporic dimensions of violent conflicts. Also, these conflicts are differentiated in the way they involve and impact on different generations, from the young to the elderly (Kurimoto and Simonse 1998; Abbink and van Kessel 2005). The question of child soldiers, on which much has been written, is only one aspect of the generational dynamics of African conflicts that require more systematic study. Estimates indicated that the conflicts of the 1980s and 1990s involved 'more than 120,000 children... For example, more than 10 percent of the fighters in the Liberian conflict are children; in Mozambique, the RENAMO rebel group had an estimated 8,000-10,000 children fighting in its force against the government; ... and in Uganda, it is estimated that around 90 percent of the soldiers in the LRA rebel force are abducted children' (Fosu and Collier 2005: 234; also see Fleischman 1994; Rone 1995; Honwana 2006).

The role of religion as a source of conflict, in objective and subjective terms, institutionally and ideologically, and at local and transnational levels and the many points in between, cannot be overemphasized (Panitch and Leys 2002). Throughout history religion has provided a powerful vehicle for instigating war, giving meaning and legitimacy to war, and in facilitating postwar reconciliation and reconstruction.[27] Wars, in turn, transform religion, bringing innovations in ideas, rituals, and institutional practices. We need to know more not only about the role of each of Africa's major religions – Christianity, Islam, and the 'traditional' religions – but also in comparative perspective. As Niels Kastfelt (2005: 1) argues forcefully and convincingly, 'many African civil wars have religious dimensions which are sufficiently important to deserve to be studied in their own right without, of course, thereby ignoring their social, economic and political context'. Examples abound. In colonial Africa there were the religiously inspired rebellions, such as the Mahdist war in the Sudan in the 1890s, the Shona-Ndebele uprising in Zimbabwe in 1896–97, the Maji Maji revolt in Tanganyika in 1905–7, and the Mau Mau liberation struggle in Kenya in the 1950s. In the postcolonial era one can point to Uganda's civil strife in which Alice Lakwena's Holy Spirit Movement and Joseph Kony's Lord's Resistance Army have played a key role, not to mention the conflicts fomented among and between Christians and Muslims that are increasingly amplified by the so-called 'war on terror'.

Some of the papers in this volume discuss the global forces and transnational networks behind violent conflicts in Africa. The tendency has been to examine the imperial and neo-colonial agendas of the major powers. More attention ought to be paid to the activities of other transnational actors including business enterprises, advocacy organizations, and even academic establishments. In this context, the role of diaspora communities, both the regional and extra-regional diasporas, needs to be accorded specific attention, as diaspora networks have become increasingly critical in fanning, facilitating and financing conflicts. For example, in the 1998 Ethiopian-Eritrean war, the diasporas of both countries played important roles in supporting their respective homelands. In the Nordic countries the Eritrean diaspora sought to raise diplomatic support for Eritrea, while in the United States elements of the more splintered Ethiopian diaspora demonstrated in Washington, DC in support of Ethiopia. The two diasporas also provided crucial financial support, which was particularly vital for Eritrea. Similarly, Somali diasporas have been critical to supporting different factions in the ongoing Somali civil war.[28]

Clearly, the research agenda on the 'root causes' of conflicts is large and complex. As with many other areas of social inquiry, conflict studies can only benefit from interdisciplinary approaches, from the collaboration of scholars from all the major disciplinary fields – the social sciences, humanities, and natural sciences – for conflicts affect all aspects of human life and the natural environment. And, of course, scholars and researchers need to engage policy-makers, national and regional security councils, social movements and rebel movements if their work is to be meaningful empirically and translate into effective policies. The challenge is to ensure that African conflicts are analyzed in their own multifaceted contexts, while avoiding seeing them as manifestations of some unique African cultural compulsion, political pathology, social sickness or moral malady. In other words, these conflicts must be understood in comparative perspective, not in isolation. Violent conflict in Africa is indeed part of the human drama, but the tendency to impose universalist models of conflict driven by stylized Western experiences or faddish theorizing must be resisted if only because, as is shown in several chapters in this volume with reference to the 'rationalist' models of neo-classical economists, such paradigms lead to poor analysis and bad policy. Conflict is too serious a matter, and its costs too grave, for glib modeling or lazy journalistic speculation uninformed by the histories of, and unmindful of the concrete conditions in, the societies under scrutiny. And history tells us that postcolonial African societies and states are not primordial fixtures frozen in splendid isolation, but complex constellations constructed out of their multiple engagements with the world.

References

Abbink, Jon and Ineke van Kessel, eds. 2005. *Vanguard or Vandals: Youth, Politics, and Conflict in Africa*. Boston, MA: Brill.

Adebajo, Adekeye and Chandra L. Sriram, eds. 2001. *Managing Armed Conflicts in the 21st Century*. London: Frank Cass.

Adebajo, Adekeye. 2002. *Liberia's Civil War: Nigeria, ECOMOG, and Regional Security in West Africa*. Boulder, CO: Lynne Rienner.

Adelman, Howard and Govind C. Rao, eds. 2004. *War and Peace in Zaire-Congo: Analyzing and Evaluating Intervention, 1996–1997*. Trenton, NJ: Africa World Press.

Afshar, Haleh and Deborah Eade, eds. 2004. *Development, Women, and War: Feminist Perspectives*. Oxford: Oxfam.

Agbu, Osita. 2004. *Ethnic Militias and the Threat to Democracy in Post-Transition Nigeria*. Uppsala: Nordiska Afrikainstitutet.

Akinrade, Sola and Amadu Sesay, eds. 1999. *Africa in the Post-Cold War International System*. London: Cassel Academic.

Akurang-Parry, Kwabena O. 2002a. 'Africa and World War I', in Toyin Falola, ed. *Africa, Vol. 3, Colonial Africa, 1885–1939*. Durham, NC: Carolina Academic Press, 53–68.

Akurang-Parry, Kwabena O. 2002b. 'Africa and World War II', in Toyin Falola, ed. *Africa, Vol. 4, The End of Colonial Rule*. Durham, NC: Carolina Academic Press, 49–62.

Alao, Abiodun, John Mackinlay, and Funmi Olonisakin. 1999. *Peacekeepers, Politicians and Warlords: The Liberian Peace Process*. Tokyo and New York: United Nations University Press.

Alexander, Martin S., Martin Evans and J.F.V. Keiger, eds. 2002. *The Algerian War and the French Army, 1954–62 : Experiences, Images, Testimonies*. New York: Palgrave Macmillan.

Amaza, Ondoga ori. 1998. *Museveni's Long March from Guerrilla to Statesman*. Kampala: Fountain Publishers.

Amnesty International. 2001a. 'The Backlash – Human Rights at Risk Throughout the World'. AI Index No. ACT 30/027/2001.

Amnesty International. 2001b. '2002 UN Commission on Human Rights: Rights at Risk', AI Index 10R 41/025/2001.

Amnesty International. 2002. 'The Arab Convention for the Suppression of Terrorism a Serious Threat to Human Rights'. http://web.amnesty.org/library/print/ENG10RS 510012002

Amnesty International. 2003. 'Tunisia: New Draft "Anti-Terrorism" Law Will Further Undermine Human Rights'. AI Index: MDE 307021/2003.

Amnesty International. 2004. 'Kenya: Draft "Anti-Terrorism" Law may Undermine Kenyan Constitution and International Law'. AI Index: AFR 32/004/2004.

Anonymous. 2004. *Imperial Hubris: Why the West is Losing the War on Terror*. Washington, DC: Brassey's.

Ardenne-van der Hoeven, Agnes van, Mohamed Salih, Nick Grono, Juan Méndez. 2006. *Explaining Darfur: Four Lectures on the Ongoing Genocide*. Amsterdam: Vossiuspers.

Arnson, Cynthia J. and I. William Zartman, eds. 2005. *Rethinking the Economics of War: The Intersection of Need, Creed, and Greed*. Baltimore, MD: Johns Hopkins University Press.

Avirgan, Tony and Martha Honey. 1982. *War in Uganda: The Legacy of Idi Amin*. Westport, CT: L. Hill.

Azar, E. and C. I. Moon. 1986. 'Managing Protracted Social Conflicts in the Third World: Facilitation and Development Diplomacy', *Millennium Journal of International Studies* 15 (3): 393–406.

Ballentine, Karen and Jake Sherman, eds. 2003. *The Political Economy of Armed Conflict: Beyond Greed and Grievance*. Boulder, CO: Lynne Rienner.

Barnes, Sandra T. 2005. 'Global Flows: Terror, Oil, and Strategic Philanthropy', *African Studies Review* 48, 1: 1–23.

BBC. 2006. 'Ethiopia "Ready for Islamist War"'. Published 11 November. http://news.bbc.co.uk/go/pr/fr/-/2/hi/africa/6175976.stm   Accessed 24 November 2006.

Bellamy, Alex J. and Paul D. Williams. 2005. 'Who's Keeping the Peace? Regionalization and Contemporary Peace Operations', *International Security* 29, 4: 157–95.

Bennis, Phyllis and IPS Iraq Task Force. 2004. *A Failed 'Transition': The Mounting Costs of the Iraq War. A Study by the Institute for Policy Studies and Foreign Policy In Focus*. Washington, DC: IPS.

Berdal, Mats and David Malone, eds. 2000. *Greed and Grievance: Economic Agendas in Civil Wars*. Boulder, CO and London: Lynne Rienner.

Bhebe, Ngwabi and Terence Ranger, eds. 1995. *Soldiers in Zimbabwe's Liberation War*. London: James Currey; Portsmouth, NH: Heinemann.

Bhebe, Ngwabi and Terence Ranger, eds. 1996. *Society in Zimbabwe's Liberation War*. London: James Currey; Portsmouth, NH: Heinemann.

Birmingham, David. 1992. *Frontline Nationalism in Angola and Mozambique*. London: James Currey; Trenton, NJ: Africa World Press.

Boahen, A. A., ed. 1990. *UNESCO General History of Africa, Vol. VII: Africa Under Colonial Domination 1880–1935* , London: James Currey.

Bonora-Waisman, Camille. 2003. *France and the Algerian Conflict: Issues in Democracy and Political Stability, 1988–1995*. Burlington, VT: Ashgate.

Borstelmann, Thomas. 1993. *Apartheid's Reluctant Uncle: The United States and Southern Africa in the Early Cold War*. New York: Oxford University Press.

Brown, Michael E., ed. 1993. *Ethnic Conflict and International Security*. Princeton, NJ: Princeton University Press.

Burnham, Gilbert, Riyadh Lafta, Shannon Doocy, and Les Roberts. 2006. 'Mortality After the 2003 Invasion of Iraq: A Cross-sectional Cluster Sample Survey'. Published online October 11. www.thelancet.com

Callaghy, T., R. Kassimir and R. Latham, eds. 2001. *Intervention and Transnationalism in Africa: Global-Local Networks of Power*. Cambridge: Cambridge University Press.

Campbell, Horace. 2003. *Reclaiming Zimbabwe: The Exhaustion of the Patriarchal Model of Libera-tion*. Trenton, NJ: Africa World Press.

Cann, John P. 1997. *Counterinsurgency in Africa: the Portuguese Way of War, 1961–1974*. West-port, CT: Greenwood Press.

Care News. 2005. 'What's Happening in the Democratic Republic of Congo?' April: 2.

Carment, David. 2006. *Who Intervenes?: Ethnic Conflict and Interstate Crisis*. Columbus, OH: Ohio State University Press.

Carmody, Pádraig. 2001. *Tearing the Social Fabric: Neoliberalism, Deindustrialization, and the Crisis of Governance in Zimbabwe*. Portsmouth, NH: Heinemann.

Carmody, Pádraig. 2005. 'Transforming Globalization and Security: Africa and America Post–9/11', *Africa Today* 52 (1): 47–68.

Cater, Charles. 2003. 'The Political Economy of Conflict and UN Intervention: Rethinking the Critical Case of Africa', in Karen Ballentine and Jake Sherman, eds, *The Political Economy of Armed Conflict: Beyond Greed and Grievance*. Boulder, CO: Lynne Rienner, 19–45.

Cilliers, Jakkie and Christian Dietrich, eds. 2000. *Angola's War Economy: The Role of Oil and Diamonds*. Pretoria: Institute for Security Studies.

Ciment, James. 1997. *Angola and Mozambique: Postcolonial Wars in Southern Africa*. New York: Facts on File.

Clark, John F. ed. 2002. *The African Stakes of the Congo War*. New York: Palgrave Macmillan.

Clarke, Richard A. 2004. *Against All Enemies: Inside America's War on Terror*. New York, Free Press.

Collier, Paul. 1999. 'On the Economic Consequences of Civil War'. Report of the World Bank: in Collaboration with the University of Oxford, *Oxford Economic Papers* 51: 168–83.

Collier, Paul. 2000. 'Doing Well Out of War: An Economic Perspective', in Mats Berdal and David M. Malone, eds, *Greed and Grievance: Economic Agendas in Civil Wars*, Boulder, CO and London: Lynne Rienner, 91–111.

Collier, Paul and Anke Hoeffler. 1998. 'On Economic Causes of Civil War'. *Oxford Economic Papers* 50: 563–73.

Collier, Paul and Anke Hoeffler. 1999. *Justice Seeking and Loot Seeking in Civil War*. Oxford: Oxford University Press, February.

Collier, Paul and Nicholas Sambanis. 2005a. *Understanding Civil Wars. Evidence and Analysis. Vol. 1, Africa*. Washington, DC: World Bank.

Collier, Paul and Nicholas Sambanis. 2005b. *Understanding Civil Wars. Evidence and Analysis. Vol. 2, Europe, Central Asia, and Other Regions*. Washington, DC: World Bank.

Collier, Paul, Anke Hoeffler and Nicholas Sambanis. 2005. 'The Collier-Hoeffler Model of Civil War Onset and the Case Study Project Research Design', in Paul Collier and Nicholas Sambanis, eds. *Understanding Civil Wars. Evidence and Analysis. Vol. 1, Africa*. Vols. 1 and 2. Washington, DC: World Bank, 1–35.

Council on Foreign Relations. 2002. *Public Diplomacy: A Strategy for Reform. A Report of an Independent Taskforce on Public Diplomacy sponsored by the Council on Foreign Relations*, 30 July. http://www.cfr.org/pubs/Task-force_final2-19.pdf

Crowder, Michael. 1978. *West African Resistance: The Military Response to Colonial Occupation*. New York: African Publishing Corporation.

Crummey, Donald, ed. 1986. *Banditry, Rebellion, and Social Protest in Africa*. London: James Currey; Portsmouth, NH: Heinemann.

Davidson, Basil. 1972. *In the Eye of the Storm: Angola's People*. Garden City, NY: Doubleday.

Davis, John, ed. 2005. *The Global War on Terrorism: Assessing the American Response*. New York: Nova Science Publishers.

De Pauw, Linda G. 1998. *Battle Cries and Lullabies: Women in War from Prehistory to the Present*. Norman, OK: University of Oklahoma Press.

Deutsch, Morton. 1991. 'Subjective Features of Conflict Resolution: Psychological, Social and Cultural Influences in R. Varynen, ed., *New Direction in Conflict Theory: Conflict Resolution and Transformation*. London: Sage, 120–35.

Dilebo, Lapiso G. 1996. *The Italo-Ethiopian War of 1887–1896 from Dogalli to Adwa*. Addis Ababa.

Dinerman, Alice. 2006. *Revolution, Counter-revolution and Revisionism in Post-colonial Africa: The Case of Mozambique, 1975–1994*. London and New York : Routledge.

Dougherty, James E. 1982. *The Horn of Africa: A Map of Political-Strategic Conflict*. Cambridge, MA: Institute for Foreign Policy Analysis.

Dudink, Stefan, Karen Hagemann and John Tosh, eds. 2004. *Masculinities in Politics and War: Gendering Modern History*. Manchester: Manchester University Press.

Eades, Lindsay Michie. 1999. *The End of Apartheid in South Africa*. Westport, CT: Greenwood Press.

Ekwe-Ekwe, Herbert. 1990. *Conflict and Intervention in Africa : Nigeria, Angola, Zaïre*. New York:

St Martin's Press.

El-Khawas, Mohamed A. 2003. 'North Africa and the War on Terror', *Mediterranean Quarterly* 14, 4: 176–91.

Ellert, H. 1993. *The Rhodesian Front War: Counter-insurgency and Guerrilla War in Rhodesia, 1962-1980*. Gweru, Zimbabwe: Mambo Press.

Elkins, Caroline. 2005. *Imperial Reckoning: The Untold Story of Britain's Gulag in Kenya*. New York: Henry Holt.

Emmett, Tony. 1999. *Popular Resistance and the Roots of Nationalism in Namibia, 1915-1966*. Basel, Switzerland: P. Schlettwein Publishing.

Fessehatzion, Tekie. 2002. *Shattered Illusion, Broken Promise: Essays on the Eritrea-Ethiopia Conflict (1998-2000)*. Lawrenceville, NJ: Red Sea Press.

Fleischman, Janet. 1994. *Easy Prey: Child Soldiers in Liberia*. New York: Human Rights Watch.

Flint, Julie and Alex de Waal. 2005. Darfur: *A Short History of a Long War*. New York: Zed Books.

Fonseca, Alroy. 2004. 'Four Million Dead The Second Congolese War, 1998–2004.' http://www.geocities.com/afonseca/CongoWar.htm

Fosu, Augustin K. and Paul Collier, eds. 2005. *Post-Conflict Economies in Africa*. New York: Palgrave Macmillan.

Francis, David J. 2005. *Dangers of Co-deployment: UN Co-operative Peacekeeping in Africa*. Burlington, VT: Ashgate.

Gawrych, George W. 2000. *The Albatross of Decisive Victory: War and Policy Between Egypt and Israel in the 1967 and 1973 Arab-Israeli Wars*. Westport, CT: Greenwood Press.

Goldstein, Joshua S. 2001. *War and Gender*. New York: Cambridge University Press.

Gordon, David F., David C. Miller, and Howard Wolpe. 1998. *The United States and Africa: A Post Cold War Perspective*. New York: W.W. Norton.

Gordon, Diana R. 2006. *Transformation and Trouble: Crime, Justice, and Participation in Democratic South Africa*. Ann Arbor, MI: University of Michigan Press.

Gorman, Robert F. 1981. *Political Conflict in the Horn of Africa*. New York: Praeger Publishers.

Gourevitch, Philip. 1999. *We Wish to Inform You That Tomorrow We Will Be Killed With Our Families: Stories from Rwanda*. New York: Picador

Gumede, William. 2005. *Thabo Mbeki and the Battle For The Soul Of The ANC*. Johannesburg: Struik Publishers.

Hammar, A., B. Raftopoulos and S. Jensen. 2003. *Zimbabwe's Unfinished Business: Rethinking Land, State and Nation in the Context of Crisis*. Harare: Weaver.

Harbeson, John W. and Donald Rothchild, eds. 1995. *Africa in World Politics: Post-cold War Challenges*. 2nd edn. Boulder, CO: Westview Press.

Harneit-Sievers, Axel, Jones O. Ahazuem, and Sydney Emezue. 1997. *A Social History of the Nigerian Civil War: Perspectives from Below*. Hamburg: LIT Verlag.

Harsch, Ernest and Tony Thomas. 1976. *Angola: the hidden history of Washington's war*. New York: Pathfinder Press.

Hawkins, Virgil. 2004. 'Stealth Conflicts: Africa's World War in the DRC and International Consciousness', *The Journal of Humanitarian Assistance* http://www.jha.ac/articles/a126.htm

Henderson, Errol A. and J. David Singer. 2002. '"New Wars" and Rumors of "New Wars"', *International Interactions* 28: 165–90.

Herbstein, Denis and John Evenson. 1989. *The Devils Are Among Us: The War for Namibia*. Atlantic Highlands, NJ: Zed Books.

Hochschild, Adam. 1998. *King Leopold's Ghost: A Story of Greed, Terror and Heroism in Colonial Africa*. Boston, MA: Houghton Mifflin.

Hoffman, Paul. 2004. 'Human Rights and Terrorism', *Human Rights Quarterly* 26: 932–55.

Honwana, Alcinda. 2006. *Child Soldiers in Africa*. Philadelphia, PA: University of Pennsylvania Press.

Horne, Alistair. 1978. *A Savage War of Peace: Algeria, 1954–1962*. New York: Viking Press.

Houston, Gregory F. 1999. *The National liberation Struggle in South Africa: A Case Study of the United Democratic Front, 1983–1987*. Brookfield, VT: Ashgate.

Human Rights Watch. 2005. *Human Rights Watch World Report 2005*. Washington, DC: Human Rights Watch.

Human Rights Watch. 2004. *Human Rights Watch World Report 2004: Human Rights and Armed Conflict*. New York: Human Rights Watch.

Human Rights Watch. 2003. *Human Rights Watch World Report 2003*. New York: Human Rights Watch.

Institute for Peace and Justice. 2005. *Peace and Justice Update* 11 (1): 1–12.

Isaacman, A. 1976. *The Tradition of Resistance in Mozambique: Anti-Colonial Activity in the Zambezi Valley, 1850–1921*. Berkeley, CA: University of California Press.

Issa-Salwe, Abdisalam M. 2000. *Cold War Fallout: Boundary Politics and Conflict in the Horn of Africa*. London: HAAN.

Iyob, Ruth and Gilbert M. Khadiagala. 2006. *Sudan: The Elusive Quest for Peace*. Boulder, CO: Lynne Rienner Publishers.

Jacquin-Berdal, Dominique and Martin Plaut, eds. 2005. *Unfinished Business: Eritrea and Ethiopia at War*. Lawrenceville, NJ: Red Sea Press.

Johnson, Douglas H. 2003. *The Root Causes of Sudan's Civil Wars*. Oxford: James Currey.

Kabwegyere, Tarsis B. 2000. *People's Choice, People's Power: Challenges and Prospects of Democracy in Uganda*. Kampala: Fountain Publishers.

Kadende-Kaiser, Rose M. and Paul J. Kaiser, eds. 2005. *Phases of Conflict in Africa*. Willowdale, Ontario: de Sitter Publications.

Kalb, Madeleine G. 1982. *The Congo Cables: The Cold War in Africa – From Eisenhower to Kennedy*. New York: Macmillan.

Kalyvas, Stathis N. 2001. '"New" and "Old" Civil Wars: A Valid Distinction?' *World Politics* 54: 99–118.

Kasozi, A.B.K. 1994. *The Social Origins of Violence in Uganda, 1964-1985*. Montreal: McGill-Queen's University Press.

Kassimir, Ronald. 2006. 'If You Are Part of the Solution, You Are Likely Part of the Problem: Transboundary Formations and Africa', in Paul Tiyambe Zeleza, ed., *The Study of Africa Vol. II Global and Transnational Engagements*. Dakar: Codesria Book Series, 45-61.

Kastfelt, Niels, ed. 2005. *Religion and African Civil Wars*. New York: Palgrave Macmillan.

Kebbede, Girma. 1999. *Sudan's Predicament: Civil War, Displacement and Ecological Degradation*. Brookfield, VT and Aldershot: Ashgate.

Kerslake, R.T. 1997. *Time and the Hour: Nigeria, East Africa, and the Second World War*. London and New York: Radcliffe Press and St Martin's Press.

Khadiagala, Gilbert M., ed. 2006. *Security Dynamics in Africa's Great Lakes Region*. Boulder, CO: Lynne Rienner.

Khalid, Mansour. 2003. *War and Peace in Sudan: A Tale of Two Countries*. New York: Kegan Paul.

Killingray, David and Richard Rathbone, eds. 1986. *Africa and the Second World War*. New York: St Martin's Press.

Kiwanuka, Semakula. 1979. *Amin and the Tragedy of Uganda*. München: Weltforum Verlag.

Kokole, Omari H. 1993. *Dimensions of Africa's International Relations*. Delmar, NY: Caravan Books.

Kraxberger, Brennan M. 2005. 'The United States and Africa: Shifting Geopolitics in an "Age of Terror"', *Africa Today* 52 (1): 47–68.

Kriger, Norma J. 1992. *Zimbabwe's Guerrilla War: Peasant Voices*. New York: Cambridge University Press.

Kurimoto, Eisei and Simon Simonse, eds. 1998. *Conflict, Age and Power in North East Africa: Age systems in transition*. Oxford: James Currey.

Kusow, Abdi, ed. 2004. *Putting the Cart before the Horse: Contested Nationalism and the Crisis of the Nation-state in Somalia*. Trenton, NJ: Red Sea Press.

Laitin, David D. and Said S. Samatar. 1987. *Somalia: Nation in Search of a State*. Boulder, CO: Westview Press.

Lan, David. 1985. *Guns & Rain: Guerrillas & Spirit Mediums in Zimbabwe*. London: James Currey.

Laskier, Michael M. 2004. *Israel and the Maghreb: From Statehood to Oslo*. Gainesville, FL: University Press of Florida.

Leys, Colin and John S. Saul. 1995. *Namibia's Liberation Struggle: The Two-edged Sword*. London: James Currey; Athens, OH: Ohio University Press.

Lezhne, Sasha. 2005. *Crafting Peace: Strategies to Deal with Warlords in Collapsing States*. Lanham, MD: Lexington Books.

Lind, Jeremy and Kathryn Sturman, eds. 2002. *Scarcity and Surfeit: The Ecology of Africa's Conflicts*. Pretoria: Institute for Security Studies.

Lorentzen, Lois Ann and Jennifer Turpin, eds. 1998. *The Women and War Reader*. New York: New York University Press.

Louw, P. Eric. 2004. *The Rise, Fall, and Legacy of Apartheid*. Westport, CT: Praeger.

Lyons, Terrence and Ahmed I. Samatar. 1995. *Somalia: State Collapse, Multilateral Intervention, and Strategies for Political Reconstruction*. Washington, DC: Brookings Institution.

Mamdani, Mahmood. 1995. *And Fire Does Not Always Beget Ash: Critical Reflections on the NRM*. Kampala: Monitor Publications.

Mamdani, Mahmood. 2001. *When Victims Become Killers: Colonialism, Nativism, and the Genocide in Rwanda*. Princeton, NJ: Princeton University Press; Oxford: James Currey.

Mamdani, Mahmood. 2004. *Good Muslim, Bad Muslim: America, the Cold War, and the Roots of Terror*. New York: Pantheon Books.

Mandela, Nelsom. 1994. *Long Walk to Freedom: The Autobiography of Nelson Mandela*. New York: Little Brown.

Maran, Rita. 1989. *Torture, the Role of Ideology in the French-Algerian War*. New York: Praeger.

Marcum, John A. 1969–78. *The Angolan Revolution*. 2 volumes. Cambridge, MA: M.I.T. Press.

Marrouchi, Mustapha. 2003. 'Introduction: Colonialism, Islamism, Terrorism', *College Literature* 30, 1: 6–55.

Marshall-Fratani, Ruth. 2006. 'The War of "Who Is Who": Autochthony, Nationalism, and Citizenship in the Ivoirian Crisis', *African Studies Review* 49 (2): 9–43.

Martinez, Luis. 2000. *The Algerian Civil War, 1990–1998*. New York: Columbia University Press.

Mazrui, Alamin. 2006. 'Africa in America's "War on Terrorism": Some Political Implications', Paper presented at a Seminar on Terrorism in Africa: Search for an African Voice, Institute for Security Studies, Kopanong, Benoni, South Africa, November 6–7.

Mazrui, Ali A. 2003. 'Introduction', in Ali A. Mazrui, ed. *UNESCO General History of Africa. Vol. VII, Africa Since 1935*. Oxford: James Currey, 1–25.

Mazurana, Dyan, Angela Raven-Roberts, and Jane Parpart, eds. 2005. *Gender, Conflict, and Peacekeeping*. Lanham, MD: Rowman and Littlefield.

Mburu, Nene. 2005. *Bandits on the Border: the Last Frontier in the Search for Somali Unity*. Trenton, NJ: Red Sea Press,

Melber, Henning, ed. 2003. *Limits to Liberation in Southern Africa: The Unfinished Business of Democratic Consolidation*. Cape Town: HSRC Press.

Melvern, Linda. 2000. *A People Betrayed: The Role of the West in Rwanda's Genocide*. New York: Zed Books.

Milkias, Paulos. 2005. *The Battle of Adwa: Reflections on Ethiopia's Historic Victory Against European Colonialism*. New York: Algora Publishing.

Miller, Charles.1974. *Battle for the Bundu: The First World War in East Africa*. New York: Macmillan.

Mills, Greg. 2004. 'Africa's New Strategic Significance', *The Washington Quarterly* 27 (4): 157–69.

Minter, William. 1994. *Apartheid's Contras: An Inquiry into the Roots of War in Angola and Mozambique*. Atlantic Highlands, NJ: Zed Books.

Mlambo, Norman. 2004. 'Rethinking Economic Agendas in African Conflicts', Paper presented at International Conference on African Conflicts: Management, Resolution and Post-Conflict Recovery and Development, organized by the Organization of Social Science Research in Eastern and Southern Africa (OSSREA), Addis Ababa, 29 November–1 December.

Moran, Mary H. 2006. *Liberia: The Violence of Democracy*. Philadelphia, PA: University of Pennsylvania Press.

Munene, G. Macharia, J.D. Olewe Nyunya and Korwa G. Adar, eds. 1995. *The United States and Africa: From Independence to the End of the Cold War*. Nairobi: East African Educational Publishers.

Nafziger, E. Wayne and Juha Auvinen. 2002. 'Economic Development, Inequality, War, and State Violence', *World Development* 30 (2): 153–63.

Namhila, Ellen Ndeshi. 1997. *The Price of Freedom*. Windhoek: New Namibia Books.

Namwambah, Tom. 2004. 'Politics of Ethnicity in Kenya: A Subjective Approach to Conflict Resolution Strategies', Paper presented at International Conference on African Conflicts: Management, Resolution and Post-Conflict Recovery and Development, organized by the Organization of Social Science Research in Eastern and Southern Africa (OSSREA), Addis Ababa, 29 November–1 December.

Negash, Tekeste and Kjetil Tronvoll. 2000. *Brothers at War: Making Sense of the Eritrean-Ethiopian War*. Oxford: James Currey; Athens, OH: Ohio University Press.

Nest, Michael. 2006. *The Democratic Republic of Congo: Economic Dimensions of War and Peace*. Boulder, CO: Lynne Rienner.

New American Century. 2000. *Rebuilding America's Defenses: Strategy, Forces and Resources for a New Century*. Washington, DC: New American Century.

Noer, Thomas J. 1985. *Cold War and Black Liberation: the United States and White Rule in Africa, 1948-1968*. Columbia, MO: University of Missouri Press.

Oberst, Timothy S. 1991. *Cost of Living and Strikes in British Africa c.1939–1948: Imperial Policy and the Impact of the Second World War*. Ann Arbor, MI: Michigan University Press.

Oded, Arye. 1987. *Africa and the Middle East Conflict*. Boulder, CO: Lynne Rienner.

Ojo, Olusola. 1988. *Africa and Israel: Relations in Perspective*. Boulder, CO: Westview Press.

Okocha, Emma. 1994. *Blood on the Niger: An Untold Story of the Nigerian Civil War*. Washington, DC: USA Africa in association with GOM SLAM.

Osaghae, Eghosa E. 1996. 'Human Rights and Ethnic Conflict Management: The Case of Nigeria', *Journal of Peace Research* 33 (2): 171–188.

Osuntokun, Akinjide. 1979. *Nigeria and the First World War*. Atlantic Highlands, NJ: Humanities Press.

Oyebade, Adebayo and Abiodun Alao, eds. 1998. *Africa after the Cold War: The Changing Perspectives on Security.* Trenton, NJ: Africa World Press.

Oyeweso, Siyan. 1992. *Perspectives on the Nigerian Civil War.* Ojokoro, Lagos: OAP Publications.

Page, Melvin E. 2000. *The Chiwaya War: Malawians and the First World War.* Boulder, CO: Westview Press.

Page, Melvin E., ed. 1987. *Africa and the First World War.* New York: St Martin's Press.

Panitch, Leo and Colin Leys, eds. 2002. *Fighting Identities: Race, Religion and Ethno-nationalism.* London: Merlin.

Patterson, K. David and Gerald W. Harting, eds. 1978. *Disease in African History: An Introductory Survey and Case Studies.* Durham, NC: Duke University Press.

Percox, David. 2004. *Britain, Kenya and the Cold War: Imperial Defence, Colonial Security and Decolonization.* New York: Tauris Academic Studies.

Peters, Joel. 1992. *Israel and Africa: The Problematic Friendship.* London: British Academic Press.

Peterson, V. Spike and Anne S. Runyan. 1999. *Global Gender Issues: Dilemmas in World Politics.* 2nd edn. Boulder, CO: Westview Press.

Prunier, Gérard. 1998. *The Rwanda Crisis: History of a Genocide.* London: C. Hurst.

Pugh, Michael and Neil Cooper. 2004. *War Economies in a Regional Context: Challenges and Transformation.* Boulder, CO: Lynne Rienner.

Ramraj, V., Michael Hor and Kent Roach, eds. 2005. *Global Anti-terrorism Law and Policy.* New York: Cambridge University Press.

Ranger, T. O. 1967. *Revolt in Southern Rhodesia, 1896–1897,* London: Heinemann.

Ranger, Terence. 1985. *Peasant Consciousness and Guerilla War in Zimbabwe: A Comparative Study.* London: James Currey; Berkeley, CA: University of California Press.

Reardon, Betty. 1985. *Sexism and the War System.* New York: Teachers College Press.

Reno, William. 1998. *Warlord Politics and African States.* Boulder, CO: Lynne Rienner.

Richards, Paul. 1996. *Fighting for the Rain Forest: War, Youth and Resources in Sierra Leone.* Oxford: James Currey.

Rone, Jemera. 1995. *Children in Sudan: Slaves, Street Children and Child Soldiers.* New York: Human Rights Watch.

Ross, M. H. 1993. *The Management of Conflict.* Cambridge: Cambridge University Press.

Ross, Michael L. 2003. 'Oil. Drugs, and Diamonds: The Varying Roles of Natural Resources in Civil War', in Karen Ballentine and Jake Sherman, eds. *The Political Economy of Armed Conflict: Beyond Greed and Grievance.* Boulder, CO: Lynne Rienner, 47–70.

Rotberg, Robert I. et al. 2000. *Peacekeeping and Peace Enforcement in Africa: Methods of Conflict Prevention.* Washington, DC: Brookings Institution Press.

Ruddick, Sara. 1989. *Maternal Thinking: Towards a Politics of Peace.* London: The Women's Press.

Sainsbury, Keith. 1979. *The North African Landings, 1942: A Strategic Decision.* Newark, DE: University of Delaware Press.

Sampson, Anthony. 1999. *Mandela: The Authorized Biography.* New York: Alfred Knopf.

Schraeder, Peter J. 2006. 'From Irredentism to Secession: The Decline of Pan-Somali Nationalism', in Barrington, Lowell W., ed., *After Independence Making and Protecting the Nation in Postcolonial and Postcommunist States.* Ann Arbor, MI: University of Michigan Press.

Seck, Diery. 2004. 'An Economic Theory of Civil War in Africa'. Paper presented at International Conference on African Conflicts: Management, Resolution and Post-Conflict Recovery and Development, organized by the Organization of Social Science Research in Eastern and Southern Africa (OSSREA), Addis Ababa, 29 November–1 December.

Selassie, Bereket Habte. 1980. *Conflict and Intervention in the Horn of Africa.* New York: Monthly Review Press.

Semujanga, Josias. 2003. *Origins of Rwandan Genocide.* Amherst, NY: Humanity Books.

Shepard, Todd. 2006. *The invention of Decolonization: the Algerian War and the Remaking of France.* Ithaca, NY: Cornell University Press.

Silverstein, Paul. 2005. 'The New Barbarians: Piracy and Terrorism on the North African Frontier', *CR: The New Centennial Review* 5 (1): 179–212.

Singer, P.W. 2001. 'Corporate Warriors: The Rise of the Privatized Military Industry and Its Ramifications for International Security.' *International Security* 26, 3: 186–220.

Sisulu, Elinor. 2002. *Walter and Albertina Sisulu: In Our Lifetime.* Claremont, South Africa: David Philip.

Skjelsbæk, Inger and Dan Smith, eds. 2001. *Gender, Peace and Conflict.* Thousand Oaks, CA: SAGE.

Sura, Vikram with Jonas Hagen. 2005. 'Fourth Committee: Special Political and Decolonization of Conflict, and Post-conflict, Situations', United Nations Chronicle [Online Edition]. Available at http://www.un.org/Pubs/chronicle/2003/issue1/0103p16.html.

Talbott, John. 1980. *The War Without a Name: France in Algeria, 1954–1962.* New York: Knopf.

Thomas, Troy S., Stephen D. Kiser, and William D. Casebeer. 2005. *Warlords Rising: Confronting Violent Non-state Actors*. Lanham, MD: Lexington Books.

Totten, Samuel and Eric Markusen, eds. 2006. *Genocide in Darfur: Investigating the Atrocities in the Sudan*. New York: Routledge.

Turshen, Meredeth. 1998. *What Women Do in Wartime: Gender and conflict in Africa*. London: Zed Books.

Twagilimana, Aimable. 2003. *The Debris of Ham: Ethnicity, Regionalism, and the 1994 Rwandan Genocide*. Lanham, MD: University Press of America.

UNESCO. 1985. *Africa and the Second World War* (Report and Papers of the Symposium Organized by Unesco at Benghazi, Libyan Arab Jamahiriya, from 10 to 13 Nov. 1980). Paris: Unesco.

United Nations. 2004. *Report of the Secretary General's High Level Panel. A More Secure World: Our Shared Responsibility*. New York: United Nations.

UNRISD. 2005. *Gender Equality: Striving for Justice in an Unequal World*. Geneva: UNRISD.

Veney, Cassandra R. 2006. *Forced Migration in Eastern Africa*. New York: Palgrave Macmillan.

Vickers, Michael. 2000. *Ethnicity and Sub-Nationalism in Nigeria: Movement for a Mid-West State*. Oxford: Worldview Publishers.

Volpi, Frédéric. 2003. *Islam and Democracy : The Failure of Dialogue in Algeria*. Sterling, VA and London: Pluto Press.

Volpi, Frédéric. 2003. *Islam and Democracy: The Failure of Dialogue in Algeria*. London: Pluto Press.

White, Mathew. 2003. 'Wars, Massacres and Atrocities of the Twentieth Century,' in *Historical Atlas of the Twentieth Century*, [Online] Available at http://users.erols.com/mwhite28/20centry.htm Accessed 28 August 2004.

White House, The. 2002. 'The National Security Strategy of the United States'. Washington, DC: The White House. http://www.whitehouse.gov/nsc/hss.html. (accessed 15 January 2005).

Zeleza, Paul Tiyambe. 2003. *Rethinking Africa's Globalization. Vol.1, The Intellectual Challenges*. Trenton, NJ: Africa World Press.

Zeleza, Paul Tiyambe. 2004a. 'Resurrecting South Africa from the Ashes of Apartheid', *Africa Development* 1&2: 7–15.

Zeleza, Paul Tiyambe. 2004b. 'The Republicanization of America.' *Codesria Bulletin*, 1&2: 40–42.

Zeleza, Paul Tiyambe. 2005. 'Human Rights and Development in Africa: Current Contexts, Challenges, and Opportunities', in Lennart Wohlgemuth and Ebrima Sall, eds. *Human Rights, Regionalism and the Dilemmas of Democracy in Africa*. Dakar: Codesria Book Series and Uppsala: Nordic Africa Institute, 57–96.

Notes

1   A perspective dubbed by Paul Richards (1996: xiii) as the 'New Barbarism' thesis.

2   A common classification is to distinguish between inter-state, intra-state and extra-state wars, see Henderson and Singer (2002).

3   There is a vast literature on struggles against apartheid, some of which is reviewed in Zeleza (2004a); also see Gregory Houston (1999), Eric Louw (2004), Lindsay Eades (1999), and the remarkable autobiography and biographies of Mandela and the Sisulus (Mandela 1994; Sampson 1999; Sisulu 2002).

4   The Rwanda genocide was the product of complex colonial and postcolonial histories, as well as internal, regional and international dynamics. Of the vast literature on the subject see some of the following: Mamdani (2001), Gourevitch (1999), Prunier (1998), Melvern (2000), Semujanga (2003), and Twagilimana (2003).

5   I discuss these developments in greater detail in Zeleza (2003, 2005).

6   All the key elements of Bush's doctrine of pre-emption articulated in a report released in September 2002, *The National Security Strategy of the United States* (White House 2002), are presaged in a 2000 report from a neo-conservative organization, the New American Century (2000: ii), called *Rebuilding America's Defenses*, which unequivocally calls for the US to rebuild, modernize and maintain its military and nuclear strategic superiority in order to sustain a Pax Americana. It has since transpired that plans for a premeditated attack on Iraq, to secure 'regime change', were in place even before Bush assumed office in January 2001 and therefore had nothing to do with the attacks of September 11, Iraq's unproven connections with Al-Qaeda, the existence of weapons of mass destruction that were never found, or the need to export democracy (Anonymous 2004; Clarke 2004).

7   Anonymous (2004: 241) tabulates them as follows: 'U.S support for Israel that keeps

Palestinians in the Israeli's thrall; US and other Western troops on the Arabian Peninsula; US occupation of Iraq and Afghanistan; US support for Russia, India, and China against their Muslim militants; US pressure on Arab energy producers to keep oil prices low; and US support for apostate, corrupt, and tyrannical Muslim governments'. That Osama bin Laden articulates and uses these grievances to mobilize his followers does not mean they are not real or shared by millions of people in the region. While some of those opposed to the US in the region are indeed terrorists, many more are ordinary nationalists fighting to liberate their countries from foreign occupation and domination.

8   This figure is from the National Priorities Project that monitors and tallies the costs of war on an ongoing basis; see its website at: http://nationalpriorities.org/index.php?option=com_wrapper&Itemid=182
    Accessed 1 November 2006.

9   This figure was widely disputed and predictably rejected by American and British leaders, the architects of the ill-fated Iraq war. It is interesting to observe the controversy about the study's methodology and conclusion, when casualty figures of African wars or the HIV/AIDS pandemic that are often based on far less rigorous research than the *Lancet* study, if not outright speculation, are largely accepted without a murmur by the so-called 'international – read Euro-American – media.

10 See the detailed report by Phyllis Bennis and the IPS Iraq Task Force (2004). At the time of writing (November 2006) the urgent need to change policy in Iraq is widely accepted even in American and British government circles, and most people in the two countries now regard the invasion as a failed adventure. As reported by the media, the quagmire in Iraq played a major role in the defeat of the Republican Party in the US midterm elections in November 2006. See the following news magazines, *Newsweek*, 'Election 2006: The Aftershocks', 20 November 2006 and *The Economist*, 'The Incredible Shrinking Presidency', 11–17 November 2006.

11 Paul Silverstein (2005) suggests, in the case of North Africa, that the 'war on terror' rekindles in the Western imaginary memories not only of Islamic invasions but also of Barbary piracy and terrorism. The literature on Africa and the 'war on terror' is growing rapidly. For a sample, see Kadende-Kaiser and Kaiser (2005); Davis (2005); Ramraj et al. (2005); Kraxberger (2005); Marrouchi (2003); Silverstein (2005); Carmody (2005); Barnes (2005); Mills (2004); El-Khawas (2003).

12 For example, Human Rights Watch (2004) has accused the UN's Security Council of disregarding human rights in the work of its Counter-Terrorism Committee and the Counter-Terrorism Executive Directorate, established by resolutions passed after 11 September 2001, both of which have to date shown reluctance to address the human rights implications of the anti-terrorism laws and strategies of member states.

13 See, for example, the reports by Amnesty International (2002, 2003).

14 Also see Amnesty International's (2002a) detailed critique of the convention adopted by the League of Arab States, which Amnesty believes presents a serious threat to human rights in Arab countries, many of which are, of course, in Africa.

15 For recent accounts and critiques of these analyses, see Kieh (2002) and Fosu and Collier (2005).

16 These wars are variously called 'new wars', 'postmodern wars', 'wars of the third kind', and 'people's wars', see Henderson and Singer (2002: 166–71).

17 Kalyvas (2001: 109) criticizes the Eurocentricism and culturalist thrust of the 'new wars' theorists and argues that 'the end of the Cold War seems to have caused the demise of the conceptual categories used to interpret civil wars rather than a decline in the ideological motivations of civil wars at the mass level'.

18 A sizeable literature has grown using this paradigm. Examples include Berdal and Malone (2000); Cilliers and Dietrich (2000); and Lind and Sturman (2002).

19 He notes that these studies have influenced the UN Security Council and General Assembly to pass resolutions prohibiting the import of conflict diamonds, to impose sanctions on rebel movements such as UNITA, and to condemn the illegal exploitation of natural resources and other forms of wealth from the Democratic Republic of Congo. Charles Cater (2003: 37) also comments on the economic predation paradigm in the UN sanctions regime, noting 'prior to 1990, the UN had only authorized sanctions twice – for Rhodesia in 1966 and for South Africa in 1977. During the 1990s, the Security Council approved sanctions relating to conflicts in twelve different countries.'

20 Michael Ross (2003) offers an interesting analysis of the varied impact of resources on separatist and non-separatist conflicts, and the different impact of various resources depending on what he calls their lootability, obstructability and legality. After examining fifteen conflicts in Africa, Asia, and Latin America he concludes, 'unlootable resources

[e.g., oil] are more likely to produce separatist conflicts, and lootable resources [e.g., diamonds] are more likely to produce nonseparatist conflicts' (Ross 2003: 67).

21 See Collier and Sambanis (2005a, 2005b). They indicate that some of the criticisms have registered, and the Collier-Hoeffler Model, as they call it, has been revised, but only on the margins. The first volume deals with Africa, and the second with the rest of the world, a division based on, we are told, mere convenience. To quote Collier et al. (2005: 26): 'There is no substantive rationale behind this organization of cases – we do not think African civil wars are different. This is simply a device to present the material effectively, given the considerable length of the book.' The other influential studies have been sponsored by the International Peace Academy through its Economic Agendas in Civil Wars program with which Collier was once affiliated; they include Berdal and Malone (2000), Ballentine and Sherman (2003), and Pugh and Cooper (2004)

22 Structural adjustment, together with the economic marginalization of border areas and the absence of regional military security mechanisms, often creates the permissive conditions for the development and sustenance of conflicts and undermines post-conflict resolution and transformation (Pugh and Cooper 2004: 35–39).

23 Regional economic networks provide channels for trade in conflict goods, smuggling and tax avoidance, and the phenomenon of displacement; military networks provide arms and mercenaries, and can create displacement effects; formal and informal political networks often reflect and reinforce regional economic and military linkages and sustain the shadow economic activities of war economies; and social networks include occupational, ethnic and diaspora affiliations that serve to underpin regional conflict complexes (Pugh and Cooper 2004: 25–35).

24 The distinction is based on the primary sources of state revenue: rentier states derive theirs from mineral rents, while merchant states derive theirs from general taxation including that of marketed peasant produce. Merchant states have to negotiate with more producers than rentier states, and therefore tend to provide more services and enjoy higher levels of social development and to boast of better human development indicators than the rentier states.

25 The UNRISD report, for which I served as one of nine members of the Advisory Group, is an invaluable source of comparative global data on 'gender, armed conflict and the search for peace', which constitute section 4 of the report (pp.205–59). The report as a whole is based on more than five dozen reports from different regions and countries, including several on Africa.

26 This is primarily because the papers were originally presented at a conference convened by the Organization of Social Science Research in Eastern Africa whose mandate is eastern and southern Africa.

27 For example, in the epic struggle against apartheid in South Africa Christian ideas inspired not only the protagonists in the conflict, but also the formation and work of the Truth and Reconciliation Commission.

28 Personal communication with Tiyanjana Maluwa, Professor of Law, Pennsylvania State University and formerly Legal Counsel, the African Union (1998–2001), 25 and 26 November 2006.

Prologue
Conflict in Africa: An Overview

ALI A. MAZRUI

As the twentieth-first century begins, Africa consists of some fifty-four countries, depending upon how you count some islands. Since independence, about one-third of these countries have experienced large-scale political violence or war (Dunnigan and Bay 1996: 651–53). This does not include those countries that have had relatively bloodless military coups or occasional assassinations. (After all, even the United States has had presidential assassinations.) It is true that not all of Africa is afflicted to the same degree. Africa is an immense continent, richly varied in its cultures and peoples. The levels of violence differ greatly. Nor can one easily predict where violence will occur. Kenya, for example, shares borders with five other countries, four of which have experienced civil wars: Ethiopia, Sudan, Somalia and Uganda. The fifth country on its borders is Tanzania, a country that was partly born out a revolution (the Zanzibar Revolution of 1964). In comparison with its neighbors, Kenya has so far been spared large-scale civil conflict. Yet the overall pattern of violence on the African continent is disturbing and deserves analysis.

The purpose of this chapter is to provide a brief overview of conflict in Africa. The first part of the chapter will focus on the causes of conflict. There are no simple and easy explanations for conflicts in Africa, and the theories that have been advanced are both numerous and contradictory. Rather than attempt to catalogue these many theories, this chapter will look at some of the rather haunting paradoxes that seem to mark conflict in Africa. The second part of the chapter will suggest some possible solutions and consider how much progress has, in fact, been made in recent decades.

The Roots of Conflict

Black Violence, White Roots
While the most lethal of all wars in Africa have been those fought between blacks, the roots of these wars lie in the white legacy. On the one hand, bloody as they were, the anti-colonial wars were less bloody than

postcolonial wars. It is true that the anti-colonial wars (primarily fought between blacks and whites) did cost a lot of lives. A case in point is Algeria, where more than a million people perished at the hands of the French. However, postcolonial wars have been fought mainly between blacks, and they have been even more ruthless.[1]

On the other hand, it must be recognized that the seeds of the post-colonial wars themselves lie in the sociological and political mess which 'white' colonialism created in Africa. The colonial powers destroyed old methods of conflict resolution and traditional African political institutions, and failed to create effective substitute ones in their place. In the West, effective states are widely perceived to be one of the major tools societies have invented for the preservation of internal stability and order. In Africa, the states founded by Europeans were not effective. They were developed in newly fashioned countries and built on fragile bases. The Africans who inherited these states from the Europeans had, moreover, little experience in governing themselves. Self-government is not something easily taught. Failing states have been one of the major sources of conflict in postcolonial Africa.

Are Borders to Blame?

While most African conflicts are partly caused by borders, those conflicts are not themselves *about* borders. Before the Western colonial powers arrived, there were virtually no boundaries in Africa. Most people lived in loose groupings. Their territories were unmarked. Empires came and went, absorbing new groups and being assimilated themselves, but possessing few, if any, rigid frontiers. But at the end of the nineteenth century the colonial West arrived. The Berlin Conference in 1885 imposed the iron grid of division upon the continent.

The political boundaries created by colonial powers in Africa enclosed groups with no traditions of shared authority or shared systems of settling disputes. These groups did not necessarily have the time to learn to become congenial.[2] In West Africa, for example, the large territory which the British carved out and called Nigeria enclosed three major nations and several smaller ones. Among the larger groups, the Yoruba in the west were very different from the Muslim Hausa in the north, who in turn were quite distinct from the Ibo in the east. This artificial mixture was to lead to one of Africa's great human tragedies, the Nigerian civil war of 1967–70. Until pictures of starving Ethiopian children shocked the world in the 1980s, the most haunting images from postcolonial Africa were those of starving Biafran children, the victims of this war.

If colonialism forced into the same political entity people who would otherwise have lived apart, it also separated people who would otherwise have lived together. A country like Somalia is in effect a nation trying to become an all-inclusive state. The Somali have scattered in four different countries, Djibouti, Ethiopia, Kenya and Somalia. Their desire for reunification has resulted in deadly conflict.

On the other hand, paradoxical as this seems, one cannot say that African conflicts are about boundaries. African governments, ironically, have tended to be possessive about these artificially created colonial borders.

They have generally resisted any challenge to them. There have been relatively few disputes about borders. The borders generate conflicts within them but have not been encouraged to generate conflict across them. The dispute between Ethiopia and Eritrea is in this regard an exception rather than the rule (Tronvoll 1999).

Religion or Ethnicity?

While the worst conflicts in Arab Africa are religious, the worst conflicts in Black Africa are ethnic. The word ethnic in this case is used in the sense of the older word, tribal.[3] By Arab Africa, we largely mean North Africa (Algeria, Libya and Egypt, for example, are Arab). Algeria is afflicted by arguably the worst conflict in Arab Africa. The conflict is between Islamicists and the military secularists, and religion, however politicized, is at its root. It is among the ugliest and most intractable armed conflicts in the world (Mortimer 1996). Religion is also at the root of the conflict in Egypt (Ansari 1984).

By contrast, the worst outbreaks of violence in Black Africa in the 1990s occurred as a result of the conflict between the Hutu and the Tutsi. The genocides in Rwanda and Burundi in the 1990s were ethnic (Nyakanvzi 1998). The conflict in Somalia was likewise ethnic or, at any rate, sub-ethnic (between clans rather than between tribes) ((Hashim 1997). The civil war between northern and southern Sudan further illustrates my point. Sudan straddles the Arab and the African worlds (Deng 1995). Is its civil war primarily ethnic or primarily religious? You may take your pick. Either interpretation is totally defensible

Resources or Identity?

While blacks clash with whites in Africa over resources, blacks clash with blacks over their identities. White and black people, in other words, fight each other about *who owns what*, but blacks fight blacks about *who is who*. Racial conflicts between blacks and whites in Africa are ultimately economic. Apartheid in South Africa, for example, was ultimately an economic war. By contrast, when you look at configurations of violence in those parts of Africa where blacks are fighting blacks, it is difficult to show that the struggles are over resources. Often there are no resources of any significance over which to fight. Sometimes it is possible see the struggle in terms of an effort to get a share of power. But for the most part, major clashes appear to be related to cultural demarcations. The struggle between the Hutu and Tutsi is one such example.

That it is culture rather than economics that matters in the politics of Black Africa can best be illustrated by looking at what happens when Africans who are left of center attempt to invoke class solidarity. When they fight somebody who invokes ethnic solidarity, the cards are stacked against them. Class symbols time and again prove inadequate in the face of ethnic sentiment. In Kenya, for example, the Luo politician Oginga Odinga used left-of-center rhetoric and appealed to all Kenyans to follow him. Despite the fact that his message ought to have appealed to the exploited, those who rallied to his cause were not the disadvantaged members of all Kenyan ethnic groups. Instead, Odinga found himself followed by Luo of all social classes. Obafemi Awolowo of Nigeria had a similar experience. He moved just a little to the left of the normal orientation of major Nigerian politicians. He warned Nigerians that they were being cheated. He too drew support, not from disadvantaged Nigerians of all ethnic groups, but from all the Yoruba. The Yoruba, moreover, came from all social classes, the rich and the poor. In other words, the ethnic messenger rather than the economic message has proved to be what counts in the conflicts among blacks.

Modern Weapons and Pre-modern Armies

At independence, weapons in Africa were in general not very advanced, but the armies were relatively disciplined and professional, in short, modem. Now the weapons have become more advanced, but the armies have become less disciplined and less professional. Both the standing army and Western weapons, it may be added, were yet another legacy of colonialism. One of the few African countries to consider, even briefly, whether to do without a standing army was Tanzania. In 1964 Julius Nyerere had the opportunity to disband his entire army and not build an alternative one. He did disband the old one, but he did not follow Costa Rica's example and do without an army. Instead he reconstructed a national army. African countries, as a whole, entered independence with this dysfunctional twin inheritance.

This combination of modern weapons and less than modem armies has proved to be a menacing and destabilizing one. Africa's rather fragile government institutions are all too easily destroyed by the predominant power in the country, the gun. Soldiers have proved to be the most power-ful force in African politics since independence. Africa has seen over seventy coups in a quarter of a century. The susceptibility of African states to military takeovers is all the more worrisome, in that militaries have not proved capable of transforming African economies. Some soldiers, it is true, have made an effort to be constructive. Jerry Rawlings of Ghana, a military pilot who seized power in Accra in the summer of 1979, sought to put his power to good use. He attempted to mobilize his people for economic development and social transformation rather than for war, and Ghana received a relatively large amount of support from the World Bank. But Rawlings' success was limited, and Ghana to this day remains impoverished.

Dualism and Pluralism

Although plural societies cause us more alarm, dual societies may in fact be more dangerous. The dangers of plural societies have been much discussed. A plural society is one which has multiple groups defined ethnically, racially, religiously, culturally, or by other parameters. The United States is a plural society. Dual societies are less numerous and less discussed than plural societies in Africa.[4] A dual society is one in which two groups (again defined ethnically, religiously, culturally, or by other para-meters) account for over 80 per cent of the population. Belgium, for example, is a dual society of Flemish and Francophone identity (O'Neill 1998).

Dual societies run a number of high risks. First, they run the risk of getting trapped in a *prolonged stalemate*. The stand-off between Greek and

Turkish Cypriots is a case in point (McDonald 1997). Second, a *culture of polarized ethnic distrust* may develop. The examples that come to mind here are outside Africa: Belgium, Guyana and Trinidad. Third, dual societies may endure *prolonged periods of tension and violence*. Outside of Africa the struggle in Northern Ireland provides ample warning of this. Within Africa, Berbers and Arabs in Algeria are on the verge of a similar struggle. Fourth, dual societies also run the risk of *separatism and secessionism*. Asian and European examples exist. Sri Lanka is still torn by the Tamil bid to secede from the Sinhalese-dominated polity (Senaratne 1997). Bosnia and Herzegovina today is split between the Muslim-Croat Federation in the west and the Serbian Republic in the east (Holbrooke 1998). Lastly, dual societies run the risk of genocide and potential genocidal reprisal. The most telling example of this is to be found in Rwanda, where the Hutu and Tutsi engaged in bloody confrontation that destabilized the region and became a key cause of the international war that later unfolded in the neighboring Democratic Republic of Congo. Meanwhile, Burundi faced acute danger of genocide until a delegation led by Nelson Mandela in 2001 helped ease ethnic tensions at least temporarily.[5]

'Ethnic' dual societies can be differentiated from 'regional' dual societies, where the division is between two regions rather than between two ethnic groups. Within Africa we may point to Sudan, Nigeria and Uganda. Northern and southern Sudan experienced civil war between 1955 and 1972 and have been engaged in civil war again since 1983 (Lesch 1998). Northern Nigeria fought southern Nigeria in a civil war (1967–70) (Cervenka 1971). While this war was not totally about divisions between north and south, it certainly included that dimension. In Uganda, there have been periodic eruptions of violence between north and south, especially since 1980. Outside of Africa, we may point to the struggle between the northern and southern US (the American Civil War) and, more recently, the tensions between North and South Korea; since their unification both Vietnam and Germany have become regional dual societies and have had to deal with the attendant problems. The evidence to date suggests that dualism may be even more dangerous than pluralism.

War: Curse or Blessing?

Africa should indeed *celebrate* the relative rarity of inter-state conflicts today. But should it also *lament* the relative rarity of inter-state conflicts in the past? Has the balance between external and internal conflict tilted too far towards the internal? Africa has, in fact, had more than its share of civil wars and, as human history has repeated time and again, civil wars leave deeper scars than most inter-state conflicts. They are more indiscriminate and ruthless than are most inter-state conflicts, with the obvious exception of world wars or nuclear wars. The US lost more people in its civil war in the 1860s than in all its other wars combined.

That Africa has had so many civil wars is, perhaps, not unrelated to the fact that it has had relatively few inter-state conflicts. The history of nation-states in Europe reveals a persistent tendency to externalize conflict and thus help promote greater unity at home. A sense of nationhood within each European country was partly fostered by a sense of rivalry and occasional conflict with its neighbors. Even the consolidation of the European state as a sovereign state was forged in the fire of inter-European conflicts. The Peace of Westphalia (1648), which launched the nation-state system, was signed at the end of the Thirty Years' War.[6]

Africa's relative dearth of external conflicts in the past may thus partly account for the prevalence of internal conflict in the present. In the modern world, however, external aggression is no longer a viable means of forging unity and building states. International war has become too dangerous. Africa must look to other solutions to bring an end to divisiveness.

Conflict Resolution

What will the future hold for Africa? The presence of violence and conflict on the African continent is obvious, but all is not self-evidently gloomy. In the past few decades, there have been signs of the winds of change blowing through the continent. Africans can point to examples of successful conflict resolution and reduction. The late Julius Nyerere, for example, has bequeathed young Tanzanians a greater self-confidence and national pride. In November 1985 he voluntarily stepped down as president of Tanzania and Vice-President Ali Hassan Mwinyi took over. Out of some 170 rulers Africa has had since independence, Nyerere was only the third to relinquish office of his own accord. By leaving the political scene, he gave the lie to the famous dictum that all power corrupts. In Ghana, Jerry Rawlings sought to eradicate corruption, tackled the economic miseries of his people and cultivated their sense of independence and initiative. In Nigeria, the civil war (1967–70), ugly and tragic as it was, did not scar the nation as it might have done. Nigerians are not noted for their restraint and discipline. Yet, the victors of the Nigerian-Biafran war were magnanimous to their enemies. They did not gloat or focus on vengeance. Yakubu Gowon and his successor Murtala Muhammed both demonstrated a remarkable ability to bring about reconciliation and, in so doing, to help heal the wounds of war.

All these examples make it clear that Africans can bring their countries to a better future. What are some of the more concrete things that can be done to achieve this goal? By cultivating toleration, developing pluralism, improving civil-military relations, and fostering innovative Pan-African solutions, African nations can make positive and constructive moves to reduce and resolve conflicts.

Toleration

One important step towards creating greater stability on the African continent is to cultivate that very elusive trait, tolerance. Tolerance is the ability to accept difference (Mendus 1988). We need to recognize that victims of intolerance do not necessarily become paragons of toleration. History has amply illustrated this fact. Christians, who suffered dreadful tortures at the hands of the Roman government, in turn inflicted the torments of the inquisition on their enemies in later centuries. The Jews, who suffered incalculable miseries under the Nazis, themselves became oppressors. As an occupying power in the Holy Land, they held thousands of Palestinians as political prisoners. The Muslims, whose entire calendar is a celebration of the Hegira as asylum, are today bombing each other's mosques across the sectarian divide. The Tutsi, as victims of yesterday, became the oppressors of today and the Hutu, as victims of today, seem destined to become the oppressors of tomorrow. Toleration can work. Kenya was once such a closed and intolerant society that the notion of a Kenyan, in Kenya, daring, as the author did in 1991, to call upon the Kenyan President to resign was seen as something remarkable. By the turn of the 2000s every second or third Kenyan was calling upon President Daniel arap Moi to step down. It was no longer of any significance. There is obviously a new level of toleration of dissent in many parts of Africa, which must be actively cultivated and institutionally enforced.

Constructive Pluralization

Another avenue that needs to be explored is what some call decentralization, and others, myself included, call the pluralization of power. Recently, power has tended to shift away from the center and become institutionalized in smaller groups. This trend is, in my view, a healthy one, and should be encouraged by promoting the development of multi-party systems, capitalism, federalism, and the political representation of women.

One of the historic problems in Africa has been the existence of one-party states that have restricted the development of multiple political organizations. Multiple parties are useful to the extent that they expand choices. Fortunately, many African countries that have previously been one-party states have become multi-party states in more recent times. They have been moving towards greater toleration of opposition parties and rival political organizations. Tanzania under Julius Nyerere and Kenya under Daniel arap Moi both illustrate this trend.[7]

So long as power is concentrated in one place, constructive pluralism cannot flourish. Constructive pluralism must be nurtured. How can this be done? One answer is to develop at least minimal degrees of capitalism. This notion is, of course, abhorrent to many African socialists. However, capitalism is the necessary 'manure' for liberal pluralistic democracy.[8] Manure may be dirty, but it does make things grow! Capitalism creates the kind of environment in which constructive pluralism can take root. It helps ensure that power is not concentrated in one particular place. A concrete example of the kind of thing capitalism can accomplish can be seen in the resignation of Richard Nixon from the American presidency in 1974. Without the newspapers, owned by private interests, he would certainly not have been obliged to step down. This does not mean that Africa should develop the same from of capitalism that exists in contemporary America. The American system demands far too little economic accountability from its citizens. Such a system would be quite destructive on this continent. What is needed is for us to develop a type of capitalism in Africa that permits us to pluralize power but which is also responsible and does not allow the desire for profit to run amok (Hirst 1998).

The concept of federalism also deserves to be given more attention. Federalism refers to the division of power between a central authority and its constituent political units. For the last thirty-five years or so, only Nigeria has treated federalism as a legitimate concept. The trouble is that Nigeria has been almost constantly governed by military rule and militarism does not go well with federalism. The rest of Africa has tended to regard the concept as anathema. And yet it does hold out some real possibilities.

Representation of Women

Another important means of creating greater stability in Africa is to give a greater voice to African women. Women need to become major voices in decisions not just about development – although that is crucial – but on other issues (including security issues). This means that women must be given power within the legislative process and in the executive branch of government, and they should be enlisted in the armed forces in increasing numbers.

African women today are, for the most part, sadly under-represented. To change the situation, some kind of direct intervention is needed. Yet this is not easy. The problem is well illustrated in India. Indians are trying to deal with the lack of female representation in their government. There is a movement afoot to have one-third of the legislative branch of government reserved for women. Despite the fact, however, that a variety of political powers claim to support such legislation, Parliament refuses to pass it. Opponents claim that the real intention of its proponents is to increase the representation of the higher caste. They point out that it would be women from the upper caste who would break into power. So, the argument goes, by increasing the representation of women you reduce the representation of the lower classes.

In Africa, too, the struggle for emancipation will doubtless encounter entrenched opposition. While there is a great deal of cultural variation in Africa, many African societies have traditionally assigned women a very subordinate place. At the same time, we need not despair. Culture is not always the insurmountable obstacle that we think it is. One of the last barriers to be broken between men and women is that of military culture. Even liberal societies have balked at the enlistment of women in the army. And yet in Somalia, women – and Muslim women at that – can at times be seen bearing arms. When the sense of urgency is great enough, traditional values are transcended.

It is clearly vital that, despite the difficulties, Africa begins to empower women. The author's recommendation is that this be accomplished gradually in a series of measured steps. In the first phase, women voters should be given the opportunity to elect women candidates. A certain percentage of seats (about 10 per cent) should be reserved for these female candidates. In the second phase, a certain portion of seats should still be reserved for women. However, women should no longer seek votes from women alone. They should attempt to reach out to men as voters and address the concerns of males as well as females. This will help close the gender gap. In the third and final phase, when it is no longer necessary, seats should no longer be reserved for women. A parallel process in Zimbabwe suggests that this could happen. Here seats were reserved on a racial basis for a while. After a point, however, such quotas ceased to be necessary.

The greater politicization and empowerment of women has direct security consequences. If women are given a greater role to play, and as they become more influential in debating, they will certainly have an effect on the choices that are made *for* war or peace. If feminist theories are correct, they may swing the balance in favor of peace. Once women have been empowered within their societies, then it may be possible to move one step further and tackle the task of empowering women in security institutions.

How far from these goals are we? Africa has, in fact, been slowly responding to the idea that women should be allowed to play a greater role in public life. There are some countries that have shown great reluctance. Nigeria, a nation in which democracy has not had much overall success, is a case in point. However, elsewhere the issue is at least being debated, as in South Africa. And some countries, Uganda for example, have already taken steps to become more representative.

Civil-Military Relations

Clearly, something must be *done* to reduce the power of the gun in Africa. African leaders have tried a variety of measures to tackle the problem of predatory militaries. Jerry Rawlings, for example, armed the ordinary people of Ghana. He worked on the assumption that an armed people would be better able to protect itself from the depredations of the military. This is an idea with which, ironically, many Americans are quite sympathetic. Their own constitution gives them the 'right to bear arms'. Whether arming the people will lead to stability in Ghana or elsewhere is, however, very much of a debatable point.

There is, however, a more central concern, and that is the power struggle between the military and civilians. A lot of African countries are 'coup-prone'. There are some things that could be done to help reduce this problem. Giving the military a share in power might reduce the temptation to intervene violently and ease the transition to civilian government. Nigeria might benefit from such an experiment. A system along the following lines might be adopted. For the next thirty or forty years (or for however long is thought necessary) civilians and soldiers could share power. A two-house system resembling that of the British Houses of Parliament could be set up. One house (the equivalent of the House of Lords) could be a 'military' house, the other an elected house. Committees, composed of elements from both Houses, could be formed. Committee members would be entrusted with the task of examining issues that have serious implications for security. They would thrash out differences until they found a solution. In addition, a civilian and a soldier might agree to run together in a presidential campaign, the civilian seeking election as president, the soldier seeking election as his vice-president. (Of course, the constitution would have to make it clear that the vice-president would not succeed the president in the event of his death. Otherwise the temptation to assassinate the president would be too great!)

Africa entered the twenty-first century restless for changes in continental arrangements. There was widespread disenchantment with the status quo. South Africa was promoting the concept of an African

Renaissance. Nigeria had embarked on the contradictory trends of renewed democratization at the national level and the establishment of Islamic law at the level of some Northern states. Senegal was pushing for a new African agenda. East Africa was moving towards a new East African community. And Libya took the initiative of hosting a special summit of the Organization of African Unity to discuss a new agenda for Africa, and new continental institutions for such an agenda. The concept of the African Union (AU) was born.

The Union was finally consummated in Durban, South Africa, in July 2002. Its ambition was much greater than the original scope of the Organization of African Unity, which the AU replaced. The Union envisaged greater economic integration, the creation of a continental banking system, the establishment of a Pan-African parliament, and eventually a monetary union with one continental currency. The concept of an African Security Council gained greater support, but its membership was still a matter of contention. If the African Security Council is to have permanent members with a veto (in the style of the United Nations) the major powers would have to include South Africa, Nigeria and Egypt.

Would such major permanent members of the African Security Council provide troops for a Pan-African interventionist force to restore order in emergencies like those of Rwanda, Liberia, Sierra Leone and Somalia in the 1990s? Such an active umbrella of Pax Africana may take time to win adequate consensus within the African Union.

The Union came into being simultaneously with the New Partnership for Africa's Development (NEPAD). This is designed as a partnership between African countries and their major donors and trading partners to help Africa exploit its resources efficiently and realize its economic potential. One important innovation in NEPAD is the peer-review mechanism. African states are to review each other's performance both economically and in terms of good governance, and pass judgment on each other. The quest for higher standards of state-behavior would include a greater effort to fight corruption and to punish its excesses. In due course the African Union would have to accept the need for collective sanctions against members who violate too many rules of good governance. If this agenda of the African Union and NEPAD is realized, Africans would at last have become truly each other's keepers. There are a variety of creative pan-African solutions that need to be considered.

Intervention

First of all, Africans can intervene to try and minimize chaos when a neighboring state collapses. There are a variety of ways in which this can be done. First, there is unilateral intervention by a single neighboring power. A famous example of unilateral intervention is the 1979 invasion of Uganda by Tanzania. On that occasion, Tanzanian troops marched all the way to Kampala and put Uganda virtually under military occupation for a couple of years (Avirgan and Honey 1982). Tanzania's intervention was very similar to that of Vietnam in Cambodia to overthrow Pol Pot, except that the Vietnamese stayed on in Cambodia a lot longer than the Tanzanians stayed in Uganda.

Another, slightly different, kind of intervention was the 1994 invasion of Rwanda by Uganda. This type of single power intervention might perhaps be dubbed a 'Bay of Pigs' style intervention. Just as Eisenhower and Kennedy trained Cubans to invade Cuba in the Bay of Pigs operation in 1961, Yoweri Museveni of Uganda trained exiled Rwandans to intervene in Rwanda in 1994. The Ugandan-based Rwandese Patriotic Front invaded Rwanda and defeated the armies of the genocidal government, the Forces Armées Rwandaises. Unlike its American counterpart, the 'Bay of Pigs' operation in Africa was spectacularly successful in achieving its objectives. It ended the genocide and permitted the return of Tutsi refugees to Rwanda. It did not, however, bring about democratization or long-term stability in the country.

The second type of intervention is regionally supported single power intervention. In this case a single power intervenes with the blessing of a wider group of states. It acts under a kind of regional umbrella. Neither Tanzania nor Uganda had the backing of a regional organization when they intervened. But Nigeria's intervention in Sierra Leone and in Liberia arguably had the blessing of ECOMOG and ECOWAS. This type of intervention likewise has counterparts outside of Africa. Here one might point to Syria's intervention in the Lebanese civil war; on this occasion, Syria had the support of League of Arab States (Rasler 1983).

A third type of intervention is what might be called 'inter-African colonization and annexation'. Africans have on occasion 'colonized' other African countries in an effort to re-establish stability. As a solution to Africa's ills, this type of intervention is controversial, but it has not been entirely unsuccessful. In 1964, for example, the Tanganyikan government annexed Zanzibar. It did so with the backing of the Western powers who were alarmed by the situation in Zanzibar. Lyndon Johnson, the US President, and Sir Alec Douglas-Home, the British Prime Minister, both encouraged the merger. They feared that Zanzibar, an island lying off the East African coast, was subversive and unstable. They wanted to avert the danger that it would become a kind of Cuba, threatening the mainland. The methods used by the Tanganyikans were very much like those used by the British in the colonial days. Just as the British had 'persuaded' African chiefs to accept treaties by which they ceased to be sovereign, the Tanganyikan ruler got the dictator of Zanzibar to agree to a treaty of Union. No referendum was held in Zanzibar to check if the people wanted to cease being an independent nation. So it is fair to see this as a colonization of sorts. But the annexation was fairly successful and did impose a kind of 'Pax Tanganyika'. Benevolent 'colonization' by Africans, for all its negative connotations, is an option worth considering.

Regional Integration

Another solution to state collapse that holds some promise is regional integration. This takes place when the state as a political refugee is integrated with its host country, when, in other words, an unstable state is assimilated by a stable state. In my estimation, the best chance of a peaceful solution of the conflict between the Hutu and Tutsi is to integrate them with such a stable society.

Rwanda and Burundi are dual societies and as a result they seem doomed to face an endless cycle of violence. A mere 'tinkering' with their internal constitutions will not solve their problems. There is every reason to fear that, while limited reforms may put a temporary halt to the violence, it will only be a matter of time before Rwanda and Burundi once again face state collapse and genocide. A more radical solution is needed. Federation could solve the problem. But federation with what state? Clearly one should not attempt to integrate Rwanda and Burundi with a 'sick', conflict-ridden society such as the Congo. This would merely add to the problems. One should also be careful not to integrate them with a relatively unstable state (like Uganda). This would run the risk of destabilizing the plural society rather than stabilizing the dual society. Federation with the Republic of Tanzania, in contrast, might work.

Interestingly, German colonial powers before the First World War had leaned towards treating Tanganyika and Rwanda-Urunda as one single area of jurisdiction. Tanzania is a stable and a plural society. Once part of a wider system, Hutu and Tutsi would compete for resources with fellow Tanzanians. They would have other political rivals. In that context, their differences would be less apparent and they might behave far differently from how they have done in the past. Hutu and Tutsi soldiers would be retrained as part of the federal army of the United Republic of Tanzania, and Hutus and Tutsis would stop having *de facto* ethnic armies of their own.

Union with Tanzania would be safer than union with the Democratic Republic of Congo (DRC), in spite of the shared Belgian connection and French language. Tanzania is a less vulnerable society and a safer haven *for* Hutus and Tutis. It is indeed significant that Hutus and Tutsis on the run are more likely to flee to Tanzania than to the DRC in spite of ethnic ties across the border with the DRC. Moreover, Hutus and Tutsis are becoming partially Swahilized and should be able to get on well with 'fellow' Tanzanian citizens. As citizens, they would be assimilated in due course; what was a refugee state would become an integrated part of their new country.

What leads one to some optimism here is the precedent in Uganda. The Bahima, who are traditionally pastoralists, and the Bairu, who are traditionally agriculturalists, are the Hutu and Tutsi by another name. They both belong to a Bantu group known as the Banyankore. The Bahima form a dominant caste, just as was traditionally true of the Tutsi. And though the Bahima and Bairu are mutually dependent in many ways, their society reflects the traditional mistrust of pastoralists and agriculturalists. However, because they are part of Uganda, on most issues they operate as one. There are occasions, of course, when they are divided, but in the wider plural society they see themselves as Banyankore and distinct from the various other ethnic groups of Uganda. They recognize their shared interests and this is reflected in their political behavior.

Clearly there are some difficulties to be overcome before federation with Tanzania is possible. The chief obstacle is that the Rwandans and Burundis are very possessive about their independence and their separate identity. It will take some compelling and well-reasoned arguments to persuade them of the need to renounce their sovereignty. Immense resources, on the one hand, will have to be made available to all three governments. They must be offered the means to build clinics, roads, schools, and other infrastructure of this sort to make palatable their sacrifices. At the same time, they must be reminded of the unbearable alternative to loss of sovereignty. Do they want their children to live constantly under the cloud of imminent genocide? Though a difficult idea to sell, federation is not one that should be lightly abandoned.

African Security Council

This author has often dreamed of an African Security Council composed of African military and civilian leaders who would focus on limiting, containing and ending African conflict. The structure would resemble that of the United Nations. Some of the more influential countries would be given permanent representation on the Council. These influential countries would likely include Nigeria (from the west), Egypt (from the north) and South Africa (from the south). It is much less easy to pick out the most influential country in the east. Ethiopia would, in some ways, be the logical choice as a permanent member, although this would anger the Eritreans, and quite likely the Kenyans who have become the most pan-Africanist and most interventionist of the countries of eastern Africa. The Ugandans, too, long the favorite of Western aid organizations, would no doubt vie for a permanent seat. There should be some non-permanent members, ranging from three to five. The principle of permanent members would be reviewed every thirty years. For example, it might be necessary to add the DRC as a permanent member to represent Central Africa.

A great deal of work would have to be done to settle the details, which are almost bound to create acrimony and rivalries. Many important issues would have to be addressed. For example, in times of crisis should the African Security Council meet at the level of heads of state? Should each permanent member have a veto or not? But the idea is certainly worth exploring. This is one area, too, in which Western cooperation would prove useful.

The establishment of a Pan-African Emergency Force might prove useful in resolving conflict. This would act as a metaphorical fire brigade, putting out fires from one collapsed war to another. It would serve to teach Africans the art of building a *Pax Africana*. Exactly what shape such a force should take is not clear. Should it be independently recruited? Should it be given specialized training? Should it be drawn from units of the armed forces of member states? How should the training, maintenance and deployment of the Emergency Force be paid for? How can Western friends of Africa like the US and the European Union help? Certainly the successes and failures of ECOMOG in Liberia should be studied carefully in preparation for this new venture (Cain 2000). There are times when renegade states are basically refugee states. Brutal villains in power are also pathetic casualties of history. The emergency force should be trained to use minimum violence.

Self-help

Another concrete proposal is a High Commissioner for Refugees and Displaced Africans under the African Union. The fact is that, although we produce a disproportionate number of refugees and displaced people,

Africans play a disproportionately limited role in helping them. A continent of one-tenth of the world's population is rapidly becoming a region of a third of the displaced people of the world. We really should organize ourselves better and tackle the refugee problem in a systematic and efficient fashion. We do not want to discourage others from helping us. But we do need to do more, and be seen to be doing more, for our own people. We need to *lead*.

Conclusion

As a final warning, let me stress the importance of moving with speed towards political reform in Africa. The English poet Andrew Marvell, once wrote to his mistress:

> Had we but world enough, and time,
> This coyness, lady, were no crime.
> But at my back I always hear
> Time's winged chariot hurrying near,
> And yonder all before us lie
> Deserts of vast eternity.
> The Grave's a fine and private place,
> But none, I think, do there embrace.[9]

Marvell's words have relevance to our own situation. Africa is a continent of immense potential. It is our obligation to move swiftly to resolve its problems and make sure that its people are given the chance to enjoy the blessings of peace and prosperity.

References

Ansari, Hamied A. 1984. 'Sectarian Conflict in Egypt and the Political Expediency of Religion', *The Middle East Journal* 38 (Summer): 18–39.

Avirgan, Tony and Martha Honey. 1982. *War, in Uganda. The Legacy of Idi Amin.* Westport, CT: L. Hill.

Cain, Kenneth L. 2000. 'Meanwhile in Africa.' *SAIS Review* 20 (1): 153–76.

Cammack, Paul A. 1997. *Capitalism and Democracy in the Third World: A Doctrine for Political Development.* London and Washington, DC: Leicester University Press.

Cervenka, Zdenek. 1971. *The Nigerian War, 1967–70. History of the War, Selected Bibliography and Documents.* Frankfurt am Main: Bernard and Graef.

Deng, Francis. 1995. *War of Visions: Conflict of Identities in the Sudan.* Washington, DC: Brookings Institution.

Dunnigan, James F. and Austin Bay. 1996. *A Quick and Dirty Guide to War.* 3rd edn. New York: WIlliam Morrow and Company.

Hashim, Alice B. 1997. *The Fallen State: Dissonance, Dictatorship and Death in Somalia.* Lanham, MD: University Press of America.

Hirst, Paul Q. 1998. *From Statism to Pluralism: Democracy, Civil Society and Global Politics.* London and Bristol: UCL Press.

Holbrooke, Richard. 1998. *To End War.* New York: Random House.

Lesch, Ann M. 1998. *The Sudan: Contested National Identities.* Bloomington, IN: Indiana University Press and Oxford: James Currey.

Lyons, Gene M. and Michael Mastanutono, eds. 1995. *Beyond, Westphalia? State Sovereignty and International Intervention.* Baltimore, MD: Johns Hopkins University Press.

Margollouth, H. M, 1971. *The Poems and Letters of Andrew Marvell.* Vol. I, 3rd edn. Oxford: Clarendon Press.

McDonald, Robert. 1997. *The Problem of Cyprus.* London: Brassey's for the International Institute of Strategic Studies.

Mendus, Susan. ed. 1988. *Justifying Toleration: Conceptual and Historical Perspectives.* Cambridge, and New York: Cambridge University Press.

Mime, R. S. 1981. *Politics in Ethnically Bipolar States: Guyana, Malaysia and Fiji.* Vancouver and London: University of British Columbia Press.

Mortimer, Robert A. 1996. 'Islamists, Soldiers and Democrats: The Second Algerian War', *The Middle East Journal* 50 (Winter): 18–39.

Moser, Robert G. 1999. 'Electoral Systems and the Number of Parties in Postcommunist States', *World Politics* 51 (3): 359–84.

Nyakanvzi, Edward. 1998. *Genocide: Rwanda and Burundi.* Rochester, VT: Schenkman Books.

O'Neill, Michael. 1998. 'Re-imagining Belgium: New Federalsim and the Political Management of Cultural Diversity.' *Parliamentary Affairs* 51 (2): 241–58.

Rasler, Karen. 1983. 'Internationalizing Civil War: A Dynamic Analysis of the Syrian Intervention in Lebanon', *The Journal of Conflict Resolution* 27 (September): 421–56.

Senaratne, Jagath P. 1997. *Political Violence in Sri Lanka, 1977–1990: Riots, Insurrections, Counterinsurgencies, Foreign Intervention.* Amsterdam: VU University Press.

Tronvoll, Kjetil. 1999. 'Borders of Violence- Boundaries of Identity: Demarcating the Eritrean Nation-State', *Ethnic and Racial Studies* 22 (6): 1037–60.

Notes

1 Recent figures include the hundreds of thousands in Rwanda and Burundi, and the tens of thousands in Algeria and the Congo. See Dunnigan and Bay (1996: 387).

2 Note that, surprisingly, an article in *The Economist* 352 (25 January 1997): 17, argues that borders have not been the primary cause of conflict.

3 The Board of UNESCO outlawed the use of the word 'tribe' for being Eurocentric. Those who do not like the word 'tribe' are largely aping a European dislike of the term. But, to avoid giving offense, the author has used the word ethnic in this paper instead.

4 These societies may also be termed 'ethnically bipolar', see Mime (1981).

5 See British Broadcasting Corporation, 'Mandela: Burundi's Gloomy Politics', BBC News, 12 October 2001; for an overview of the situation in the Great Lakes, consult the special issue of the *African Studies Review* 41 (1) (1999): 1–97.

6 The Westphalian compact established the principle that national sovereignty was inviolable. It became customary for the international community to avoid intervention if this meant infringing state sovereignty. Internal excesses may, however, be testing this custom. See Lyons and Mastanutono (1995).

7 Robert G. Moser (1999) provides an interesting comparative analysis of how different types of electoral systems affect the number of political parties in regions once governed by a single party system.

8 The debate on the linkages between economic freedom and political freedom is historic and relevant; for a recent example, see Cammack (1997).

9 These lines are taken from Andrew Marvell's 'To A Coy Mistress', in H. M, Margollouth (1971: 27–28).

1

When States Implode
Africa's Civil Wars
1950–92

ERROL A. HENDERSON

Africa has been the site of some of the world's most deadly conflicts in the last few decades, with those in Angola, Ethiopia, Mozambique, Rwanda, Somalia, Sudan and Uganda each resulting in the deaths through battlefield casualties or war-induced famine and disease of 500,000 to 1,000,000 persons. Stedman (1996: 237) notes that '[i]n 1995, there were five on-going wars (in Angola, Liberia, Sierra Leone, Somalia, and Sudan), several countries that were candidates for state collapse or civil war (Burundi, Cameroon, Kenya, Nigeria, Rwanda, Togo, and Zaire), and a host of other countries where low-level ethnic and political conflict remained contained but unresolved (Chad, Congo, Djibouti, Ethiopia, Malawi, Mali, Mozam-bique, Senegal, South Africa, and Uganda)'.

Although African states continue to experience these horrific wars, scholars have generated relatively few systematic, large-N, data-based analyses of the correlates of African civil wars that could inform policy to prevent them. Many studies of Africa's large-scale domestic conflicts during the Cold War era focused on their presumed 'ethnic' nature, or insisted that they were epiphenomena of the underlying geopolitical gamesmanship of the superpowers (i.e. proxy-wars). By contrast, I would contend that African civil wars in the post-Second World War era largely emerged from domestic political factors related to state-building and nation-building. Drawing on this theoretical argument, I derive several testable propositions on the correlates of these wars and test them against the empirical record from 1950 to 1992.

The remainder of this chapter is organized in a number of sections. Initially, I discuss how decolonization contributed to the political, economic, and cultural disparities that have given rise to African domestic conflict. Next, I provide a brief discussion of the theoretical point of departure of the study. Following that, I present several propositions on the putative corre-lates of Africa's civil wars and I evaluate the propositions using logistic regression analyses. After presenting the findings, I discuss their implica-tions for future research and policy, and conclude with a brief summary of the main points of the paper.

Civil War & African Politics

Decolonization led to the creation of more independent states in Africa than in any other continent during the postwar era. With independence, the leaders of African states faced the dual challenges of building the institutional apparatus of the state (state-building), while simultaneously constructing an overarching national identity among disparate cultural groups (nation-building). While most developed states had had difficulty responding to these demands separately and sequentially, the newly independent African states were required to respond to both simultaneously. However, colonialism was not aimed at creating strong, viable, autonomous states. The newly independent African states were usually left with little institutional support, wealth or university-trained specialists from the departing colonizers. Holsti (1996: 62) agrees that '[t]he colonial state's main purposes had nothing to do with preparation for ultimate statehood, and everything to do with economic exploitation, building some infrastructure and communication, settling migrants, organizing plantation agriculture, introducing extraction of surplus through taxes, organizing some semblance of lower-level education and religious activity, and providing "law and order" so that these tasks could go on unhindered' (p. 62).

Colonial underdevelopment resulted in the political decapitation of African elites from their citizens and the coupling of African governments to the interests of the former colonial powers. An institutional vacuum was created within African states, which left them as relatively easy prey for organized insurgency. Moreover, the failure of state-building exacerbated problems of nation-building. Colonialism had arbitrarily fused dramatically disparate societies into single states that seemed doomed to fracture (although colonial boundaries were largely accepted by African elites under the principle of *uti possidetis*). In many of these newly independent and culturally diverse states, culture became the primary criterion for political association, and political competition took on the complexion of inter-cultural competition. Without the support of integrative state institutions to exert countervailing pressures, fissures in the fragile state system fractured. Many of the African states thus affected disintegrated violently into civil war.

The simultaneous challenges of state-building and nation-building were further complicated by the demands on African elites to provide economic development for their states. Economic development, which tends to reduce violence in the long term, can exacerbate tensions in the short term, because uneven growth in different sectors of the economy may intensify existing cleavages and lead to increasing inequality as the economy expands. The resultant asymmetrical development may engender frustration and conflict among competing groups (Gurr 1970). In addition, rivalry over economic spoils is a primary basis for ethnic mobilization (Hechter 1978), and discrimination with respect to the dispensation of goods (and 'bads') across different identity groups is viewed as a chief cause of 'ethno-political conflict' (Gurr 1993).

Although the discussion up to this point reminds us that various political, economic, and cultural factors may each contribute to the onset of African civil wars, many of the arguments on the causes of these wars suggest that they are simply 'ethnic conflicts'. For example, Mazrui (1986: 291) insists that '[a]ll civil wars in Africa have been substantially ethnic'. However, it is not clear to what extent cultural factors are more consequential than political or economic ones in generating civil wars in Africa. Before one can reliably suggest that African civil wars are simply 'ethnic conflicts'. it is necessary to conduct a systematic examination of the role of cultural factors in these wars, controlling for political and economic factors that might also contribute to their onset. Once one controls for non-cultural factors, the impact of culture may become insignificant. On the other hand, if, after controlling for non-cultural factors, the relationship between culture and civil war is significant, then we would have empirically established the link between culture and African civil wars. This study provides such an analysis.

In addition, only by including the various political, economic and cultural factors in a single model can we usefully distinguish among them and determine their individual impact on the probability of civil war. Distinguishing the effects of each class of variables will not only allow us to better determine the processes giving rise to African civil wars, it will also provide a clear direction for policy to reduce the likelihood of them. For example, if African civil wars primarily result from political factors, then policies aimed at democratization or the removal of exploitative political linkages should be our primary concern. On the other hand, if economic factors are more critical in African civil wars, then policies that focus on economic development or changes in domestic spending priorities should be pursued initially. If cultural factors are more important, then African states should focus on policies that provide redress for the claims of aggrieved ethno-political groups.

Before conducting the empirical analysis of the relationship among political, economic and cultural factors and the onset of African civil wars, it is necessary to flesh out the linkages between each of these factors and domestic conflict. This requires an elucidation of the theoretical argument that links these various factors in a coherent explanation of civil war onset. As discussed above, I contend that African civil wars largely result from the failed policies of state leaders in response to the dual challenges of state-building and nation-building. In the next section, I flesh out this theoretical argument.

Theoretical Point of Departure

Of the very few large-N, longitudinal, data-based studies of civil wars (e.g. Hegre et al., 1997; Henderson and Singer 2000; Rummel, 1997), most do not focus on a single region. Of the few that focus on African civil wars specifically (i.e. Collier, 1998; Collier and Hoeffler, 1998), they do not address the relative impact of the varied political, economic, and cultural factors that I wish to examine in this study. The focus on political,

54 Errol A. Henderson

economic and cultural factors is born of the viewpoint that all of these classes of factors are interconnected and that, without controlling for each of them, one may draw spurious inferences regarding the correlates of African civil wars. Furthermore, I maintain that African civil wars largely result from internal factors within African states; specifically, from the failure of African states to respond adequately to the simultaneous challenges of state-building and nation-building. Let us explore this claim more fully.

To be sure, when one considers the number of African civil wars in the postwar era, one is immediately confronted by the bloody record of Soviet and US involvement in these wars. Although foreign intrigue often played a major role in the *expansion* and *escalation* of African civil wars, international factors were rarely associated with the *onset* of these wars. Ayoob (1995: 189) agrees that '[t]he internal vulnerabilities of Third World states are primarily responsible for the high level of conflict in many parts of the Third World', while Brown (1996: 582), Luard (1989) and Holsti (1996) make similar claims for postcolonial conflicts, in general. Focusing on African armed conflicts, in particular, Stedman (1996: 238) notes that their origins 'lie principally' with 'policies pursued by elites to gain and consolidate power'.

The crux of the view that African civil wars result largely from domestic factors is the thesis that tensions related to the challenges of state-building and nation-building comprise the 'taproot of insurgency' (see Cohen et al., 1981; Henderson, 1999). For example, European states had many decades – for some, centuries – to develop effective institutions of governance and a domestic environment in which the central government was the primary institution to which citizens swore fealty. Moreover, among European states, state-building preceded and facilitated nation-building; European elites were therefore able to address and resolve problems associated with each sequentially. African states not only had a much shorter time horizon in which to build effective state structures and cohesive national identities, but they usually had to accomplish both simultaneously. One result was that African political elites faced a 'state-strength dilemma', wherein by attempting to create strong states they engendered resistance that further weakened them, due to the competition and conflict among their diverse and often disputatious groups that did not swear fealty to the central government (Holsti 1996: 128).

Further complicating this process was the perception among many African leaders that there were disincentives to the development of legitimate political institutions. Chief among these disincentives was the fear that such development might lead to the construction of rival power centers that might threaten the political elite's incumbency. Subsequently, instead of creating strong, economically developed, democratic states, they erected weak, economically marginalized, autocratic and heavily militarized regimes that were more geared toward providing for the personal predilections of the ruling elite rather than the welfare of the vast majority of its citizens. In light of popular political mobilization from a disaffected, generally poor, and often heterogeneous citizenry, many African elites utilized repression to insure their regime's security, while devoting resources to the military to stave off insurgency. Ironically, the result was often the very insurgency that the governing elites' policies were intended to deter.

In sum, African insurgency should be viewed as a result of the lingering legacy of colonialism and the failure of African elites to respond adequately to the dual and simultaneous challenges of state-building and nation-building. With this theoretical argument in mind, one can devolve several propositions on the correlates of African civil wars that focus on the internal characteristics of African states themselves. Moreover, we can clearly delineate the political, economic and cultural variables that are operative in these wars. In the next section, I discuss several of these prospective correlates of African civil wars before testing them against the empirical record of the postwar era.

Correlates of African Civil War

Among the political, economic and cultural factors most consistently implicated in civil wars are those related to a state's regime type (Auvinen, 1997; Hegre et al., 1997; Henderson and Singer 2000; Rummel, 1997), its level of economic development (Collier, 1998; Collier and Hoeffler, 1998; Henderson and Singer 2000), and/or its cultural composition (Auvinen, 1997; Collier, 1998; Collier and Hoeffler, 1998; Rummel, 1997), respectively. Turning first to the political factors, several studies maintain that full-fledged democracies are less prone to large-scale domestic conflict due to the availability of legitimate channels for dispute resolution while autocracies are resistant to civil war because their use of repression stifles dissent. Interestingly, the relationship between regime type and war for states with an intermediate level of democracy – semi-democracies – has gained increasing attention in the literature. Semi-democracies are states that are neither fully democratic nor strongly autocratic. Previous empirical findings indicate that semi-democracies are more prone to civil war because they have neither the range of legitimate institutionalized channels found in full-fledged democracies nor the expansive repressive machinery of full-fledged autocracies to deter insurgency (Hegre et al., 1997; Henderson and Singer 2000). Therefore, dissidents in semi-democracies rarely have their demands effectively addressed through the limited (and often resource-strained) governmental channels available to them, but they also do not face an overarching repressive state apparatus; consequently, they are more apt to mobilize their dissent and pursue insurgency.

The conflict-exacerbating role of semi-democracy appears to be evident in African states (Mazrui 1986: 181–6). For example, Uganda's nascent democracy was felled by the civil war in the summer of 1966; Nigeria's Third Republic was overthrown by the civil conflict of 1984; Burundi's civil war was precipitated by the assassination of its first democratically elected president; Angola's civil war was rekindled following the refusal of the insurgent UNITA forces to accept the outcome of internationally observed elections; and the civil war in Congo-Brazzaville began in 1997 shortly after the country's first democratically elected president took office. Therefore I posit that:

Proposition 1.1: Presence of semi-democracy increases the likelihood of civil war.

Another important political variable that has been associated with African domestic conflict is the colonial experience of the state. As noted above, colonial policies, in their entirety, often exacerbated problems related to the construction of viable African states. Stedman (1996: 236) notes that '[l]egacies from colonialism predisposed much of Africa to violent conflicts'. Holsti (1996: 62) reminds us that the 'actual patterns of exploitation' under colonialism varied from colony to colony, ranging from the British policy of 'indirect rule' to the Belgian policy in the Congo, which he characterizes as 'little more than an organized system of theft based on forced labor to benefit the Belgian crown' (p. 62). In the latter case, Holsti is too kind; recent research has revealed that among the horrific atrocities committed by the Belgians in the Congo there are estimates of 10 million Africans killed (see Hochschild 1998).

The practices of European and American colonizers left a destructive legacy that had a deleterious impact on African state-building and nation-building initiatives. Among imperialist states, Britain is often credited with promoting a highly rational colonial policy focusing on indirect rule; however, Mazrui anc d Tidy (1986: 84) maintain that, although the British often supported federations, they also used their tactic of 'divide and rule' within African states and they supported 'ethnically based political parties as a tactic to weaken and divide nationalist opposition to colonial rule', most notably in English-speaking West Africa, but also in Uganda, Kenya and Zambia. The horrific Biafran civil war and the enduring domestic conflicts in Uganda are associated with British colonial policy with respect to Ibos, Yorubas, and Hausa-Fulani in Nigeria and the relationship between Baganda and Nilotics in Uganda, respectively.

Most imperialist states maintained informal or neo-colonial relationships with their former colonial subjects. While independence for Africans in the Belgian Congo brought invasion by Belgian (and US) troops, and Africans in each of the Portuguese colonies had to fight prolonged and bloody wars to end their colonial domination, colonial powers often used economic measures to maintain their dominance in their former colonies. For example, the French tied their former colonies to the CFA franc and also bound their politico-economies to the Communauté Economique de l'Afrique de l'Ouest (CEAO). Similarly, the political economy of Liberia was tied so tightly to the US through Firestone Rubber Company that the African state was 'subject to a mightier economic imperialism than could be imposed in Africa by European colonial powers' (ibid.: 29). In addition, colonial legacies often had an even more direct military impact on the likelihood of civil war. For example, British troops disarmed East African mutineers in 1964 and France used force liberally in its former sub-Saharan colonies, most notably in Cameroon, Niger, Gabon, Chad, and the interlacustrine states where it assumed the former role of Belgium.

To my mind, the relative impact of the distinct colonial legacies of African states is more likely a function of the extent to which the colonial power either facilitated or circumscribed the state-building and nation-building processes in its former colonies. Although the data analysis (see below) will allow us to determine the relative impact of different colonial experiences on the likelihood of civil war, what is of primary importance is to determine the extent to which colonialism evinced an enduring impact on the conflict-proneness of African states at all. While it is often assumed to be the case, this assumption has not been tested across the range of African civil wars.[1] Therefore, I test the following proposition:

Proposition 1.2: Colonial legacy is associated with the likelihood of civil war.

Collier and Hoeffler's (1999) analysis clearly implicates economic factors in African civil wars, while Mullins (1987) concludes that in many African and Third World states, in general, internal conflicts result largely from the uncoupling of economic development from military capability. Following Tilly (1975), he argues that during state formation in Europe leaders were compelled to provide some measure of economic development so that taxes could be raised from the citizenry in order to provide for the state's professional military forces. This security function encouraged development, since resources to pay professional militaries could be more readily secured through domestic taxation rather than from foreign adventure. In this way, economic development became tied to the state's military capability; however, in African states, political elites are often unable to extract sufficient resources from their poor societies to support their bloated militaries. Furthermore, leaders of postcolonial African states rarely fear external aggression since major power (or regional) patronage – as well as international law – protects their sovereignty. This is reflected in the fact that African states have experienced fewer than 2 per cent of all inter-state wars from 1946 to 1992, while experiencing almost 30 per cent of all civil wars during that era. Since African elites have few worries that their regimes will be brought down by external aggression, their policies are not informed by the security-development nexus; they can therefore pursue their own myopic interest of protecting their regime from insurgency, with little regard for larger development issues. This relationship inverts Eurocentric security/development strategies in Africa and results in both greater insecurity for the vast majority of African citizens and the underdevelopment of the economies of African states. Both of these factors increase the likelihood of insurgency in African states.

The significance of economic factors as precipitants of civil war also derives from the view that the economic health of the state is the chief responsibility of the political leadership. Citizens facing economic privation are likely to hold the incumbent political regime responsible for their hardship. Moreover, economically marginalized citizens often provide fodder for insurgency. Unlike more developed states that have resources that can be redistributed to marginalized or disaffected groups to maintain their support of the status quo, African states are generally resource-strained and, therefore, have few resources to utilize in this way. Further complicating this process, African regimes often divert their limited revenue to military spending, which both truncates economic development and provides resources to the armed elements of the society that are often eager to usurp political authority. Nevertheless, the conflict-dampening impact of economic development is evident among African states such as

Botswana where it has contributed to that state's greater stability. Empirical studies largely support the view that economic development reduces the likelihood of insurgency (Collier and Hoeffler 1998). Therefore I posit that:
Proposition 2.1: The greater a state's level of economic development, the lower its likelihood of civil war.

The level of military spending in African states is an additional economic factor that is associated with African civil wars. As suggested above, military spending in African states is usually not aimed at external enemies but at internal ones. Furthermore, African political elites often privilege their militaries in their budgeting decisions (Gyimah-Brempong, 1992); however, this may often have a negative impact on investment and growth (Deger, 1986; Lebovic and Ishaq, 1987). In addition, increased military spending often crowds out social welfare, health and education expenditures. Heo's (1998) and Frederickson and Looney's (1983: 637) findings indicate that the opportunity costs of military spending are most evident in resource-constrained countries such as those found throughout Africa. I maintain that the socio-economic dislocations wrought from increased military spending are likely to heighten the probability of insurgency. Therefore, I posit that:
Proposition 2.2: The greater a state's level of military spending, the greater its likelihood of civil war.

Turning to the role of cultural factors in African civil wars, although Africa's domestic conflicts are often assumed to be largely ethnic in nature, there are competing findings on the relationship between cultural factors and civil wars in the region. For example, Barrows (1976: 165–6) found that neither linguistic nor ethnic fractionalization had a consistent significant impact on domestic violence in sub-Saharan Africa. Later, Collier (1998) and Collier & Hoeffler (1998: 570–71) suggested an inverted U relationship between ethno-linguistic homogeneity and civil war in sub-Saharan Africa, but added that the war proneness of these regimes was more a function of their poverty than of ethnic factors. On the other hand, Schlichte's (1994) case studies of conflicts in Africa suggest that ethnicity was not a salient factor in several ostensibly 'ethnic' conflicts, while Fearon and Laitin's (1996) analysis revealed that interethnic cooperation in Africa is much more prevalent than interethnic conflict.[2]

Of the different explanations for the conflict-exacerbating role of cultural factors in Africa's civil wars, the rationale provided by Collier and Hoeffler (1998) is the most theoretically compelling. They suggest that the most likely candidates for civil war in Africa are those states that are ethnically polarized with two relatively equal but distinct cultural groups accounting for most of the state's population. Their basic contention is that co-ordinating insurgency is facilitated where rebels are bound by a common identity distinct from that of their adversaries, and common culture – especially common language – is assumed to provide a basis for such self-identification. Since heterogeneous societies are more likely to be fractionalized, they offer little prospect for successful insurgency, and culturally homogeneous states lack cultural fissures and thus face few if any cultural challengers. Therefore, one would expect that:

Proposition 3.1: The greater the cultural polarization in a state, the greater the likelihood of civil war.

In addition, since Gurr (1994) suggests that the presence of certain types of 'politicized ethnic groups' or 'ethno-political groups' is associated with domestic conflict, a useful measure of the extent to which cultural factors are associated with civil wars should focus on the impact of these groups on the likelihood of insurgency. Gurr (1993, 24) notes that in the early 1990s there were 74 politicized communal groups in the region (comprising more than 40 per cent of the total population of sub-Saharan Africa) involved in various types of 'ethnopolitical conflict'. Scarritt (1993: 254) maintains that the prevalence of minorities at risk is greater in Africa than in most other regions of the world, and points out that in three African countries all of the population is at risk, in eight over half, and in four over 40 per cent. Twenty-nine of the thirty-six countries in the region have 'at risk' populations of more than one million, the second highest percentage among world regions (p. 255). One may assume that the prevalence of ethnopolitical groups within African states increases the probability of large-scale conflict (i.e. civil war), especially since African conflicts are widely assumed to derive from ethnopolitical factors. Therefore, one would expect that:

Proposition 3.2: The presence of ethno-political groups increases the likelihood of civil war.

Having derived propositions on several ostensible correlates of African civil war, what is left is to evaluate systematically the extent to which these propositions are borne out empirically. In the next section, I outline the research design that is utilized to determine the significance of the political, economic and cultural factors in African civil wars.

Research Design

Definition of Civil War
The Correlates of War (COW) project provides an operational definition of civil war as sustained military combat, primarily internal, resulting in at least 1,000 battle deaths per year, pitting central government forces against an insurgent force capable of effective resistance, determined by the latter's ability to inflict upon the government forces at least 5 per cent of the fatalities that the insurgents sustain (Small and Singer 1982: 210–20). The COW definition has been utilized in quantitative as well as case-study analyses of civil war (e.g. Collier and Hoeffler 1998; Henderson and Singer 2000; Licklider 1993; Regan 1996).[3]

Outcome Variable
This study examines cases of African civil wars from 1950 to 1992, beginning with the civil war of 1960 and ending with the Congolese (DRC) war in Angola in 1992.[4] The unit of analysis is the state-year, which is the annual observation for each of the 46 independent African states in the

data set.[5] There are a total of 963 state-years for which we have complete data, and our analysis is conducted on this population. The outcome variable is the onset of civil war (*Civil War*) and is coded as '1' if a civil war began during the year and '0' if it did not; war data are from Singer and Small (1994).[6]

Predictor Variables

The first political variable, *Semidemocracy*, is constructed in several steps. The extent of democracy is measured as the difference between the state's 11-point democracy and autocracy scores (both range from 0 to 10) using the codings from the Polity III data set (Jaggers and Gurr, 1995). This difference is called the 'regime score' and it is measured on a 21-point scale, which assumes values from −10 (the highest level of autocracy) to +10 (the highest level of democracy). From there, I construct a dichotomous variable which equals '1' for those cases where the regime score ranges from 0 to +5, and otherwise equals '0'. That is, the range of *Semidemocracy* includes regime scores of 0, 1, 2, 3, 4, or 5 on the Polity III scale. Using this coding, I capture the intuitive notion that semi-democracies are neither full-fledged democracies (conventionally, a 'coherent democracy' requires a regime score of at least +7 on the Polity III scale) nor are they strongly autocratic (by virtue of their non-negative regime scores). For the other political variable(s) in the model, I construct five dummy variables (*Belgian, British, French, Portuguese, US*) to designate the former colonizer of each post-colonial African state. Where there was more than one colonizer, such as in the case of the former German and Italian colonies, the more recent colonial power was used.[7]

A state's level of economic development, *Development*, is measured as the log of the ratio of the state's energy consumption as a proportion of its total population. The military spending variable, *Milspending*, is measured as the log of the ratio of a state's military expenditures (in constant, 1990 US dollars) to its total population. Data for these two variables are from the COW Material Capabilities data set (Singer and Small, 1995).

Cultural polarization, *Polar*, is a dummy variable that reflects the extent that the distribution of a state's culture groups approximates a 50-50 split. Specifically, polarized states are those in which the sum of the squared percentage shares of the two largest cultural groups is at least 50 per cent of the total population, with group B (the second largest group) having no less than half the population of group A (the largest group) and group C (the third largest group) having no more than half the population share of group B. Following these coding rules, states with distributions such as 50-50, 40-40-20, or 45-45-10 are polarized, while states with distributions such as 70-30, 40-35-25-5 are not. Polarized states are coded '1' and those that are not polarized are coded '0'. The polarization measures are estimated using data for each state's language groups and come from the COW cultural composition data set (Singer, 1996).

An additional cultural variable is the presence/absence of an 'ethno-political group' in the state. Gurr and Harff (1994: 190) define ethno-political groups as 'ethnic groups that have organized to promote their common interests', and it is these groups that engage in 'ethno-political conflict.'

There are four types of ethno-political groups; among them, ethno-nationalists and communal contenders are most often associated with conflict. Gurr (1994: 355, 360) contends that '[o]f the 233 politicized communal groups included in the Minorities at Risk study, eighty-one pursued ethno-national objectives; their conflicts were on average more intense than those in which other issues were manifest and increased markedly in numbers and magnitude from the 1950s to the 1980s.' Communal contenders were also involved in a high degree of ethno-political conflict, according to Gurr (1994: 354–55). Therefore, the second cultural variable, *Ethnopolitical Group*, is a dummy variable that is coded '1' for those postcolonial states that contained either ethno-nationalists or communal contenders in the 1990s as reflected in the Minorities at Risk data set and coded '0' for states that do not.

Data Analysis

A multivariate logistic regression model is estimated to evaluate the propositions. The logistic regression model takes the following form: $\text{Pr}(Civil\ War) = 1/(1+ e^{-Zi})$ where $\text{Pr}(Civil\ War)$ is the probability that the outcome variable (the onset of civil war) equals 1; and Z_i is the sum of the product of the coefficient values (b_i) across all observations of the predictor variables (X_{ik}), that is: $\alpha + \beta_1 Semidemocracy + \beta_2 Belgian + \beta_3 British + \beta_4 Portuguese + \beta_5 US + \beta_6 Development + \beta_7 Milspending + \beta_8 Polar + \beta_9 Ethnopolitical\ Group.$[8] ``

Findings

The findings from the logistic regression model are reported in Table 1.1. The model performs well with respect to its log likelihood score and X^2 significance level and all but three of the variables are significantly associated with the probability of civil war.[9] Taking each in turn, I find that *Semidemocracy* is not significantly associated with the likelihood of civil war, and this is inconsistent with *Proposition 1.1*. This finding is surprising, given both the previous research on the relationship between semidemocracy and civil war (i.e. Hegre et al. 1997; Henderson and Singer 2000) and the apparent relationship revealed by comparing the distribution of regime types in African states to the incidence of civil war on the continent.

For example, autocracies are the most prevalent regime type in Africa in our temporal domain, with 78 per cent of African state years coded as autocratic. By contrast 13 per cent of African state years are coded as semidemocratic and 9 per cent are coded as democratic. When we compare the distribution of regime types to the distribution of war onsets, we find that 67 per cent of the state years marked by war onsets are coded as autocratic, 29 per cent are coded as semidemocratic, and the remaining 4 per cent are coded as democratic. Starting with the democracies, these data reveal that war onsets occur in only 4 per cent of those state years marked by a democratic regime, which represents less than half of the total number of state years during which there is a democratic regime (9 per cent). This suggests that democratic regimes have a reduced incidence of war onsets. Autocracies likewise experience a reduced incidence of war onsets, since they comprise 78 per cent of the total number of state-years in sub-Saharan Africa but experience only 67 per cent of the state years of civil war. On the other hand, it is clear that semidemocracies are much more prone to civil war. In fact, although semidemocratic regimes comprise 13 per cent of the total number of the state years in Africa, they experience more than twice as many state years of civil war (i.e. 29 per cent).[10]

In light of the apparent relationship between semidemocracy and civil war, I estimated a revised model that included separate democracy and autocracy variables. The findings revealed that, although the general direction of the relationship between regime type and civil war follows the broad outline suggested by the semidemocracy-civil war thesis (i.e. that both democracies and autocracies are less war-prone than semidemocracies), this relationship was clearly not significant for African states. Therefore, although the comparison of regime type and civil war onset seems to provide a modicum of support for the view that semidemocracies are more war-prone, it is nevertheless clear that the relationship is not statistically significant once one controls for the range of factors included in our analysis. The results reported in Table 1.1 provide another example that relationships evident in other regions of the world are often not borne out in Africa.

Moving to the other predictor variables in the model, the results reveal that each of the colonizer state variables is significantly associated with the likelihood of civil war and since each of the coefficients is estimated using French colonies as the baseline, then their positive relationships should be considered relative to the experience of French colonies.[11] These findings provide strong support for *Proposition 1.2* in that colonial legacy is strongly associated with the probability of civil war, and they also indicate that the non-French colonies were more likely to experience civil war. The latter conclusion should not be construed as support for the view that French colonies are peaceful, in general. One is reminded that France was heavily involved in the civil war in Chad, and a civil war raged in the former French colony of Congo-Brazzaville. The findings probably reflect the greater deterrent value of France's military presence in its former colonies, including the secondment of French troops, which may have contributed to the lower incidence of full-scale civil war in the Francophone states as compared with the Anglophone or Lusophone states.[12] In addition, it should be remembered that most of the French colonies on the continent were in West Africa where there was a historical Islamic politico-religious influence. French colonial policies often allowed them to overlay their administration on an extant Islamic one that persisted into the independence era. In this way, the presence of indigenous politico-religious structures may have alleviated some of the problems associated with the lack of institutional development and comprehensive cultural identity that exacerbates state-building and nation-building initiatives – which my theoretical argument suggests leads to civil war.

The findings also indicate that increased development is associated with a decreased likelihood of civil war, which is consistent with *Proposition 2.1*. I re-estimated the original model to include the annual percentage rate of change of *Development* in order to determine whether 'growth' rather than

Table 1.1. Logistic regression of factors associated with civil war, 1950–92

Variables	Coefficients
Semidemocracy	.41
	(.91)
Belgian	3.18***
	(.86)
British	1.88***
	(.73)
Portuguese	2.25*
	(1.35)
US	4.27***
	(1.24)
Development	−.1.53**
	(.63)
Milspending	1.38**
	(.60)
Ethnopolitical Group	1.12
	(.68)
Polar	.51
	(.57)
Constant	−9.19***
	(1.56)
-2 Log likelihood	173.71
N	959
X^2	28.32***

Standard errors are in parentheses; *p < .10, **p < .05 level, ***p < .01 level.

'development' had the strongest conflict dampening impact on African civil war. I find that, controlling for the factors listed in Table 1.1, growth is not significantly associated with the likelihood of African civil war, while *Development* remains negative and highly significant. It appears that development more than growth reduces the probability of the onset of civil war in Africa.

I also find that *Milspending* is significantly associated with an increased likelihood of civil war, which is consistent with *Proposition 2.2*. The latter finding challenges the view that by privileging the military in their budgetary decisions, political elites stave off potential insurgency (e.g. Gyimah-Brempong, 1992). In fact, hyper-spending on the military probably increases the likelihood that the military itself, fat on the largesse provided by the political leadership, will eventually move on its patrons.

Considering the prevalent view that assumes the salience of cultural variables in African domestic conflicts, it is interesting that neither cultural variable is significantly associated with the probability of civil war (these findings refute *Propositions 3.1* and *3.2*).[13] In the case of polarization, the findings suggest that civil wars may emerge within polarized or non-polarized states, or in those characterized by a wide range of cultural distributions (see Horowitz, 1985). The absence of a significant relationship between *Ethnopolitical Group* and *Civil War* is particularly interesting since Scarritt (1993: 254) maintains that the prevalence of minorities at risk is greater in Africa than in most other regions of the world. Since the coefficient for *Ethnopolitical Group* is just barely insignificant with a p value of .10, I conducted sensitivity tests to attempt to determine the robustness of this nonsignificant finding. I disaggregated the temporal domain and examined the relationship between *Ethnopolitical Group* and *Civil War* for the periods from 1960 to the present, 1970 to the present, 1980 to the present, and 1990 to the present; yet, there was no significant relationship between *Ethnopolitical Group* and *Civil War* for any of these time periods (p. values were consistently greater than .30 across each of the time periods). I conclude that the findings reported in Table 1.1 are robust and that there is no significant relationship between the presence of a mobilized ethno-political group and the probability of civil war in African states.

To my mind, the latter findings suggest that cultural factors are only likely to be associated with civil war when fused with political and economic factors. Therefore, when one controls for political and economic factors, as is done in this study, the impact of cultural factors is insignificant. Nevertheless, one should not infer from these findings that a policy aimed at reducing the likelihood of African civil war should not focus on the protection of the rights of ethno-political groups (see Gurr and Harff 1994; Henderson, 1999); one should simply not assume that the distribution of culture groups or the presence of 'politicized ethnic groups', in and of themselves, are portents of civil war. Moreover, one should not assume that African civil wars are simply 'ethnic conflicts'.

Beyond the significance of the predictor variables, it is also important to determine their relative impact on the likelihood of civil war. Although the beta coefficients from logistic regression are not directly interpretable, techniques are available that allow us to determine the independent impact of each predictor variable on the probability of the outcome, holding the other variables constant at their mean or modal values (Menard, 1995). Table 1.2 lists the marginal impact of each significant predictor variable in our model, *ceteris paribus*, on the probability of civil war.

The results indicate the greater role of political – more than economic or cultural – variables on the likelihood of civil war. Specifically, the four colonizer state variables have the greatest marginal effects on the likelihood of civil war when holding other variables constant at their mean or modal values. For example, a unit change in the value of *US* (i.e. a change from the absence of US colonization '0', to the presence of US colonization '1') is associated with a 9 per cent probability of civil war when the other variables are held at their mean or modal values. This represents more than a sixty-fold increase in the likelihood of civil war as compared with the baseline probability of civil war (which is .14 per cent). *Belgian* has the

Table 1.2. Marginal impact of predictor variables on the probability of civil war, 1950–92

	Marginal Probability of War	Difference in Marginal Probability as Compared with the Baseline Probability of War
US	9.00%	+8.86%
Belgian	3.20%	+3.06%
Portuguese	1.30%	+1.16%
British	.90%	+.76%
Milspending	.30%	+.16%
Baseline Probability of War	.14%	-
Development	.06%	−.08%

second highest marginal impact on the likelihood of civil war, followed by *Portuguese* and *British*. Among the remaining variables, *Milspending* is associated with a .3 per cent likelihood of civil war while *Development* is associated with a .06 per cent likelihood of civil war, which represents a .08 per cent decrease in the probability of civil war as compared with the baseline probability. All told, the findings indicate that the less developed, militarized states that were not colonized by the French have been the most likely candidates for civil war in Africa.

Discussion

Of the political, economic and cultural factors widely assumed to be associated with the onset of civil war in Africa, the results indicate that the lingering impact of colonialism was the most powerful precipitant of civil war. The findings clearly implicate the disparate colonial legacies of African states as significant precipitants of African civil wars. To my mind, one of the most significant aspects of the colonial legacy was that it saddled African states with the burden of simultaneously erecting legitimate political institutions of governance, while incorporating diverse peoples into a single political entity to which they would swear fealty. The strongest European states had centuries to respond to the dual demands of state-building and nation-building; however, African states have had only a few decades. The fact that the colonial powers left Africa with a plethora of very weak states (Holsti 1996: 99–100) only exacerbated these difficulties. The findings suggest that much of the armed conflict that we are viewing in Africa today is the result of this historic and ongoing political underdevelopment (also see Nkrumah 1965; Rodney 1980).

The problems associated with the simultaneous challenges of state-building and nation-building continue to confront African states with enormous demands on their brittle polities and often lead their elites to eschew democracy and to ignore the popular demands of their disaffected citizenry. Nevertheless, African elites also have themselves to blame for some very poor choices and policies, including the militarization of their societies and the failure to expand their economies – both conditions which increase the likelihood of civil war. The militarization of African societies – especially during the Cold War – did not provide greater security for the citizens of African states but primarily facilitated the longevity of corrupt leaders. Many African citizens were held hostage by political elites – who were often supported by the West – including some of the postwar era's worst dictators, murderers and kleptocrats. Their bloated militaries gave them an awesome capacity for domestic destructiveness and they fought (and in several cases continue to fight) some of the most brutal and protracted wars against their own citizens. As was so often the case, the former colonial powers and their allies threw gasoline on the smoldering conflicts in African states. During the Cold War era the superpower rivalry and the proxy-wars carried out in African states gave truth to the African saying, 'when two elephants fight, it is the grass that suffers'.

Ironically, the end of the Cold War and the rapprochement between the superpowers did not bode well for African development either, which supports the corollary to the maxim stated above: 'when two elephants make love, it's also the grass that suffers.' African states continue to be hamstrung by huge debts and poor economies while development aid floods into Eastern Europe and away from the South (Ihonvbere, 1998: 11–12). One result is the further widening of the gap between North and South, and the further immiseration of Africa, in particular. For example, Broad and Cavanagh (1998: 19) point out that 'in 1960 developing countries' gross domestic product (GDP) per capita was 18 per cent of the industrial nations; in 1990, at 17 per cent, the gap was almost unchanged'. More telling was Broad and Landi's (1996: 8) finding that, from 1980 to 1991, per capita GNP in the North increased at an average rate of 2.3 per cent. Over the same period, per capita GNP in the South had an average rate of increase of only 1 per cent; however, African states did not even realize that minuscule level of growth as their per capita GNP actually *declined* by 1.2 per cent.

The findings remind us that African states require a multifaceted strategy for development and demilitarization in order to reduce their likelihood of experiencing civil war. Such an approach is further necessitated because 'remedies' intended to alleviate a problem related to one class of factors (e.g. economic development) too often exacerbate difficulties related to other factors (e.g. political stability). For example, states that attempt to develop economically are often compelled to appeal to international organizations for assistance; however, Auvinen's (1996: 395) analysis of 70 less developed states from 1981 to 1989 implicated the IMF's high-conditionality structural adjustment programs in generating political protest even in more developed and democratic Third World states. It is these types of linkages that keep many African states severely hampered from ending their immiseration and the domestic conflict that it often generates.[14] These linkages, which are largely colonial and neocolonial in origin, also make it quite difficult to develop local initiatives that can provide for demilitarization and development, which are both important deterrents to civil war. In my view, Africans will have to rely on their indigenous resources and mechanisms in place in the region to insure against another half-century of civil wars, because, as Stedman (1996: 264) notes, the resolution of Africa's problems will ultimately depend on the development of regimes 'that have the capabilities to carry out the tasks that modern states are expected to perform'. Nevertheless, the lingering impact of colonialism on the prospect of African civil wars makes it imperative that Africans carve from their own experience a path to peace that privileges and strengthens their viable indigenous institutions because, as Ugandan leader Yoweri Museveni correctly pointed out: '[in Africa] We are building Afrocentric, not Eurocentric countries' (quoted in McGeary 1997).

Conclusion

In this chapter, I have systematically examined the extent to which political, economic and cultural factors are associated with civil wars in sub-Saharan African states. Drawing on a theoretical argument that associates the likelihood of civil war with the tumult that arises from the simultaneous challenges of state-building and nation-building, I derived several testable propositions on the correlates of African civil wars. Results of logistic regression analyses indicated that previous colonial experience is a significant predictor of the likelihood of civil wars. I also found that economic development reduces the probability of civil war, while militarization increases it. Interestingly, neither regime type nor cultural factors played a significant role in African civil wars.

All told, the findings lend greater support to those who emphasize the centrality of political and economic factors over cultural ones in explaining the incidence of African civil wars. In fact, the major contribution of this study is that it challenges the view that African civil wars are fueled by 'ethnic tensions', belying the notion that Africa's wars are simply 'ethnic conflicts'. Most importantly, the findings reinforce the view that African political elites must devise and implement more effective strategies to respond to the challenges of state-building and nation-building or face many more decades of civil wars on that battered and conflict-torn continent.

References

Auvinen, Juha, 1996. 'IMF Intervention and Political Protest in the Third World: A Conventional Wisdom Refined', *Third World Quarterly* 17 (3): 377–400.

Auvinen, Juha, 1997. 'Political Conflict in Less Developed Countries, 1981–89', *Journal of Peace Research* 34 (2): 177–95.

Ayoob, Mohammed, 1995. *The Third World Security Predicament*. Boulder, CO: Lynne Rienner.

Barrows, Walter, 1976. 'Ethnic Diversity and Political Instability in Black Africa', *Comparative Political Studies* 9 (2): 139–70.

Beck, Nathaniel, Jonathan Katz and Richard Tucker, 1998. 'Taking Time Seriously in Binary-Time-Series-Cross-Section Analysis', *American Journal of Political Science* 42 (4): 1260–88.

Broad, Robin and John Cavanagh, 1998. 'Don't Neglect the Impoverished South', in Robert Griffiths, ed., *Annual Editions: Developing World 98/99*. Guilford, CT: McGraw-Hill, 18–25.

Broad, Robin and Christina Landi, 1996. 'Whither the North-South Gap', *Third World Quarterly*

17 (1): 7–17.

Brown, Michael, 1996. 'The Causes and Regional Dimensions of Internal Conflict', in Michael Brown, ed., *The International Dimensions of Internal Conflict*. Cambridge, MA: MIT Press, 571–601.

Cohen, Youssef, Brian Brown and A. F. K. Organski, 1981. 'The Paradoxical Nature of State Making: The Violent Creation of Order', *American Political Science Review* 75 (4): 901–10.

Collier, Paul, 1998. *The Political Economy of Ethnicity*, Working Paper Series 98–8, Oxford: Centre for the Study of African Economies (April).

Collier, Paul & Anke Hoeffler, 1998. 'On Economic Causes of Civil War', *Oxford Economic Papers* 50 (October): 563–73.

Deger, Saadet, 1986. *Military Expenditure in Third World Countries*. London: Routledge & Kegan Paul.

Eichenberg, Richard, Brigitta Widmaier and Ulrich Widmaier, 1984. 'Projecting Domestic Conflict Using Cross-Section Data: A Project Report', in J. David Singer and Richard Stoll, ed., *Quantitative Indicators in World Politics*. New York: Praeger, 11–33.

Fearon, James and David Laitin, 1996. 'Explaining Interethnic Cooperation', *American Political Science Review* 90 (4): 715–35.

Frederickson, Peter and Robert Looney, 1983. 'Defense Expenditures and Economic Growth in Developing Countries', *Armed Forces and Society* 9 (4): 633–45.

Gurr, Ted, 1970. *Why Men Rebel*. Princeton, NJ: Princeton University Press.

Gurr, Ted, ed., 1993. *Minorities at Risk: A Global View of Ethnopolitical Conflict*. Washington, DC: US Institute of Peace.

Gurr, Ted, 1994. 'Peoples Against States: Ethnopolitical Conflict and the Changing World System', *International Studies Quarterly* 38 (September): 347–77.

Gurr, Ted and Barbara Harff, 1994. *Ethnic Conflict in World Politics*. Boulder, CO: Westview Press.

Gurr, Ted and Mark Lichbach, 1979. 'Forecasting Domestic Political Conflict', in J. David Singer and Michael Wallace, eds, *To Augur Well: Early Warning Indicators in World Politics*. Beverly Hills, CA: SAGE, 153–93.

Gyimah-Brempong, Kwabena, 1992. 'Do African Governments Favor Defense in Budgeting?', *Journal of Peace Research* 29 (2): 191–206.

Hechter, Michael, 1978. 'Group Formation and the Cultural Division of Labor', *American Journal of Sociology* 84, 2: 293–318.

Hegre, Havard, Tanja Ellingsen, Nils Petter Gleditsch and Scott Gates, 1997. 'Towards a Democratic Civil Peace? Democracy, Democratization, and Civil War 1816–1992', Paper presented to the Annual Conference of the Peace Science Society (International), Indianapolis, IN, November.

Henderson, Errol, 1998. 'The Impact of Culture on African Coups d'Etat, 1960–1997', *World Affairs* 161 (1): 10–21.

Henderson, Errol, 1999. 'Civil Wars', in Lawrence Kurtz, ed., *The Encyclopedia of Violence, Peace and Conflict*. San Diego, CA: Academic Press, 279–87.

Henderson, Errol and J. David Singer, 2000. 'Civil War in the Postcolonial World, 1946–92', *Journal of Peace Research* 37, 3: 275–99.

Heo, Uk, 1998. ''Modeling the Defense-Growth Relationship around the Globe', *Journal of Conflict Resolution* 42 (5): 637–57.

Hochschild, Adam, 1999. *King Leopold's Ghost*. New York: Houghton Mifflin.

Holsti, Kalevi, 1996. *The State, War, and the State of War*. Cambridge: Cambridge University Press.

Horowitz, Donald, 1985. *Ethnic Groups in Conflict*. Berkeley, CA: University of California Press.

Ihonvbere, Julius, 1998. 'The Third World and the New World Order in the 1990s', in Robert Griffiths, ed., *Annual Editions: Developing World 98/99*. Guilford, CT: McGraw-Hill, 8–17.

Jaggers, Keith and Ted Gurr, 1995. 'Tracking Democracy's Third Wave with the Polity III Data', *Journal of Peace Research* 32 (4): 469–82.

Lebovic, James and Ashfag Ishaq, 1987. 'Military Burden, Security Needs, and Economic Growth in the Middle East', *Journal of Conflict Resolution* 31 (1): 106–38.

Licklider, Roy, ed. 1993. *Stopping the Killing: How Civil Wars End*. New York: New York University Press.

Luard, Evan, 1989. *The Blunted Sword*. New York: New Amsterdam Books.

Mazrui, Ali, 1986. *The Africans: A Triple Heritage*. Boston, MA: Little, Brown and Co.

Mazrui, Ali and Michael Tidy, 1986. *Nationalism and New States in Africa*. London: Heinemann.

McGeary, J. 1997. 'An African for Africa', *TIME* 150, 9: 36-40.

Menard, Scott, 1995. *Applied Logistic Regression Analysis*. Beverly Hills, CA: SAGE.

Morrison, Donald and Hugh Stevenson, 1971. 'Political Instability in Independent Black Africa: More Dimensions of Conflict Behavior within Nations', *Journal of Conflict Resolution* 15 (3): 347-368.

Muller, Edward and Erich Weede, 1990. 'Cross-National Variation in Political Violence: A Rational Actor Approach', *Journal of Conflict Resolution* 34 (4): 624-651.

Mullins, A. F., 1987. *Born Arming: Development and Military Power in New States*. Palo Alto, CA: Stanford University Press.

Nkrumah, Kwame, 1965. *Neo-Colonialism: The Last Stage of Imperialism*. London: Panaf.

O'Kane, Rosemary. 1993. 'Coup d'état in Africa: A Political Economy Approach', *Journal of Peace Research* 30, 3: 251-70.

Regan, Patrick, 1996. 'Conditions of Successful Third-Party Intervention in Intrastate Conflicts', *Journal of Conflict Resolution* 40 (2): 336-59.

Rodney, Walter. 1974. *How Europe Underdeveloped Africa*. Washington, DC: Howard University Press.

Rummel, Rudolph. 1997. 'Is Collective Violence Correlated with Social Pluralism?', *Journal of Peace Research* 34 (2): 163-75.

Scarritt, James, 1993. 'Communal Conflict and Contention for Power in Africa South of the Sahara', in Ted Gurr, ed., *Minorities at Risk*. Washington, DC: US Institute of Peace, 252-89.

Schlichte, Klaus, 1994. 'Is Ethnicity a Cause of War?', *Peace Review* 6 (1): 59-65.

Singer, J. David, 1996. *Cultural Composition of States Data, 1820–1990*. Correlates of War Project. Ann Arbor, MI: University of Michigan, Department of Political Science.

Singer, J. David and Melvin Small, 1994. *International and Civil War Data, 1816–1992. Correlates of War Project*. Ann Arbor, MI: University of Michigan, Department of Political Science.

Singer, J. David and Melvin Small, 1995. *National Material Capabilities Data, 1816–1992. Correlates of War Project*. Ann Arbor: MI: University of Michigan, Department of Political Science.

Small, Melvin and J. David Singer, 1982. *Resort to Arms: International and Civil Wars, 1816–1980*. Beverly Hills, CA: SAGE.

Stedman, Stephen, 1996. 'Conflict and Conciliation in Sub-Saharan Africa', in Michael Brown, ed., *The International Dimensions of Internal Conflict*. Cambridge, MA: MIT Press, 235-65.

Tilly, Charles, ed. 1975. *The Formation of National States in Western Europe*. Princeton, NJ: Princeton University Press.

Weede, Erich, 1981. 'Income Inequality, Average Income, and Domestic Violence', *Journal of Conflict Resolution* 25 (4): 639-54.

Notes

1   The ambivalence regarding the extent of the impact of colonialism on independent African states is captured by Mazrui (1986: 14) in his discussion of whether the colonial period is best depicted as an 'epic' or an 'episode'. In the former case, colonialism represented a revolutionary period for Africa by incorporating the continent into the global political economy through the Atlantic Slave System and, later, formal colonialism. In the latter case, its impact is assumed to have been disruptive but more tenuous. For example, Mazrui (p. 14) reminds us that the colonial period was so brief that '[w]hen Jomo Kenyatta was born, Kenya was not yet a crown colony. Kenyatta lived right through the period of British rule and outlasted British rule by fifteen years.' He adds, "[I]f the entire period of colonialism could be compressed into the life span of a single individual, how deep was the impact?'

2   These inconsistent findings are not surprising in light of the disagreement on the role of cultural factors in other forms of African conflict such as coups d'etat (see Henderson 1998).

3   In this study, I focus on civil wars as a distinct form of domestic armed conflict in accordance with Gurr's (1970: 334) and Morrison and Stevenson's (1971) admonition that scholars distinguish among different forms of domestic violence because their correlates vary. For example, democracy *increases* the probability of protests but *decreases* the probability of rebellions (Gurr and Lichbach, 1979); economic development *reduces* the likelihood of internal wars but *increases* the likelihood of protests, demonstrations, and strikes (Eichenberg et al., 1984).

4   The findings reported in Table 1.1 are consistent when using either 1950 or 1960 as the initial year of the analysis; however, by beginning with 1950 data, we do not arbitrarily exclude observations for several African states that were already independent (i.e. Ethiopia, Ghana, Guinea, Liberia, Somalia, South Africa, Sudan).

5   All states that were colonies in 1950 enter the data set at independence. The spatial domain includes the following states: Angola, Benin, Botswana, Burkina Faso, Burundi, Cameroon, Cape Verde, Central African Republic, Chad, Comoros, Congo, Djibouti, Equatorial Guinea, Ethiopia, Gabon, Gambia, Ghana, Guinea, Guinea-Bissau, Ivory Coast, Kenya, Liberia, Lesotho, Madagascar, Malawi, Mali, Mauritania, Mauritius, Mozambique, Niger, Nigeria, Rwanda, São Tomé and Principe, Senegal, Seychelles, Sierra Leone, Somalia, South Africa, Sudan, Swaziland, Tanzania, Togo, Uganda, Zaire, Zambia, Zimbabwe.

6   Africa's civil wars (with starting dates) include: DRC, 1960; Sudan, 1963; Rwanda, 1963; Uganda, 1966; Nigeria, 1967; Burundi, 1972; Zimbabwe (Rhodesia), 1972; Angola, 1975; Mozambique, 1979; Chad, 1980; Nigeria, 1980; Uganda, 1980; Somalia, 1982; Sudan, 1983; Nigeria, 1984; Burundi, 1988; Liberia, 1989; Rwanda, 1990; Burundi, 1991; Liberia, 1992; Angola, 1992.

7   Ethiopia, Liberia and South Africa are coded as former Italian, US and British colonies, respectively (I also alternated codings with South Africa as a Dutch colony but the findings were consistent with those in Table 1.1). Although these states were not colonized in the traditional sense, nevertheless a case can be made that their autonomy, development and civil-military relations were constrained by processes quite similar to those of more traditionally colonized states. If Liberia is not included as a US colony, then the findings with regard to the US are moot; otherwise the exclusion of the Liberia/US case does not affect the direction or significance of the other variables in the model with the exception of the *Portuguese*, which remains positive but is not significant.

8   I do not include all of the colonizer state variables in the same equation because that would create a perfect linear combination and preclude estimation; I therefore exclude *French* from the regression equation, so that it can be used as the baseline with which we can determine the impact of the other regional variables.

9   I examine the tolerance levels among the predictor variables in order to gauge the extent of multicollinearity (see Menard, 1995: 66) and they are consistently above .30; thus, the findings appear to be robust with respect to potential problems of multicollinearity. I also apply Beck et al's (1998) diagnostic for autocorrelation and I find that the direction and significance of the coefficients of the variables in the original model are consistent with those that include the diagnostic. Including a lagged dependent variable in the original model also does not affect the direction or significance of the variables in the original model reported in Table 1.1 (the lagged dependent variable is insignificant, as well). I therefore conclude that the findings are also robust with respect to problems of autocorrelation. In addition, the original model is robust with respect to the inclusion of annual lags on the predictors; one may therefore conclude that the impact of the predictors appears to be temporally prior to the onset of the outcome.

10 The semidemocratic African states that experienced civil war were DRC in 1960, Uganda in 1966 and 1980, Zimbabwe in 1972, Chad in 1980, and Liberia in 1992.

11 There is a negative relationship between *French* and *Civil War*.

12 O'Kane (1993) suggests that such deployments reduced the probability of coups d'état.

13 In addition, the insignificance of either cultural variable is not affected by the inclusion or exclusion of either variable in the same regression equation.

14 With respect to international assistance, if the experience of the last half-century is any indication, then Africans will have to devise new strategies to confront a largely indifferent – if not hostile – international environment. Nevertheless, many Africans have begun to increase their appeal to their diaspora – especially in the US – both to provide support for indigenous African initiatives and to lobby their governments for African development programs – most importantly, debt forgiveness on the part of European and American governments, which, in this time of controversy over debt repayment, have yet to repay the awesome debt owed to Africa for the holocaust of enslavement and colonization.

2

Multiple Complexity
& Prospects for Reconciliation & Unity
The Sudan Conundrum

ABDEL GHAFFAR M. AHMED

Rather than considering the Sudan as a country shaped by 'multiple marginality' (Mazrui 1971),[1] this chapter attempts to examine the multiple complexities of the issues that characterize its environment and its people. The country is the largest in Africa[2] and is characterized by geographical diversity ranging from tropical forests in the South to sand desert in the North. This diversity is reflected in its people who are multi-cultural, multi-ethnic, and multi-lingual. Most of the country is sparsely populated because of the arid conditions and the substantial rural-urban migration and displacement in recent years (Eltigani1995). Though Sudan is endowed with natural resources, the vast majority of the population is poor. Inequalities in resource sharing and the effects of the civil war have left a large part of the population in extreme poverty (Ali et al. 2002).

Like several other African countries, it has experienced many years of political tension and civil war since its independence in 1956. The first civil war started in 1955, a few months before the country declared its independence, and lasted for 17 years. The Addis Ababa Peace Accord signed in 1972 led to the settlement of this war and helped bring about eleven years of relative peace (Alier 1990, 1992). During this period South Sudan enjoyed autonomy under Nimeri's regime and a different system of governance from the North. 'The situation amounted then to an island of liberal parliamentary democracy in an ocean of one party dictatorship and the personal rule of Nimeri in the whole country. What this rule lacked, or was denied, was the economic power and resources to sustain and develop the Southern Region. This was marked by deterioration in the conditions of living in the South, economic stagnation and social anarchy' (Nyaba 2000: 21). The struggle for power among the Southern elite and the mobilization of support on the basis of ethnic relations, together with the passing of Islamic laws by Nimeri, created a favorable climate for a resumption of the conflict.

By 1983 hostilities broke out again, leading to another prolonged civil war. It is estimated that during the twenty years of this war 2 million people died and 4 million became internally displaced (IDP), with no

71

sustainable source of income or adequate services. They remained vulnerable to widespread famine and disease. Most of them joined the increasing number of the urban poor located in various camps in Khartoum state and other urban areas in the country. A number of peace initiatives were undertaken, reaching their climax in the latest three, namely, the IGAD-Naivasha, Abuja and Cairo initiatives outlining the framework of a peace settlement. With the imminent settlement, the IDPs are expected to repatriate, relocate or integrate themselves in the setting where they are currently residing. In such circumstances the key ingredient for preventing the resumption of hostilities is building confidence in the body politic in a way that assures the society that every community and every interest group enjoys equality of opportunity. Yet that in itself is not a sufficient condition, as a structure of authority needs to be put in place that ensures that individuals and communities feel that they are part of the wider system and therefore develop a sense of belonging that enables them to perceive any conflict situation as being detrimental to their own interests. This will call for the institutionalization of power-sharing mechanisms and mechanisms for the transfer of development resources from the center to the localities in a way that ensures equity in their allocation to meet the cost of providing for basic human needs, such as education and health care.

Interaction between a diversity of ethnic groups in the IDP camps has led to the gradual fading of ethnic boundaries. Individuals and groups in these camps express a high degree of tolerance and a desire for peaceful coexistence regardless of the region of origin, cultural background and system of organization of each group. They have exhibited an ability to survive in a new environment, to adopt new values, to develop new systems of organization and to allow for the emergence of new leadership to match the new setting. This experience opens up a window of opportunity that the national political elite can use to bring about reconciliation and demonstrate that unity in diversity is a viable alternative for holding the Sudan from falling apart.

Background: Re-reading History

Continuity is a striking feature of the history of the Sudan. This history consists of a series of episodes dating back a number of centuries, that still contribute to the present shaping of relations and the conflict situation in different parts of the country. Without knowledge of the dynamic inter-action between people during these episodes, it is difficult to understand the multiple complexity of the present state of affairs. An analysis of the historical background to the Sudanese conflict suggests a number of pre-conditions that have militated against peace since the dawn of independence. These include the polarization in the diversity alluded to earlier. As such, a war based in the South against a North-dominated government is bound to be an ethnic war of identity or a' war of visions', as has been recently characterized by a leading Sudanese scholar (Deng 1995). Religious composition is also a major contributor to this polarization, where three religions can be found competing, namely, a dominant Islam followed by a large percentage of followers of indigenous beliefs and a Christian minority, the latter two found mainly in the South. Linguistic diversity also contributes to this polarity, with approximately 134 living languages dividing the population (Ali et al. 2002).[3]

Population mobility has been a major feature of Sudan's history. Under the Kushites attempts were made to move northwards into Egypt, expanding the domain of influence and creating various ethnic relations. 'Towards the end of the third century the Axumites made a direct attack on Meroe in order to protect the Beja.... About the same time, either shortly before or shortly after, the Meroe area suffered a heavy infiltration of a people called Nuba who came from Kordofan' (Conte 1976: 29). Centuries later, Arab penetration followed through the coastal region, the North and later the West. Ethnic groups from the South moved in to establish the Fung Kingdom of Sinnar in alliance with Arab nomadic ethnic groups. Central Sudan became a melting pot where different ethnic groups started competing for its rich natural resources. Adjustment in ethnic and social spheres was taking place, accompanied to some extent by a revival in the political sphere where a new ethno-cultural identity had been established. Such encounters led to a national rebirth, which might be considered a gradual neutralization of those elements that had broken up the Meroitic civilization and paved the way for Fung rule.

This mobility was also followed by matching changes in beliefs. From worshiping divine kings, an idea borrowed from the Egyptian civilization in the North, to the advent of Christianity and later Islam, the population in Central Sudan was continuously coping with tremendous shifts. Christianization of Nubia was a slow process that started in the second century AD and gradually went on to establish its dominance in the kingdoms that lasted up to the sixteen century. The same path was followed by Islam that started penetrating the place some time during the seventh century together with a slow process of Arabization of the population in the center. The settlement of the Arabs in Northern and central Sudan caused the displacement of the local people who scattered in all directions, especially towards the South and the West. The alliance between local ethnic groups and Arab groups eventually resulted in the emergence of the Islamic states of Eastern and Western Sudan.

The polarization of the Sudan goes beyond these issues of ethnicity, religion and language to cover the fields of economics, politics and the system of administration that are major determinants of the daily lives of its people. The difference between the North and the South of the country is greatly influenced by the inequity in economic development, the different systems of government in the local communities, and the dominant political parties that have essentially been confined to the North and have not to the present day penetrated the South in an effective manner (Ahmed and El Nager 2003). Hence, during the limited period when democracy was given an opportunity to rule the country after independence, these Northern parties essentially determined the political bargaining processes (Mohamed Salih 2001: 76–106).[4] It is not surprising that this state of affairs has ignited grievances among the people of Southern Sudan and led to many disagreements and great distrust (Alier 1990).

The situation was further exacerbated by the lack of economic development in the Southern region. It is true that all indicators suggest that Sudan was at independence, and still is, desperately poor (Ahmed 1989, 1992; Ali 1992). However, this state of affairs is more conspicuous in the South than in the North.[5] It came about as a result of the concentration of the major agricultural development schemes in the Central region, a policy started by the colonial administration and later followed by the national ruling elite after independence. At the moment, it can be estimated that the South has an average per capita income less than half the national average. The economy was also dependent on primary products, especially in the Southern and Western regions with total dependence on the Central and Eastern regions where irrigated and rain-fed agriculture is flourishing. This dependence has been deepened even further now that Sudan is an oil-producing country. However, the oil can be considered 'conflict' oil, since most of the proven reserves are in the South and control over this resource is in the hands of the central government that is using the revenues to strengthen its power and authority in relation to all other parts of the country. When considering the services that depend on the country's economic ability, the gap between the regions widens further over time and the South has significantly lagged behind.[6]

Large population movements within the country and across its borders impacted on its economy, political system, social life and the health of its inhabitants. More importantly, the unabated civil conflict during the past decades has had a negative impact on the country's social and economic development. Decades of political and economic deterioration have left their mark on the infrastructure and on human capital, leading to the impoverishment of the masses and the alienation of the educated groups. Conflicts and internal displacement of civilians have resulted in food insecurity in parts of the country and continue to cause egregious suffering and loss of life. Against this background, poverty is widespread and the country suffers from a weak and uneven economic base and infrastructure. GDP per capita for 2001 was estimated at US$395 (World Bank 2003).

In early January 2005 negotiations between the government and the Sudan People's Liberation Army (SPLA)[7] were concluded, leading to the Comprehensive Peace Agreement that brought to an end the longest civil war in Africa. However, a new situation of similar nature based on similar grievances to those in the South started in early 2003 in Dar Fur leading to what the international media termed a 'humanitarian crisis'. Indigenous efforts and international pressures have brought the government and the fighting parties, the Sudan Liberation Army (SLA) and the Justice and Equity Movement (JEM), to the negotiating table in Abuja in the hope of reaching an agreement along the lines of what took place between the central government and the SPLA in Kenya.[8] There were hopes and expectations that these talks would lead to a settlement of the longest civil war in Africa (1955–72 and 1983 to date). However, while peace is necessary, it is not sufficient to ensure sustainable development of the country. For such a peace to be sustained, it needs to be accompanied by major reforms in all aspects of life. When dealing with human development under such circumstances, special attention should be paid to the situation within which the IDPs survive. The goal should be to improve their living conditions in the short run and offer them better opportunities in the future. To achieve this, there is a need to take decisions based on deep understanding and evidence-based knowledge of the complex reality of the scenes of the different conflicts. In the following sections of this chapter an attempt will be made to highlight the multiple complexity of the country and to reflect on its impact on the possible opportunities for reconciliation and unity.

The Multiple Complexities

As stated above, the Sudan is characterized by cultural diversity, different systems of livelihood (i.e. the economy) and social organization of the various ethnic groups, and enormous variations of the physical environment, all of which affect the daily lives of its inhabitants. The interaction between these factors leads to the multiple complexity that faces students and observers of Sudanese society. Many dichotomies can be drawn between the different parts of the country as well as between its ethnic groups. However, in reality these dichotomies do not necessarily explain in full the kind of conflict that arises between the different peoples in the country. It is only when these factors are combined with resources and wealth differentials or the perceived sense of group inequalities, and other such socio-economic conditions, on the one hand, and a particular configuration of society such as the presence of geographical homogeneity in the distribution of ethnic aggregates, that they can account for, and cause, conflict (cf. Adekanye 1997).

The conflict in Southern Sudan that started in 1955, a few months before independence, was basically characterized as a conflict that can be expressed in three major dichotomies. Most of the literature and the international media present it as a conflict between Arabs and Africans, Muslims and Christians, and oppressors and oppressed. Though there may be elements of each of these dichotomies in the situation, none of them offers a thorough explanation of the root causes of the conflict. The issue of underdevelopment and economic marginalization embedded in the notion of oppressors and oppressed is more relevant as an explanation of what went on over the decades.

Contrary to what most people believe, the Sudan is not racially or culturally divided into clear-cut Arab-North and African-South factions. There is certainly a foundation for this dichotomy, but it has been largely overplayed to the point of confusing realities, aggravating differences and generating tension and conflict. It is correct to assume that the start of the infiltration of Muslim Arabs and their gradual inter-mixing with the indigenous population have left considerable elements of Arab ethnic and cultural identification throughout the North. There is enough evidence from historians and anthropologists to invalidate any of the claims of purity of blood, as Arabs intermarried and integrated with the indigenous population. The Arab element eventually became more emphasized than the Negroid elements in the process of political development and competition. Perhaps the only group that can claim purity of Arab blood is the Rashayda of Eastern Sudan whose migration into that area took place less than two centuries ago.[9]

In addressing the dichotomy based on religion, the elements of continuity and peaceful co-existence between different beliefs over centuries seem to be glossed over by most of those who want to utilize this issue for political purposes, whether this is Christianity, Islam, or traditional beliefs. Religion is an important part of the identity of Sudanese people. It is difficult, however, to isolate religion from other aspects of Sudanese life (Voll and Voll 1985: 15–16). While traditional beliefs have survived through centuries and they are still able to adjust and co-exist with changing circumstances, this has not been the case with Christianity and Islam in Northern Sudan. 'Arabization, in the mixed religious- cultural- and racial sense it now has, was not to come until the seventh century when Justinian sent Missionaries from Egypt to convert the Nubians. Meeting with success, the Nile Valley from Arabia to Abyssinia became Christian. Three Christian kingdoms were established – Alawa, Muqurra, and Maris – which survived the spread of Islam for several centuries' (Deng 1973: 12). These kingdoms managed to resist the penetration of Islam and it was only in the fifteenth century that an Islamic kingdom was able to establish bases itself in central Sudan.[10] The dichotomy on religious grounds is a recent creation brought about by the colonial administration. In its support of the missionary activities, the administration considered Islam the greatest stumbling block in the way of Christian penetration into the region. Thus the eradication of Islamic influence became a major concern of missionaries and their allied administrators, and certain steps were taken to secure that end (Ministry of Foreign Affairs 1973: 25).

It is the Southern Sudan policy starting from 1922 until its reversal in 1947 which explains that it was not the above dichotomies but rather the deliberate policy to separate the South from the North which is the root cause of the conflict. This separatist policy 'was heavily influenced by the administration's desire to block out Arabism and Islam from Black Africa. The idea of preventing the penetration of Arab influence into the interior of Africa had existed long before the conquest of the Sudan'[11] (Ruay 1994: 38). According to this policy southerners were forbidden to assume Arabic names or to adopt Northern attire. The use of Arabic, formerly the *lingua franca* of the South, was greatly discouraged. Emigration from South to North was forbidden and persons found guilty of crossing the fictitious dividing line between the two regions were fined or imprisoned. 'The implication of the South-North separate policy was not clear to the British, but the possibility of the South being eventually linked to East Africa seems to have been contemplated. Southern Governors were not as a rule required to attend the annual meeting of Governors in the North, but to coordinate their work with their colleagues in East African British colonies' (Deng 1973: 33).

Another important effect of this colonial policy in the South on the development of North–South relations came though its impact in the field of education. Christian missionaries were assigned the complete monopoly of running the school systems. With this type of education, Southerners were discouraged from engagement in politics, political debate and action, and anybody found practicing political dissent was punished and dismissed from either school or job (Nyaba 2000: 16). In line with the contemplated link with East Africa, graduates from Southern intermediate schools went to Makerere College in Uganda for their higher education (Deng 1973: 33).

The colonial Southern policy, as noted by Ali et al. (2002), had no economic development objectives apart from restriction of trade and mobility of labor. This is the point at which the two parts of the country started drifting apart in terms of economic development. The development of irrigated agriculture and the building of transport systems were not a deliberate policy to develop the North, but rather an effort to make the colony pay for itself through the use of local cheap labor. The start of rain-fed agriculture in Eastern Sudan during the Second World War was also put in operation not for the sake of the food security of the population but to secure the necessary food for the fighting forces in North Africa. In the South, economic development was limited to small projects such as small cotton growing and rubber and coffee plantations. It was thought that it would be a disaster to allow the people of the South to obtain wealth that brings 'various luxuries of civilization'.[12] Reversal of the policy came in 1946, but by then the damage was already done and the gap between the two parts of the country had become too difficult to bridge.

Perplexed attempts have been made recently to characterize the case in Dar Fur, using the dichotomy of Arabs against Africans, or Muslims against non-Muslims. Such attempts cannot be quantified. The parties to the conflict are for the most part a mixture of African and Arab ethnic groups which can only be differentiated by their livelihoods systems. It is possible to refer to a dichotomy of herders and farmers. There can be no reference to a religious dichotomy, since all groups in the region are Muslims. A conflict that started as competition for decades over resources (Suliman 2000; Ahmed and Harir 1983) has been driven by both internal and external forces to reach its present critical state. In reality, the issue is one of the marginalization of people in peripheral regions exhibiting a case of acute poverty, lack of development and exclusion from participation in decision-making. However, the articulation of these issues by the leadership of the rebelling groups is poor and the central government is exploiting this situation to its advantage by engaging in promoting a counter leadership by its own party members in the region to express to the local people and the international community the lack of consistency in the rebels' position.

A dichotomy that adds to the complexity of the Sudan case is the growing rift between rural (traditional) and urban (modern) areas. It is perhaps correct to assume that urban areas have been exploiting rural areas for many decades now. This has been an historical role of small and large urban centers (Ahmed 1979a, 1979b; Southall 1998). The rural population have recognized the exploitation process and have had to live with it, and have stayed in their locations. However, under the pressure of environmental calamities, civil war and ethnic conflicts resulting from competition over resources, growing numbers have moved to seek refuge in urban areas. This kind of movement led to the increasing number of displaced people around small and large urban centers and ultimately the ruralization of the urban setting (Mohamed Salih 1985; El Nager 2001). It is hardly possible to draw a significant distinction between rural and urban lifestyles in most of the present settlements in Sudan.

The point to emphasize here is that attempts to express the conflict in various parts of the country on the basis of the three often mentioned dichotomies, i.e. race, religion and oppression, without looking in-depth at elements of the history that brought them about is a simplistic way of addressing the problem. The complexity goes beyond these elements that are used to mobilize support and win followers to the position of the exponents of each argument. The root causes of the conflict in each region and among the different ethnic groups may have some elements of the dichotomies expressed in that case. However, in all cases it can be more clearly expressed if the dominant elite at the center, who control the positions of power and authority and manage the resources to their own advantage, address it as an issue of underdevelopment, exploitation and marginalization of rural regional people. This elite, the majority of whom come from the North and Central regions of the country, still maintains some representation of other parts of the country.

Failing Elite, Self-Promotion & Opportunism

Apart from the dichotomies, the reality of the social and political structures characterizing the social map of present-day Sudan, the role of the elite becomes a key factor in explaining the country's conundrum. The egregious suffering of the various regions can be attributed to the status and roles of the modern political elite who are assuming power and authority and controlling productive resources from the capital or in regional urban centers. This elite is vigorously manipulating ethnic identities in its attempt to sustain authoritarianism, no matter what that does to the system of governance it claims to pursue. Even when political parties were established, each party[13] was affiliated to a certain ethnic or religious group, often with a certain geographical territory. The party claims monopoly over that ethnic group or geographical region where the ethnic group originates. Even the elite leading the SPLA are not able to avoid such a situation. '

> Despite many years of common historical development, including fighting together for a common nationhood, many intellectuals now, more than ever before, still identify themselves first as Dinka, Nuer, Moro, Shilluk, Zande, etc., and then south Sudanese, even when interacting with each other. This alienation was accentuated by the experience South Sudanese went through in the Southern Regional Government in Juba following the Addis Ababa Agreement in 1972. The political elite who took over the power structure in the South emphasized their tribal attributes and unity with the North at the expense of and against the South Sudanese nationalism which started developing on the eve of independence of Sudan. (Nyaba 2000: 6–7)

This manipulation of ethnicity and the egocentric struggle for state power are closely linked to, and perhaps best explained through, under-standing the bases upon which colonial education in Sudan was founded.

Education played a critical role in colonial state development. To satisfy the need for skilled and literate employees in the lower and middle tiers of the bureaucracy, the colonial regime in Sudan, as in many other colonies, founded government institutions that groomed young men for clerical, judicial and technical posts (Sharkey 2003: 40). The students selected for such institutions in the early stages were sons of the leaders of ethnic groups or came from the ranks of the 'detribalized' population in major urban centers. The selection and grooming of this nucleus of elites has had a profound impact on the development of the political life of the country up to the present. The emphasis was on acculturation, which the colonial power aimed for, rather than the formation of an organic educated elite, which became the prime concern of the postcolonial era. The contact with Egypt played a significant role in the elite formation and influenced the progress toward the creation of an active political and labour movement.

Education in the South, which was the monopoly of the missionaries, followed the same direction and pattern in the process of selecting the sons of ethnic leaders. It pursued the aims of Southern policy and did not allow for any contact with the educational system in the North. This not only increased the gap between the North and the South, but also produced apolitical, docile civil servants (Nyaba 2000:16). The graduates of such education were discouraged from engagement in politics and were punished if they did so.

A notable feature of the development of these elites is their tendency to be 'detribalized' through the process of education that moves them out of their communities. In most cases they do not return after receiving such education in the urban centers. Long periods of absence and being subjected to an education that has no relevance to the livelihood systems in their local areas lead to a total break from their group values and lifestyles. Few members of this elite group maintain ties and regular contacts with their home areas and therefore eventually lack understanding of the processes of change that are taking place in their regions of origin. They develop a lack of touch with the impact of environmental changes, civil wars and inter-group conflicts on local communities and pay little or no attention to the needs of the rural population.

The decades of political turmoil and the attitudes of the national political parties and military regimes that have ruled the Sudan have capitalized on the 'detribalized' elites as agents of control of their ethnic groups. Such elites are frequently sent back, at times of crisis, to their areas to propagate the views of the powers that be in the centers by offering as many promises as they can, which are never fulfilled. In doing so, they work for their own self-promotion and that of their parties. They exploit the trust of the local communities in an opportunistic manner to build power positions for themselves within the centers. They only recognize how marginalized and oppressed the remote regions are when they start to be marginalized in the power positions they gained as rewards for manipulating their ethnic connection to strengthen the powers at the center. This is the time, as can be seen from recent events, when such elites attempt to go back to their remote regions and start mobilizing the masses against the center. However, without minimizing the case of the marginalization of the regions, the Dar Fur case can be cited to illustrate this point.[14] But even more serious is the case of the elite in the Diaspora. Having lost touch with events in their areas of origin, most of them exhibit a clear lack of understanding of the real events in the region they claim to represent to the international community.[15] This drives them to positions where they knowingly or unknowingly serve the interest of external powers rather than that of their own people.

The New Reality in IDP Communities

Population displacement is caused by a number of factors, some of which are sudden while others may be the result of a slow process of accumulation over time. It is a form of interaction between the individual, the community and the environment. It is also an indicator of the lack of sustainability of the environmental resource base, the production system and the cultural and political setting. As a sudden mass movement of people, it became a conspicuous phenomenon of the Sudan, especially during the last two decades, to the extent of drastically changing the demographic features of many of the regions (Abu Sin 1998; Ibrahim 1995).The civil war in the South and the drought in the East and the West are the major causes of population mobility and the population displacement taking place today. A number of families and individuals have had to leave their places of residence and abandon their traditional means of livelihood and join the multitude of displaced people around urban areas. In their new settlement areas they depend on the government and NGOs, and await food relief and the extension of services. However, because of limitations on what can be provided by the government and national and international NGOs, after being in the settlement for a while they seek opportunities for income generation and devise their own coping strategies in order to stay alive.

IDPs at the individual and community level undergo a number of changes in their values and systems of organization. Major among these are the changes in gender relations as well as the system of cooperation among the group in the new locality (El Nager 1992; Assal 2004; Ibrahim 1995). Having had to reside in camps where groups from different ethnic and cultural backgrounds find themselves packed into the same limited physical space, they are forced to develop mechanisms of adjustment whereby they can make the necessary changes in their values to accommodate the 'others'. In their struggle to survive, they also have to learn new concepts and develop new skills that they did not know or appreciate when they were in their home areas. Changing, for example, from being pastoralists or farmers in rain-fed areas to having to manage in an urban setting has been a challenging task for these individuals, families, and communities.

Leaving their area of habitation and moving to the camps arranged for the displaced away from the centers of urban areas, they can no longer maintain their organizational structures as they used to do in their home areas. Adjustments to new systems of organization and new structures of administration in the camp area become essential for existence. They are faced with new structures which include more than one ethnic group under one administrative unit. This, in turn, leads to the emergence of a new type of leadership, since the traditional leaders do not necessarily come to the camps with the group. Usually such traditional leaders, in the case of those from regions other than the South, move to residences they already owned in the small urban areas of their own regions. In many ways this is a change that will have its impact on the future structure of local administration within these communities whether they stay in their place around the urban centers where they are now, or relocate to their home areas. Given the dynamics of change and the experience gained during this period in the areas where the IDPs have settled, it is not surprising to see the rise of new types of leadership among the newly-formed communities. Values, relations and expectations of the leadership in the camps have changed, and this has paved the way for the emergence of leaders who are able to articulate the needs and grievances of the camp members and communicate them to the relevant authorities and NGOs and extract as much benefit as possible for their constituency.

Education is a key factor in the process of building multi-cultural, multi-ethnic groups out of the younger generation of IDPs. It offers an opportunity for some to assume leadership positions in the camps and beyond. The availability of primary level education, for example, is evident from the number of schools in each camp of the four major camps around Khartoum. 'It is reported that 67.6 percent of children in 6–18 age category have attended primary schools, but only 5.9 percent attended high school' (Assal 2004:35).[16] Although the quality of education is poor because of the lack of resources and trained teachers, by using the national curriculum these schools become a major instrument of integration and a significant tool in breaking down ethnic boundaries and a mechanism for introduction to the wider national community. The fact that schools in the IDP camps use Arabic as a medium of instruction brings to the fore the issue of contested identities among the younger generation of IDPs. However, it is mastering the language and acquiring the general knowledge of relevance to life in an urban setting offered in these schools which is the major force behind survival in the camps and the rise of new leadership.

Between Reconciliation & Unity or Fall Apart

The future of the IDPs is riddled with challenges. Displacement as a process has changed the demographic map of the country. Different groups that may never have come close to each other are currently living in the same camps. Although displacement has had many negative effects on individuals, families and communities, some positive aspects can be seen as a result of the transformation that took place in the cultural values and structural organization of the IDPs. The imminent end of the civil war in the South between the SPLA and the central government and the prospect of settling the question of Dar Fur in the West, as well as the improvement of the environment in the degraded areas, may provide the opportunity for the IDPs to return to their localities or resettle in new areas away from the urban areas where opportunities for survival are limited.

The debate on the IDPs' future, which is focused on the three options of repatriation, relocation or integration, has its political overtones. However, the reality is that the IDPs will need to take into consideration the cultural change they have undergone during the time when they had to settle in camps and interact with other ethnic groups, the kind of skills they gained and the relevance of such skills to the livelihood systems in their home areas as well as the kind of services they may find if they repatriate or relocate. Integration into the present setting requires full adaptation to the new realities, and poses a challenge to the state authorities advocating this policy. If anything, the experience of displacement has shown that tolerance of the other and co-existence between ethnic groups as diverse as those currrently in the camps are possible. Such attitudes are good indicators that reconciliation and unity are not a remote prospect in the near future. Unity in diversity is as possible to obtain in the future of the Sudan as it was in the past.

The role of the elite is key to stability and sustainable peace. This applies to the modern political elite exercising power and authority in the center and the regions or the traditional and the newly emerging elite in the IDP camps. It is important to remember here that it is not all the members of a given group, but rather their elite who are the ones involved in the management of the conflicts that lead to major population mobility and displacement. Although the interests, goals and objectives that competing elites pursue tend to be mostly self-regarding and in fact transcend those of their particular groups, somehow these elites have little or no problem in reconciling their rational, self-calculating interests as individuals with the collective interests of their ethnic groups. This is a significant aspect of the process of ethnic mobilization, which is part of these groups' historical experience that was adopted and utilized by the colonial powers and continued even after the country gained its independence. The traditional elite, categorized as the historical product of colonialism, have come to assume a reality of their own and are accepted in their communities as moderators of conflicts and facilitators of contacts with the central authorities.[17]

The dilemma of the modern elite lies in their structure and origin and the opportunistic manner in which they have learned to operate. While disasters such as civil wars and famines devastated remote parts of the country, politicians were fighting at the center for power positions on the basis of self-interest. The fighting forces in the war zones are not in a better situation. Political maneuvering and unworkable sect-based coalitions brought paralysis to the country and retarded its development. The chieftain mentality inherent in the origin of the educated elites is in evidence today and seems to dominate the behavior of the present leadership and that of the political parties or the fighting groups to which they belong.[18] With the exception of the Sudanese Communist Party and the NIF (splitting into the National Congress and the Popular Congress), the dominant leadership is either family-, ethnic-, and/or religious-based. It is this social network rather than political awareness, in a country whose population is mostly illiterate, that has guided the political scene. A large sector of society

– women – is mostly drawn into the political process through this means, rather than through choice resulting from awareness as to how things ought to be. If settlement is reached and attempts at reconciliation are to be taken seriously, the modern elite in the center and their counterpart in the war zone have to find ways and means to come to grips with the new realities brought about by the demographic mobility resulting form the process of displacement. The newly emerging leadership in the IDP camps, together with the leadership of the burgeoning civil society organizations, have to be given the opportunity to become active players in the national political game.

The new leadership in the IDP camps have gained significant skills in dealing with the urban authorities and making forceful presentations of the claims of the communities they represent. The interaction and daily encounters in the camps exhibited the magnitude of the tolerance and the ability of the individuals and groups in the camps to accept the 'other' values, beliefs and respect for order in daily life. They developed new values and traditions as a result of being together that are shared by most if not all in the 'new home' from home. Reconciling with different new beliefs and values as well as a new system of administration shows that new types of communities are emerging, something that the political elite must recognize and be able to work with for the resolution of conflict and shaping the future. By moving towards the central parts of the country it can be argued that the IDPs have 'voted with their feet' for reconciliation and perhaps unity in the future. Such a move has been prompted by the realization that the Central region is endowed with many resources and the availability of social and other services. This has also brought them closer to the decision-makers and power-holders and given them a sense of security in a multi-ethnic and multi-cultural setting. In taking such steps, the IDPs have offered the national political leadership at the center and the marginalized regions an opportunity to reconsider their policies and step up their efforts towards creating unity, before such an opportunity is lost like the many similar ones in the recent past.

The repatriation policy advocated by the international NGOs and supported, according to recent studies, by a majority of the residents in the camps can lead to serious problems (Assal 2004). Many people may not be able to return to their previous localities due to environmental degradation as a result of the civil war or drought and desertification. The presence of unmarked landmines is going to force some groups to resettle in different areas from the ones they originally left. Such a situation can be riddled with uncertainty and may lead to the recurrence of inter-ethnic conflicts if not handled cautiously.

The present state of affairs exhibits multiple complexities as already alluded to, and things may fall apart. Given the existing circumstances, the possibility of seeing many Sudans rather than the proposed 'one country two systems' will soon emerge. Progress on this front will depend on the seriousness of the elite that led the negotiations in Naivasha and Abuja and their ability to be more concerned with serving the interest and the welfare of their general public rather than their own self-interest. The protocols of power and wealth-sharing[19] seem so far to address the concerns of the elite rather than those of the general public. No mention is made of the wealth accumulated by some on both sides of the conflict divide and whether they should be held accountable and asked to explain how they amassed all this wealth when their constituency was suffering from hunger (Nyaba 2004). Reconciliation in the case of the Sudan has to be reconciliation with justice, and compensation has to be offered.

Conclusion

In attempting to highlight the complexity of the present state of affairs in the Sudan with special reference to the displaced population, emphasis is focused on the interaction between cultural variables such as ethnicity, language, beliefs, values and resources and their interplay with politics. Within this framework of interaction there appears to be a clear element of actual and perceived group inequalities and an exploitative relationship between the center and the periphery leading people from marginal regional areas to flock towards the center. The demographic changes resulting from the displacement process have changed the features of the different ethnic groups and their relations and the way they organize themselves in their new areas of residence. Tolerance and co-existence are prominent features of the camp community. New leadership with capacity to deal with emerging issues in the new setting has taken shape, and the traditional and modern elites and their political parties have to adjust their activities in a manner that accommodates these new realities.

The question of policy towards the displaced has a serious undercurrent of political overtones that are embedded in the interaction of the central and regional elite, the international NGOs, and the newly emerging elite in the IDP camps. These political overtones are centered on questioning the legitimacy of the state, leading to the argument for the right of self-determination for all self-appointed groups. However, the idea of legitimate multi-ethnic states is a fundamental principle on which the international community rests. Recognition of this principle is of great relevance to the Sudan case at the present moment. Different ethnic groups have shown amazing tolerance of each other and share resources, though not in an equitable manner. Building on this foundation, the possibilities for reconciliation exist and some form of unity in diversity can be one viable alternative for keeping the Sudan from falling apart.

References

Abu Sin. 1998. 'Sudan', in Charles R. Lane ed., *Custodian of the Commons: Pastoral Land Tenure in East and West Africa*. London: Earthscan, 120–49.

Adekanye, Boya. 1997. 'Interaction of Ethnicity, Economy and Society in Separatist Movements in Africa', in Trude Andersen et al. eds, *Separatism: Culture Count, Resource Decide*, Bergen: Chn. Michelsen Institute, 72–105.

Ahmed, Abdel Ghaffar. 1974. *Shaykhs and Followers: Political Struggle in the Rufa'a El Hoi Nazirate in the Sudan*. Khartoum: Khartoum University Press.

Ahmed, Abdel Ghaffar. 1979a. 'Tribal Elite: A Base for Social Stratification in the Sudan', in S. Diamond, ed., *Towards a Marxist Anthropology*, Amsterdam: Mouton Press, 321–35.

Ahmed, Abdel Ghaffar.1979b. 'Small Urban Centers: Vanguards of Exploitation, Two Cases from the Sudan', *Africa* 49 (3): 258–71.

Ahmed, Abdel Ghaffar. 1989. 'Ecological Degradation in the Sohel: the political dimension', in A. Hjort and M. A. Mohamed Salih, eds, *Ecology and Politics*, Uppsala: Scandinavian Institute of African Studies.

Ahmed, Abdel Ghaffar. 1992. 'Rural Production Systems in the Sudan: a general perspective', in Martin Doornbos et al. eds, *Beyond Conflict in the Horn*, Trenton, NJ: Red Sea Press, 133–42.

Ahmed, Abdel Ghaffar and Samia El Nager. 2003. 'When Political Parties Fail: Sudan's Democratic Comundrum', in Mohamed Salih ed., *African Political Parties*, London: Pluto Press.

Ahmed, Abdel Ghaffar and Sharif Harir. 1983. *Sudan Rural Society and its Dynamics*, Khartoum: DSRC University of Khartoum (in Arabic).

Akol, Lam. 2001. *SPLM/SPLA: Inside an African Revolution*. Khartoum: Khartoum University Press.

Ali, A. Ali, Ibrahim Elbadaur, and Atta El-Batahani. 2002. 'On the Causes, Consequences and Resolution of the Civil War in Sudan', Manuscript presented to UNDP office, Khartoum.

Ali, A. Ali. 1992. *Structural Adjustment Programs and Poverty in Sudan*. Cairo: Arab Research Center.

Alier, Abel. 1990. *The Southern Sudan: Too Many Agreements Dishonored*. Exeter, UK: Ithaca Press.

Alier, Abel. 1992. 'Comment on Prospects for Peace', in Martin Doornbos et al. eds, *Beyond Conflict in the Horn*, Trenton, NJ: Red Sea Press.

Andersen et al. Bergen, Norway: Michelsen Institute, pp 72–105.

Asad, Talal. 1970. *The Kababish Arabs*. London: Hirst.

Assal, Munzoul. 2004. *Displaced Persons in Khartoum: Current Realities and Post-war Scenario*, Report to the Middle East Awards Program. Cairo: Population Council.

Beshir, M. O. 1968. *Southern Sudan: Background to Conflict*. Khartoum: Khartoum University Press.

Collins, Robert, 1971, *Land Beyond the Rivers: The Southern Sudan, 1898–1918*, New Haven, CT: Yale University Press.

Conte, Carmelo. 1976. *The Sudan as a Nation*, trans. Richard Hill.Topografia Mori & C.snc, Varese: Giuffre Editore.

Cunnison, Ian. 1966. *The Baggara Arabs*. Oxford: Clarendon Press; Cairo: Dar Turath (in Arabic).

Deng, Francis M. 1973. *Dynamics of Identification: A Basis for National Integration in The Sudan*. Khartoum: Khartoum University Press.

Deng, Francis M. 1995. *War of Vision: Conflict of Identities in the Sudan*. Washington, DC: The Brookings Institution.

El Nager, Samia. 1992. 'Children and War in the Horn of Africa', in Martin Doornbos et al. eds, *Beyond Conflict in the Horn*, Trenton, NJ: Red Sea Press, 15–21.

El Nager, Samia. 2001. 'Changing Gender Roles and Pastoral Adaptations to Market Opportunities in Omdurman, Sudan', in Mohamed Salih et al. eds, *African Pastoralism*, Pluto Press in association with OSSREA, pp 247–77.

El Nager, Samia. 2001. 'Displaced Women in Khartoum: Problems of Analysis and Recommendation for Action'. Report to the World Food Program, Khartoum. Unpublished.

Eltigani, E., ed. 1995. *War and Drought in Sudan: Essays on Population Displacement*. Gainesville, FL: University of Florida Press.

Gurdon, Charles, ed. 1994. *The Horn of Africa*. London: UCL Press.

Ibrahim, S. 1995. 'War Displacement: The Socio-Cultural Dimension', in E. Eltigiani, ed., *War and Drought in Sudan*, Gainesville, FL: University of Florida Press.

Khalid, Mansour, 2003, *War and Peace in Sudan: A Tale of Two Countries*, Cairo: Dar Turath.

Kulusika, Simon E. 1998. *Southern Sudan: Political and Economic Power Dilemmas and Options*. London: Minerva Press.

Mazrui, Ali A. 1971. 'The Multiple Marginality of the Sudan', in Yusuf F. Hassan, ed., *Sudan in Africa*, Khartoum: Khartoum University Press. 240–55.

Ministry of Foreign Affairs. 1973. *Peace and Unity in the Sudan: An African Achievement*. Khartoum: Khartoum University Press.

Mohamed Salih, M. A. 2001. *African Democracies and African Politics*. London: Pluto Press.

Mohamed Salih, M. A. 1985. 'Pastoralist in Town: Some Recent Trends in Pastoralism in North West of Omdurman District.' *Pastoral Development Network*. London: ODI.

Niblock, T. 1987. *Class and Power in the Sudan*. Albany, NY: State University of New York Press.

Nyaba, Peter A. 2004. 'We Will Only Declare Our Wealth: Evening Out Social and Economic disparities in Post-war South Sudan.' Paper presented to RWCMEA workshop, Ahfad University, Omdurman, 2–3 September.

Nyaba, Peter A. 2000. *The Politics of Liberation in South Sudan: An Insider's View*. Kampala: Fountain Publishers.

Ruay, Deng d. Akol. 1994. *The Politics of Two Sudans: The South and the North 1821–1969*. Uppsala: The Scandinavian Institute for African Studies.

Sharkey, Heather J. 2003. *Living with Colonialism: Nationalism and Culture in the Anglo-Egyptian Sudan*. Berkeley, CA: University of California Press.

Southhall, Aidan. 1998. *The City in Time and Space*. Cambridge: Cambridge University Press.

Suliman, Mohamed. 2000. *Sudan Civil Wars: New Perspective*. Cambridge: Cambridge Academic Press (in Arabic).

Voll, John ed. 1991, *Sudan: State and Society in Crisis*. Bloomington, IN: Indiana University Press, in association with the Middle East Institute, Washington, DC.

Voll, John and Sarah Voll. 1985. *The Sudan: Unity and Diversity in a Multicultural State*. Boulder, CO: Westview Press.

Woodward, Peter. 1979. *Condominium and Sudanese Nationalism*. New York: Barnes and Noble Books.

World Bank. 2003. *Sudan Stabilization and Reconstruction: Country Economic Memorandum*. Report No. 24620-SU, Washington, DC: World Bank.

Notes

1 Rather than accepting the reference to the Sudan as a bridge between Africa north and south of the Sahara, Mazrui (1971) preferred to give emphasis to the marginality of the Sudan in relation to the two parts of the continent. He used the 'term marginality to denote specific traits in the Sudan which place it significantly in an intermediate category between two distinct sectors of Africa. Sometimes the intermediacy gives the Sudan a double identity as in her capacity as both an African country in a racial sense and an Arab country in a cultural sense. But essentially the notion of marginality we intend is that which places the Sudan on a frontier between two distinct African universes: a frontier which shares some of the characteristics of both of those universes' (Mazrui 1971: 240–55).

2 Sudan has an area of 2.5 sq km. and its population is estimated at 32.5 million, with an annual rate of growth of approximately 2.6 per cent (World Bank 2003). It neighbors nine countries and shares an equal number of ethnic groups or more with these neighbors.

3 According to Ali et al. (2002) the number of languages listed for the Sudan is 142, of which 134 are living languages and 8 are extinct. Languages in the Sudan belong to three linguistics families, namely Afro-Asiatic, Nilo-Saharan, and Niger-Congo. Other sources give different figures (see Mohamed Salih 2001: 84; and Voll and Voll 1985:13).

4 Mohamed Salih gives an in-depth analysis of the role of political parties in Sudan showing the way alliances are made and dissolved during different periods, leading to what he rightly characterizes as a circus.

5 The only major exception in this case of investment in a large project is the Zandi scheme, the first integrated agricultural development scheme of its kind in the country. However, this scheme did not last for long since it was destroyed during the first civil war starting 1955. A similar fate a decade later faced the Jongoli project, which had the promise of offering an enormous opportunity for developing the Southern region.

6 The substantial economic marginalization of the South diminishes the opportunity cost of a rebellion. As the leader of the SPLA states, 'the burden and incidence of neglect and oppression by successive Khartoum clique regimes has traditionally fallen more on the south than on other parts of the country. Under these circumstances, the marginal cost of rebellion in the south became very small, zero or negative; thus, in the south it pays to rebel.' John Garang de Mabior (unpublished ms.) quoted in Ali et al. (2002).

7 The SPLA is the main fighting group leading the civil war in Southern Sudan. It has dominated the scene since its emergence in the closing months of 1963. It 'declared itself as a socialist movement fighting not for the separation of the South, as the Southerners expected, but for a united Socialist Sudan. It was to wage a protracted armed struggle

starting from the South but which would engulf the whole country in a socialist transformation' (Akol 2001: 13).

8   The two movements in Dar Fur insist they are not fighting for self-determination but for equitable share of resources and power, especially when it comes to governing their region. While the SLA seems to represent a multitude of different groups and a left-of-center ideological orientation, as indicated by the history of the political leanings of its leaders, the JEM is rumored to be part of the Turabi party, given the fact the its leader was part of the ruling party before its split.

9   According to the 1956 population census, the only census in the history of the country that included a question on ethnic and racial origin, there were nearly 600 'tribes' making over 50 'tribal' groups. Racially the population is divided into Hamitic, Semitic, Nilotic, Bantu and a number of other ethnic groups, resulting in a very heterogeneous country (See Voll 1991; Ministry of Foreign Affairs 1973).

10 It was only in 1504 that the Fung, in alliance with nomadic Arab groups, were able to overthrow the Christian kingdoms which were reduced and weakened by then, and establish their Islamic Kingdom with its capital in Sinnar some 250 km south of Khartoum. The origin of the Fung remains a contested issue among historians. The most accepted theory suggests that they were Shilluk. The Fung dominated the whole area except for Dar Fur which was under rulers (Sultans) who claimed Arab descent but looked more Negroid than Arab.

11 The idea of blocking the Arabs from having an influence on Africans can be seen in a memorandum by General Kitchener in 1892. He warned that 'unless the Christian powers hold their own in Africa, the Mohammedan Arabs will I believe step in and in the center of the continent will form a base from which they will be able to drive back all civilizing influences to the coast, and the country will then be given up to slavery and misrule as is the case in the Sudan at present', quoted by Ruay (1994:38) from Collins (1971:17).

12 This attitude was clearly expressed by the Governor of Upper Nile province in his 1925 report in which he states, 'to provide means for the present generation to acquire sufficient wealth to enable them to obtain all the various luxuries civilization brings and to make it possible for such comparative wealth to be easily gained, would in my opinion, be disastrous. For this reason I am anxious that the price for cotton should not be too high;' as quoted in Ali et al. (2002) with a reference to Beshir (1968: 44–5). For more on the Southern policy refer to Beshir (1968).

13 The exceptions to this case are the Sudanese Communist Party and the National Islamic Front. These two parties have attempted to establish themselves among the students, civil service employees, army personal, labour and farmers' unions.

14 Until recently leading figures in JEM were active members of the National Islamic Front (NIF) and held positions as high as ministerial posts. It was only when the NIF split and they found themselves on the losing side of Turabi that they went back to lead a rebellion.

15 Many articles, posted by Sudanese groups or individuals in the diaspora on the Internet, carry misjudged information and call for unrealistic solutions to the problems of different regions in the country.

16 Regarding high schools, Assal (2004:35) observes that, 'there are no high schools in the camps. To go to high school, students have to travel for long distances. The cost of transport can be prohibitive.' This explains the low percentage of those who attend such schools.

17 This role of the traditional elite and their relation to the colonial administration can be seen in a number of anthropological monographs. These include Cunnison (1966), Asad (1970) and Ahmed (1974) to name just a few.

18 Politics in Sudan and the role of political parties and their elitist leadership have been a subject of debate and analysis involving many scholars interested in the country. Mohamed Salih (2001) provides the most comprehensive analysis of the present situation. For more on the role of political parties, see Niblock (1987), Woodward (1979), Khalid (2003), Kulusika (1998), Akol, (2001) and also the articles on Sudan in the book edited by Charles Gurdon (1994), just to mention a few.

19 These protocols were signed by the Government of Sudan and the Sudan People's Liberation Movement in May 2004 in Naivasha, Kenya.

3

'You Don't Belong Here'
Citizenship, the State & Africa's Conflicts
Reflections on Ivory Coast

JOHN AKOKPARI

Although conflicts are not unique to Africa, its conflicts are somewhat unique. This uniqueness is reflected in the dramatic increase in the number of conflicts in recent decades – approximately 80 between 1960 and the 1990s (Adedeji 1999: 3), a good proportion of which occurred in the post-Cold War era. Also, in contrast to Europe whose history has been marked by inter-state conflicts, the majority of conflicts in Africa are intra-state. For example, of the total of 16 wars occurring in Africa in the seven years between 1990 and 1997, only two – Chad/Libya and Rwanda/Uganda – were interstate; the rest were internal conflicts (Laremont 2002: 3). Furthermore, only a small number of African countries have so far escaped destructive conflicts of one type or another.[1] Even Zimbabwe and Ivory Coast, once the epitome of political stability and economic development in Southern and West Africa respectively, are now an integral component of the continent's growing conflict statistics. Equally unique yet disconcerting are the systematic rapes, the brutal maimings and amputations as well as the persistent use of child soldiers, which have become defining characteristics of African conflicts (Laremont 2002: 14).

Africa's conflicts have generally wrought destruction of property and human lives and adversely affected the nascent institutions of governance. While intellectual analysis and mainstream literature have to an appreciable degree engaged the causes of these conflicts, there are other dimensions that have either remained unobtrusive or have been only marginally captured by the discourse. The question of citizenship, along with the attendant notion that some constituencies are 'strangers' and therefore should be content with the status of second-class citizens, remains at the heart of many of the conflicts in Africa. Potentially volatile, this notion is aggravated by the state's inclination to manipulate associated ethnic and chauvinistic sentiments to its advantage. A good number of Africa's intra-state conflicts, including that in the Ivory Coast, vividly demonstrate the trappings of the 'citizen-stranger' dichotomy and its manipulation by the state.

This essay offers a close examination of the conflict in Ivory Coast and argues that the citizen-stranger dichotomy and its manipulation by the elite lie at the heart of the conflict. It argues further that such manipulation has been aimed at excluding certain constituencies from competing in the political space. Consequently, any initiatives aimed at sustainable peace in Ivory Coast must first and foremost address this hidden dynamic. The essay begins with a cursory review of some of the dominant explanations of conflicts. It then explains the notion of citizenship and demonstrates how this has provided both the context and pretext for conflicts. Finally, it subjects the conflict in Ivory Coast to a case study to demonstrate the degree to which citizen-immigrant dichotomy and its manipulation by political elites have contributed not only to the eruption of the conflict, but also to the difficulty of negotiating a durable peace.

Conventional Explanations of Africa's Conflicts

The causes of Africa's conflicts are complex and defy the explanation of any single analytical perspective. While some see the causes of Africa's conflicts as economic and linked to poverty, debt and structural adjustment (Brown 1995; Adekanye 1995), others reduce them to political and governance-related factors such as the struggle for power, the fragility of the African state and ethnicity (Adedeji 1999; Lake and Rothchild 1996; Copson 1994). Yet others point to ecological factors such as competition over farming and grazing lands and other natural resources (Hyden 2000; Suliman and Omer 1994; Obi 1997). At a deeper lever, however, these seemingly discrete factors overlap and reinforce each other. For the purpose of this study, three popular sets of causal factors, which do not necessarily preclude economic and political factors, are highlighted. These are Africa's colonial experience, the failures of the state, and external factors. It is surmised that, with the exception of the latter, the causes of conflicts linked to Africa's colonial experience and the failures of the state are often fuelled by tensions between indigenes and settlers. In demonstrating this and related arguments, we first consider some of the widely presented causes of conflict in Africa.

The artificiality of the African state, which in contrast to the European state was a colonial construction, is a frequently cited cause of conflict. According to this argument, the African state assumed characteristics that were largely inimical to stability. The carving out of states was hasty and ill-conceived, as boundaries parcelled out homogenous groups into different states while re-grouping different, often mutually hostile, entities within the same territorial boundaries. These boundaries were, however, accepted by African leaders at independence and were sanctioned by the OAU in 1963, ostensibly on the grounds that tampering with the borders would generate new conflicts (Guest 2004).[2] Yet, while such arbitrary borders served the geo-economic and geo-political interests of Europe they undermined the natural process of state creation and nation-building in Africa (Laremont 2002: 3). Thus as Wiseman (1990:14) notes, African states are 'archetypal examples of states without nations'. Because of arbitrary borders, the typical postcolonial African state contains heterogeneous entities that have little in common. Not only does such heterogeneity set the stage for mutual suspicion and conflicts, but it also incites communities to rally in support, even in defence, of relatives and ethnic kin in neighbouring countries deemed to be persecuted, thus helping conflicts to spread.

A further set of explanations relate to the failures of the state. First, there is the state's failure to carefully manage the complexities and contradictions associated with diversity and heterogeneity. In sharp contrast to the states in Europe, which are inclined towards relative neutrality and impartiality in the distribution of resources among competing constituencies, the postcolonial state in Africa has been excessively partisan, favouring certain constituencies over others (Akokpari 1998). The Liberian conflict, for example, was rooted in President William Tolbert's inclination to entrench the Americo-Liberian's dominance in politics and the economy and the consequent marginalization of the other fifteen identifiable ethnic groups (Ofuatey-Kudjoe 1994). Similarly, Somalia's seemingly intractable conflict originated from former strongman Siad Barre's choice of privileging only three of Somalia's numerous clans – those of Barre, his mother and his principal son-in-law – and marginalizing the rest (Adam 1995: 72). Such politics of exclusion had the predictable consequence of fuelling inter-clan animosity and violence. In general, marginalized communities resort to various tactics, including voting with their feet and strengthening allegiance to sub-state leaderships. This is the case in Africa where people feel more loyalty to their ethnicity than to the young nation-states of which they are citizens (Thomas 2004: 80). This dual allegiance undermines the legitimacy of the state.

Second, since independence, the postcolonial state has emerged as the main employer, provider and distributor of resources. The private sector, which should serve as an alternative source of employment and an engine for growth, has been small, fragmented and weak and has in many cases depended on the state for capital and direction. This has created a perception of the state as a channel of accumulation and a source of contestation. The struggle for the state is fierce and considered a matter of life and death because 'political power is sought in order, *inter alia*, to acquire control over the means of production. Those who win in the intense and brutal political power competition no longer need to exert themselves in furthering their economic well-being. Those who lose are not just immiserated and pauperised but run the risk of losing their lives' (Adedeji 1999: 12). Bayart's (1993) euphemistic depiction of the conjuncture between politics and the African state as 'politics of the belly' is an apt summation of the dominant motive for accessing the state. Competition raises the stakes over the state and creates a paranoid perception that politics is not a game of winners and losers but warfare between victors and vanquished.

Third, and related to the state's partisan posture, is its failure to fulfil its social contract with citizens. Generally, the legitimacy of the state is enhanced if it provides basic services and creates reasonable economic conditions for development (Stewart 2002: 343). Often described as 'failed' (Mutisya 1998: 9), many African states are weak and show a growing incapacity to provide minimal services, including basic security for their population, a fact which further deepens the state's legitimacy crisis. While the inverse link between legitimacy and good governance, on the one hand, and conflict, on the other, is indisputable, African leaders have in many respects compromised good governance. This has created an environment riddled with authoritarianism and antagonism. State partisanship and social exclusion are exacerbated by lack of good governance (Stedman 1991: 373; Adedeji 1999: 15). Without credible avenues to vent grievances, disaffected constituencies are forced to resort to violence as a way of rectifying grotesque imbalances and injustices. Thus, conflicts and bad governance are cyclical and mutually reinforcing. While bad governance increases the risk of conflicts, the latter undermine the development of governance institutions, making cause and effect almost inseparable. Also, conflicts, as in the cases of Somalia, Liberia and Sierra Leone, lead to state collapse – a situation where the structure, authority, law and political order have fallen apart and must be reconstructed in some form or another (Zartman 1995), or the state is too incapacitated to perform its basic functions (Hyden 1992). State collapse is characterised by anarchy in which factions vie for control of the state, ending up with enclaves of authority. However, although it promotes further conflicts, state collapse is a consequence rather than a cause. Yet, once in place, state collapse and conflict may reinforce each other and seriously undermine efforts at reconstruction.

Africa's conflicts have also been known to be externally inspired. Indeed, Great Power involvement in Africa's conflicts prior to the abatement of the Cold War could neither be disputed nor ignored. Many African countries gained independence during the Cold War and some of them witnessed internal conflicts that were fought within the Cold War context (Nabudere 2003). The US and the Soviet Union waged proxy-wars in Angola and Ethiopia in a contest to establish ideological dominance. The abatement of the Cold War has hardly reversed the continent's susceptibility to conflict. On the contrary, the easing of East-West tensions has produced new conditions and pretexts for contestation. The demise of the strategic salience of certain regimes and the concomitant retreat of Western military support not only increased the vulnerability of these states to rebellion by constituencies they once repressed, but also truncated their ability to annihilate insurgencies. At the same time, the susceptibility of regimes emboldened disaffected constituencies who believed that access to the state was no longer beyond their reach (Jackson 2002). In other cases the termination of external military support inspired the involvement of neighboring and often opportunistic states in local conflicts, thereby escalating or prolonging them. Also, some of the conflicts in West Africa and the Great Lakes region have either been caused or escalated by forces external to their borders but internal to Africa.

An emerging paradox in Africa is that the ubiquity of mineral resources, which should ideally help the course of development and consequently mitigate violent contestations, has rather served to catalyze distributional conflicts. As Hyden (2000: 2) notes, Africa's conflicts are increasingly over natural resources. Africa's conflicts, are now increasingly referred to as resource conflicts, as in the case of 'conflict diamonds'.[3] Controlling the sources of natural resources has become a popular method of financing war machines. It is widely believed that the involvement of former Liberian President, Charles Taylor, in the Sierra Leonean war was motivated by a desire to gain access to the country's diamond mines. Similarly, to finance his war effort, Jonas Savimbi and the defunct UNITA movement fought, over, controlled and accounted for 80 per cent of Angola's diamond output in 1996 (Laremont 2002: 13). The DRC is no exception. The involvement in the country of Angola, Uganda, Rwanda and Zimbabwe was motivated, despite claims to the contrary, by interest in Congo's vast diamond and other mineral resources (Nabudere 2003). Such resource-inspired interventions either escalated or prolonged conflicts in these countries. The irony is that while resource-poor countries go to war over scarce resources, competition over resources can engender violent conflicts in those that are resource-endowed. The saddening reality is that neither the abundance nor the scarcity of mineral resources guarantees peace in Africa. Such competing claims to the state and resources have sometimes been inspired by simultaneous contestations over citizenship, and who is entitled to its related rights, or simply who legitimately should be part of the contest.

Citizenship & Conflicts: Context & Controversy

The tendency for African elites to manipulate citizenship to advance a particular agenda suggests that the concept is either being abused, exaggerated, or incorrectly understood. Conventionally, citizenship refers to a person's *bona fide* membership in a state. Historically, however, the term 'citizen' derived from the word 'city' was first used during ancient and classical times in Europe to refer to members or dwellers of a city (Borja 2000). Citizenship, the status of being a citizen, was confined to free adult males. Individuals captured during the inter-city wars and who became slaves could not acquire citizenship of the captors' city. Moreover, the dominance of patriarchy as a social ideology in the ancient European world ensured that women remained excluded from the paraphernalia of rights associated with citizenship, such as the right to elect councillors and members of the city's administrative structures as well as the opportunity to speak at public assemblies. Although citizens differed in wealth and intelligence, a fundamental feature of citizenship was equality, which ideally meant that all free adult males were equal before the law, equal in enjoying the democratic values of the city, and equal in accessing the opportunities for self-fulfilment (Minogue 2000: 10).

As the highest structures of authority demanding the allegiance of citizens, cities performed a variety of functions, including the maintenance of order and *ipso facto* the protection of citizens. Moreover, cities created and facilitated the environment for equality and justice and were the agencies by which the identities of citizens were bound. Cities conferred rights and privileges on citizens and demanded duties and responsibilities in return. The duties of the citizen to the city included attending and contributing at public assemblies, giving allegiance and loyalty and defending it against enemies. Since states in the modern sense did not exist during the ancient and medieval eras, cities literally performed the traditional functions of the modern state. Citizenship therefore remained the main connecting thread between the individual and the city, or more precisely, the basis of social contract between the city and its citizens.

With the legal arrangements under the Treaty of Westphalia in 1648, however, cities became part of the larger territorial entity called the state. The state is generally described as an entity with a recognizd geographical territory, a population, and a government that enjoys sovereignty in its internal and external dealings (Russett and Starr 1988: 49-50; Mingst 2004: 101). This new entity became the main recipient of the allegiance and loyalty previously reserved for the city. Today, citizenship is used exclusively in relation to states, which like cities before them confer a variety of rights and privileges on citizens. Against this background, Albert Hornby (1989: 203) defines a citizen succinctly as 'a person who has full rights as a member of a country either by birth or by being granted such rights'.

Like the city, the modern state demands both civic and political duties from citizens, including the payment of taxes, loyalty, allegiance, the defence of the state and voting, among other things. Characteristic of most modern states is their heterogeneity. Many states are composed of individuals who belong to or identify with various sub-national communities. Although different, these sub-national communities are tied to the state through the common identity of citizenship. A key principle in the discourse on modern citizenship is for the state to provide equal opportunities – political, economic and social – to every member of the state or political community, irrespective of gender, race, religion or any such basis of identity. In many African countries, this truism has been open to cruel misinterpretations, providing auspicious pretexts for denial of certain rights to particular communities. This has particularly been the case where the old and familiar dichotomy between indigenes and settlers is used as an exploitable resource by political elites.

Conflicts and economic and environmental conditions in Africa since the colonial era have increased migration patterns. In some cases, immigrants were assimilated into host communities through intermarriages and other cultural exchanges, thereby blurring distinctions among communities over time, which led to the emergence of new identities and the evolution of new cultures. In other cases, newly arrived communities kept their separate identities while maintaining harmonious relations with the original inhabitants. However, in many post-independence states the political elite, in their unbridled desire to gain power, are prepared to disrupt harmonious inter-communal relations even if it is at the risk of sparking violent inter-communal conflicts.

A number of issues have emerged to compound the nuances and contestations about citizenship in Africa. Three are particularly germane to the current discussion. The first is the nebulous nature of the nation. Unlike the state, a nation is a group of people claiming common history, beliefs and traditions (Plano and Olton, 1988: 3). Many groups of people defined generically as nations or ethnic groups in Africa lack clearly defined geographical boundaries. The feeling of oneness among members of a nation often translates into nationalism – the feeling that nations should constitute their own states and determine their modes of government. It was this feeling of nationalism, for example, that led to the unification of Italy and Germany in the nineteenth century (Mingst 2004: 102). The majority of ethnic groups in Africa traverse and overlap many state boundaries. The secession of Eritrea from Ethiopia and Somaliland from Somalia, for example, illustrates the power of ethnic nationalism and how it can potentially alter state boundaries. Yet, even in relatively homogenous nations various subdivisions exist, which can pursue divergent interests that may sometimes clash, leading to heightened mutual suspicion, animosity and intra-communal conflicts. The seemingly intractable conflict in Somalia, the perennial political tensions in Lesotho and Swaziland, which are culturally homogenous by African standards, offer pertinent examples.

The traversing character of nations in Africa has introduced a curious but dangerous dynamic in the continent's politics. While citizens recognize and show allegiance to the territorial state within which they reside, they simultaneously empathize with members of their communities in neighboring countries. Strong attachments with community members in other countries have caused communities in one state to develop interest in, or even to attempt to influence the politics of, countries beyond their borders. For example, it is often the feeling of ethnic Tutsis in Rwanda to support the cause of fellow Tutsis in the neighboring Democratic Republic of Congo (DRC) or Uganda, and vice versa. In cases of state implosion, neighboring states get involved in their politics either by supporting rebel factions or by direct military intervention. Either scenario widens the arena of contestation of the troubled state and often culminates in the spilling over of the conflict into neighboring states (Zartman 1989).

The second issue confounding citizenship relates to its mode of acquisition and the rights associated with it. As already noted, citizenship in the city was acquired through birth. Since city-states were innately patriarchal, an individual had to be born to a free adult male to become a citizen. That a slave would marry a woman born of free parents was unthinkable let alone possible, eliminating any possibility of doubt about one's citizenship. In the modern state, however, the rise of legal prescriptions and regulations in response to the growing complexities of international relations and human rights has introduced additional criteria for citizenship. Today, there are three popular ways of acquiring citizenship. Through birth (*jus soli*), by descent or ancestral claims (*jus sanguinis*), and by naturalization (Adejumobi 2001: 154). The third mode is acquired either through residence or by the conferment of refugee status, which over time gives the emigrant citizenship of the host country. The issue of residence has proved contentious in many African countries, which has, in turn, generated profound implications for conflicts. Many African countries contend with the reality of settler or immigrant communities, which have lived side by side with the indigenes for a long time, sometimes predating colonial rule. The poignant question here is whether or not these communities should be considered legitimate citizens with fully accorded political and civic rights. This delicate question has to be addressed against the background of the fact that some of the settler communities have been part of either the struggle against colonial rule or their countries' efforts in postcolonial construction and reconstruction.

There is a tendency for states faced with crucial political choices to manipulate the question of citizenship. Political expediency often dictates the fate of settler communities where such choices are to be made. As Mamdani (2002: 496-7) notes, the Yoweri Museveni-led National

Resistance Movement (NRM) initially used residence as the basis for citizenship rights in Uganda. This enabled it to elicit the support of all settler communities, including the Banyarwanda, the largest immigrant community in Buganda. In 1986 the NRM assumed power after a success-ful resistance campaign. However, following tensions between indigenous and settler communities (the latter including a section of the Banyarwanda) over land rights in 1990, the NRM government, in its bid to honour earlier campaign promises over land holdings and rights, changed residence to ancestry as a basis for citizenship rights. This policy shift effectively stripped the Banyarwanda, who, in addition to fighting the war, were also part of the post-conflict reconstruction project in Uganda, of their citizenship rights and consequently condemned them to 'second-class' citizen status.

Some argue that the changing focus of citizenship from being an individual phenomenon (where it defined the relationship between the individual and the state) to a group phenomenon (identifying a particular group or constituency within the state) is a key cause of the frequent manipulation of the rights of citizenship. Adejumobi (2001) contends that the shift from individual to group identity emerged when rights were denied to certain individuals. Such individuals articulated their grievances through groups, thus making sub-national identities both the support and the base for resistance against the state. He concludes that 'it is the consciousness of the denial of citizenship rights by a people which usually facilitates the transformation of sectarian groups like racial and ethnic groups from being "groups in themselves" into "groups for themselves"' (Adejumobi 2001: 156). In other words, in the practical dynamics of governance in Africa, marked by state partisanship, marginalization, and exclusions, citizens are forced to find alternative ways of reasserting themselves. Group identity becomes the solace, but in the process it supplants individual identities as the basis for confronting such perceived injustices.

Colonial rule created dichotomies between rural and urban, and natives and settlers, that left lasting legacies. Consistent with the policy of divide and rule, colonialism engendered what, in regard to the Tutsi-Hutu dichotomy, Mamdani (2002: 498) calls 'political identities' – identities that were based neither on culture or race nor the market but were informed by an orchestrated policy to facilitate colonialism. In such cases colonialism conferred rights and privileges associated with citizenship, such as access to land and political office, on natives or the indigenous population and denied them to the settlers. Under colonialism, then, indigeniety rather than residence was the basis for citizenship rights. In apartheid South Africa, however, the reverse was the case. While apartheid conferred rights and privileges linked to citizenship on settlers, it denied these to the natives. Thus under apartheid indigeniety became the basis of exclusion, while group rather than individual identity became the basis for enjoying citizenship rights. The apartheid state carefully used race-based group identity in the definition of citizenship rights as a basis for maintaining the *status quo*. It will be shown that in Ivory Coast the contestation over rights is based neither on race nor on the divide between indigenes and colonizers, but rather that between indigenes and immigrants.

The third issue complicating the modern notion of citizenship relates to the overarching impact of globalization on the state but also on the nature and future of the latter's relation with citizens. Globalization is a wide and embracing term, whose precise definition remains a matter of debate. In the most simplistic terms, Giddens (1990: 64) defines globalization as 'the intensification of worldwide social relations which link distant localities in such a way that local happenings are shaped by events occurring miles away and vice versa'. Visibly, globalization is characterized by inter-nationalization, i.e., the intensification of cross-border interaction between countries; liberalization, i.e., its emphasis on deregulation of the political and economic spaces; universalization, i.e., its capacity to spread experiences of one region to all corners of the globe; and deterritorialization, i.e., its capacity to render territorial borders obsolete (Scholte 2001: 14). The dynamics of globalization have intricately linked economies and peoples across the globe, such that the world has become a 'global village'. Globalization also produces other effects, the most salient for this analysis being its capacity to undermine the state's monopoly over citizens and consequently vitiate the relevance of the conventional discourse on citizenship. This occurs in various ways.

In the first place, globalization is increasingly creating a world of virtual borders, thus challenging the established assumptions of the Westphalia state system. This has been reflected, among other things, by the cross-border movements of factors of production and especially by the state's waning control over such movements. Secondly, by its very logic, globalization spawns the emergence of regional organizations and common markets. These, in turn, establish supranational bodies, which assume some of the traditional functions of the territorial state, including legislation and the provision of security. The European Union (EU), whose parliament promulgates binding legislation on citizens of the Union, is a good contemporary example in this regard. Thirdly, the inevitable fact of international migration, also an indirect, but sometimes a direct consequence of globalization, is compelling states to concede to the reality of dual citizenship for immigrants not wishing to divest themselves of membership of their original home countries (Akokpari 2000). Many EU countries have decriminalized dual citizenship, as are some African countries, including Ghana, Nigeria, South Africa, Kenya and Zimbabwe, to name just a few (Akokpari 2005). The phenomenon of dual citizenship also attenuates the orthodox assumptions on the state-citizen relationship. Furthermore, globalization, in the case of Africa, is gradually transferring the state's control over economic issues to markets (Akokpari 2001). Cumulatively, these delegitimize the state and undermine its previously unquestioned control over citizens. Consequently, globalization plunges the very notion of citizenship into crisis. David Scobey (2001: 13) could not have been more correct in depicting citizenship as an 'endangered species'. The Ivorian political elite, as will be shown shortly, however, have not come to terms with these sobering realities about the changing meanings of citizenship. They continue to manipulate citizenship and its accompanying tensions between indigenes and immigrants. The consequence of this development is turning a once politically stable and economically flourishing country into a shadow of its former self.

Ivory Coast

On 24 December 1999, a military coup led by General Robert Guei toppled the government of Henri Konan Bédié, the successor of the country's founding President, Houphouet Boigny. This forced Konan Bédié into exile. The coup effectively ended Ivory Coast's 39 years of stability. Since that coup, peace in the country has remained fragile at best, as a succession of attempted coups, tensions and sometimes violent conflicts between government and opposition supporters have dominated the country's political landscape. In September 2002, violent clashes between government and rebel forces occurred, which not only unearthed the simmering contradictions in Ivorian politics, but also underscored the growing tensions and mutual suspicions among the Ivory Coast's established ethnic communities. The upheavals also revealed the escalating xenophobia against communities in the north who came to be depicted as 'foreigners'. Above all, the series of political upheavals revealed the inclination of the state to instigate and exploit the native-foreigner tensions. Yet, this succession of events, which culminated in the current conflict between government and rebel forces, has to be understood within the broader context of the country's political economy, at the centre of which was the philosophy of Félix Houphouet Boigny, Ivory Coast's first post-independence President.

By 2000 the political traditions left behind by Houphouet Boigny, aptly referred to as Houphouetism, had been supplanted by a new identity rhetoric centring on the question of citizenship in Ivory Coast – referred to as 'Ivoirité' – the indigenous Ivorian. Houphouetism, according to Francis Akindès (2004: 7–8) 'is a social and political construction built on a certain colonial ethnology and the process of inventing the political Côte d Ivoire'. Practically, Houphouetism was a leader-forged ideology whose doctrines, having permeated the Ivorian body polity, became unquestionable. Houphouetism imparted certain core ideals in the economic, social and political realms of Ivorian life. Economically, it stood for a liberalized capital-driven market system, although ironically the political space remained rigidly circumscribed and dominated by the Democratic Party of the Ivory Coast (PDCI). Politically, Houphouetism was based on a system of patronage by which Houphouet Boigny held a heterogeneous and theoretically fractured country of sixty ethnic groups together. Socially, it was informed by a thinking that some constituencies in Ivory Coast, the predominantly Christian Akans led by Houphouet Boigny's own ethnic group, the Baoule, were predestined to rule. In terms of citizenship rights, Houphouetism stood for an open and quite generous mode of acquisition based on birth, ancestry or residence. Moreover, Houphouetism prioritized the individual over groups on citizenship rights. These principles were successfully championed by Houphouet Boigny and the PDCI and led to a harmonious relationship among the various constituencies, including Ivory Coast's growing immigrant community. However, the failure of successive leaders to manage the complexities associated with the ethnically diverse country and especially one with a huge and expanding migrant community, had damning implications for inter-communal relations.

The Immigrant Factor

The attraction of Ivory Coast to immigrants predated the country's independence in 1960 and was motivated by the dynamics of the Ivorian colonial economy. Between the late 1800s and the early 1900s, agricultural production in Ivory Coast, especially in cocoa, coffee, rubber and palm oil, rose dramatically in response to international demand. This in turn created a demand for labor in the agricultural sector. Between 1920 and 1940, the Ivorian labor market was composed of two categories of workers – voluntary and forced migrant labourers. The latter were compulsorily requisitioned with the assistance of traditional leaders in Upper Volta (now Burkina Faso). This was possible because until its independence Ivory Coast, together with other French West African countries, was part of a larger French administrative unit, the federation of Afrique Occidentale Française – AOF (Campbell 1978:68). These voluntary and forced workers ensured a regular supply of labor to Ivorian agriculture and the equally expanding construction industry (Akindès 2004: 8). The buoyancy of the Ivorian economy also attracted extra-African economic migrants such as Lebanese, and to a lesser extent Syrians, who took advantage of the economic environment (Bierwirth 1997).

The state's receptivity to foreign labor and its generally market-friendly policies continued and indeed intensified after independence under Houphouet Boigny. Consequently, Ivory Coast attracted not only immigrants but also considerable quantities of foreign direct investment (FDI) from the West and especially France. These, together with industrial expansion and high agricultural productivity, provided Ivory Coast with spectacular growth figures. For example, between 1960 and 1975, Ivory Coast recorded an annual GDP growth of more than 7 per cent, a remarkable figure by any standards (Zartman and Delgado 1984; Durufle 1989). Economic development in Ivory Coast accelerated remarkably during the 1975–77 boom in agricultural prices of cocoa, coffee and timber (Durufle 1989). Ivory Coast was clearly a success story of growth. While the Ivorian economy prospered and created room for migrant workers, the economies of the majority of West African countries plummeted under the combined weight of political instability, mis-management, and self-destructive economic policies. Ivory Coast thereupon became a centripetal axis attracting immigrants not just from French West Africa but also from English-speaking West African countries. Ghana and Nigeria, whose post-independence economies teetered on the brink of collapse in the 1970s and 1980s, respectively, were the major sources of immigrants to Ivory Coast from Anglophone West Africa. By 1998 immigrants constituted a critical constituency, accounting for 26.03 per cent of the 15,366,672 Ivorian population. While Ghanaians and Nigerians constituted 5.5 per cent and 1.7 per cent respectively of the immigrant population, the bulk came from Burkina Faso and Mali who together accounted for 75.8 per cent of all immigrants in the country (Akindès 2004: 10).[4] The latter settled in the predominantly agricultural regions of northern Ivory Coast.

The Baoule Hegemony

Although politically stable, the privileging of the Baoule under Houphouet Boigny's rule laid the foundation for future contestations and conflict among Ivorian communities. Houphouet Boigny's regime deliberately ranked Ivorian ethnic groups in terms of their relative importance and competence. Consistent with this ideology, the Baoule community was extolled as superior to other ethnic groups. This superiority was re-invented and sometimes explicitly articulated in Houphouet Boigny's speeches (Akindès 2004: 13). The Baoule were more or less accepted as the supplier of political elites, and this remained unchallenged, at least openly. While the Akan ethnic stock in general and the Baoule in particular were ranked at the top of the social hierarchy, the predominantly Muslim Dioula were ranked at the bottom. Dioula is a socially constructed term used to describe amorphously a collection of ethnic and religious groups with markedly similar characteristics. Akindès (2004:14) notes that Dioula was 'the professional name for traders and a family name in the Kong Manding dialect, but used here as a popular and pejorative reference to all Mandé and Gur people from the north and, therefore, to all Muslims'. The Dioula was predominantly immigrants who arrived in Ivory Coast over time. Literally 'disqualified' from competing in the political space, the Dioula suffered discrimination and marginalization. Their bottom ranking was justified on frivolous grounds such as their alleged unreliability, promiscuousness and lack of education. Part of a state-propagated ideology, these facile perceptions were nonetheless imbibed by ethnic groups across the country.

In spite of their marginalization and exclusion, Houphouet Boigny could count on the acquiescence and loyalty of the Dioula through a constructed system of patronage by which he held the diverse ethnic groups together. The patronage scheme involved a complex mix of bribery, threats, intimidation and detention of opposition elements. For example, he jailed Laurent Gbagbo, his most outspoken critic, in 1969 and detained him again from 1971 to 1973 (Rake 2000: 43). He also offered appointments to potential competitors as part of a grand co-optation strategy. Under this, he offered high-profile jobs to members of marginalized communities, notably Alassane Dramane Ouattara, to assuage the Dioula community's sense of marginalization (Doudo, 2000: 32).[5] Thus, even prior to Houphouet Boigny's exit from the political scene, contradictions in the Ivorian polity were already palpable; differences among its competing constituencies in terms of rights and access to the state had been firmly established. In the 1990s the dichotomy between the Akans and the other ethnic groups became an outright dichotomy between indigenous Ivorians (Ivoirité) and the 'strangers'. This generated considerable anxiety among the Dioula who, perceived as strangers, became victims of state-engineered discrimination, exclusion and xenophobia.

Ivoirité & Xenophobia

Although explained variously by Ivorian scholars, Ivoirité can broadly be taken to represent a nationalist ideology, which defines who an Ivorian is. In this sense, Ivoirité defined citizenship, its attendant rights and by logic 'the criteria for participation in the distribution of scarce resources' (Akindès 2004: 26). Moreover, by defining citizenship, Ivoirité also established the relationship between individuals and the state. As a doctrine contrived and propagated by the state, Ivoirité quickly gained acceptance among the majority of the Ivorian population. In perspective, the rhetoric of Ivoirité was first brought into the public domain and made a state doctrine by Henri Konan Bédié. Although speculation is wide about its motivation, it is apparent that political reasons were its main cause, notwithstanding the evocation of economic justifications. The major economic reason was based on the fact that the once prosperous Ivorian economy had been going through recession since the late 1980s, one of the effects of which was to widen the gap between immigrants who were generally more willing to take up low-paid jobs, on the one hand ,and native Ivorians who were inclined towards high-paid white-collar jobs, on the other. The Economic and Social Council of Ivory Coast noted, for example, that unemployment was 6.3 per cent among Ivorians and 3.6 per cent among foreigners. It also noted the larger participation in the economy by foreigners than by Ivorians (Akindès 2004: 27–8). Thus in providing economic justification for Ivoirité, one pro-Ivoirité Ivorian historian argued that the larger participation of foreigners in the Ivorian economy threatened the jobs of indigenous Ivorians (Loucou 1996). The imperative to increase the participation of native Ivorians in the economy is, according to this view, the motive behind Ivoirité. Historically, African countries confronted with shrinking employment opportunities have resorted to the expulsion of immigrants. This was what Ghana and Nigeria did in 1969 and 1983–5 respectively in the face of deteriorating economic conditions (Essuman-Johnson, 1996: 68–9). In Ivory Coast, however, concerns about unemployment resulted not in expulsions but in exclusions, suggesting other sinister motives behind the policy.

It is argued that a poignant explanation for Ivoirité was the orchestrated desire of the Ivorian elite to disqualify and thus exclude credible opponents from political contestation over state power. This has to be understood in context. The wave of democratization and multi-partyism which swept across Africa from the late 1980s liberalized the Ivorian political space and threatened the dominance of the PDCI and the Akan aristocracy. New political parties emerged and those hitherto operating clandestinely resurfaced. Notable among them were the Ivorian Popular Front (FPI) led by Laurent Gbagbo, the Ivorian Workers' Party (PIT) led by Francis Wodie, and the Rally of the Republicans (RDR) led by Alassane Dramane Ouattara. The latter broke away from the PDCI after serving as Prime Minister under Houphouet Boigny from 1990 until 1993. The RDR enjoyed a great deal of support from the disaffected and marginalized ethnic groups from the north. Konan Bédié's policy of Ivoirité was thus aimed at preserving Baoule dominance by foreclosing the political space to potential contenders, especially Alassane Ouattara.[6] In 1995, Ouattara, along with Gbagbo, boycotted the presidential election after accusing Konan Bédié of electoral manipulation. Despite this, his RDR party polled over 50 per cent of the popular vote. Ouattara was certainly a threat to Bédié's presidential ambitions. His re-entry into the presidential race in 2000 meant that Bédié needed a new strategy of exclusion. This he found in Ivoirité. In mid-July 2000 Guei supervised a nation-wide referendum, which approved new clauses on citizenship in the Constitution, notable among them Article 35, which spelt out who could contest the presidency. It stated that 'The President of the Republic must be of an Ivorian origin, born of a father and mother who are also Ivorian by birth' (cited in Akindès 2004: 30). The Constitution effectively reversed the long-standing mode of citizenship acquisition based on residence. The general thrust of Ivoirité also deprived the Dioula, regarded as foreigners, of their rights as citizens of Ivory Coast. The Constitution came into effect in time for the general election of 22 October 2002. The coup that toppled Bédié was widely known to have been organized by northern elements in the military, although they rebelled under the leadership of General Guei, who was not himself a northerner.

General Robert Guei who replaced Konan Bédié as head of state also sought to manipulate the already contentious citizenship issue to his advantage. Coming from non-Akan ethnic stock and taking over power by means of a military coup, he needed to quickly strengthen his authority and also broaden his support base. But in practice his options in attaining these objectives were severely truncated. To pacify the Akans and the Baoule, he needed to identify with Houphouetism, but at the cost of incensing other ethnic groups, which had hoped for a termination of Baoule dominance with the demise of Bédié's regime. On the other hand, appeasing other groups meant that he had to completely repudiate and, in fact, distance himself from the legacies of Houphouet Boigny at the risk of Akan resentment and possible backlash. Faced with these choices, Guei sought to experiment precariously with both options. First, he projected himself into Houphouetism by identifying with the Akan, although he understood the political risks in contemplating, let alone restoring, Akan hegemony. Suspicions about his intentions strengthened the opposition against him, whereupon he tactically retracted from Houphouetism and embarked on a new policy direction that involved undermining the traditions of Houphouetism such as strict interpretations of the criteria for Ivorian citizenship. Here, too, the result was the heightening of suspicions of not only communities from the north but also the large number of African immigrants who had acquired Ivorian citizenship by residence. In Guei's quest to satisfy constituencies at both ends, he ended up satisfying none. His re-visitation of the Ivoirité policy further undermined the already tenuous relations between northern and southern communities and between Christians and Muslims. In a surprise move, and an untrammelled desire to prolong his stay in power, Guei reverted to the PDCI, the party he had overthrown from power, and presented himself as its presidential candidate in the 26 October elections. This exasperated the rank and file of the PDCI who declared: 'we are not going to let our father's assassin marry our mother' (Michaud 2000:13).

On 6 October 2000 the Supreme Court, headed by General Guei's former legal adviser, disqualified Alassane Ouattara from contesting the election under the new citizenship provisions in the Constitution, much to the chagrin of the Dioula and the entire Ivorian immigrant community.

Ouattara was claimed to be a non-Ivorian. Surprisingly, this was a politician who had been Ivory Coast's Prime Minister for three years and represented the country on important international bodies during the reign of Houphouet Boigny. The five rival candidates of the former ruling PDCI were also disqualified, leaving in total five presidential contestants. Among these, the race became a straight two-way contest between General Guei and Laurent Gbagbo. The disqualifications, in the meantime, left profound implications for regional and ethnic representivity in the contest. One supporter of Ouattara bemoaned the effect of the Supreme Court's decision: 'the north, the centre and the east of Côte d'Ivoire have no representatives in the race; that is to say more than 80 per cent of the population is excluded from the vote, which will be run by representatives from the west (Gbagbo and Guei)' (*West Africa* 16–22 October 2000: 7). In an ethnically conscious society, where group identities provided constant political reference points, these grotesque exclusions were a blueprint for conflict. Guei's final miscalculation was the dismissal of the National Electoral Commissioner, after sensing his imminent defeat at the polls. He then ordered the Interior Ministry to announce carefully manufactured figures to show that he had won. Laurent Gbagbo and the FPI organized a popular revolt against Guei, who fled after defections by his key officers, some members of his bodyguard, and an entire battalion of the military. Laurent Gbagbo, who polled 59.4 per cent of the popular vote, was subsequently declared the winner.[7]

By the time Laurent Gbagbo assumed the presidency on 26 October 2000, the stage had already been set for further inter-communal conflict. The politics of marginalization and exclusion pursued by Konan Bédié and General Guei under the xenophobia-inspired citizen question had left the residue of a deeply fissured Ivorian society, characterized by suspicion and discontent. Yet, Laurent Gbagbo, like his predecessor, has been content to maintain a hardline posture on the exclusionist citizenship policy. When, following the exit of General Guei, the combined voice of the UN Secretary General, the OAU, President Thabo Mbeki and Western governments urged fresh elections in which Ouattara would be a contestant as a stratagem to restore peace to Ivory Coast, Gbagbo's response was predictable:

> The answer is the constitution, the law. Alassane Ouattara called on the people to vote yes to the constitution. The Supreme Court excluded him based on the criteria outlined in the constitution. I don't have anything to say about that. ... The presidential elections are gone, forget about that, it's all behind us. I went to the elections and I won. I shall exercise power in line with the constitution and the people's will (Rake 2000: 44).

Sadly, the uncompromising position on the citizenship issue has not helped the cause of peace in Ivory Coast. Skirmishes and clashes between supporters of Gbagbo and Alassane Ouattara have remained much in evidence. They came to a head in September 2002 when rebels and government forces exchanged gunfire in Abidjan. General Guei was killed in the ensuing clash. Tensions and insecurity then escalated, along with confusion and uncertainty. Since September 2002, real peace has eluded Ivory Coast; nor has Gbagbo's government been able to assert firm control over the entire country. The north remains firmly under the control of the Patriotic

Movement of the Ivory Coast (MPCI), the main rebel group. Two additional rebel movements – the Movement for Justice and Peace (MJP) and the Popular Movement of Ivory Coast's Far West (MPIGO) – emerged in late November 2002 both in western Ivory Coast, dedicated to avenging the death of General Guei.

The timely intervention of French troops in the face of ECOWAS procrastination and incapacity has kept the warring factions apart. A series of French and ECOWAS-initiated peace attempts have had minimal effect, leaving Ivory Coast divided between government forces and the MPCI. Adedeji (1999) has cautioned that it is imperative to comprehend, master and transcend conflicts as a precondition to lasting solutions. With the controversy around Ivoirité at the heart of the conflict, the Ivorian state may need to speedily revisit the citizenship question if there are to be any hopes of a long-term solution.

Conclusion

This essay has shown that Africa's conflicts have increased both in number and in scale in recent years. This has been caused by a conjuncture of factors, including the artificiality of Africa's colonial borders, the failures of the state to deal adequately with the complexities of African politics; and external factors. But running through these seemingly discrete factors is the struggle over the state and resources. At times, this has been exacerbated by a struggle over citizenship and, more specifically, who is legitimately entitled to participate in the struggle. It has been demonstrated that in the case of Ivory Coast, the notion of Ivoirité has been central to the conflict. This has been aggravated by the unending predilection of the Ivorian political elite to employ it as a weapon for excluding opponents from the contest over state power. It was argued that, although economic arguments were made to justify Ivoirité, the most probable reasons were political – the physical exclusion of political rivals. As evident under the regimes of Konan Bédié, Robert Guei and Laurent Gbagbo, the doctrine of Ivoirité was used to exclude Alassane Ouattara, perceived as the greatest threat to their ambitions.

Yet, it was also noted that the notion of citizenship is slowly but surely retreating under the weight of globalization and liberalization. The former in particular is unleashing threatening forces not only on the state but also on the very foundations of citizenship. These have severely undercut the state's dominance and exclusive control over citizenship. The Ivorian civil war is being fought over a cube of ice which is gradually melting under the heat of globalization and which will sooner or later cease to exist. It is suggested that the citizenship issue, which lies at the heart of the Ivorian conflict, be given another look by Ivorians. The Economic Community of West African States (ECOWAS), the African Union (AU), and international efforts assisting Ivory Coast to end the conflict must help the country address, or even reverse, the policy on Ivoirité in order the better to deal with the contradictions it has generated. Otherwise, Ivory Coast, once the envy of Africa, could slip further into a bottomless pit of self-destruction.

References

Adam, H.M. 1995. 'Somalia: a Terrible Beauty Being Born', in W Zartman, ed., *Collapsed States: The Disintegration and Restoration of Legitimate Authority*, Boulder, CO: Lynne Rienner, 69–89.

Adedeji, A. 1999. 'Comprehending Africa's Conflicts', in Adebayo Adedeji, ed., *Comprehending and Mastering African Conflicts: the Search for Sustainable Peace and Good Governance*, London: Zed Books, 3–21.

Adejumobi, S. 2001. 'Citizenship, Rights and the Problem of Conflicts and Civil Wars in Africa', *Human Rights Quarterly* 23(1): 148–70.

Adekanye, J. 1995. 'Structural Adjustment, Democratisation and Rising Ethnic Tensions in Africa.' *Development and Change* 26: 335-374.

Akindes, F. 2004. *The Roots of the Military-Political Crisis in Côte d'Ivoire*. Uppsala: Nordiska Afrikainstitutet.

Akokpari, J. 1998. 'The State, Refugees and Migration in sub-Saharan Africa', *international Migration Review* 36(2): 211–31.

Akokpari, J. 2000. 'Globalisation and Migration in Africa', *African Sociological Review* 4(2): 72–92.

Akokpari, J. 2001. 'Globalisation and the Challenges for the African State', *Nordic Journal of African Studies* 10(2): 188–209.

Akokpari, J. 2005. 'Strangers in a Strange Land: Citizenship and the Immigration Debate in Lesotho', *Development Southern Africa* 22(1): 87–102.

Bayart, Jean-Francois. 1993. *The State in Africa: The Politics of the Belly*. London: Longman.

Bierwirth, C. 1997. 'The Initial Establishment of the Lebanese Community in Cote d'Ivoire, ca. 1925–45.' *The International Journal of African Historical Studies* 30(2): 325–48.

Borja, J. 2000. 'The Citizenship Question and the Challenge of Globalisation.' *City* 4(1): 43–52

Brown, M.B. 1995. *Africa's Choices: After Thirty Years of the World Bank*. Harmondsworth: Penguin Books.

Campbell, B. 1978. 'Ivory Coast', in John Dunn, ed., *West African States: Failures and Promise*, London: Cambridge University Press, 66–116.

Copson, R. W. 1994. *Africa's Wars and Prospects for Peace*. New York: M.E. Sharp.

Doudo, C. 2000. 'Who Wants to Burn Côte d'Ivoire?' *New African* (London) November: 32–3.

Durufle, Gillies. 1989. 'Structural Disequilibria and Adjustment in Ivory Coast', in Bonnie Campbell and John Loxley, eds, *Structural Adjustment in Africa*, New York: St Martins Press, 132–68.

Essuman-Johnson, E. 1996. 'Refugees and Migrants in West Africa', *University of Ghana, Faculty of Social Studies–FASS Bulletin* 1(1): 64–73.

Giddens, A. 1990. *The Consequences of Modernity*. Cambridge: Polity Press.

Guest, Robert. 2004. *The Shackled Continent: Africa's past, present and the future*. Basingstoke: Macmillan.

Hornby, A.S. 1989. *Oxford Advanced Learner's Dictionary*. Oxford: Oxford University Press.

Hyden, G. 1992. 'Governance and the Study of Politics', in Goran Hyden and Michael Bratton, eds. *Governance and Politics in Africa*, Boulder, CO: Lynne Rienner, 1–26.

Hyden, G. 2000. 'Post-War Reconstruction and Democratisation: Concepts, Goals and Lessons Learnt.' Paper presented at a Seminar on After War: Reconciliation and Democratisation in Divided Societies, Solstrand, Norway, 27–29 March.

Jackson, R. 2002. 'Violent Internal Conflicts and the African State: Towards a Framework of Analysis', *Journal of Contemporary African Studies* 20(1): 29–54.

Lake, D.A and D. Rothchild. 1996. 'Containing Fear: the origin and management of ethnic conflicts', *International Security* 21(2): 41–75.

Laremont, R.R. 2002. 'The Causes of Warfare and the Implications of Peacekeeping in Africa', in Ricardo René Laremont, ed., *The Causes of Warfare and the Implications of Peacekeeping in Africa*, Portsmouth, NH: Heinemann, 1–18.

Loucou, J.N. 1996. 'De l'Ivoirité', in *L'Ivoirité ou l'espirit du nouveau contrat social du président Henri Konan Bédié*. Abidjan: PUCI, 19–24.

Mamdani, M. 2002. 'African States, Citizenship and War: A case-study', *International Affairs* 78(3): 493–506

Michaud, P. 2000. 'Guei: I'm the Man', *New African* (London), September: 13.

Mingst, Karen A. 2004. *Essentials of International Relations*. 3rd edn. New York: W.W. Norton.

Minogue, Kenneth. 2000. *Politics: A Very Short Introduction*. Oxford: Oxford University Press.

Mutisya, Godfrey. 1998. 'Conflict Watch', *Conflict Trends* (October): 4–5.

Nabudere, D. 2003. *Conflict over Mineral Wealth: Understanding the Second Invasion of the DRC*. Occasional Paper No. 37. Johannesburg: Institute for Global Dialogue, September.

Obi, Cyril. 1997. 'Economic Adjustment and the Deepening of Environmental Conflict in Africa.' *Lesotho Social Science Review* 3(1): 13–29.
Ofuatey-Kudjoe, W. 1994. 'Regional Organisations and the Resolutions of Internal Conflict: The ECOWAS Intervention in Liberia', *International Peacekeeping* 1(3): 261–302.
Plano, J. and R. Olton. 1988. *The International Relations Dictionary*, 4th edn. Oxford: ABC-Clio.
Rake, Alan. 2000. 'The Rise and Rise of Laurent Gbagbo.' *New African* December: 43–4.
Russett, B and H. Starr. 1988. *World Politics: the menu for choice.* 2nd edn. New York: W.H. Freeman and Co.
Scholte, J.A. 2001. 'The Globalisation of World Politics', in John Baylis and Steve Smith, eds, *The Globalisation of World Politics: An introduction to international relations.* 2nd edn, New York: Oxford University Press, 13–32.
Scobey, D. 2001. 'The Spectre of Citizenship', *Citizenship Studies* 5(1): 11–26.
Stedman, Stephen J. 1991. 'Conflict and Conflict Resolution in Africa: A Conceptual Framework', in Francis M. Deng and William Zartman, eds, *Conflict Resolution in Africa*, Washington, DC: The Brookings Institution, 367–99.
Stewart, F. 2002. 'Root Causes of Violent Conflicts in Developing Countries', *British Medical Journal* 324 (7333): 342–45.
Suliman, M and A. Omer. 1994. 'The Environment: a new dimension in Sudan's political and social landscape', *Africa World Review* November–April: 23–5.
Thomas, T. 2004. 'Reviewing Africa's Tribes and Borders', *Contemporary Review* 285 (1663): 79–82.
Wiseman, J. 1990. *Democracy in Black Africa: Survival and Revival.* New York: Paragon House Publishers.
Zartman, W. 1989. *Ripe for Resolution.* 2nd edn. New York: Oxford University Press.
Zartman, W. 1995. 'Introduction: Posing the Problem of State Collapse', in I.W. Zartman, ed., *Collapsed States: The Disintegration and Restoration of Legitimate Authority.* Boulder, CO: Lynne Rienner, 1–11.
Zartman, William and Christopher Delgado, eds. 1984. *The Political Economy of Ivory Coast.* New York: Praeger Publishers.

Notes

1   It has been noted that, in 1994, no fewer than 12 of the 48 countries in sub-Saharan Africa were at war; two were in the post-war phase, while 14 had a previous or current experience with political violence (Adejumobi 2001: 149).
2   In a short yet succinct article, Tony Thomas (2004) argues for the re-drawing of some of Africa's borders to avert conflicts and economic adversities. In particular, he identifies Nigeria and the Sudan as countries requiring new borders.
3   Concerns by the international community that diamond sales by rebels have been responsible for the sustenance of conflicts led to the establishment of the Kimberley Process in May 2000. The Kimberley process is an initiative taken by governments, NGOs and the international diamond industry to prevent the flow of diamonds controlled and sold by rebel movements (in Angola, the Democratic Republic of Congo and Sierra Leone) to finance wars against legitimate governments. The Kimberley Process led in 2002 to the Kimberley Process Certification Scheme, which requires all participants in the Kimberley Process (now numbering 50) to certify international shipments of diamonds to ensure that these are not from rebel-held territories. See http://europa.eu.int/comm/external_relations/kimb/intro/ (8/10/04)
4   In fact, Campbell (1978: 103) contends that 50 per cent of the labor force employed in the Ivorian agricultural sector by 1970 was non-Ivorian.
5   Alassane Ouattara, who was claimed to belong to the Dioula, had served as Prime Minister in Houphouet Boigny's government between 1990 and 1993. Prior to this, he worked with the International Monetary Fund (IMF) in Washington as its deputy director, and with the West African Central Bank. Appointments into prominent financial institutions require the support of the applicant's home government. See Doudo (2000: 32).
6   See 'Alassane Ouattara: The outsider' (http://news.bbc.co.uk/2/hi/africa/954870.stm) (20/07/05)
7   The true election results showed General Robert Guei in second place, with 32.7 per cent of the votes, followed in third place by Francis Wodie with 5.7 per cent. The remaining 2.2 per cent of the votes was shared by the smaller parties (http://www.electionworld.org/ivorycoast.htm) 20/10/04

4

The Terrible Toll of Postcolonial Rebel Movements
Towards an Explanation
of the Violence against the Peasantry

THANDIKA MKANDAWIRE

A disturbing feature of some of the post-independence armed rebel movements in Africa has been the extremely brutal and spiteful forms of violence that they have unleashed and inflicted on fellow citizens. One of the lessons Mao bequeathed to those who, together with the peasantry, take up arms against authority was that they must enjoy the explicit support, or at least the tacit complicity, of the population among whom they live, if they are to swim among the masses like fish in the water. The work of one of Africa's most successful guerrilla leaders, Amilcar Cabral, is replete with injunctions on the transformation that the 'petty bourgeoisie' would have to undergo in order to be at one with the peasantry. They were called upon to commit 'class suicide' by immersing themselves in the lives of the peasantry and seeing the world from the peasantry's perspective. The PAIGC (African Party for the Independence of Guinea-Bissau and Cape Verde) was legendary for its meticulous political work among the peasantry before embarking on military actions (Chaliand 1969; Davidson 1969). However, in the case of postcolonial Africa, over and over again, armed movements have appeared as anything but fish, violating Mao's basic injunction by murderously wading into still waters to wreak havoc and cause enormous suffering. The human emergencies caused by these conflicts have generated a slew of studies on the 'root causes' of these wars. Although this chapter looks critically at some of these studies, it is not so much about such 'root causes' as about the wanton violence associated with many of the conflicts.

The main argument of the chapter is that, to understand the actions of the rebel movements and their violence, we must understand not only the elites and the intra-elite conflicts that produce their leaders, but also the actions and responses of the wider population. More specifically, we need to know, on the one hand, the nature of the rebel movements – the thinking, composition, actions and capacities of the leaders of the insurgent movements – and, on the other hand, the social structures of the African countryside in which they often operate. I argue that the social terrain of rural Africa is highly unsuitable for classical guerrilla warfare and that, combined with the urban origins of rebel movements, this generates self-defeating behavior on the part of armed groups, and terrible suffering for rural populations.

I also argue that, fatally flawed and morally reprehensible though these movements may be, one needs to take their political roots and ideological cognitive components seriously, even as their banditry confounds their political agenda. The failure and even degeneration of these movements should not lead us to deny or downplay the objective conditions that create the discontent, which is the fuel of conflict.[1] This should be obvious enough, and most students of rebel movements in Africa would share Christopher Clapham's (1998a:5) suggestion that 'insurgencies derive basically from blocked political aspirations, and in some cases also from reactive desperation'. Regrettably, the recent focus on the means of financing rebel movements and the failure of most movements to coherently articulate, let alone achieve, their proclaimed objectives have encouraged an easy dismissal of the politics of such movements and an inclination towards economistic, culturalistic and militaristic interpretations of the conflicts.

The paper is divided into two main parts. In the first part I review some of the major accounts of the 'root causes' of civil wars in Africa and the violent turn they take. Considerable space is devoted to the 'rational choice' explanation, partly because it seems to be widely accepted in the policy-making world, but also because it exemplifies an abstract and deductive neoclassical style of discourse that has informed the study of policy-making and attempts to understand Africa. In the second part I offer an alternative approach that builds on the interaction between the largely urban origins of conflicts, and the rural terrains in which these conflicts are violently played out. Underlying this discussion is a concern for the crucial integrative role and fiscal needs of the state, on the one hand, and its capacity to play this role, on the other. I also underscore the different types of rebel movement that have emerged in Africa.

Current Explanations

The Apocalyptic View

The initial reaction to wanton violence is often total bewilderment, encapsulated in the view that we are witnessing a senseless madness taken, in the words of Hans Magnus Enzenberger (1993), to *reductio ad insanitatem*.[2] This apocalyptic vision has been most vividly captured by Kaplan's 'The Coming Anarchy' (1994) – a study that combines passion, prejudice, ignorance, pop-ecology and good writing to enormous effect. For Kaplan, the experience of a number of African countries is merely a dress rehearsal for an ecological fate towards which humanity is ineluctably moving. This image has also been widely conveyed by the international press as part of a journalistic genre that has peddled 'Afro-pessimism', such as that which induced *The Economist* (13 May 2000) to emblazon its cover page with the headline 'The Hopeless Continent'.

The Culturalist View

In some essentialist (and often poorly veiled racist) accounts, it is suggested that there is something fundamentally wrong with African culture – and that senseless violence is an undisavowable excrescence of that culture. Such accounts attempt to search some distant past for culturally encoded genes for the perpetration of atrocious acts and plunder to explain the recurrence of such deeds today. Some authors even resort to what borders on instant historical anthropology: having identified cases of plunder in Liberia's troubled past, Stephen Ellis (1998: 169) concludes: 'There is an obvious echo of this historical tradition in the practice of present-day warlords'. Patrick Chabal and Jean-Pascal Daloz (1999: 2) concur with Ellis when they conclude that the 'seemingly 'barbaric' violence' is 'an instrumentally plausible retraditionalisation of society'. That is how 'Africa works', and all the conflicts 'are part of everyday calculus of power in contemporary Africa' (Chabal and Daloz 1999: 82). Much of this writing takes historical continuity and cultural relativism to absurd extremes, to say the least, and in its journalistic rendition attains racist proportions.[3]

Neopatrimonialism and Civil Wars

In response to racist and essentialist views of African conflicts, there have been other attempts at explanation, often prompted by the laudable intention of reaffirming the humanity of Africans, even as fellow citizens commit inhuman acts. The first set of these explanations has strong culturalist overtones, as it builds on the paradigm that argues that neo-patrimonialism is, in the words of Michael Bratton and Nicholas van de Walle (1998: 277), 'the distinctive institutional hallmark of African regimes'. In such neopatrimonial regimes the chief executive maintains authority 'through personal patronage, rather than through ideology or law.' The ineluctable process of decline engendered by neopatrimonialism is said to generate a range of responses among citizens, including 'voice', through which citizens openly articulate their discontent, and 'exit', whereby citizens sullenly withdraw from spaces dominated by states. According to some analysts, immanent in such rule is the 'violence of everyday life' (Chabal and Daloz 1999), and the violence of rebels is viewed as the mirror image of the violence of the state.

Chris Allen (1999: 377) builds on this paradigm to argue that the endemic violence found in a number of countries is to be sought in the 'internal dynamics of 'spoils politics' in which the primary goal of those competing for political office or power is self-enrichment'. He argues that the unravelling of these patron-clientelist relations is the logical outcome of the elite rapacity and structural violence that characterize neopatrimonial states. In such regimes, corruption is 'massive and endemic' but highly concentrated. Over time, the self-destructive logic of prebendalism that accompanies such relationships undermines the fiscal capacity of the state, and the state ceases to provide the most basic social services. This induces conflicts, which may assume violent forms and warlordism. The state may in the process lose control over the means of coercion. During this 'terminal' phase, the characteristic features of the spoils system are intensified, and violence becomes the 'dominant feature of political interaction and change'. There is apparently some length of time over which such states may exist without violence. Prolongation beyond this period will lead to state collapse.

While this analysis captures some of the African political reality, it cannot explain the cases of collapse of putatively patron-clientelistic states that have not led to violence. A significant number of transitions have been relatively smooth, leading in some cases to more democratic forms of government. The cases involved are numerous enough to warrant serious consideration as counterfactual evidence (Bratton and van de Walle 1998; Diop and Diouf 1999). Since neopatrimonial regimes have taken a wide range of turns, including violent collapse, bureaucratisation and democratization, one is only able to read the causal processes and to know whether the 'spoils system' has been excessively prolonged *post factum*.

Rational Civil Wars

This set of explanations seeks to find the rational kernel to violent acts. It is often driven by the need to allay the fears of donors who might be paralyzed in their funding by the portrayal of the situation as merely chaotic and idiosyncratic. Because conflicts loom large in humanitarian emergencies, donor perspectives play an inordinately important role in driving the research agenda. The view of some policy-oriented researchers seems to be that, if the nature of the conflict were posed in an understandable (read 'rational') way, potential for its rational resolution would elicit international support because the cause-effect nexus would be obvious. Thus David Keen (1998: 5) states:

> The task of reviving the analysis of war from a political and economic perspective is all the more urgent since the portrayal of war as chaos and 'sheer madness' seems to play a part in paralysing international response. If the portrayal of war as chaos suggests that 'nothing can be done' then it may follow that no structured intervention can be made. This may sometimes serve as a convenient excuse for international inaction.

Consequently, various authors have sought to establish that what was happening was either perfectly human or rational under the circumstances, or was comparable to some familiar case. Paul Richards (1995) pushes the logic of the model furthest, and surmises from interviews that cutting off hands was a rational act intended to dissuade the population from voting.[4] And so against the view that these wars have been 'mindless violence', Keen prefers to describe them as a 'particularly organised kind of chaos, particularly rational kind of madness'. The oxymoronic expressions should in themselves be suggestive of the misuse to which Keen has put the idea of rationality.

In more anthropologically informed explanations, the usual way of establishing the rationality of rebel behavior has involved tracing war or its pursuit to some self-interest whose existence could be established by actual material gains or testimonies by individuals engaged in war (Keen 1998; Richards 1995, 1998). Often conclusion is reached without any attempt at process-tracing to determine if the participants in the rebellion made choices in the manner depicted by the model. In the absence of such evidence, anecdotes and stylized facts are often marshalled to clinch the argument. However, methodologically, this is not satisfactory. First, for every anecdote pointing in one direction, another can be found pointing in the opposite direction. Which anecdotes one deems credible will ultimately depend on one's predisposition. Second, one needs to know in advance the independent evidence of the preferences of the individuals in question. In a situation where individuals commit terrible crimes, the need for rationalization is enormous, so that one cannot take the *ex post* explanations of individuals as evidence for the sequence of their reasoning. A retrospective account of what drove them to commit the crimes is likely to be self-serving.[5] And the motives and opportunities for concealing what one did and why are virtually unlimited. To confound issues further, the 'incomes' being pursued are apparently not entirely material, but include psychic ones as well. It is difficult enough to establish the nexus of rationality between wanton violence and economic gain, let alone that between violence and psychic income, as some try to do. The problems start from the view that by enumerating the uses to which war may be put by individuals (economic gain, psychic relief, revenge, 'Rambo demonstration effect', escape from rural boredom, etc.), one establishes the rational nature of the pursuit of particular wars.[6]

A second set of explanations under this rubric has been advanced by economists – including, significantly, World Bank economists – who have deployed their analytic tools towards a more rigorous and quantitative rational-choice explanation of the violence of rebel movements in Africa. This approach uses, in a more or less consistent manner, the rational-choice framework in which social action is derived from an individual's calculation of self-interest and personal gain. On the basis of the universality of core premises about individual behavior and pursuit of self-interest, such economists, unlike historians and anthropologists, have not been bothered by the empirical foundations of the 'rationality' hypothesis, and have simply proceeded to treat rebels as 'an enterprise' out to maximize profits. Rebel movements are then an aggregation of such interests. Their behavior has a utilitarian rationality explicable in neoclassical utility-maximization behavior.

I shall focus on the World Bank papers of Paul Collier and his associates (Collier 1999, 2000; Collier and Hoeffler 1998, 1999, 2001), because of the institution within which they have been produced and their acceptance by a surprisingly large number of donors as a major explanation of conflicts in Africa – as evidenced by the fact that these studies have been given wide publicity by the Bank itself (see World Bank 2000), and picked up by a number of influential newspapers.[7] In one paper, Collier and Hoeffler (1999) present two models of rebellion: a 'looting model of rebellion', in which the objective of rebellion is simply 'the capture of loot,' and a 'justice-seeking model', in which the rebels are driven by the desire to rectify perceived injustice. The authors dismiss the latter model, and stick to the looting model,[8] in which it is assumed that the loot is acquired during the process of rebellion rather than being dependent upon prior victory. The looting 'sector' is treated like any industry, so that looting is a positive function of 'rebel labor' and the presence of lootable resources, and a negative function of the government resources devoted to protection. The resultant function obeys the standard neoclassical assumption of diminishing returns, and in equilibrium the marginal product of rebel labor for a given g (government protection) and N (lootable resources) is equated with its opportunity cost.[9] The model suggests that rebels start off as ordinary robbers. However, driven by economies of scale, they become bigger and after a certain threshold of killing and looting they attain the status of rebels. Not surprisingly, the only difference that the model is able to make between rebels and criminals is the level of violence. There is one empirical point worth highlighting here: no known rebel movement in Africa possesses these features of a crime syndicate that has grown into a rebel movement simply by the logic of economies of scale. And, in any case, the model definitely does not relate to Angola and Sierra Leone, which the authors cite explicitly. Although these studies do not specifically address the issue of violence against civilians, it can be surmised that this is more likely in the looting model. Such violence would presumably be the logical outcome of the preferences and rationality of rebels.

The authors argue that economic inequality, as measured by the Gini coefficient, is not a significant determinant of conflict, but that poverty is – not because it is associated with injustice and inequality, but because it produces the cannon fodder for conflicts.[10] It is necessary to point out, *en passant*, that the measure of inequality is obviously irrelevant in this case, and is too blunt to capture the politically salient distinctions among inequalities. Vertical inequality measured by the indices used in such analyses is rarely as explosive as horizontal inequality among ethnic groups.[11] The 'class consciousness' required to address vertical inequality is known to be more difficult to inculcate than other forms of consciousness to address religious, ethnic or regional inequality. The same is true of authoritarian rule. It matters whether authoritarian rule is ethnic-based and its repression is largely directed against other ethnic groups, as was the case in South Africa, Rhodesia, Rwanda, Burundi and Liberia, or is generalized as in Malawi under Banda.

It should be noted that, although this research merely addresses issues of the probability of war and the correlation of such a probability with a number of political and economic factors, the political reading has been that we are actually dealing with causes, leading to the conflation of a causal explanation of wars with 'enabling conditions'. According to Collier and Hoeffler (2001: 2):

> Our results thus contrast with conventional beliefs about the causes of conflict. A stylised version of these beliefs would be that grievance begets conflict, which begets grievance, which begets further conflict. With such an analysis, the only point of intervention is to reduce the level of objective grievance. Our model suggests that what is actually happening is that opportunities for primary commodity predation cause conflict, and that policy intervention points here are reducing the absolute and relative attraction of primary commodity predation, and reducing the ability of diasporas to fund rebel movements.

The 'rational choice' model is a very demanding taskmaster. If one resorts to rational choice as a fundamental premise, then one must insist on its consistent use. One cannot simply switch it on and off without undermining the applicability of predictions based on self-interest. If one relaxes any of the assumptions, then one gets 'multiple equilibria,' and all sorts of indeterminacies crop up. In such a situation, logical deduction cannot tell us which equilibrium will be reached, nor can we, knowing one equilibrium, retrace the path back to a unique point of departure. The multiplicity of equilibria, and of paths leading to any one equilibrium, deprives the rational approach of its claimed strength: that it can be a guide to policy because it establishes a cause-effect nexus. Furthermore, rational choice's claim to dominance has always been based upon both the parsimony of its assumptions and the universality of its conceptualization of human beings. The behavior of both leaders and followers must be deducible from the logic of instrumental behavior. Although the World Bank economists assume rationality on behalf of rebel leaders, this faculty seems to be denied to political supporters. To sort out the problems, they drag in a *deus ex machina*: leadership and propaganda. The rational rebel leaders are able to inculcate in their followers a 'subjective sense of injustice whether or not this is objectively justified' (Collier 2000: 5); or, if the followers are in the diaspora, they may be, at best, 'useful fools', suffering a form of 'false consciousness' so severe that they are simply taken in by what rebels say.[12]

Collier (2000) cites Lenin on the importance of indoctrination to suggest that rebels not only make up the grievances, but also create the aggrieved groups. However, if one is to take Lenin as a serious theoretician of rebellion, one must also recall his insistence on the need for 'concrete analysis of concrete conditions'. Lenin would probably have considered the activities of many African postcolonial movements as 'adventurist', and as suffering from serious 'infantile disorders'. In any case, the view that the manipulations of rebel leaders can move an otherwise inert mass to do what they command suggests, on the one hand, a view of human conduct which credits leaders with more instrumental rationalism than they deserve, while, on the other hand, failing to account for the irrationality of the followers. All this, of course, undercuts the rational-choice basis of the analysis by bringing back moral agency and ignorance, and robs it of its claim to parsimony.

Furthermore, this apportionment of rationality ultimately involves arbitrary 'domain restrictions' (over who can be rational and who cannot), such that the analysis cannot but lead to the 'pathologies' that Green and Shapiro (1994) so eloquently warn against.[13] Why is rationality deployed in one context for self-interest and in another context for collective interests? Why is it that self-interested rebels not only ignore the collective discontent of their communities, but even turn against these very same communities whose material relationship with the state is, to say the least, tenuous? And even if one accepts that the rebels (or the youth that join them) act rationally, why should we privilege their 'rationality' over that of the community as a whole? One asks these questions because, in some writings, there is also a conflation of individual and collective rationality, such that perverse individual rationality based on calculability is extrapolated to define whole cultures. In most of the countries concerned, the wayward behavior of youth and the mayhem they have perpetrated symbolize a breakdown of order, an erosion of values and a definite confounding of collective wisdom. In such situations where the bonds of community are undone and diabolical forces are unleashed, it is a trifle pointless to place the rebels on any scale of rationality. Not surprisingly, in some societies the re-integration of youth and children has called for nothing less than an appeal to the gods and ritual cleansing. In any case, there is a touch of arrogance to the view that a visiting scholar sees 'rationality' where no one else sees it. There is a political message here: against the putatively instrumental rationality of rebels, there is another rationality, which is likely to be based on goals and values, and which can be politically mobilized to shield communities against predation and violence.

The rational-choice school has also argued that rationality must extend to expectations as well, so that individuals should not rationally engage in actions that can rationally be expected to undermine their programmes. Amartya Sen (1977: 12) reminds us that 'rational choice must demand something at least about the correspondence between what one tries to achieve and how one goes about it. Where such correspondence is missing, the zealous rational pursuit of self-interest can only produce 'rational fools'.[14] Where a huge gulf persists between the rhetoric of a movement and reality, rationality needs to be revisited. We therefore have to juxtapose the postulated rationality of rebels not only against the outcomes of their action, but also against what is known about successful guerrilla warfare. During the last forty years there have been a wide range of conflicts in Africa, and not all of them have exhibited the wanton destructiveness of some of the more recent postcolonial wars.

Laudable though the view that Africans are 'just like us' may be, it accepts as a benchmark a highly stylized 'homo economicus' view of 'Western' man and woman – a view whose appropriateness for any actually existing human society is highly contested, to say the least. Constraining rebel actions for the pursuit of material interests leaves out a whole range of things that drive rebel movements – 'passions', moral agency, 'false consciousness' – which are important in untangling the many complex conflicts afflicting Africa today. Devoid of any historical sense, the rationality assumption cannot explain the differences among the combatants in different times and places in Africa, except to assert in a tautological sense that the circumstances must have been different, accounting for the fact that rationality explained the different behavior. The ultimate effect of such a view is Panglossian; every war becomes the best of all possible wars, and every act in the pursuit of that best of all wars becomes the best of all possible acts. Reduced to this, the argument is not falsifiable and has little empirical or moral sense. Rationality is emptied of any social and empirical meaning, which perhaps explains the procrustean dimension that rationality ultimately acquires, stretchable to accommodate any position *post factum*.

Towards an Alternative Explanation

The Urban Roots of Rebellion
Three types of postcolonial rebel movements have dominated the armed conflict scene in postcolonial Africa. The first are the secessionist regionalist

movements, or those seeking greater autonomy for a particular (often ethnically specific) area. The second are those which have become rural-based following defeat in urban confrontations. The third are externally supported movements returning from exile, and passing through the countryside on their way to the urban areas.

Except perhaps for the secessionists, a common feature of all these movements is that they are driven by essentially urban issues, few of which have much resonance in the countryside. As a general proposition, one can state that 'urban crisis ' (rather than agrarian crisis) is the source of rebel movements in Africa.[15] It is the urban origin of these struggles that accounts for their 'national' character, since the ultimate purpose of the belligerents is not merely to liberate one area but to assume political power in the national capital. Such urban origin of rebels is, of course, not peculiarly African,[16] nor is the retreat to the countryside. And of course not all urban 'disturbances' spill over to the rural areas.[17] What may be specific to individual countries are the social character of the urban movements, the rural terrain to which they withdraw and within which they must perform, and the responses of the denizens of the countryside.

Two major sources of conflict in the urban areas often feed into each other, producing a downward spiral of dislocation. Ethnic conflicts are the first of these, often as a consequence of intra-elite conflicts. The literature on ethnic conflict is replete with accounts of elite mobilization of ethnic identities in the urban areas, which then spill over into rural areas.[18] These types of conflict are usually the result of the failure by the political system to manage the social pluralism of their respective countries and the erosion of the 'political pacts' that nationalists had carved to achieve much-vaunted 'national unity'. The struggle has been for power or the resolution of some conflict in the capital city. The conflict may be over failed decolonization processes in which a disunited nationalist movement is unable to share political power, or over postcolonial social discontents. In both cases, the locus of discontent is urban. The struggle for spoils often leads to what Nnoli (1998) calls 'ruling class fractionalism'.

The second source of conflicts stems from the two-decade-long economic crisis, and the structural adjustment measures adopted to address it, which together have put enormous pressure on the African body politic. They have, as elsewhere, increased income inequality and favoured dramatic increases in luxury consumption among the *nouveaux riches*, the inter-national businessmen and employees of international organisations and NGOs that have multiplied in numbers. This has intensified the sense of 'relative deprivation'. The dramatic increase in conspicuous consumption in the cities juxtaposed against deepening squalor has led to the unravelling of the 'social pacts' – be they populist, corporatist or patron-clientelist – that up to then provided a modicum of peace in the postcolonial era. Currency devaluation and the removal of subsidies have at times led to sharp increases in the prices of basic commodities, sometimes provoking 'rice riots' that have been, as in Liberia in 1979, the proximate trigger of a chain of events that eventually led to civil war (Dunn 1999).

Much of this increased social differentiation in the urban areas has been policy-induced, although it is often presented as the result of the ineluctable forces of globalization. Already in the 1970s, international organizations such as the International Labour Organization pointed to growing urban poverty and informalization of the economy, and to the fact that patterns of development were generating social structures that were politically dangerous. These concerns disappeared in the early 1980s, however, and since then the standard argument has been that the African crisis, and more specifically the agrarian manifestations of that crisis, has been caused by 'urban biases' in policies (Bates 1986; Corbridge 1982; Kydd 1988; Lofchie 1988; Peterson 1986). It has thus been argued that the removal of such a bias would benefit rural areas. One consequence of this focus on the urban–rural divide has been to underestimate or overlook intrasectoral differentiation, especially in urban areas, thus blinding policy-makers to the deleterious effects of new policies on the social coherence and political stability of the urban areas themselves. Adjustment policies have been totally oblivious to the urban ferment.[19] The crisis is also producing a marginalized youth likely to engage in criminal activities or join rebel movements.[20] Their discontent has often expressed itself in various forms, such as participation in democratic movements, looting and riots. African scholars, especially those writing on Sierra Leone (see especially Abdullah 1997; Bangura 1997; Kandeh 1999; Rashid 1997), have tended to advance a sociologically anchored explication of the composition and behavior of these young people, stressing their 'lumpen' character and paying attention to their ideological discourses. At the ideological level, the 'organic intellectuals' of such movements espouse versions of radicalism.[21] In most cases, the urban poor and 'lumpens' are mobilized by political elites for conflicts that at times turn violent. In a number of cases armed conflicts can emerge in which groups fight one another *within* the urban environments themselves, as was the case in Brazzaville. And in other cases, the losers may be forced to retreat to the countryside or go into exile.

Significantly, despite their urban origins, there are no urban guerrilla movements in Africa in the sense of movements whose fighting terrain is urban (as were the Tupamaros in Uruguay, for example). Urban violence has often occurred between communal or ethnic groupings, in which, in the worst case as in Congo Brazzaville, highly politicized militias have confronted each other. Generally, however, the fighting takes place in the countryside until such time as it is deemed appropriate to make the final assault on the urban areas. It is therefore necessary to consider the social structure of rural Africa and the propensity of African peasants *not* to adhere to rebellions.

The Hostile Rural Terrain
There are two striking features of the African countryside that have shaped the prospects and conditions for rebellion. The first is that peasants still have direct access to the main means of production – labor and land; and the second relates to the links between the state and the countryside. With the exception of countries of settler agriculture and concessions, production of export crops in much of colonial Africa has remained in the hands of peasants. Capitalist relations of production entailing mass land alienation are thus rare. Although the post-independence era saw many attempts to

expand capitalist agriculture, posing a real threat to peasant access to land for the first time, many such schemes depended heavily on state subsidies and could not survive the removal of them that accompanied structural adjustment. It is on the basis of this peculiar position of the African peasantry that Goran Hyden (1980) could talk of an 'uncaptured peasantry'. The exploitation of peasants does not generally involve the direct extraction of surplus by a landlord or feudal class. It is almost invariably mediated by 'markets' and by other extra-economic exaction encapsulated in what Mamdani (1996) refers to as 'decentralized despotism'. However, such local 'decentralised despotism', whether invented by colonial masters, as suggested by Mamdani, or resting on tradition, is usually not made of the nasty stuff that has provoked peasant revolt elsewhere in the world.[22] Indeed, we have many cases where 'traditional' authorities have been able to rally the local population against marauding rebel movements.[23] Such sweeping measures as declarations by governments claiming to be the sole owners of all national land have had little effect on the usufructuary rights of African peasants. In any case, insecurity over land is not a major preoccupation of African peasants.

Peasants' access to land has had enormous implications for the fate of rebel movements in Africa. It has denied them that most potent of revolutionary slogans – 'land to the tiller' – that was so vital to the classical peasant-based guerrilla movements of Latin America or Asia, and to national liberation movements, even when their leaderships were urban. Interestingly, none other than Che Guevara (2000: 221) drew the lessons for African rebels. His diary entry on his Congo adventure captures the essence of the problem:

> The peasants pose for us the most difficult and absorbing problems of a people's war. In all wars of liberation of this type, a basic element is the hunger for land, involving the great poverty exploited by latifundistas, feudal lords and, in some cases, capitalist-type companies. In the Congo, however, this was not the case, at least not in our region, and probably not in most of the country.

After noting that feudalism may have been more developed in Bukova, he remarks, 'in the mountainous region where we live the peasants are completely independent'. Capitalism, he notes, 'operates only in superficial forms, trades and the demonstration effect of certain items used by the peasantry', and 'imperialism gives only sporadic signs of life in the region' (Guevara 2000: 222, 223). He then asks a central question:

> What could the Liberation Army offer these peasants? That is the question which always bothered us. We could not speak here of dividing up the land in an agrarian reform, because everyone could see that it was already divided; nor could we speak of credits for the purchase of farm tools, because peasants ate what they tilled with their primitive instruments and the physical characteristics of the region did not lend themselves to credit-fuelled expansion (Guevara 2000: 223).

Noting that they had little to offer the peasantry, he concludes (ibid.):

> I think that some deep thought and research needs to be devoted to the problem of revolutionary tactics where the relations of production do not give rise to land hunger among the peasantry. For the peasantry is the main social layer in this

region; there is no industrial proletariat and the petty bourgeoisie of middlemen is not very developed.

The second feature is the linkage between the state and the countryside, which is shaped by variations in the fiscal exigencies of the state that determine whether to tax or subsidize the rural sector. The state's usual method of capture has been through marketing boards and other mechanisms for manipulating the terms of trade against agriculture. Much has been made of this source of extraction as a form of exploitation that has stifled agricultural production (Bates 1981). Exploitative though this has been, there are two features that have prevented it from becoming a source of peasant revolt, or encouraging peasants to embrace armed groups aimed at toppling the exploitative state. First, contrary to the urban-bias thesis, African governments' attitudes towards the extraction of surplus from the peasant are characterized by ambiguity, as evidenced by the taxation of peasants, on the one hand, and the provision of subsidized inputs and welfare services, on the other. There is a widespread view that African states have extracted inordinately high levels of surplus from the peasantry through unfavourable terms of trade induced by price controls and overvalued foreign exchange. This assertion is widely accepted 'even though no study ever succeeded in bringing fully convincing evidence allowing not only for direct and indirect taxation but also for direct and indirect subsidies to farmers, as well as for funds channelled through international aid projects and programmes' (Platteau 1996: 191). The World Bank's own MADIA (Management of Agricultural Development in Africa) studies have questioned the validity of the 'agricultural-squeeze' thesis both in terms of actual levels of taxation and of the impact of such taxation on variations in the performance of crops (Lele 1990). In any case, by the mid-1980s and 1990s, state capacity to extract surplus from the peasantry had been severely eroded both by structural adjustment programs and by the general curtailing of the state's reach in most African countries. Peasants had also contributed to the erosion of state capacity by simply withdrawing from state-controlled markets, a point captured by the 'lame-Leviathan' thesis (Callaghy 1987). Therefore, even if in the past African states could be seen as exploitative Leviathans weighing heavily on the peasantry, shredding of the state apparatus by both the economic and political crisis and the liberalization policies pursued to address the crisis, have 'de-captured' the peasantry.[24]

There were a number of factors determining this vacillation in state policies towards the rural sector. The first was the social base of the nationalist movement and the 'nation-building' project through which the new states sought to extend their reach. The problems of the state extending its authority over daunting geographical and cultural terrain have been underscored by the new interest in geography as an important constraint on socio-economic development (Herbst 2000; Sachs and Warner 1995). Although some of this literature succumbs to geographical determinism, the more nuanced accounts, such as those of Jeffrey Herbst, highlight the real difficulties that precolonial, colonial and postcolonial states have faced in extending themselves without thereby denying the wide range of responses to geography. Policies such as pan-territorial pricing, whereby the state guaranteed to pay the same price for all products regardless of the costs imposed by geography, are a good example of policy responses to geographical dispersion and the exigencies of nation-building.

The second is that not all African states need agricultural surpluses for their survival or their projects of industrialization. In the mineral-rich countries, while 'Dutch disease' effects may have imposed indirect taxes on agriculture, the imperative guiding state policies towards the sector was not surplus extraction. In two earlier papers on the state and agriculture and on the fiscal capacity of the African states, I have used the distinction between 'rentier' and 'merchant' states to underscore the importance of the revenue base of policies and responses to crises (Mkandawire 1987, 1995).[25] The rentier state relies on revenue from rents from the mining sector, while the merchant state relies on a broad range of taxes, especially on peasant farmers taxed through marketing boards (as in Angola, Botswana, Gabon, Congo, Nigeria, Sierra Leone and Liberia).

One interesting phenomenon is that rentier states have been much more prone to rebellion than merchant states. While this may seem to support Collier and Hoeffler's looting model of rebellion, the explanation actually lies elsewhere – namely, in the enclave and exclusivistic nature of the social structure of accumulation in such economies, which leads to virulent urban discontent among the youth, and in the politically salient economic neglect of the countryside. Because of the external nature of 'rents', it is much easier to concentrate wealth in a few hands, partly because the production of such rents does not require much labor. Usually wealth is highly concentrated, economic enclaves and the urban centers of rentier states tending to have much more skewed income distribution. Richard Auty (1998) notes that income inequality is markedly higher in resource-rich countries than in resource-deficient ones. He cites the study by Nankani (1979) which, drawing on data for the 1960s and 1970s, concluded that the mineral-rich countries exhibited relatively high levels of income inequality, as well as significantly lower levels of social development. Similar results are reported by Moore et al. (1999), who find that mineral dependence leads to low human development indicators. It is this pronounced relative deprivation in the urban areas of rentier states that partly explains their proneness to rebel movements.

To compound matters, although mineral-rich countries have a readily taxable asset, they do not necessarily collect a larger share of GDP in taxation, precisely because easy access to this one source of revenue reduces the fiscal imperative to broaden the tax base by developing the necessary apparatus for effective collection of taxes beyond the mineral enclave. As Cheibub (1998) argues, it is because governments derive income from large mineral sectors that they may be in a position to avoid the politically sensitive task of taxing their population.[26] The neglect of the countryside may not only *not* lead to peasant rebellion in the countryside (in fact, it rarely does in Africa), but it may leave the countryside wide open for urban-based rebellions. There are, however, two contradictory processes in such economies that impinge on rebellion: while the greater level of inequality within the urban areas is likely to generate urban conflicts that may spill over to the countryside, the wide urban-rural divide is likely to make such urban conflicts irrelevant to rural communities.

Where the state has to raise revenue over vast areas, over which its control is usually tenuous anyway, some form of 'quasi-voluntary' compliance, to use Margaret Levi's (1988) expression, is necessary. The merchant state has to negotiate with a much larger number of producers than does the rentier state. In such cases, there is always a need for some political presence. A kind of bargain often develops, in which governments promise to provide public goods that are positively valued, in exchange for tax payments. The state has to maintain marketing board depots, post offices, police stations, and so forth. These bureaucratic structures, tattered though they may seem, constitute the political infrastructure that suggests the presence of the state. The much deplored and vilified patron-client relationships extend their reach and presence to the rural areas, and provide some antennae for listening in on the rumblings in the countryside and for pre-empting some of the more violent manifestations of protest.[27] It is also in such merchant states that a rapacious state or misguided policies are most likely to cause harm to and alienate the peasantry. The wanton violence in the countryside of Uganda's Milton Obote, and FRELIMO's failed socialization of agriculture in Mozambique, are cases in point. Both gave rise to rebel movements with tacit or open support from peasants who had been hurt by violence or reforms. Predation in these circumstances has entirely different political consequences from neglect and marginalization in enclave rentier states, and provokes entirely different political responses from the peasantry. It does, at least, provoke passive support of rebel movements with the tacit and circumstantial connivance of peasants.

The point here is not to suggest that African peasants have no grievances (God knows they do!), still less that they are passive and never resort to violence.[28] In situations where agrarian relations have been similar to those in Asia or Latin America, African peasants have actively participated in armed struggle. Even ethnic conflicts where the key players vie not only for political power at the central government level, but also over material causes at the local level, take on many characteristics of 'peasant wars' (Buijtenhuijs 2000). So-called communal conflicts, for example, often over access to natural resources, including land and water, are a common example. The most violent ones occur between 'settlers' and populations which have claims to 'indigenous' rights. Mamdani has written extensively on this type of conflict. Another type of conflict occurs when governments or businesses encroach on the rights of the peasant or cause ecological damage. In general, however, neither the intensity of these grievances nor the political consciousness or judgement of the peasants has predisposed them to protracted rebellions against the state or the ruling classes. African peasants, with all their grievances, are not dry grass that can be set on fire by simple revolutionary sparks. Much of the violent response of African peasants has tended to be sporadic, highly localized and quite distant from classic 'peasant revolts'. One reason is that it is difficult to mobilize against the particular forms of oppression and exploitation to which they are subjected. This is definitely the case with exploitation through the 'market', partly because of the illusion of voluntary involvement in it, partly because of the diffusiveness of its exploitative processes, and partly because of the 'free rider' problems that organizers against it have to face. Instead, peasants have generally resorted to a whole range of 'everyday forms of resistance', to borrow James C. Scott's (1985) felicitous expression. Such forms of resistance are well-known: tax evasion, withdrawal from official markets, deception, pilfering, dissimulation, feigning loyalty, theft, and exit from the national territorial or officially assigned spaces. These forms of resistance may once in a while erupt into acts of violence, but rarely lead to armed rebel movements, although many writers have been tempted to wring from these actions a few precious drops of revolutionary action.

To conclude, the grievances that rebel movements claim to seek to address are often not salient in local political situations.[29] There is no landlord from whom to free the masses or upon whose surpluses guerrillas can survive. Guerrillas cannot offer an immediate end to predation by local potentates, since such predation hardly exists; nor can they liberate peasants from the heavy exactions of national governments, since African governments have only extracted surplus through the market and not by direct taxation at the level of production. If anything, 'revolutionary movements' in the postcolonial countryside are solutions in search of a problem – and in the process they become the first external agent to 'capture' the peasantry. In many cases, they have constituted the first postcolonial imposition of forced labor through requisition of surplus. Rebel movements stepping into a rural environment such as that described above find no obvious targets other than some state functionaries and other (often dilapidated) physical signs of state presence, which they tend to burn down rather than occupy.

Stationary and Roving Rebels

Before discussing the implications of the urban origins of rebel movements in a hostile rural environment, let me outline the two major forms that rebellion takes in the African countryside. To explain the different behavior of rebel movements, I will borrow Mancur Olson's (1997, 2000) useful distinction between 'stationary' and 'roving' bandits, which he used to explain the popularity and unpopularity of different warlords in Chinese history. Stationary bandits are dependent on the prosperity of the communities that they inhabit, and will therefore adopt measures that facilitate such prosperity, such as ensuring that law and order and productive activities are maintained and expanded. Setting up rudimentary structures of governance becomes an important task of the political arm of such movements. The ideal is to extend the area over which one is stationary until the whole country is 'liberated'. Roving bandits, in contrast, are constantly on the move, extracting resources through robbery, taxation and pillaging as they move to the scene of the next confrontation. They thus tend to be extremely predatory and destructive.

Of course, no movement completely fits into either category. Every rebel movement aspires to some form of sedentary existence or respite in 'liberated zones'. Thus the RUF in Sierra Leone has had, from time to time and in some areas, zones in which it assumed the role of stationary rebel.[30]

In practice, many movements are partly roving and partly stationary. And most change from one form into another, depending on a whole range of factors – the geographical origins of the movement, the resource base, the response and support from the local population, and the counter-insurgency strategies and strength of government forces. However, one can distinguish movements according to their most pronounced characteristics with regard to activities and organization.

With all these caveats, I shall use these spatial characteristics to classify African rebel movements into stationary and roving rebels. My main argument is that, in Africa, postcolonial rebel movements have drifted towards the 'roving' type. This is largely explicable by the following factors: (a) the urban origins and agendas of African rebel movements; (b) their ideological fuzziness and leadership problems; (c) the non-correspondence of the questions addressed by the movements, and the projects or agendas of rural societies; and (d) the extreme ethnic fragmentation of the African countryside. The social composition of the 'vanguard' of these movements and the social structure of the African countryside mean that most movements are condemned to the status of roving rebels. African rebels are anything but Eric Hobsbawm's (1996) 'social rebels', who are often peasants on the run from local landowners and the government, who regard them as criminals.[31]

The quintessential 'stationary rebels' are secessionist/regionalist movements. Such movements have often emerged in extreme situations where historical grievances against central authority are serious. Contrary to widespread perceptions, 'secessionist' peasant revolts have rarely driven rebel movements in Africa. Such movements often establish themselves in a specific area where they enjoy support, and where – as in Eritrea or Biafra – they may appeal to ethnic sentiments to strengthen that support. This also applies to irredentist movements – a rare species in Africa. It also applies to situations where, often as the result of colonial policy, a large part of a country feels itself to be under what is almost an occupying force composed of an army from another part of the country. Uganda under both Obote and Idi Amin is a case in point. In such situations, given the congruence of interests, peasants would at worst be indifferent, and in many cases would give positive support to the movements. The guerrilla movements' own political understanding of the situation is that they enjoy support, or that they can garner it, with sufficient political work. Political work of 'conscientization' and mobilization is seen as rewarding in such a context, a fact that gives considerable authority to the political wing of such movements. The Eritrean and Tigrayan Liberation movements (Pool 1998; Young 1998) and Uganda's NRM (Mamdani 1995; Ngoga 1998) are prime examples whose exemplary disciplined behavior has been widely commented upon.[32]

Perhaps the best known of the stationary rebels in Africa is UNITA. Over the years, UNITA has established a complex support system, which has included not only diamond mining but also large farms. It has reportedly not only 'mobilized' local populations but also uses labor from the Democratic Republic of Congo – and even distant Senegal – to dig for diamonds (Le Billon 2000; Potgier 2000). For years now, UNITA has controlled large chunks of Angola that are rich in diamonds. This stationariness has been facilitated partly by its revenue base – diamonds, as well as South African and CIA support over the years – and partly by its long organizational experience. In addition, there has been the ethnic factor: the core of the area occupied by UNITA is that of Jonas Savimbi's ethnic group. The movement's wealth has enabled it to establish a regular army relying much less on forced recruitment than is the case in many guerrilla movements.[33] In addition, mercenaries have played a much more important role than is usually the case in Africa. However, the 'enclave' nature of the source of revenue tends to obviate the need to organize or negotiate with a large number of dispersed peasant producers, and pushes the movement towards an essentially regular army structure.

It should, however, be noted that the regional and ethnic attachment of these movements means that they can only attain the status of stationary rebel in one area, and that outside the confines of the ethnic/regional boundaries such movements will be fish on dry land (to continue along the lines of Mao's metaphor). And the more intensely an ethnic group feels it must take to arms to right some wrong, the more alienated it becomes from other ethnic groups that might be seen as beneficiaries of the extant political dispensation. The dynamics of affirmation of its own identity mean that it will tend to describe the 'other' as the enemy or collaborator with the state, which, in turn, rightly or wrongly, is associated with some ethnic groups. And so, as it ventures out of the original ethnic confines, the movement is confronted with real or imagined adversaries. In these circumstances, a stationary guerrilla movement which seeks to move beyond its liberated zones is likely to end up in some other area in which it enjoys neither traditional authority nor communal usufructuary rights to land. Establishing new liberated zones and staying put would therefore involve challenging local custom with respect to both authority and property – a treacherous exercise in Africa where neither of these is characterized by predation. The result is violence against local populations. Even the relatively successful rebellion in the former Zaire, led by Pierre Mulele, one of the few postcolonial movements to have absorbed Maoist teachings,[34] was to run into this problem. Nzongola-Ntalaja (1987: 132) gives as one of the reasons for the failure of the rebellion, the choice by Pierre Mulele and Antoine Gizenga of their own regions of origin as their revolutionary base. He writes:

> Although it did appear sensible for all revolutionaries to start the struggle in their own areas with the aim of eventually merging all of the revolutionary bases in a truly mass-based national struggle, the fact that a revolutionary leader of Mulele's stature was to be mainly identified with his own and allied ethnic groups proved detrimental to the struggle, as other groups were encouraged to feel excluded from it by the enemies of the revolution.

UNITA has suffered from the same problem, so that as it moves from its enclave (to capture more towns or dislocate the government's infrastructure and political reach), it is inclined to force peasants out of their home areas, a very un-Maoist practice generating the large numbers of displaced persons in Zambia, Congo and Namibia.

The rarity of secessionist/regionalist armed movements in postcolonial Africa has tended to encourage roving rebel-type movements. Two kinds of roving rebels have occupied centre-stage in recent African history: one consisting of movements returning from exile, and the other of urban groups that shift their struggle to the countryside. In the case of the first group, the roving rebels know full well that they will be traversing areas in which the population is, at best, indifferent, but more probably hostile. The speed with which the rush to the capital is executed often leaves little room for 'politicization' or winning the hearts and minds of local populations. Indeed, in such movements the political agenda is invariably compromised by the military and economic agenda. Moreover, the logic of these movements is heavily influenced, if not determined, by their foreign allies, further undermining their local or national anchoring. Recent examples include the Rwandese and the anti-Mobutu movements and, later, the anti-Kabila movement. The Rwanda Patriotic Front (RPF) has probably been the most successful of this genre. The account of the RPF by Gérard Prunier (1998: 132), a sympathetic observer, is telling in this respect:

> How can one assess the place of the RPF among the African guerrillas? Obviously it is an oddity because of its peculiar origins and recruitment and because of the bizarre political framework in which it operated. On the ground it was closer to a (good) classical jungle army than to a guerrilla force, and it fought a mostly conventional war. It never had to face all the problems of the relations with the local population, which are the daily fare of practically all guerrilla movements. It always operated in a vacuum, both physically and intellectually.

The success of the RPF was to inspire, first, the anti-Mobutu movement and later, the anti-Kabila movements supported by Rwanda and Uganda. The anti-Kabila rebels were initially literally going to march to Kinshasa but instead 'stumbled' into guerrilla warfare. Their association with foreign troops increased their ideological 'distance' from the local communities through which they passed. Here the peasants were simply the grass under two fighting elephants – a fact demonstrated spectacularly by the all too frequent skirmishes in Kisangani by contending foreign allies and, even more brutally, by the many intra-rebel ethnic massacres in the eastern regions of the country.

It is significant that the choice of areas to be 'liberated' is often guided neither by the perceived need for liberation of an exceptionally exploited area, nor by the revolutionary potential of that area. At first, this statement may seem contradicted by the fact that, in many cases, the areas where revolts start are indeed poor. Some writers have variously sought to give this more political and strategic importance than is warranted, suggesting that these are areas where the sense of alienation from the state is likely to be strong. However, this choice is more the result of security considerations than of political analysis. Remote areas, which often happen to be poor, are often far from the reach of the state security system and, therefore, as good a starting point as any. The subsequent focus is on areas likely to ensure the provisioning of the rebel army by whatever means possible. Not surprisingly, mineral-rich areas have turned out to be major targets of rebel movements. Diamonds, being highly portable and valued, are a favourite target, as we have seen in Angola, Sierra Leone and Congo.[35] Obviously, in this rush to capture mineral wealth, such movements neither have the need nor the time to engage in the niceties of ' political conscientization' of the peasantry through whose fields they must literally march, and to whose crops they invariably help themselves. It is this behavior that gives some credibility to the looting model of rebellion.

Where movements are initially composed of urban groups that have escaped to the countryside following defeat in urban skirmishes or a decision to shift the terrain of the struggle, alienation from the local rural population is inevitable. Many movements of urban origin have become rural following defeat in urban confrontations. Mao Tse-Tung's retreat to the countryside and guerrilla strategy was the consequence of a 'spectacular failure' of insurrection in the cities (Hobsbawm 1996). Asian history is full of rebellions that turn to banditry, and most of Mao's injunctions on revolution are derived from the bitter history of failed rebellions in China and some of the lessons from past social banditry.[36] The romantic image of youthful revolt has been that of radical urban youths responding to the clarion call of peasant uprisings. The situation in Africa has been different; here it is the urban youth seeking to persuade the peasants to respond to the exigencies of urban revolt. They come to the rural areas convinced that the peasants are desperately in need of liberation. Persuaded not only of the necessity but the actuality of the revolution, they will tend to consider reluctant peasants as enemies or traitors, with death the usual penalty. In this state of mind and imbued with the contempt for the rural folk so common among urban populations everywhere, their encounter with rustic indifference or passivity can be unsettling, to say the least. They will easily resort to force and coercion.[37]

One should note here the problems of discipline that plague both stationary and roving rebel movements. Recruits to any movement come with a wide range of motives (individual and collective), and different levels of consciousness and understanding of the issues. It is the capacity of the movement's 'vanguard' to shape these diverse and divergent interests into a fighting force that ultimately determines its coherence. The product is rarely the simple arithmetical sum of individual rationality that is suggested by anecdotal interviews with individuals in the movements. The motley crew of alien urban youth and alienated local youth that constitute the majority of many movements accounts for the fuzziness of their cause, and reflects the peculiar position in the social order – a position laden with ambiguities, contradictions and extreme uncertainty. How does a movement discipline the youthful 'lumpens' who are most likely to be its first adherents? The work on both successful and unsuccessful movements testifies to the centrality of this concern. The task of 'taming' these elements so as to constitute a coherent and disciplined fighting force is a Herculean task that every successful revolution has had to carry out. Failure to do so can lead to defeat.

In the earlier rebellions in the Democratic Republic of the Congo, for example, the problems of indiscipline played a devastating role. Writing on the problems of the Conseil National de Libération, one of the Lumumbist rebel movements (in which, interestingly Laurent Kabila played a part), Nzongola-Ntalaja (1987: 134) states:

CNL leaders were not in a position to control their middle cadres effectively. These cadres were recruited among clerks, primary school teachers, ex-soldiers, ex-policemen and leaders of the *jeunesse*. For most of these partisans, as for their leaders, the concept of 'second independence' meant their turn to enjoy the fruits of independence formerly monopolised by reactionary politicians that had been removed from power. The idea that the new order was to serve all the people was lost in a youthful population given to excesses of brutality and savagery once it fell under the influence of hemp. *The lack of discipline was a critical factor in the progressive alienation of the masses from an army that they had considered as their liberator from the brutal and repressive ANC.* (emphasis added).

Museveni (1997: 85, 90) recalls the following:

We recruited 54 boys, mostly from Bugisu, and started training them at Nachingwea. Unfortunately, once again, these boys had not been well selected. They had been working mostly in towns like Nairobi and had a *kiyaye* (*lumpen proletariat*) culture. They began misbehaving in the Frelimo camp and soon after their training, the Tanzanian government dispersed them. ...

I took personal charge of the Montepuez group and stayed with the boys during the training months in Mozambique because I feared that some of the recruits might be undisciplined *bayaaye*, like those of 1973, and they might have caused us problems. With my presence in the camp, however, we were able to suppress most of their negative tendencies and attitudes.

It should be borne in mind that virtually all African rebel movements have been aware of the need for discipline (see the various cases in Clapham 1998b). Even the notorious RUF tried to set up a 'civil administration,' and to raise the level of consciousness of its recruits through its so-called 'ideology system', the central motto of which was 'arms to the people, power to the people, and wealth to the people'. Abdullah and Muana (1998) report that, under this ideology system, combatants were ordered not to take 'even a single needle' from the local population.

Compounding matters is the relative mobility of African peasants, who can take up the 'exit' option against the predation or violence of either state or non-state actors.[38] The porousness of African borders, the relative abundance of land, and the transboundary ethnic loyalties still prevailing make African peasantries more mobile than peasants elsewhere. Such peasant mobility means that guerrillas are likely to be roving rebels, stationary predation having been emptied of all purpose by the mobile prey. It is difficult to be stationary when the population (or Mao's 'water') is highly mobile and subject to tidal movements. For most guerrillas this mobility of the peasantry can be devastating, since it denies them the water that they need if they are to be anything like Mao's fish.[39] The incredible sight of the massive return by Rwandese peasant refugees to their homes despite pressures from the Interahamwe provides poignant evidence of this. By their departure, they suddenly exposed the Interahamwe 'fish' to attacks by Rwandese forces. Earlier, the RPF itself had been confronted by similar problems. Mamdani (2001: 188) notes that the RPF 'consistently failed to translate RPF military victory on the field into political gains within the population. The reason was simple. Every time the RPF captured a new area and established military control, the population fled.'

The ultimate effect of this was that there were:

no liberated zones where alternate modes of governance were introduced under the benevolent eye of a new administration. There were no Resistance Councils and Committees as in the Luwero Triangle, no effort to reach out to mobilize peasants politically, so as to transform them into a human resource for the struggle. There was not even an effort to establish administrative structures in the areas over which the RPF had military control. If anything, there was – unlike in most previous cases – a distrust of the peasantry, for the peasants were predominantly Hutu and they showed no enthusiasm at being 'liberated'... The object of this liberation was no longer the population, but the territory. Thus, liberation turned out to be a combination of occupation and displacement: occupation of the land and displacement of the people. (ibid.)

As suggested above, the resource base of the movements impinges on their comportment and their relationship with the peasantry. For instance, control of diamonds and the ability to purchase arms can lead to a hasty transformation of guerrilla movements to conventional warfare, with the military side overshadowing the political side as movements become less solicitous of peasant support. The same is true of external financial support. The case of RENAMO is interesting in this respect.[40] This movement was constituted partly by discontented FRELIMO elements, but later heavily supported by Rhodesia and South Africa. In the earlier phases, RENAMO targeted state institutions and public infrastructure, which was also part of South Africa's 'destabilization' strategy in Southern Africa. RENAMO had no particular need for surpluses from peasants. With the end of financial support from South Africa and Rhodesia, however, the movement increasingly had to extract surpluses from peasants. It also sought to undermine the legitimacy of the state in the countryside by destroying whatever social services the government had provided in the post-independence era. One result was the flight of more than a million refugees to Malawi and Zimbabwe. It also became government policy to deny RENAMO the ability to become implanted in any given area, and thus to deny it any success as a stationary rebel movement.[41]

Conclusion

The first message of this chapter is that, while the focus on raw materials in some of Africa's major wars has usefully drawn attention to the need to cut off the access of rebel movements to these 'conflict' resources, and while the denial of access to relatively easily cornered, portable and marketable products can severely undermine the military capacity of rebel movements, they are not the cause of wars, any more than the banks, whose 'expropriation' was fashionable among urban guerrillas in Latin America, caused urban guerrilla movements. Different movements finance their rebellions in different ways, and the fixation with modes of financing may blind us to the true 'root causes.'

The second point is that, to understand the terrible toll of rebel movements, we must consider both the structural conditions that are propitious to insurgency, and the agency of individuals and social movements. Consequently we need to understand the explosive nature of the combination of the urban crisis and the social composition of these movements and their essentially 'urban' agenda, on the one hand, and, on the other, a rural social landscape that may be indifferent to these agendas, at best, and more often than not hostile to them. The roots of revolt in most African countries lie in the cities, and more specifically, the capital cities. Most guerrillas are merely 'passing through' the countryside on their way to capture power in the city, or some natural resource deemed necessary for the prosecution of war. This, together with the movements' unclear political agendas, the apathy or hostility of local communities, and the complexities and peculiarities of the African rural societies, produces a volatile combination that has led to so much unnecessary suffering. We have argued why many rebel movements are likely to degenerate into banditry. One clear message for urban rebel movements seeking mechanically to apply revolutionary theories is that rural Africa is a treacherous environment, which will not only erode their political agenda but also reduce them to despicable criminals and bandits.

A third message of the chapter is that, incoherent as the rebels' objectives may sound, they reflect a serious urban malaise that should not be lightly dismissed by reducing the members of these movements to simple criminals. These rebels – uncouth, brutal, difficult to grasp and hard to sympathize with – are unlikely to attract analyses that seek to understand the sources of their grievances. The temptation is to dismiss their political motivations. But we must not lose sight of the political factors behind such conflicts. The view that these conflicts are merely driven by greed is not merely cynical, but can only lead to fatal political blindness.

Finally, the threat of revolt and conflict hangs like a Damocles' sword over many African countries. Understanding the 'root causes' of revolt is, therefore, an important task, and more work on this should be encouraged. Such work will be useful if it avoids stereotyped views of African politics and the excessively deductive accounts of the relationships between the economy and politics. What is required is more historically contextualized analysis, drawing on both African and non-African experiences, and taking national politics seriously. This paper will have served its purpose if it contributes towards a shift in that direction.

References

Abdullah, I. 1997. 'The Bush Path to Destruction: the Origins and Character of the Revolutionary United Front (RUF SL).' *Africa Development* 22 (3/4): 45-76.

Abdullah, I. and P. Muana. 1998. 'The Revolutionary United Front in Sierra Leone: a revolt of the lumpenproletariat', in C. Clapham, ed., *African Guerrillas*. Bloomington, IN: Indiana University Press, 172-93.

Abdullah, I. and Y. Bangura. 1997. Special Issue of *Africa Development* on 'Youth Culture and Political Violence: the Sierra Leone civil war.' Dakar: CODESRIA.

Adam, H. 1999. 'Somali Civil Wars', in T. Ali and R. Mathews, eds., *Civil Wars in Africa: Roots and Resolution.* Montreal: McGill-Queens University Press, 169-92.

Addison, T., P. Le Billon and S. M. Murshed. 2000. 'On the Economic Motivation for Conflict in Africa.' Paper presented at Annual Bank conference on development economics Europe 2000. Paris: World Bank.

Ali, T. and R. Mathews, eds 1999. *Civil Wars in Africa: roots and resolution.* Montreal: McGill-

Queens University Press.

Allen, C. 1999. 'Warfare, Endemic Violence and State Collapse in Africa.' *Review of African Political Economy* 26 (81): 367-84.

Amanor, K. S. 1999. *Global Restructuring and Land Rights in Ghana*. Uppsala: Nordiska Afrikainstitutet.

Auty, R. 1998. *Resource Abundance and Economic Development: Improving the Performance of Resource-rich Countries*. Helsinki: UNU/WIDER.

Bangura, Y. 1997. 'Understanding the Political and Cultural Dynamics of the Sierra Leone War: a Critique of Paul Richard's *Fighting for the Rain Forest*', *Africa Development* 22 (3/4): 117-48.

Bangura, Y. 2000. 'Strategic Policy Failure and Governance in Sierra Leone', *Journal of Modern African Studies* 38 (4): 551-77.

Bates, R. 1981. *Markets and States in Tropical Africa*. Berkeley, CA: University of California Press.

Bates, R. 1986. 'The regulation of rural markets in Africa', in S. Commins, M. Lofchie and R. Payne, eds. *Africa's Agrarian Crisis*. Boulder, CO: Lynne Rienner.

Bratton, M. and N. van de Walle. 1998. 'Neopatrimonial regimes and political transitions in Africa', in P. Lewis, ed. *Africa: The Dilemmas of Development and Change*. Boulder, CO: Westview Press.

Buijtenhuijs, R. 2000. 'Peasant Wars in Africa: Gone with the Wind? ' in D. F. Bryceson, C. Kay and J. Mooij, eds. *Disappearing Peasantries ? Rural labour in Africa, Asia and Latin America*. London: Intermediate Technology Publications.

Callaghy, T. 1987. 'The State as Lame Leviathan: The patrimonial administrative state in Africa', in E. Zaki, ed., *The African State in Transition*. London: Macmillan.

Chabal, P. and J.-P. Daloz. 1999. *Africa Works: Disorder as Political Instrument*. Oxford: James Currey.

Chaliand, G. 1969. *Armed Struggle in Africa*. New York: Monthly Review Press.

Chege, M. 2000. 'What's really wrong? ' *The Times Literary Supplement*, London, 22 September: 8.

Cheibub, J. A. 1998. 'Political Regimes and the Extractive Capacity of Governments: Taxation in democracies and dictatorships ', *World Politics* 50, 3: 349-76.

Clapham, C. 1998a. 'Introduction: analysing African insurgencies ', in C. Clapham, ed. *African Guerrillas*, Oxford: James Currey, 1-18.

Clapham, C., ed. 1998b. *African Guerrillas*. Oxford: James Currey.

Collier, P. 1999. 'Doing Well out of War', Paper prepared for Conference on Economic Agendas in Civil War. London: World Bank.

Collier, P. 2000. *Economic Causes of Civil Conflict and Their Implications for Policy*. Washington DC: World Bank, Development Research Group.

Collier, P. and A. Hoeffler. 1998. *On Economic Causes of Civil War*, *Oxford Economic Papers* 50: 263-73.

Collier, P. and A. Hoeffler. 1999. *Loot-seeking and Justice-seeking in Civil War*. Washington, DC: World Bank, Development Research Group.

Collier, P. and A. Hoeffler. 2001. *Greed and Grievance in Civil War*. Washington, DC: World Bank, Development Research Group.

Corbridge, S. 1982. 'Urban Bias, Rural Bias and Industrialisation: an appraisal of the work of Michael Lipton and Terry Byres', in J. Harriss and M. Moore, eds., *Rural Development: Theories of peasant economy and agrarian change*. London: Hutchison University Library.

Daloz, J.-P. 1998. 'Mise' re(s) de l'africanisme ', *Politique Africaine* 70: 105-17.

Davidson, B. 1969. *The Liberation of Guinea* . Harmondsworth: Penguin.

Diop, M.-C. and M. Diouf. 1999. *Les figures du politique en Afrique: des pouvoirs hérités aux pouvoirs élus*, Dakar: CODESRIA.

Duffield, M. 1998. 'Post-modern Conflict: Warlords, post-adjustment States, and Private Protection', *Civil Wars*, 1, 1: 65:105.

Dunn, E. 1999. 'Civil War in Liberia', in T. Ali and R. Mathews, eds., *Civil Wars in Africa*, Montreal: McGill-Queens University Press, 89-121.

é Nziem, I. N. 1998. 'Du Congo des rébellions au Zaire des pillages'. *Cahiers d'Etudes Africaines* 38, 2-4: 417-39.

Economist. 2000. 'The Hopeless Continent'. London, 13 May, front cover.

El-Kenz, A. 1996. 'Youth and Violence', in S. Ellis, ed., *Africa Now: People, Policies, Institutions*. London: James Currey, 42-57.

Ellis, S. 1998. 'Liberia's Warlord Insurgency', in C. Clapham, ed. *African Guerrillas*, Oxford:

James Currey, 155-71.

Enzenberger, H. M. 1993. *InboX rdeskrig*. Stockholm: Norstedts Storpocket.

Fyle, C. M. 1993. *The State and the Provision of Social Services in Sierra Leone since Independence, 1961-91*. Dakar: CODESRIA.

Green, D. and I. Shapiro. 1994. *Pathologies of Rational Choice Theory: A critique of applications in political science*. New Haven, CT: Yale University Press.

Guevara, E. C. 2000. *The African Dream: The diaries of the revolutionary war in the Congo*. London: Harvill.

Gugler, J. 1988. 'The Urban Character of Contemporary Revolutions,' in J. Gugler, ed., *The Urbanisation of the Third World*. Oxford: Oxford University Press.

Herbst, J. 2000. *States and Power in Africa: Comparative lessons in authority and control*. Princeton, NJ: Princeton University Press.

Hirschman, A. 1970. *Exit, Voice and Loyalty: Responses to decline in firms, organizations and states*. Cambridge, MA: Harvard University Press.

Hobsbawm, E. 1996. *The Age of Extremes: A history of the world, 1914-1991*. New York: Vintage.

Hyden, G. 1980. *Beyond Ujamaa in Tanzania: Underdevelopment and an uncaptured peasantry*. Berkeley, CA: University of California Press.

Kandeh, J. D. 1999. 'Ransoming the State: Elite origins of subaltern terror in Sierra Leone', *Review of African Political Economy* 26, 81: 349-66.

Kaplan, R. 1994. 'The Coming Anarchy', *The Atlantic Monthly*, 273, 2: 44-76.

Keen, D. 1998. 'The Political Economy of War', Paper presnted at Workshop on Economic and Social Consequences of Conflict. Queen Elizabeth House, University of Oxford.

Kydd, J. 1988. 'Zambia', in C. Harvey, ed., *Agriculture Pricing Policy in Africa: Four country case studies*. London: Macmillan.

Le Billon, P. 2000. 'The Political Economy of Resource Wars', in J. Cilliers and C. Dietrich, eds., *Angola's War Economy: The role of oil and diamonds*. Pretoria: Institute of Strategic Studies.

Lele, U. 1990. *Agricultural Growth and Assistance to Africa: lessons of a quarter century*. San Francisco, CA: International Center for Economic Growth.

Levi, M. 1999. 'Death and taxes: extractive equality and the development of democratic institutions', in I. Shapiro and C. Hacker-Gordon, eds., *Democracy's Value*. Cambridge: Cambridge University Press.

Lofchie, M. 1988. 'Tanzania's Agricultural Decline'. in N. Chazan and T. Shaw, eds. *The Political Economy of Food in Africa*. Boulder, CO: Lynne Rienner.

Mamdani, M. 1995. *And the Fire Does Not Always Beget Ash*. Kampala: Monitor Publications.

Mamdani, M. 1996. *Citizen and Subject: Contemporary Africa and the legacy of late colonialism*. Princeton, NJ: Princeton University Press; Oxford: James Currey.

Mamdani, M. 2001. *When Victims Become Killers: Colonialism, nativism, and the genocide in Rwanda*. Princeton, NJ: Princeton University Press; Oxford: James Currey.

Mkandawire, T. 1987. 'The State and Agriculture: Introductory remarks', in T. M. a. N. Bourenane, ed., *The State and Agriculture in Africa*. Dakar: CODESRIA.

Mkandawire, T. 1995. 'Fiscal Structure, State Contraction and Political Responses in Africa', in T. Mkandawire and A. Olukoshi, eds., *Between Liberalisation and Repression: the politics of adjustment in Africa*. Dakar: CODESRIA.

Moore, M., J. Leavy, P. Houtzager and H. White. 1999. *Polity Qualities: How Governance Affects Poverty*. Washington, DC: World Bank.

Museveni, Y. 1997. *Sowing the Mustard Seed: The Struggle for Freedom and Democracy in Uganda*. London: Macmillan.

Mustapha, A. R. 1992. 'Structural Adjustment and Multiple Modes of Social Livelihood in Nigeria', in P. Gibbon, Y. Bangura and A. Ofstad, eds., *Authoritarianism, Democracy and Adjustment: The politics of economic reform in Africa*. Uppsala: Nordiska Afrikainstitutet.

Nankani, G. T. 1979. *Development Problems of Mineral Exporting Countries*. Washington, DC: World Bank.

Natsios, A. 1995. 'Humanitarian Relief Interventions in Somalia: The economics of chaos'. Paper presented to the Princeton University conference, 'Learning from Operation Restore Hope', April.

Ngoga, P. 1998. 'Uganda: the National Resistance Army', in C. Clapham, ed., *African Guerrillas*, Oxford: James Currey, 91-106.

Nilsson, A. 1999. *Peace in Our Time: Towards a holistic understanding of world society conflicts*. Gothenburg: PADRIGU.

Nnoli, O. 1998. *Ethnic Conflicts in Africa*. Dakar: CODESRIA.

Nzongola-Ntalaja. 1987. 'The Second Independence Movement in Congo-Kinshasa', in P. Anyang' Nyongo, ed., *Popular Struggles for Democracy in Africa*. London: Zed Books.

Obi, C. 2001. *The Changing Forms of Identity Politics in Nigeria Under Economic Adjustment: the Case of the Oil Minorities Movement of the Niger Delta*. Uppsala: Nordiska Afrikainstitutet.

O'Brien, D. B. C. 1996. 'A Lost Generation: Youth identity and state decay in West Africa', in R. Werbner and T. Ranger, eds., *Post Colonial Identities in Africa*. London: Zed Books.

Olson, M. 1997. 'The New Institutional Economics: The collective choice approach to economic development', in C. Clague, ed., *Institutions and Economic Development: Growth and governance in less developed and post-socialist countries*. Baltimore, MD: Johns Hopkins University Press.

Olson, M. 2000. *Power and Prosperity: Outgrowing communist and capitalist dictatorships*. New York: Basic Books.

Osaghae, E. E. 1994. 'Towards a Fuller Understanding of Ethnicity in Africa: bringing rural ethnicity back in ', in E. E. Osaghae, ed., *Between State and Civil Society in Africa*. Dakar: CODESRIA.

Peters, K. and P. Richards. 1998. 'Why we Fight: the voice of youth combatants in Sierra Leone', *Africa* 68, 2: 183-210.

Peterson, S. 1986. 'Neglecting the Poor: State policy towards smallholders in Kenya', in S. Commins, M. Lofchie and R. Payne, eds., *Africa's Agrarian Crisis*. Boulder, CO: Lynne Rienner.

Platteau, J.-P. 1996. 'Physical Infrastructure as a Constraint on Agricultural Growth: The case of Sub-Saharan Africa', *Oxford Development Studies* 24, 3: 189-220.

Pool, D. 1998. 'The Eritrean People's Liberation Front', in C. Clapham, ed., *African Guerrillas*, Oxford: James Currey, 19-35.

Potgier, J. 2000. '"Taking Aid from the Devil Himself": UNITA's support structures', in J. Cilliers and C. Dietrich, eds., *Angola's War Economy: The role of oil and diamonds*. Pretoria: Institute of Strategic Studies.

Prendergast, J. and M. Duffield. 1999. 'Liberation politics in Ethiopia and Eritrea ', in T. Ali and R. Mathews, eds., *Civil Wars in Africa*, Montreal: McGill-Queens University Press, 35-51.

Prunier, G. 1998. 'The Rwandan Patriotic Front', in C. Clapham, ed., *African Guerrillas*, Oxford: James Currey, 119-33.

Rashid, I. 1997. 'Subaltern Reactions: lumpens, students, and the left ', *Africa Development* 22, 3-4: 19-44.

Richards, P. 1995. 'Rebellion in Liberia and Sierra Leone: a crisis of youth', in O. Furley, ed., *Conflict in Africa*. London: I.B. Tauris.

Richards, P. 1998. 'Sur la nouvelle violence politique en Afrique: le sectarisme séculier au Sierra Leone', *Politique Africaine* 70, June: 85-103.

Sachs, J. D. and M. Warner. 1995. *Natural Resources and Economic Growth*. Cambridge, MA: Harvard Institute for International Development.

Saul, J. and C. Leys. 1999. 'Sub-Saharan Africa in global capitalism ', *Monthly Review* 51, 3: 13-31.

Schaffer, J. 2001. 'Guerrillas and Violence in the War in Mozambique: De-socialisation or Resocialisation ', *African Affairs* 100, 399: 215-37.

Scott, J. C. 1985. *Weapons of the Weak: Everyday forms of peasant resistance*. New Haven, CT: Yale University Press.

Sen, A. 1977. 'Rational Fools: A Critique of the Behavioural Foundations of Economic Theory', *Philosophy and Public Affairs* 6, 4: 317-44.

Sen, A. 1987. *On Ethics and Economics*. London: Blackwell.

Sesay, M. 1995. 'State Capacity and Politics of Economic Reform in Sierra Leone', *Journal of Contemporary African Studies* 13, 2: 165-92.

Stewart, F. 1998. *The Root Causes of Conflict: evidence and policy implications*. Helsinki: UNU/WIDER.

Vines, A. 1992. *RENAMO: Terrorism in Mozambique*. London: James Currey.

World Bank 2000. 'Greed for diamonds and other 'lootable' commodities fuels civil wars: new report challenges popular notions about origins of civil conflict'. Washington DC: World Bank.

Young, J. 1998. 'The Tigray People's Liberation Front', in C. Clapham, ed., *African Guerrillas*, Oxford: James Currey, 36-52.

Notes

1 This point is eloquently made by Abdullah and Muana (1998: 193) in the conclusion to their paper on the RUF: 'Despite the limitations and failures of the RUF, the country – indeed the continent – will have to pay more attention to the frustrated energies of the lumpen revolutionaries who are asking a poignant question about how the nation is being governed ... moving onto the centre stage in the historical process, as opposed to being marginal – is not only a RUF agenda but the lumpen project writ large.'

2 Enzenberger is describing a global phenomenon, which he associates with Hanna Arendt's view of the banality of evil.

3 Commenting on the sweeping generalizations made about Africa, Michael Chege (2000: 8) observes: 'No one would countenance sweeping statements of this kind about, say, Asians, Americans or Jews. No one suggests that violence in Sri Lanka or the depravity of the Khmer Rouge reflect an "Asian" cultural affliction. Yet, according to the conventional wisdom of the new discipline of all-Africa catastrophe studies, the shocking human mutilation and senseless carnage of Sierra Leonean and Liberian warlords are all symptomatic of "Africa" in chaos.' The purveyors of this 'all-Africa catastrophe' view go to inordinately great lengths to pre-empt accusations that their writing panders to racism. Thus Chabal and Daloz (1999: xx) state: 'We are, of course, aware that our emphasis on disorder may prompt ideologically motivated or intellectually torpid readers to draw unwarranted normative conclusions about Africa and Africans. This is a danger that is impossible to avoid since such interpretations are driven by the need to belittle Africa and demean Africans – a need as powerful as that which fuels racism in our own countries. To desist because of such a danger would be a dereliction of our responsibility as Africanist scholars.' Or 'For decades, it was virtually unacceptable seriously to consider such issues since they would almost inevitably have been regarded as remnants of an imperial outlook or even racist prejudices' (Chabal and Daloz 1999: 129). The point is echoed in the conclusion, when the authors state 'it is worth stating again that our argument cannot be used as evidence to support the view either that Africans are 'inherently' different from us or that that they are 'inherently' incapable of changing the condition of the countries in which they live' (ibid.: 163). Anyone who does not share their interpretation is a victim of 'intellectual sloth,' 'paternalism,' or 'prêt-à-penser' of others. In a separate article, Daloz (1998) accuses those not holding their self-proclaimed 'heretical' but scientific stance of seeking to be 'politically correct' or being afflicted by blinding 'third worldism'. I believe the authors protest suspiciously too much.

4 In response to Paul Richards's strenuous efforts to depict obviously barbaric acts as rational and 'devilishly well calculated', Yusuf Bangura (1997: 123) points out: 'The cutting off of hands to prevent adult villagers from voting may be a rational RUF strategy, as Richards insists, but one would have to stretch rationality to its limits to explain the logic behind the decision to subject to the same treatment 9 and 10 year-olds who do not vote.' Here the outcomes of the postulated 'rationality' lend credence to Amartya Sen's (1977) observation that the completely 'rational individual is close to being a social moron'.

5 These problems are underscored by Jessica Schaffer (2001) in her study which, on the basis of interviews after the war in Mozambique, challenges the accounts about the motivations and attitudes of young men who participated in the war. The responses depended on such factors as time, location and audience.

6 One source of the problem is that a number of writers tend to treat rationality and self-interest as synonymous. They are, however, distinct. As Amartya Sen (1987: 320) points out, the rationality criterion is purely procedural. It specifies nothing about the content of pursued goals. In principle, there is nothing inconsistent about rational behavior that tries to advance the wellbeing of others, nor is there anything that says that the pursuit of self-interest is rational.

7 There have been other attempts to provide the economic motivation for conflict in Africa in similar game-theoretical frameworks. See, for instance Addison et al. (2000).

8 In the justice model, the authors identify three types of grievances: those arising from hatreds between social groups, those provoked by repression in the process of political

decision-making, and those engendered by poor economic outcomes. After some rather heroic assumptions about preference and production functions, they prefer the 'looting model' over the 'justice-seeking model,' partly because in the latter model rebels face serious collective-action problems, given Africa's ethnic fractionalization and political repression, and partly because none of the proxies of intensity of grievance (extent of inequality, social fractionalization or poor past economic performance) significantly increase the risk of war.

9   The assumption that the social behavior and organization of rebel movements can be derived from underlying micro-level individual rationality often involves a leap of faith which is unproblematic only within the neoclassical paradigm.

10 There is a suggestion that the poor have 'little to lose' from joining either rebel or government forces. This would seem to go against the well-argued view that the poor are generally risk-averse. And it turns out that part of the violence by rebel movements can be accounted for by this reluctance on the part of the poor to join movements that purportedly fight in their name.

11 This is the message of the UNU/WIDER studies summarized by Frances Stewart (1998). One should also add here that the same Gini coefficient could be generated by a wide range of social relations with entirely different political implications. Thus the high Gini coefficient of apartheid South Africa has entirely different political implications from the equally high one of Botswana.

12 This is a rather cynical view. One of the sources of 'diaspora' support is increased information, facilitated partly by the very means of communication that rebels use - the Internet, for example. Furthermore, here we run into a failure to recognize endogeneity. Diasporas are in many cases the result of conflict and the repression of minorities, and are thus a poor independent variable. Indeed, many of the people in diasporas have ended up abroad as refugees.

13 They criticize the tendency of rational-choice theorists to conceal their assumptions about actors' information sets, risk levels, desires and goals, and decision-making capacities, which means that one can admit disconfirming evidence without abandoning one's core beliefs.

14 As Sen (1987: 13) notes: 'If a person does exactly the opposite of what would help achieving what he or she would want to achieve, and does this with flawless consistency (always choosing exactly the opposite of what will enhance the occurrence of things he or she wants and values), the person can scarcely be seen as rational even if that dogged consistency inspires some kind of astonished admiration on the part of the observer.'

15 There are, of course, many cases of violent protests of rural origin in Africa. Intercommunal or inter-ethnic ones, waged over natural resources, are a common form. The most vicious are those between 'indigenous' populations and 'settler' groups. Mamdani (2001) has given this interpretation to the conflicts in the Great Lakes region. There are also cases of revolts by peasants against incursions into their communal property by the state or foreign capital, such as the peasant response to the Bakalori project or 'oil minorities' such as the Ogoni people in Nigeria (Obi 2001). Another example is that of the 'rice fires' in Ghana in the 1980s, when the expropriation of 9,000 hectares by the government to establish a palm oil project led to the phenomenon of 'night harvesters' – young people who 'sleep during the day and rising in the evening... descend on GOPPDC plantation in groups to plunder oil palm branches' – rationalizing their activities by arguing that the land belongs to them and was unfairly expropriated (Amanor 1999). However, most of these acts of rebellion remain localized. The episodic and highly local character of peasant revolt and its rarity may account for the tendency among scholars of a teleological bent to celebrate and oversell its significance.

16 On the urban character of many contemporary revolutions, see Gugler 1988.

17 Thus, for instance, the spontaneous forms of violence in Mobutu's Congo – the looting, 'journée morte' and other forms – were almost exclusively an urban phenomenon (É Nziem 1998).

18 There is no suggestion here that ethnic politics is an exclusively urban phenomenon. Eghosa Osaghae (1994) has persuasively argued for the salience of rural ethnicity in Africa politics, and shown how it forms the ethnic grid within which much of African politics is played out. However, in many cases urban politics have given greater poignancy to rural ethnic identities, and made them a national concern.

19 Thus while Sierra Leone scholars bemoaned the catastrophic decline in social services

caused by both the crisis and adjustment (Fyle 1993), a combined International Monetary Fund/World Bank team visiting Sierra Leone in the midst of the unrest described the severely austere economic measures of the NPRC government as 'a feat of outstanding performance' (cited in Sesay 1995). As Sesay laconically remarks, 'The good results accruing from the Fund's policies and overall good intentions are countered by the unsavoury social, economic and political consequences.' One salient feature of the adjustment process has been increased 'informalization' of the economy, which has played a significant role in wars in Africa by providing perfect cover for the movement of resources to finance arms purchases and by further eroding the reach of the state. The informalization of the diamond industry in Sierra Leone is a telling case (Bangura 1997).

20 On the political salience of youth in African politics, see Abdullah and Bangura 1997; El-Kenz 1996; O'Brien 1996; Peters and Richards 1998; Richards 1995. Youth politics is strongly affected by a country's political culture and civil society. In Nigeria, with a dense civil society and a broad political/ideological spectrum, youth politics has usually been harnessed through these political channels. Where youth are constrained within a non-existent or extremely restrictive political culture, they are likely to swallow poorly digested lessons from elsewhere or create their own political spaces and cultures that can be asocial or hostile to 'business as usual', which they consider as repressive and prone to docility or fatalism.

21 In the case of Sierra Leone, researchers have recounted the ideological developments of these movements in impressive and informative detail (see especially Abdullah 1997; Abdullah and Muana 1998; Bangura 1997; Kandeh 1999; Rashid 1997). Abdullah (1997: 53) informs us that the 'lumpen' leaders 'were conversant with the political philosophy of some distinguished Africans. They knew the history of the slave trade and the dehumanisation of the African which it entailed. They could make connections between the colonial past and the post-colonial present and generally espouse some form of pan-Africanism. (Their) discourse was spiced with generous quotes from Marcus Garvey, Bob Marley, Kwame Nkrumah, Wallace-Johnson, and, at times, Haile Selassie. Some of (them) had read Kwame Nkrumah and Frantz Fanon, a little of Che Guevara and Fidel Castro, and some undigested Marx and Lenin.'

22 One should note that revolts, even in countries where peasant conditions have been much worse than those prevailing in Africa, are a rare occurrence. In most cases, peasants are engaged in what Hobsbawm (1969) describes as 'working the system to their minimum disadvantage'. This, of course, is the point that Scott (1985) has eloquently made in recounting the 'prosaic but constant struggle between the peasantry and those seeking to extract labour, food, taxes, rents, and interest from them'. One should add here that by tending to treat each peasant act that is in some sense dysfunctional to state projects or interests as 'resistance', many studies exaggerate the 'militancy' of the peasantry even in this prosaic form of resistance. Thus, withdrawal from the market when prices are bad may be no more than the rational behavior of neoclassical economics, and reading resistance into it is misleading – and, in a sense, renders resistance meaningless.

23 This definitely seemed to have been the case in Sierra Leone, where the 'traditional' Kamajo fighters joined in the fights against RUF rebels, and in Ethiopia when the TPLF (Tigray People's Liberation Front) recruited priests of the Ethiopian Orthodox Church, which was generally viewed as the bastion of Ethiopian feudalism (Young 1998).

24 Most of the neoliberal reforms were premised on the ineffectiveness of state pricing policies. Consequently, it was assumed that withdrawal of the state from markets would lead to improved prices for the peasants and provide the necessary stimulus for increased production. In the event, this has not happened, partly because much of the production had been traded at world prices in parallel markets and was, therefore, unlikely to benefit from the incentives.

25 I have further argued that actual policies pursued by each of these regimes will also depend on distinctions in the strength of their civil society or political life (Mkandawire 1995).

26 One should add here the effect of the revenue base on the state's responses to rebellion, since it also affects the capacity of the state to wage war. The government's relative bargaining power issues from the resources it controls, increasing when it does not depend on resources – economic, political and otherwise – that are controlled by individuals and groups in society. More specifically, where the state's revenue is unaffected by the massive

destruction of physical infrastructure or loss of territory, the urgency of negotiations is not as compelling. The contrasts between the governments of Angola and Mozambique can partly be explained by this difference in fiscal base. In Angola the state was able to obtain vast amounts of money despite its loss of control of some of its most productive territory. In Mozambique, in contrast, the war undermined virtually all of the state's revenue bases: peasant surpluses, ports cut off from the hinterland and landlocked neighbors, the Cabora Bassa dam. Under these conditions, the FRELIMO government was compelled not only to negotiate the end of conflict, but also to abandon its ideological posture.

27   After I had finished writing this paper I ran into this remarkably similar analysis by John Saul and Colin Leys (1999: 25), who make the following observation: States that relied on peasant export production for revenue and growth had had to build robust links with the rural areas and these proved surprisingly resilient, even in the face of the acute stresses of structural adjustment, especially when centralized bureaucratism had maintained a degree of prudential control over inequality and injustice in the way state patronage was deployed. States that depended on mineral exports from foreign-run mining enclaves, however, had not needed to develop such widespread networks of support, and this proved a crucial weakness in the new situation. Moreover, mineral exports offered extremely rich and vulnerable pickings to well-armed gangs that armies were less and less able or willing to combat; indeed, in many cases the new warlords were former military officers who had struck out on their own as army pay and privileges dried up and armies disintegrated in the wake of coups, counter-coups, and civil wars. It is therefore in mineral-rich countries like Angola and Congo DRC, with less developed political links to the rural areas – and especially where extreme 'spoils politics' had already ruined the state (as in Sierra Leone and Liberia) – that warlordism, fuelled by oil and diamonds, threatens to become endemic.

28   See, for instance Mamdani (1996) and Mustapha (1992) on various forms of exploitation faced by peasants in Africa. These go beyond the 'taxes ' imposed through the marketing and exchange-rate policies of African governments.

29   In the African case, one should contrast this with national liberation movements, which fared better with respect to the responsiveness of the peasantry. In the anti-colonial struggles where taking up arms became a necessity, the 'national' issues had some local anchoring and as such were usually understood at the local level. Peasants usually shared the grievances of the nationalist movements, or were at least fertile ground for nationalist propaganda and agitation.

30   On the behavior of the RUF when stationary in some areas see Bangura (2000). In such areas they have often taxed trade and ensured that some production takes place. Under these conditions of stationariness, the rebels have behaved unusually decently.

31   Hobsbawm (1996) portrays the social rebel thus: 'He is an outsider and a rebel, a poor man who refuses to accept the normal roles of poverty, and establishes his freedom by means of the only resources within reach of the poor: strength, bravery, cunning, and determination. This draws him close to the poor: he is one of them. It sets him in opposition to the hierarchy of power, wealth and influence.'

32   The behavior of the EPLF and TPLF is such that Prendergast and Duffield (1999) go as far as arguing that the manner in which they fought the long-standing armed struggle 'calls into question the conventional wisdom on the consequences of war and famine – that war is the antithesis of development'.

33   There is evidence of forced recruitment of youths. However, in a number of cases this was with the connivance of the traditional authorities and even of parents.

34   According to Nzongola-Ntalaja (1987), 'His teachings, as found in the lecture notes of some cadres, display a successful attempt at systematisation in Marxist-Leninist-Maoist terms of the egalitarian, ascetic, communitarian and other ideas of ordinary people in revolt against exploitation, conspicuous consumption, and oppression. State employees, teachers, students, and the unemployed urban youth joined peasants in what became a profoundly popular and rural insurrection.'

35   The targeted area need not be one with diamonds, but any from which rebels can extract surplus. Somalia is also a case where defeated elements retreated to the countryside, often their home district. Siyad Barre tried to lead an assault on Mogadishu from his clan homeland before he finally fled to Kenya. Interestingly, 'Hardest hit by these two deadly circumstances was the area between the Juba River and Shebeli River further north. This

interriverine area contains the country's richest agricultural land and serves as its breadbasket. The area is inhabited by the Bantu and Benadir people who are outside the clan structure and by the Rahanwin clan ... Rahanwin and Bantu farmers were caught in the clan feud between Darod and Hawiye ... Barre's retreating troops targeted the Rahanwin for massacre. These warring clans took, then lost, and took again this farming area from each other; each time the area changed hands the supplies of food dwindled' (Natsios 1995, cited in Adam 1999: 180).

36   Eric Hobsbawm informs us that Mao Tse-Tung was strongly influenced by the great Chinese novel of social banditry, *The Water Margin*.

37   They may attract some rural youth who see arms and Nike shoes as symbols of modernity and urban promise – a point that those with a postmodernist anthropological perspective have, in my opinion, overworked.

38   The notion of 'exit' is borrowed from Albert Hirschman (1970). This is in contrast to the 'voice' option. It is interesting that Hirschman explicitly observes the ubiquity of such an option in Africa. Jeffrey Herbst (2000) also stresses this 'primacy of exit' as one of the consequences of Africa's geography. One conspicuous effect of all this is the high level of refugees and internally displaced persons generated by African civil wars. African refugees are usually running away, not from repressive regimes, but from non-governmental forces that target civilian populations.

39   An even more recent experience of RUF rebels underscores the point of Mao's 'fish'. In an article headlined 'Hungry rebels attack, burn Sierra Leone villages', the Associated Press (27 June 2000) reported: Hungry rebels attacked and burned villages in government-held areas of central and north western Sierra Leone, UN officials said Tuesday. The Revolutionary United Front rebels, who re-ignited Sierra Leone's long civil war this spring, have been going hungry because their main source of food – farmers and villagers – have mostly fled rebel-held areas. Monday's attacks followed a reported build-up of rebels near government-held towns where relief groups have been feeding refugees from the fighting. RUF fighters looted food and burned down the villages of Komrabai, Mamilla and Robis near the strategically important government town of Mile 91, 60 miles east of Freetown, the capital, UN spokeswoman Hirut Befecadu said. It was unclear if there were any casualties.

40   For a systematic discussion of RENAMO and the conflict in Mozambique, see Nilsson (1999); Vines (1992).

41   The effect of resources on strategic and organizational options for rebel movements is also illustrated by the rebel movements in Chad, where the once undernourished rebels of FROLINAT – also known as the 'thin ones of Ibrahima Abatcha' – changed strategy and behavior as Colonel Qadafi substantially improved its coffers. The resultant reduced dependence on peasant support actually eroded the discipline of the movement: 'Gone forever was the FROLINAT of the early days which advanced the claims of peasant communities and whose members behaved as 'bandits of honour'.' Alongside the collapse of the discipline with respect to the peasantry, there was also a breakdown in FROLINAT's chain of command' (Buijtenhuijs 2000: 116).

5

Fanon & the African Woman Combatant
Updating Fanon's Psychological Perspectives on Anti-Colonial & Postcolonial Wars

AARONETTE M. WHITE

Frantz Fanon, the Black psychiatrist, is upheld as a primary anti-colonial revolutionary theorist because he articulated the underlying psychological justification for people's wars among colonized peoples in Africa. However, despite the seemingly historical and political effectiveness of revolutionary violence, to what degree does Fanon's rhetoric regarding the psychological effectiveness of violence match the realities of war and its aftermath, particularly among African women soldiers today? African and African-American nationalists are inclined to canonize Frantz Fanon (Gibson 1999; Gordan et al. 1996; Jinadu 1986), while European and White American feminists and Marxist political theorists are more likely to vilify him (Arendt 1970; Nghe 1963; Sharpley-Whiting 1998). However, it is possible to achieve balance in evaluating Fanon's analysis of the debilitating psychological effects of 'colonized identity' and the role of revolutionary violence in its healthy transformation.

To his credit, Fanon acknowledged the important role women played in the Algerian revolutionary struggle. He witnessed the psychological transformation of some Algerian women during the war and wrote about their right to exist as autonomous human beings in *A Dying Colonialism* (1967a). Unlike French archival records and the Algerian Ministry of Veterans' official accounts of the war, Fanon resisted the patriarchal tendency to exclude women from history. His writings acknowledge every role Algerian women played during the national war of independence, including the revolutionary role of the sex worker ('prostitute') as a political actor (ibid.: 60). He also noted how Algerian women's participation in the armed struggle altered their 'feminine' colonized identities and family relationships in positive ways that challenged feudal, and thus patriarchal, traditions (ibid.: 99-120).

> In Algerian societies stories were told of women who in ever greater numbers suffered death and imprisonment in order that an independent Algeria might be born. It was these militant women who constituted the points of reference around which the imagination of Algerian feminine society was to be stirred to boiling point. The woman-for-marriage progressively disappeared, and gave way to the woman-for-action. The young girl was replaced by the militant ... The

woman ceased to be a complement for man. She literally forged a new place for herself by her sheer strength (ibid.: 108-9).

However, Fanon's writings on the colonized mentality and its transformation through war omit other important gendered psychopolitical factors that exacerbate the negative effects of war on African women combatants. Today, Algerian feminists criticize Fanon for overstating the relationship between national liberation and women's liberation, overestimating Algerian women's military roles as combatants, and assuming that women's military status was equal to that of men (Helie-Lucas 1988; Lazreg 1994). I believe his optimism reflects how much he underestimated the strength of patriarchy as a component of the colonized mentality of men and its relationship to nationalism, violence and militarism.

Fanon emphasized the racialized psychological effects of colonial subjugation on the colonized, referring to the resultant inferiority complex as 'the epidermalization of inferiority' (1967b: 13). Accordingly, liberation wars provide the colonized with a sense of agency and the recognition of their humanity in ways that transform a colonized identity into a revolutionary one. However, in addition to these racialized effects of colonial subjugation, I argue that gendered psychological effects and what I refer to as 'the androcentricization of inferiority' among many colonized men must also be taken into consideration, and are exacerbated by war. African men's struggles over the recognition of their *masculine* identities are just as important during the revolutionary struggle, and shape the efforts of women to achieve gender equity before, during, and after such wars. Specifically, the extremely patriarchal aspects of the mentality of colonized men – neglected by Fanon and reinforced by African 'customary law', nationalism, war and militarism – have profound implications for African women freedom fighters and the equal recognition of their basic human rights.

The 'androcentricization of inferiority' among some colonized African men results in a militarized, neo-colonized mentality following liberation wars, despite different historical periods and regardless of the type of liberation war (e.g., liberation from Europe, widespread settler colonialism, an African dictator being used as a 'puppet' by former colonial powers, or from a federation [secessionist wars] based on former colonial agreements, as with Eritrea and Ethiopia). Although Fanon theorized about anti-colonial wars of independence *per se*, the wars of Africa today are historically connected to the aftermath of colonial subjugation and the unfinished business of the former anti-colonial, independence wars. Thus, many African nationalists (and Fanon was considered an African nationalist) view postcolonial African wars as merely mutations of the former anti-colonial wars, given their complex interconnections (Mama 2001; McFadden 2005; see also MacLean, Chapter 6 and Zeleza, Introduction in this volume). The continued economic, political and military interests of the former colonial powers and their direct and indirect support of 'the opposition' in newly independent (neo-colonial) African countries make clear that the anti-colonial wars are continuing (after all, how can one define a war as 'civil, intra-state conflict' when the oppositional military force is totally trained and funded by foreign powers associated with former colonial regimes?).[1]

Therefore, 'the colonized mentality' that Fanon theorized about is directly related to 'the neo-colonized and militarized mentality' of many African men today, contrary to the romanticized revolutionary one he envisioned.

Admittedly four decades after Fanon's initial theorizing, this chapter examines the distinctively patriarchal aspects of armed struggles in African countries that intersect with racial and economic factors affecting the possibilities of gender equity and justice that African women combatants seek. Radical African feminist perspectives, a review of published first-hand accounts of the experiences of African women ex-combatants, archival research of government documents, reports by various human rights organizations, plus current psychological research on military combat support my argument regarding the patriarchal aspects of the colonized mentality and challenge some of Fanon's earlier claims. The point is not to blame Fanon for what he did not know in the 1950s, but to update what he wrote based on women combatants' war experiences.

Gendering African 'Civil,' 'Uncivil' & 'Silent' Wars

Many contemporary African women war veterans served in African liberation armies that struggled for political independence from European colonial rule (Adugna 2001; Arthur 1998; Cock 1991; Lyons 2004; Musialela 1983; Helie-Lucas 1988; Kanogo 1987; Urdang 1979). African women have also served (voluntarily and by force) in government militia and counter-insurgent paramilitary forces (including 'civilian' defense forces) during post-independence wars (Halim 1998; Hammond 1990; Houten 1998; Mugambe 2000; McKay and Mazurana 2004; Wilson 1991). However, their war stories are rarely read or heard because the existing literature on African women combatants is scattered across scholarly journals, government and human rights organizations' reports, newspaper and magazine articles, and isolated chapters in edited collections and anthologies. In addition to the scattered nature of the literature, the bulk of it is (i) disconnected from important national and international inequities that shape and reflect local realities; (ii) policy-oriented, based on internationally donor-funded development initiatives that are well-intentioned but often limited in scope; and (iii) atheoretical, partly due to the misconception that African gender development initiatives do not require rigorous intellectual analysis and evaluation (see Lewis 2004). In addition, first-hand accounts of African women combatants are often collected by war journalists, humanitarian workers, and other independent authors whose writings are largely descriptive. Although valuable in their own right, they often leave the complex effects of war on African women soldiers unaddressed.

There is also an assumption that women, African and otherwise, are simply victims of war, not active agents in war. Scholars have now documented the degree to which women have been critical to the economy of armed forces, troop morale, and their survival (De Pauw 1998; Enloe 1983; Goldstein 2001; Moser and Clark 2001). Current research reveals African women's strong sense of political agency and how they enter fighting forces to (i) demonstrate their support for revolutionary ideology, (ii) gain protection for self and/or family from local or state violence, (iii) avoid problems in the home, (iv) earn money, (v) fulfill compulsory service, (vi) improve education options and (vii) improve career options (Keitetsi 2002; Lazreg 1994; Lyons 2004; Veale 2005).

Women also provide 'unofficial' and thus unacknowledged military support to wars as domestic servants, porters, messengers, intelligence officers, disseminators of propaganda, combat trainers, sex workers and recruiters of other women and children military personnel (Adugna 2001; Goldman 1982; Kanogo 1987; Turshen and Twagiramariya 1998). Moreover, the number of girls and women in all fighting forces is routinely underestimated, given the emphasis on their roles as 'sexual slaves,' 'wives of commanders', 'prostitutes', and 'camp followers'; in particular, use of the term 'camp follower' obscures the roles women play during war (Enloe 1983; McKay and Mazurana 2004). Furthermore, when actual sex workers are involved in war, their multiple roles and political commitments as spies, assassins, decoys, and in some instances combat fighters are understated (McKay and Mazurana 2004; Kanogo 1987; Kesby 1996).

Silence surrounds the military participation of African women also because many are recruited or forced to join very young, in violation of the United Nations recommendation that enlisted soldiers be aged 18 or more (UNICEF 1997). Recent reports indicate that African girl soldiers served specifically as combat fighters in 11 African countries between 1990 and 2003 (McKay and Mazurana 2004: 25). Countries' efforts to conceal their breach of international law regarding the use of child soldiers results in many girls and women being unaccounted for after years of military service.

Therefore, African women and girls have been some of the most courageous and fierce fighters in armed struggles. However, we need to be careful not to romanticize their lives (e.g., the posters that displayed 'a liberated African woman with her baby in one hand and her rifle in the other'), lest we fail to remember where power really lies in military organizations. The words of Thandi Modise, South African National Congress member of Parliament and former Umkhonto we Sizwe guerrilla commander, highlight previously overlooked gendered factors that have affected African women combatants:

> Women face far more difficulties in going underground ... they have to contend with the traditionally strict attitudes in the society towards women – that we should stay at home and have children ... even though that sort of thinking is challenged by the liberation army not all comrades have unlearned their previous conditioning ... in becoming a guerrilla, there is a strong possibility that you will lose your family, your home, and all security ... men are expected to be away from home earning the money or protecting our nation ... they know that whatever happens to them, their wives will still look after the children (Curnow 2000: 39–40)

Missing from the literature are analytical approaches grounded explicitly in radical African feminist scholarship and the experiences of women cultural workers and fighters like Thandi Modise who played significant roles in shaping and challenging European colonialism. Radical African feminists and some Western feminist scholars argue that we must examine power relations between women and men as well as how 'femininity' and 'masculinity' are constructed and re-inscribed during revolutionary movements. In other words, in order to understand the factors that placed African women at risk of becoming disproportionately *disempowered* during various anti-colonial struggles – particularly in the role of combat fighters – we must also understand if and how African men were disproportionately *empowered* by the same factors. Both perspectives are crucial in assessing the contemporary relevance of Fanon's theories regarding the therapeutic role of revolutionary violence, and help to disentangle the rhetoric and assumptions about violence propagated by the state as well as liberation armies (Enloe 2004a). Radical African feminist perspectives also reflect the need as well as the potential for international feminist solidarity when resisting global militarization.

Highlighting the Works of Radical African Feminists

We must reject the argument that Africa is not ready for radical feminism ... our sexuality has a whole lot to do with women's oppression. We can see it in ideologies such as 'heteronormativity,' 'marriagenormativity,' and 'mothernormativity.' (Sylvia Tamale, Ugandan feminist, 2006: 40)

Radical feminists in the Movement are not going to go away, and no one can tell me that the African Women's Movement is only for moderate and conservative women; not when I work 25 hours a day in that Movement. So, the ideological differences have to be confronted. (Patricia McFadden, Swazi feminist, 1997: 5).

Not all feminists, whether they describe themselves as 'Western', 'Third World' or 'African', share a commitment to *radical* critiques of society. Like North American feminisms, African feminist thought is heterogeneous (Mikell 1997; Nnaemeka 2004; Salo 2001). This chapter selectively highlights the works of *radical* African feminists, while simultaneously including the works of relevant Western feminist scholars. The term 'radical African feminist' is used here in the historical sense, not as a biological (essentialist) description and not to promote divisiveness. Rather, it refers to feminists whose theorizing grew primarily out of their experiences with independent and postcolonial movements in Africa, and who dispel myths regarding the inevitability of African women's oppression, consider diversity among African women across various ethnic, national and sexual locations, and challenge the Western misconception of 'one essential' African culture (Lewis 2004; Meena 1992; Salo 2001; Thiam 1995). Their perspectives fit squarely within a history of international 'Black' radicalism characterized by an opposition to 'all forms of oppression, including class exploitation (Wilson 1991), racism (Kabira and Nzioki 1993), patriarchy (Thiam 1995), homophobia (Potgieter 1997; Tamale 2003), anti-immigration prejudice (McFadden 2005), and imperialism (El Saadawi 2004)' (Black Radical Congress, 1998).

Most important, critical African feminists challenge binary formulations and dichotomous thinking that oversimplify African realities and the messiness of war. They underscore frequently neglected interconnections, contesting either/or conceptualizations such as 'anti-colonial vs postcolonial conflict,' 'traditional' versus 'modern' African societies, soldiers vs. civilians, freedom fighters vs terrorists, rebels vs. murderers, victims vs perpetrators, 'just wars' vs 'dirty wars,' and 'state' vs 'individual' violence (El Saadawi 2004; Halim 1998; Honwana 2000; Mama 2001).

Together, radical African feminists and some Western feminist scholars argue that we must move away from an exclusive focus on women's disadvantage and examine power relations between women and men and how the gender identities between the two are socially constructed and manipulated before, during and after the war. In addition, radical African feminist perspectives on war connect the realities of local African women to the realities facing women globally – particularly those women who join military forces and who, while not officially enlisted, are affected by the spread of militaristic ideology and the expansion of the power of military institutions. Their views are uniquely relevant for analyzing and contextualizing Frantz Fanon's psychological perspectives on political violence and the spread of wars today.

Gendering Fanon's Psychological Perspectives on War
Although writing on Fanon emphasizes his social and political thought, he was first and foremost a psychiatrist. His psychological works were published in psychiatric, medical and political journals, and his books incorporated psychological dimensions to complement, illustrate and concretize the macro-social experiences he sought to explain and transform (Bulhan 1985). Thus, placing Fanon in his professional context enhances our understanding of the questions he asked and the psychological theorizing that runs through his better-known works (Fanon 1967a, 1967b, 1967c, 1968).

Frantz Fanon, grandson of a former slave, was born in 1925 in the former French colony of Martinique.[2] After specializing in psychiatry at the University of Lyon in France, he became clinical director of the largest psychiatric hospital in Algeria in 1953. During this period, the Algerian struggle for national independence from France was gaining mass support. Fanon argued that the French used violence to usurp Algerian land, deny Algerians full citizenship, and denounce their religious and cultural practices; this violence had profound psychological implications. Lacking the economic and military power necessary to institutionalize their own cultural values and beliefs, many indigenous Algerians – after generations of colonial oppression – accepted what the French colonizers described as their 'racial inferiority' and repressed any revolutionary counterviolent urges. Fanon calls this debilitating psychological capitulation the 'epidermalization of inferiority' (1967b: 13), characterized by fear and the adoption of a variety of behaviors to avoid direct confrontation with the source of their fear, the colonizer. Rather than strike out directly, the colonized repress their counterviolent desires for justice. The cumulative impact of oppression and repressed urges results in the colonized turning their anger, fear and frustration inward, resulting in alcoholism, depression, stress-induced physical ailments and intracommunal homicides (1968: 54). Conversely, Fanon also observed how Algerians who developed a political consciousness were able to use violence to transform their colonized identity into a revolutionary, nationalist one. By redirecting repressed urges outward and towards the appropriate target (the colonizer), the power of the colonizer is demystified and self-confidence is restored, promoting a strong collective (nationalist) identity among the colonized. Fanon notes that when the colonized begin to fully identify themselves with their 'wretchedness' – realizing they have nothing to lose, given the daily erosion of their lives under colonial conditions – revolutionary violence becomes pivotal in transforming their previously self-destructive identity (1968: 35-106). Liberation wars allow the colonized to regain their sense of agency and dignity and become creators of history, rather than remaining victims of historical conquest. They learn that dignity and equality are more important than life itself, and hence become willing to risk their lives in war for these values. As a result, counterviolence ultimately purges the colonized of their fear of the colonizer and, paradoxically, restores their humanity, after experiencing the dehumanizing conditions of colonial subjugation. Fanon boldly states, 'Violence is a cleansing force. It frees the native from his inferiority complex and from his despair and inaction; it makes him fearless and restores his self-respect' (1968: 94). Furthermore, he views the violence of the colonized as 'humanistic,' given its ability to restore balance in everyone's perceptions (e.g., the colonized overcome inferiority complexes and the colonizers overcome superiority complexes). Accordingly, he argues, this balance cannot be 'granted' by the colonizer; it must be fought for by the colonized.

Did Fanon use psychological jargon merely to romanticize violence and glorify it for its own sake, as his critics suggest? A series of clinical cases in the last section of *The Wretched of the Earth* casts serious doubt on what may be an unfair and oversimplified reading of his work by critics like Hannah Arendt (1970) and others (see Bulhan 1985 for an overview of Fanon's major critics).[3] Series A deals with reactive psychosis, e.g., a traumatized Algerian fighter whose wife was tortured and raped by the French authorities following the discovery of his guerrilla activities and a French police interrogator and torturer who ended up torturing his wife and children (Fanon 1968: 254–70). Series B cases have forensic and clinical implications, e.g., children murdering children during the war and how children on both sides cope with the murder of their parents (see Bulhan 1985: 203 and Fanon (1968: 270–79). Series C describes the psychological reactions of torture victims and the various techniques of torture (1968: 280–89). Series D includes psychosomatic disorders experienced by war veterans (1968: 289-310).

The cases reveal Fanon's sensitivity to the brutality of violence and its potentially corrosive effects on the colonizer and the colonized (Bulhan 1985). Yet, the cases also show the degree to which Fanon believed that politically conscious and goal-directed violent confrontation by the colonized against their colonizers was unavoidable and – *despite* the risks – could have profoundly rehabilitative psychological effects. Thus, he concluded that colonial violence was so great and so impervious to reason that only violence in return would transform the oppressive order. The colonizer understands and depends on violence; therefore, 'Violence alone, violence committed by the people, violence organized and educated by its leaders, makes it possible for the masses to understand social truths and gives the key to them' (1968: 147).

Fanon's psychological perspectives were influenced by the master-slave paradigm presented in Hegel's *The Phenomenology of the Mind* (1966: 229–40). Hegel's influential ideas on the dynamics of bondage (also referred to as Hegel's master-slave dialectic) argued that man becomes conscious of himself only through recognition by the other.[4] However, when this desire for recognition is denied, a conflict and a struggle ensues. The person who attains recognition without reciprocating becomes the master, and the other who recognizes but is not recognized in return becomes the slave. Fanon reconceptualized and extended Hegel's paradigm by highlighting the racial superiority complex of the White colonizer and the inferiority complex of the Black colonized. By demanding that the colonized not only recognize their colonizers but also serve them through their labor, White colonizers stubbornly refuse to acknowledge even the slightest possible humanity of the Black people they have colonized. Efforts of the colonized to create reciprocal recognition by reasoning with their colonizers are futile and meet with piecemeal attempts at reform followed by increased repression (Bulhan 1985). Thus, violent confrontation becomes necessary for mutual recognition.

Fanon died from leukemia less than a year before Algeria won its independence, and did not witness the challenges that faced it after the war.[5] In my reanalysis of Fanon's psychological perspectives, the colonized mentality of many African men under European rule can best be described by a combined approach, taking both race and gender into account. Unlike Fanon, however, I believe that some African men are able to resist these psychological processes, due to current empirical research that suggests racial and gender identities are multidimensional (Fischer et al. 2000; Jackson and Smith 1999; Sellers et al. 1997). Thus, not all African men internalize this mentality. However, the diversity among African men is beyond the scope of this chapter and the assumption is that *most* men do succumb psychologically.

The following sections address Fanon's underestimation of (i) the extreme distortion of gender relations during the colonial period, which relied on violence, European versions of patriarchy, and manipulated versions of precolonial African patriarchal customs that produced 'African customary law'; (ii) patriarchal nationalisms due to the nature of wars, militarism, and military forces, which mobilize and sustain gendered relations during revolutions; and (iii) African men's resistance to transforming entrenched neo-colonized and militarized mentalities that support the militarization of postcolonial African states specifically, and global militarization generally.

Pre-War Realities:
The Differential Worth of the Wretched

The decision to become a guerrilla is not one that a woman can take lightly. She has so much more to lose than a man. (Marie Jose Arthur, FRELIMO woman soldier, Mozambique, 1998)

Two phenomena that shape the pre-war colonized mentality of many African men, but to which Fanon gave insufficient weight, are the colonial invention of African 'customary law' and the gendered, patriarchal under-pinnings of most nationalisms. Precolonial social divisions among African peoples (often a complex mix of generation, genealogy, gender and geography) were exploited, racialized, and gendered in extreme ways by Europeans during colonization (Lazreg 1994; Meena 1992; Tamale 1999). Thus, despite geopolitical, ethnic and national differences, as African feminist Amina Mama (1997: 47) states, 'being conquered by the colonizing powers; being culturally and materially subjected to a 19th century European racial hierarchy and its gender politics; being indoctri-nated into all-male European administrative systems and the insidious paternalism of their new religious and educational systems; and facing the continuous flow of material and human resources from Africa to Europe' reflect the shared experiences of most African peoples.

As products of Victorian social mores, most European men did not view women of any race as equal to men; thus, their racial bigotry only compounded their low opinion of African women as they quickly replaced African versions of patriarchy with their own (Kabira and Nzioki 1993; Mama 1996; Schmidt 1991; Tamale 1999). Colonists generally sought to subordinate African men under European rule in order to exploit their cheap labor; however, facilitating their own economic interests also required appeasing chiefs, headmen (e.g., heads of wards, villages and lineages), and other important elder men (Mama 1996; Schmidt 1991; Tamale 1999). These African men experienced loss of status and material resources as a result of forced resettlement, imposed taxation, and the disruption of traditional territorial lineages linked to land ownership, which led to deep resentments. Rather than destroying precolonial African male authority entirely, the colonizers strategically maintained some semblance of law and order by allowing African men to retain varying degrees of authority in their homes and villages (Banda 2005; Mama 1996; Schmidt 1991).

African 'customary law', the result of this strategic compromise, was constructed by colonialists in consultation with the chiefly elite and elder African men of importance (Chanock 1989; Cock 1991; Schmidt 1991). It represented written versions of precolonial African customary practices, revised African practices based upon newly imposed European colonial policies, and created entirely new practices that resulted from the clash of European and African cultures (Bourdillon 1975; Chanock 1989; Mbilinyi 1988). These invented rules were (i) less flexible than the original precolonial customs; (ii) invariably favored fathers, husbands and sons over mothers, wives, and daughters; (iii) were designed to bolster old bases of power and establish new ones among African men; and (iv) were a collaborative means of promoting European interests, appeasing an otherwise antagonistic group of powerful African men by allowing them some familiar degree of control over African women (Bourdillon 1975; Chanock 1989; Schmidt 1991). However, despite the opportunity to reassert their masculinity in the private sphere, most African men were rendered politically powerless under colonialism by the exploitation of their labor. This racial, gendered and economically-related subordination, in turn, led African men to express their grievances in newly formed nationalist organizations designed to gain their independence as *Africans* and as *men* from European control.

The status of African women under colonial subjugation was particularly diminished under newly evolved fusions of European and African authority (Kabira and Nzioki 1991; Mama 1996; Tamale 1999). African women resisted these laws through protests, creative entrepreneurship (e.g., beer brewing), militia activity, relocation to urban areas, and even religious conversion and commitment to convent life (Adugna 2001; El Saadawi 2004; Kanogo 1987; Lazreg 1994; Schmidt 1991). Yet, their legalized status as minors and their lack of independent access to land, housing or wage employment made effective resistance difficult. Colonial efforts to keep African women in rural areas and in the private, domestic domain by allowing many African men the opportunity to remain petty chiefs in their homes contributed greatly to an androcentric colonized mentality and patriarchal practices among African men. Unlike many African men, African women's opportunities to express – and act on – their gender-specific grievances are drastically hampered by their isolation from public spaces as legal minors and their related absence from early meetings and decisions regarding the leadership of revolutionary organizations (particularly their absence from the circle of intellectuals drafting position papers and advising the organization on policies; see Lazreg 1994: 139). Thus, sociocultural and political processes during colonization are intimately tied to how nationalisms are constructed. They shape the degree of commitment to gender equity and gender-specific political education during pre-war mobilization, the liberation war itself, and gender relations after it (Arthur 1998; Halim 1998; Kesby 1996; Lazreg 1994; Mugambe 2000). As a result, nationalism is gendered and often harbors a distinctly patriarchal thrust and corresponding agenda.[6]

Nationalism can be a powerful, politically mobilizing and identity-shaping tool for people whose way of life has been demeaned and controlled by others (West 1997). However, nationalism has often enabled African men, regardless of status, to reclaim both the 'imaginary' and the 'real' status they had prior to colonization, and induces nostalgia for a romanticized past 'when they controlled the land and the women' without any interference from European men (Lazreg 1994; Meena 1992; Maitse 2000). African men were clearly aware that African women's status as *Africans* and as *women* had also been negatively affected; thus, Fanon, the FLN, and many other revolutionary movements mobilized African women to join armed struggles with rhetoric equating national liberation with their liberation as women:

> An article in the FLN newspaper claims, 'The Algerian woman does not need emancipation. She is already free because she takes part in the liberation of her country of which she is the soul, the heart, and the glory' (Lazreg 1994: 130).

> Samora Machel, President of FRELMO, the Front for the Liberation of Mozambique, emphasized: 'The liberation of women is a fundamental necessity for the Revolution, the guarantee of its continuity and the precondition for its victory' (Isaacman and Isaacman 1984: 174).

Amilcar Cabral, President of PAIGC, the Party for the Independence of Guinea-Bissau and Cape Verde, insisted that party mobilizers understand and accept the need for the liberation of women and stood behind a PAIGC directive of the early 1960s which stated, 'Defend the rights of women, respect and make others respect them (whether as children, young girls, or adults) (Urdang 1979: 124).

The African National Congress's (ANC) most famous 1955 South African document – The Freedom Charter – states, 'Every man and woman shall have the right to vote and stand as a candidate for all bodies which make the laws' (Cock 1991: 47–8).

The 1977 National Democratic Programme of the Eritrean People's Liberation Front (EPLF) assured 'women full rights of equality with men in politics, economy, and social life as well as equal pay for equal work' (Wilson 1991: 161).

The South West Africa's People Organization (SWAPO) spoke of Namibia's 1976 political programme aimed 'to combat all reactionary tendencies of individualism, tribalism, nepotism, racism, sexism, chauvinism, and regionalism' (Becker 1995: 44).

Robert Mugabe, current President of Zimbabwe and former leader of the Zimbabwe African National Union (ZANU) argued that 'the national struggle, therefore, especially at its highest level, when it became the armed national struggle, became as much a process towards the liberation of the nation as towards the emancipation of the woman' (Lyons 2004: 47).

Revolutionary rhetoric regarding women's equality was similar across various African liberation movements, due to socialist influences that shaped political objectives during the early days of the movement and the close proximity of their clandestine military training camps that influenced their ideologies about revolutionary war.[7] Thus, despite different historical periods and the type of liberation war, most revolutionary rhetoric regarded women's emancipation as a part of national liberation. Radical African feminists, however, have argued that African national liberation and African women's liberation movements are related, but they are not identical social processes (Lazreg 1994; Mama 2000; Maitse 2000). The assumption that Fanon and other African revolutionaries also make is that women's identities are at the heart of any gender struggles during anti-imperial revolutions. However, recent scholarship suggests that African men's struggles over their own masculine identities are just as important during liberation wars and shape the efforts of women to achieve gender equity before, during and after such wars (Campbell 2003; Mama 2000; Meena 1992; McFadden 2005).

Despite the historical period in which he was writing, Fanon did not totally ignore the gendered aspects of nationalism. However, they were sorely understated. Fanon attributed any narrowness within nationalism mainly to class issues, in particular the myopia of the national bourgeoisie (1968: 148–205). Nevertheless, he warned the colonized not to perpetuate 'the feudal tradition which holds sacred the superiority of the masculine over the feminine' in their efforts to create the new government (ibid.: 202). Despite this warning, Fanon's failure to address the gendered struggles of African men under colonial subjugation as thoroughly as their race and class struggles contributed to his excessively optimistic expectations regarding gender relations during and after the Algerian war. The andro-centric aspects of African men's colonized mentality may also explain why the active roles African women played during the war failed to culminate in gender parity after it.[8] Androcentric mentalities are further entrenched by the intricate relationships among patriarchy, nationalism, war and militarism.

Active War Realities: Shooting Democracy in the Foot

The patriarchal nature of war, nationalism and militarism appear to perpetuate violent injustices and entrench the colonized mentalities Fanon predicted they would eradicate (Campbell 2003; Mama 1997; de Waal 2002; Ochieng 2002). An androcentric, colonized mentality among many African men, shaped sharply during the colonial period, is further reinforced during the revolutionary war period as the nationalist conscious-ness becomes 'militarized' through values imparted by the armed forces (Cock 1991; Enloe 2004b; de Waal 2002). Military forces as social institu-tions are not gender-neutral; together, the ideology of militarism and the military organizations it produces, interact, mobilize and construct gender identities in ways that promote patriarchal ideology and practices (Cock 1991; de Waal 2002; Enloe 2004b). Militarized patriarchal ideology and practices work against democratic values associated with revolutionary transformation; thus, revolutionary parties that engage in armed struggle often end up 'shooting democracy in the foot' (Mama 2000: 3).

First-hand accounts of anti-colonial African women combatants suggest that military values often undermine their sense of agency, in particular because such values disproportionately increase their vulnerability to gender-specific human rights abuses by the enemy as well as alleged comrades. These abuses include rape, torture, brutal abductions, forced pregnancies, forced sex work and other forms of sexual harassment, sexual molestation and sexual discrimination. Understanding war involves under-standing militarism and how it shapes military forces. Thus, military values require further analysis in order to understand how Fanon may have overestimated the psychologically transformative power of violent struggles among the colonized, in particular, women.

As an ideology, militarism accepts violence as characteristic of courage, virility, chivalry, superiority and ideal masculinity (Enloe 2004b; de Waal 2002; Mama 2000, 2001). In addition, authoritarianism (power based on absolute authority, hierarchy and obedience) and the notion of combat as 'men's work' promote narrow, hypermasculine views of manhood (e.g., manhood as aggressive, competitive, stoic and the opposite of anything feminine) and a sexual division of labor, that, together, work against the equal recognition of women by men in military forces. Authoritarianism, and thus any effective military organization, works against democratic values associated with civil society, such as free expression, consensus, egalitarianism and transparency in decision-making (de Waal 2002). Such authoritarian values are important to military organizations because war is about gaining and exercising power, and combat is the manifestation of power at its most brutal and uncompromising (de Waal 2002). Authoritarianism molds a soldier who will obey orders without thinking and will internalize unquestioning loyalty to his superiors in ways that minimize the chance that he will flinch in combat (de Waal 2002). Rather than increasing a soldier's sense of agency, military values work against autonomy among soldiers, regardless of gender, in ways that foster blind compliance.

In addition to the authoritarianism that pervades the military as a social institution, the stereotype of the 'super macho combat soldier' perpetuates hypermasculine attitudes and values that also work against a male soldier's recognition of a woman soldier (or any woman) as his equal. South African feminist sociologist Jacklyn Cock (1991) elaborates: 'War does not challenge women to prove that they are women, whereas wars have been historically symbolized as the touchstone of "manliness". The concept of war as this proving ground of manliness has centered on the notion of combat. Combat is understood to be the ultimate test of masculinity, and thus crucial to the ideological structure of patriarchy' (1991: 235–6).

Interestingly, guerrilla warfare tactics in most of Africa's revolutionary wars do not rely on hand-to-hand combat. Instead, they often rely on ambushing patrols, sabotaging communication and transportation lines, and making hit-and-run attacks against enemy posts – tasks that women are fully capable of carrying out (Cock 1991; Goldman 1982; Goldstein 2001). Yet, the myth of combat as 'men's work' dies hard; even with today's technologically sophisticated war weaponry, the 'presumption that a man is unproven in his manhood until he has engaged in collective, violent, and physical struggle against someone categorized as the enemy' is widespread (Enloe 1983: 13). Moreover, Fanon's perspectives on war deeply entail such masculinist overtones.

Masculinist notions also serve as powerful tools for making men into soldiers because military forces also encourage aggressiveness, competitiveness, the censure of emotional expression, and images of weak soldiers as effeminate (Cock 1991; Enloe 1983; Goldstein 2001). Combat readiness, male bonding and social cohesion are achieved through military training by emphasizing the 'otherness' of both women and the enemy: women represent the weaker sex, home and hearth, and the need to be protected, while the enemy represents the weaker force to be dominated and conquered (Cock 1991; Enloe 1983; Goldstein 2001). Given the interactive relationship among militarism, military forces as social institutions, and combat as the test of a man's masculinity, women are almost always excluded from combat, whether in conventional or guerrilla armies (Cock 1991; Goldstein 2001; Goldman 1982).[9]

The Sexual Division of Labor: Blurring Private and Public Spheres
Although wars have produced some powerful new identities for women, military forces remain distinctively patriarchal institutions by maintaining a sexual division of labor. Most women occupy subordinate positions resembling stereotypical female employment in the civilian sector (e.g., clerks, nurses, social workers, cooks). By keeping women out of top levels of policy and decision-making roles and most forms of combat, military

forces simply re-inscribe and expand traditionally gendered roles, instead of fundamentally challenging patriarchy (Cock 1991; Enloe 1983; Goldstein 2001).

First-hand accounts of African women combatants emphasize how the men did so out of desperation and necessity, not enlightenment or feminist consciousness:

> When the women first joined [the Eritrean Patriotic Liberation Front, EPLF], the men thought, 'What can they do, these women?' Then the men saw what women could do – in the clinics and as dressers and at the front line. They saw them fight, take prisoners, capture tanks; they saw them when they lost their legs, their eyes... (Chu Chu, EPLF guerrilla soldier, Eritrea) (Wilson 1991: 98–9).
>
> There was strong opposition to our participation in combat because that was against our tradition. We started a campaign explaining why we also had to fight ... we as women were even more oppressed than men and therefore had the right as well as the will and the strength to fight. We insisted on our military training and being given weapons. (FRELIMO woman guerrilla soldier, Mozambique) (Issacman and Issacman 1984: 158)

Women who are channeled into 'masculine' military roles, including combat, are seen as exceptions, and their activities in these capacities are often interpreted as temporary and as 'helping the men' (Isaacman and Isaacman 1984; Lazreg 1994; Lyons 2004). Therefore, even though African women in many revolutionary armies were taught to use weapons, they were often deployed in supportive roles, were ordered to fight only when necessary, and often were assigned secondary roles as cooks, child-care providers, laundry workers and porters. Algerian feminist Marie-Almee Helie-Lucas (1988:175–6) notes,

> Since 'there is no humble task in the revolution' we did not dispute the roles we had ... what makes me angry, in retrospect, is not the mere fact of confining women to their place, but the brain-washing which did not allow us, young women, to even think in terms of questioning the women's place. And what makes me even more angry is to witness the replication of this situation in various places in the world where national liberation struggles are still taking place – to witness women engaged in liberation fronts covering the misbehavings of their fellow men, hiding, in the name of national solidarity and identity, crime which will be perpetuated after the liberation.

The sexual division of labor and the secondary roles of African women combatants have been documented across various countries and armies in Africa including Algeria (Lazreg 1994), Ethiopia (Adugna 2001), Guinea-Bissau (Urdang 1979), Kenya (Kanogo 1987), Mozambique, Sierra Leone and Northern Uganda (McKay and Mazurana 2004), Somalia (van Houten 1998), Southern Sudan (Halim 1998), Zimbabwe (Lyons 2004), and South Africa (Cock 1991). Thus, although revolutionary rhetoric suggests that every role in the revolution is *valued*, every role is certainly not *equally* valued.

African feminist historian Tabitha Kanogo explains how women who took part in the anti-colonial war in Kenya struggled to counter men's stereotypes of them. However, male fighters continued to view them as sexual objects:

Since traditionally women did not participate in warfare, their status and roles were initially 'highly ambiguous' and tended to shift as the battle lengthened. At the beginning, they were allocated domestic chores, including fetching firewood, cooking, washing, and cleaning. In certain camps, male leaders were each allowed to choose a woman... who as well as seeing to the other needs of the leader was also expected to meet his sexual needs. Women were induced to fulfill such 'tasks' for 'the good of the cause.' As one Mau Mau woman stated, 'Generally, I would think of sleeping with a man as an individual concern. Here, it seems to me that the leaders consider this as part of the woman's duty in the [Mau Mau] society. I believe that since I could not do any other better service to my people, I would then willingly accept it as my contribution to society' (1987: 87–8).

Although pre-war gender norms of behavior instructed most African women to be demure, congenial, faithful and to resist men's overtures, the military camps created different mores for women as well as men. In some instances, communal living patterns in the military camps and the stress of war led to relaxing some traditional gender norms. This, in turn, served as a catalyst for the creation of marriage codes that challenged African customary law (Hammond 1990; Lazreg 1994; Wilson 1991). However, most marriages among combatants highlighted how practices lagged behind revolutionary rhetoric. As one FRELIMO woman combatant lamented:

While many of the male guerrillas accept the fact that women had the right to fight, within the household our husbands continued to treat us as if they were still 'petty chiefs'...we women were still expected to fetch water, clean house, prepare dinner and take care of the children as well as fight for the nation...in general, they didn't do anything in the home and we did not demand that they do anything (Isaacman and Isaacman 1984: 168).

For some women, regardless of the incongruence between rhetoric and reality, marriage, especially to a commanding officer, was one way to survive military camp life:

I met the father of my first two children during the war. He was a commander, and I got with him because he was single and so was I, and I thought, I had better get hooked with someone so the other men wouldn't put pressure on me... (Lyons 2004: 195).

Although some comrades created stable unions, the emphasis on nationalism and newly militarized masculine identities, coupled with revolutionary militancy and an absolute commitment to the struggle, provided many male combatants with a convenient excuse for irresponsibility toward the mothers of their children and the children themselves (Kesby 1996; Lyons 2004; Shikola 1998). Some commanders had as many as fifteen or eighteen children (Shikola 1998: 143).[10] Yet, many African armies did not promote contraception as a matter of policy because it was expensive, access to it was unreliable, and they associated it with prostitution, and in some cases, with an attempt by colonizers to reduce the number of Africans (Lyons 2004). Pregnant women were often sent to special camps stigmatized as a place for prostitutes (Lyons 2004). Many men denied paternity; when a pregnant woman was sent to the camp, this created 'a vacuum for the guy', he would 'get involved with some other new recruit', and end up with 'maybe three or four babies' in the women's camp (Lyons

2004: 201). The official policy of most African armies *not* to promote contraception or abortion created additional vulnerabilities on women soldiers regarding sex, contraceptives, pregnancy, birth and parenting. These same policies, however, expanded men's autonomy and contributed to counter-revolutionary hypermasculine attitudes and sexual practices in the camps. Women combatants' ability to achieve mutual recognition is highly improbable under such circumstances.

Torture, Rape, and Abduction by 'Friends' and Foes
In addition to a sexual division of labor, military forces engaged in Africa's wars reinforced patriarchal values and practices through the use of torture, the abuse of military rank to justify rape, and the abduction of civilians. Some torture techniques were also used against men; however, the same technique had different meanings for women and men. Moreover, specific techniques targeted women's sexuality. Male interrogators relied on deep-rooted cultural concepts of a woman's shame and honor to break women combatants. Thus, most women were raped when taken prisoner by enemy forces as a South African woman fighter confirms:

> I don't know what was the worst in jail, the constant threat of being raped or the actual incident itself! Women were made to stand the whole day with blood [from their menstrual cycles and the rapes] flowing down and drying on their legs. Did they gain strength from looking at [and] asking us to drink our own blood? (Krog 2001: 204–5).

In addition to sleep deprivation, physical beatings, and electric shocks to genitals, male guards have engaged in humiliating body searches and vaginal examinations, inserted foreign objects including rats into women's vaginas, repeatedly raped women prisoners and forced women to have intercourse with other prisoners for the 'entertainment' of prison personnel (Lazreg 1994; Goldblatt and Meintjes 1998; Krog 2001). Women's fallopian tubes have been flooded with gushing water, often resulting in their inability to bear children (Goldblatt and Meintjes 1998). Most women combatants are ashamed to speak about these incidents, so first-person accounts are few, and are often kept brief and confidential. Psychological reports verify how these forms of violence traumatize rather than transform and leave enduring emotional scares on soldiers that political independence after such wars cannot erase (Goldblatt and Meintjes 1998; Krog 2001).

Most egregious, however, are repetitive testimonies by women indicating that the sexual torture and abuse of women combatants were not confined to the activities of enemy forces. Revolutionary armies too have engaged in horrific human rights abuses including rape, torture and brutal abductions (Cock 1991; Lyons 2004; McKay and Mazurana 2004). Rufaro, abducted from her school by guerrilla soldiers of the Zimbabwe People's Revolutionary Army seeking recruits, became committed to the armed struggle after being 'politically educated'. She later insisted on being trained for combat:

> I went to the Botswana/Zimbabwe border and crossed the river with over 200 children from the school. The guerrillas took us.... When we reached Zambia we were taken to Victory Camp. This camp was used by MPLA [Movement for the Popular Liberation of Angola] freedom fighters. We found other children from the

> Manama Mission, who were captured by the same guerrillas who captured us...
> We used to cry saying, 'Why are you discriminating us from men. Men are
> training in the camps, you just keep us here in Victory Camp... Please we want
> to train as soldiers (Lyons 2004: 122).

Most abducted students were held against their will. Abductions occur
on both sides as the war escalates and human resources are needed (Halim
1998; Kanogo 1987; Lyons 2004; Keitetsi 2002). After Mozambique's
independence from the Portuguese, FRELIMO, the former revolutionary
army, officially became the government army. Interviews with former girl
soldiers who fought in the civil war that erupted after independence
confirmed the following report:

> Throughout the civil war in Mozambique (1976–92), young women and girls
> were involved in fighting for the government forces of FRELIMO and the rebel
> group RENAMO. Although RENAMO made considerably greater use of children
> in its forces than FRELIMO, in 1975 FRELIMO began recruiting and abducting
> girls into their forces. FRELIMO recruiters with buses arrived at schools and
> asked girls to volunteer for the military; when few volunteered, a number of girls
> were rounded up and forced onto the buses, despite protests from the teachers
> and the girls. This process was repeated at a number of schools until the buses
> were full. The girls were then brought to and held at the Mowamba military base
> (McKay and Mazurana 2004: 107).

Abductions are the antithesis of the human agency Fanon predicted.

Among their own comrades, women combatants have been subjected to
forced marriage, combat duty as well as sexual duty, and sexual politics
that require marrying a commanding officer in order to rise through the
ranks (Halim 1998; Kanogo 1987; Lyons 2004; McKay and Mazurana
2004). These double standards make clear that, regardless of their training
and status as fighters, women are primarily expected to care for, serve, and
comfort men (Cock 1991; Halim 1998). From the beginning of her military
training and throughout her years as a military commander, Thandi
Modise knew that she had to protect herself from the South African
apartheid enemy forces as well as her own comrades. Modise recalled fights
among male soldiers as to whether the women soldiers should be used
sexually when the male soldiers were bored and felt sexually frustrated in
the isolated military camps; several incidences of sexual molestation and
harassment were ignored by the ANC leadership (Curnow 2000). Girl
soldiers were particularly at risk of rape. The African girls and women who
fought on the front lines were often the poorest, youngest, most illiterate,
and thus most vulnerable to such human rights abuses (ibid.; Lyons 2004;
Kanogo 1987). Margaret Dongo, former ZANLA guerrilla soldier and the
first female and independent member of the Zimbabwean Parliament
recalled:

> When I got to the camps, I was asked who I was, to surrender what little,
> whatever I had, and choose a name for myself, a pseudonym...From here, I am
> cutting the story short. I am not talking about the experience I got in those days.
> It was very nasty ... And then I went to the barracks – shelter – thinking I would
> have somewhere nice to sleep, only to find someone say, 'Well there is your grass
> ... so you get this grass to make your mattress ... and you can make your bed ...
> I had to learn to live with it. Nobody forced me to come. ... I had to adjust, and

I did adjust...We could stay for two weeks without enough food, feeding on water or skimmed milk (Lyons 2004: 115–16).

Later in the interview, Margo admitted to being raped by a comrade. 'China,' a former 13-year-old girl soldier of the Ugandan National Resistance Army, recalls:

We had many brutal officers. I remember one whose name was Suicide. He was a war hero, a mad one. Suicide had the power to do anything. He could rape civilian and army girls and nothing would happen to him because he was a good soldier... We female soldiers had to offer sex to more than five officers in one unit. Nearly every evening an officer would come and order you to report to his place, usually at 9 pm. It would have been a little easier on us if it had been one or two afandes (officers) but every day of the week we had to sleep with different afandes against our will! If we refused our afandes' orders, we would have to say goodbye to visiting our families. On top of that, the abuse would turn violent and we would get extra duties... We lived in fear all day thinking about 9 pm... Our male comrades knew about the abuse. They called us *masala ya wakubwa* and *guduria*, the 'food of the afandes,' the big pot from which all the soldiers ate their fill (Keitetsi 2002: 127–8).

Feminist Sudanese lawyer Asma Abdel Halim notes, 'The [sexual] violation of the woman by friends [comrades] seems to be a part of her duties' (1998; 97). She is expected to give her body willingly to men in her fighting unit, but to protect her body with her life when it comes to the men of the enemy forces (Halim 1998). Aroghu, of the Sudanese People's Liberation Army, reported her grievances to a human rights agency:

Lack of promotion was not the only problem faced by women rebels... I remember during our training in 1986 in the bushes of the Equatoria, some of us were sexually abused not only by the Sudanese trainers, but also by Ugandan soldiers who were training us (Halim 1998: 96).

Many women had to negotiate their survival by acquiescing. One woman fighter for the Zimbabwe African National Liberation Army also noted:

Women were given equal treatment ... going through military training. We were just being mixed up with the men and if we show that military commander we can command and everybody will be saluting you and everything... But [what] was disappointing was that they would try to fall in love with [you] or to make you love the guys and ... when you're in the hardships promising you that you can have soap, you can have ... luxury ... even sugar ... where you could go for four days without food ... so they started kind of buying women (Lyons 2004: 191).

Teckla, formerly of the People's Liberation Army of Namibia, avoided being raped. However, her testimony highlights how abuses can occur because the training and discipline required to fight wars allow little room for dissent and insubordination:

... Sometimes, when you are coming from home, you are new, and they train you in the army to say 'yes'. Whenever someone in charge calls you, you shouldn't refuse, you don't say no, you have to go. You feel scared of saying no, you cannot talk directly to a commander. Sometimes the chiefs would call out these poor young girls fresh from home. The chiefs made love to them and the women became pregnant without knowing the person who impregnated them, sometimes they didn't even know his name (Shikola 1998: 143).

When authoritarian values and violence become internalized, a code of silence and aspects of the 'warrior ethos' manifest themselves in unexpected and sometimes twisted ways (Grossman 1995). Rita Mazibuko, a military-trained South African cadre of the African National Congress, was detained by her own people after nine comrades close to her had been shot. Accused of being a spy, she was tortured and raped:

> They pushed a pipe with a condom in and out of my vagina. While they did it, they asked how it felt ... someone called Desmond raped me nine times ... Comrade Mashego ... raped me until I approached the authorities. And then, Tebogo, who was also very young, he raped me and cut my genitals – he cut me from number one to number two. And then he put me in a certain room, he tied my legs apart ... then poured Dettol [an antiseptic] over my genitals (Krog 1998: 207–8).

Despite Fanon's rhetoric characterizing revolutionary violence as a 'cleansing force', war is a dirty business. Rather than becoming a psychologically transformative, humanistic force, violence often becomes a degenerative one (Grossman 1995; Honwana 2000; Mama 2000; Ochieng 2002). The trauma and humiliation that remain as a result of certain debilitating violent acts leave many women soldiers feeling unworthy of *any* recognition, let alone mutual recognition.

Revolutionary Warfare: An Oxymoron?

Contrary to Fanon's major theoretical premise, 'revolutionary warfare' may be a contradiction in terms. The values and brutal tactics needed for effective warfare (authoritarianism, elitism, secrecy and tight control of information for fear of spies and leaks, torture to get information from enemies,) contradict the values and practices needed for effective revolutionary social transformation (egalitarianism, freedom of expression, consensus, dissent, transparency in government decisions and policies).

Thus, the progressive ideological goals of a revolution are diametrically opposed to the tactics taught to achieve victory in warfare. Such contradictions may explain why some of the most visionary revolutionary organizations and their leaders begin, over time, to mimic the authoritarian, elitist, and violent characteristics of the regimes they are striving to overthrow – despite their sloganeering, best intentions, and just causes for going to war initially (Campbell 2003; de Waal 2002). Although anti-colonial revolutionary wars are motivated by the desire to right perceived wrongs and are often driven by an agenda of progressive social transformation, they still encourage violence and militaristic values that often increase the chance of post-independence violent conflict (de Waal 2002).

Civilians caught in combat zones attest to the difficulty in defining 'who the real enemy is', especially during various postcolonial civil wars. Ugandan refugees explain:

> We had a lot of problems from all the fighting forces here; both the rebels and the NRA (National Resistance Army) kept us moving up and down and running for dear life. They [both groups] robbed people of their goats, cows, and sheep (Rose, Uganda, in Bennet et al. 1995: 107).

After one serious fight between the rebels and the NRA in our village, the NRA started questioning [civilians] about how these rebels could move through the villages to come and attack them. In retaliation, most civilians in the village were victimized. The NRA started burning houses, robbing property, and killing indiscriminately. Even the very old, the blind, and the disabled, who could not run, were killed. The government was convinced that the rebels were our sons, so all of us were assumed to be rebels. (Olga, Uganda, in Bennet et al. 1995: 107–8).

Contemporary postcolonial civil wars in Africa are more complex and difficult to identify as 'liberatory' or 'people's wars' even though their leaders refer to them as such. The initial 'revolutionary causes' of the civil wars in Liberia, Sierra Leone, Somalia, and the Ethiopian-Eritrean 1998-2000 conflict often disappear; former allies end up fighting one another, and economic motives interwoven with political ambitions have created an entirely new generation of warlords whose self-proclaimed revolutionary visions are purely economic (de Waal 2002; Mama 2000; van Houten 1998).

Differences of opinion and the discussion of potentially divisive issues such as gender relations are discouraged during active war under the pretext of safeguarding national unity (Kabira and Nzioki 1993; Lazreg 1994; McFadden 2000). Thus, most revolutionary organizations lack clear active policies regarding gender-specific political education and trans-formation. 'Equal rights for women' is often a revolutionary call asserting 'women's equal right with men to take up arms against repression' (Cock 1991: 197). This narrow, militaristic interpretation of equal rights paves the way for the marginalization of women after the war and the perpetuation of an androcentric, militarized neo-colonized mentality among many men during postwar reconstruction.

Postwar Realities: Gender Segregation, Militarization, War Mutations

Contrary to Fanon's prediction that revolutionary violence would create a 'new man', the idealization of ultra-masculine, rebellious and violent attitudes has created successive generations of African male leaders who justify militarism and dictatorship as the only appropriate defense against imperialism and other remnants of colonialism (Campbell 2003; Kebede 2001; Longman 2006; Mengisteab and Yohannes 2005). The former 'colonized mentality' of men morphs into a 'militarized neo-colonized mentality' after independence that (i) encourages a backlash against African women combatants in efforts to put them 'back in their place', (ii) promotes an ongoing culture of violence and mental health challenges due to the traumatic effects of war on combat soldiers that often go un-addressed, and (iii) supports the proliferation of non-conventional fighting forces across Africa and mutations of the former anti-colonial wars driven, in part, by the continued interference and involvement of former colonial powers and the growing worldwide trade in weapons fueling global militarization (de Waal 2001; Volman 1998; UNRISD 2005). Furthermore, although individual African women combatants describe their war experiences as empowering, violence was not integral to the empowerment they describe.

The Postwar Censorship of African Women Combatants

Radical African feminists have noted how 'androcentric, militarized men' also require feminine embodiments of womanhood that complement them; thus, women combatants are expected to make the necessary practical and emotional adjustments and go back to their traditional roles as mothers and wives (Mama 2000; McFadden 2000; Tamale 1999). Their visions of social change and gender equity must compete with popular patriarchal yearnings to return to 'normal,' usually defined as putting down their weapons, returning to the domestic sphere, and bearing children for the new, post-independent society (Enloe 2004b; Lazreg 1994; McFadden 2005). Destruction of extended family networks through revolutionary wars (forced removals, detention) make family life a practical and empowering choice for many African women ex-combatants. However, motherhood and wifehood are not presented as options, but as mandates linked to respectability (McFadden 2005). Herein lies the source of postwar censorship of women combatants as equal contributors to the revolution; while African men often collectively return as 'heroes' and use their roles as fighters to fortify their evolving masculine identities, the evolution of female ex-fighters' identities as women is thwarted (Curnow 2001; Gaba 1997; Shikola 1998).

After the war, African women soldiers are usually regarded with contempt by civilians and even their fellow comrades, as 'women with declined status or loose morals', 'women associated with the spread of AIDS', 'prostitutes', 'too feisty and difficult' for marriage, barren if they do not have children and bad mothers if they do but have left them with family members in order to fight (Cock 1991; Isaacman and Isaacman 1984; Lyons 2004; West 2000). Many end up concealing their roles as former combatants (Lyons 2004; McKay and Mazurana 2004). Moreover, the shaming process ensures that women fighters are not recognized as restoring their dignity through war, but as having compromised it by their participation. Engaging in warfare restores an African male combatant's dignity in ways that uphold society's vision of his masculinity, while simultaneously detracting from an African woman combatant's dignity because of the perception that she has lost her femininity. Becoming 'respectable' wives and mothers and lying about their war experiences are presented as options to avoid being ostracized permanently (Lyons 2004). With few exceptions, former 'creators of history,' as described by Fanon, are pressured to disappear *again* from history (see Gaba 1997).

Postwar Research on the Adverse Psychological Effects of Combat

Most damaging to Fanon's perspectives on war is the fact that the psychologically transformative effects of political violence have not been clinically substantiated by psychological research for women or men. In fact, the opposite appears to be the case, suggesting that Fanon overgeneralized the results of his clinical observations of the Algerian war

(Grossman 1995). Fanon did not live long enough to conduct any long-term follow-up investigations of Algerian combatants (Kebede 2001). Today, psychological research suggests that learning to kill exacts a high psychological price from soldiers, their families, and society at large (Grossman 1995; Honwana 2000; Mama 2000; Ochieng 2002).

Historian, soldier, and psychologist, Lieutenant Colonel Dave Grossman's (1995) comprehensive psychological study of the nature of killing in combat suggests that 98 per cent of all soldiers involved in close combat become psychiatric casualties while the remaining 2 per cent who endure sustained combat already have a predisposition toward 'aggressive psychopathic personalities' (43–4). At close range, the screams and cries of the enemy can be heard and add to the trauma experienced by the soldier (116). Soldiers who have been involved in close combat 'suffer higher incidences of divorce, marital problems, tranquilizer use, alcoholism and other addictions, joblessness, heart disease, high blood pressure, and ulcers' (283). These negative effects reflect the dehumanizing nature of violence rather than its 'humanistic' potential that Fanon hypothesized, thereby creating additional challenges when postwar societies attempt to rebuild respect for human rights within the population at large, particularly among former combatants, members of the security forces, and the judicial system (Grossman 1995; UNRISD 2005).

The Absence of Gender Reconciliation Amid Ongoing Militarization
Fanon understood that African independence alone was not enough to create a revolution; however, he appears to have overestimated the psychological significance of violence for psychological transformation, thereby unwittingly contributing to the postcolonial evolution of the militarized, neo-colonized masculine mentality that makes it difficult to nurture a human rights culture. Although different African nations have approached 'reconciliation' in a number of ways, the specific need for *gender* reconciliation is rarely addressed (UNRISD 2005).

The growth of the militarized, neo-colonized mentality and its patriarchal underpinnings has not been adequately addressed via any postwar gender-specific political education campaign. Shaped by the invention of African 'customary' law during colonial subjugation, patriarchal African nationalisms, and the patriarchal nature of war, militarism, and military forces, postcolonial masculinity paves the way for the ongoing militarization of African states, in the context of global militarization.

Many African governments have heads of state who are current or former military officers/liberation fighters and whose governance styles are militaristic (e.g., characterized by the lack of transparency in decision-making, the promotion of military-focused budgets at the expense of civilian development projects, authoritarian and dictatorial leadership styles, etc; Campbell 2003; Longman 2006; Mengisteab and Yohannes 2005). Although the military cannot and should not be eliminated, the problem arises when military attitudes and practices are reproduced at most levels of society as a justification for completing the so-called unfinished business of the revolution (e.g., excessive stockpiling of military weapons, organizing new security forces and party militias, and the authoritative advocacy of only one correct party line in educational institutions, see de Waal 2002 for additional characteristics). Furthermore, militaristic governments tend to be intolerant of their domestic critics, thereby creating factions and the likelihood of military coups and civil war (de Waal 2002). When any disagreement with the 'party line' or 'correct analysis' becomes tantamount to treason, disgruntled rival groups declare their own 'liberation war' and often gain military support from foreign allies (e.g., former colonial powers, other foreign superpowers or African countries with similar political and economic interests). Once again, the violence of the state drives marginalized peoples to the point of armed resistance, and the cycle of violence continues (de Waal 2002; UNRISD 2005).

With militarized masculinities intact – and in public office – most states sideline women's issues after the revolution, retain discriminatory African customary law as a part of their legal systems, support cosmetic legislative reforms that are not enforced, facilitate changes in the electoral system that increase only a token number of female parliamentarians, reward a few high-ranking women combatants with government positions, and engage in other symbolic gestures that do not essentially change structural gender inequities (Banda 2005; McFadden 2005; Mama 2000). Therefore, when postcolonial African states are militarized, the likelihood that women will achieve gender equity decreases, regardless of the roles they played during the revolution. To what degree, then, does participation in revolutionary military action empower women and restore their recognition as equal human beings? Was Fanon right about *anything*, regarding how violence can transform the colonized mentalities of African women?

Individual Empowerment vs Widespread Social Change
Fanon correctly emphasized that political education must accompany the armed struggle, and, despite overwhelming challenges, individual women do sometimes emerge empowered from that struggle. Furthermore, new constitutions and laws with radical provisions for women might not have occurred so quickly had there not been a war or major upheaval in countries like South Africa, Zimbabwe, Eritrea, Namibia, Uganda, Rwanda and Mozambique (UNRISD 2005). Moreover, these legal changes have helped some women gain a stronger political voice and higher levels of representation in government than was possible before the war (UNRISD 2005). However, how have African women *combatants*, in particular, fared after the war? Fanon's perspectives specifically theorize about fighters engaged in political violence, therefore the test of his theory rests on the aftermath of the lives of women combatants, not women in general.

African women ex-combatants vary in age, educational level, social class, rural or urban background, marketable skills, physical ability, and both personal and political aspirations (Cock 1994). Hardships they may have endured include physical illnesses like malaria, hunger, imprisonment, sexual abuse, and ongoing fear of death at the hands of the enemy and some comrades (Cock 1994; Lazreg 1994; Lyons 2004). Many suffer from post-traumatic stress disorder, while others face permanent physical disabilities. However, isolated accounts of personal empowerment exist from women who were able to benefit from leadership positions during the war

(Curnow 2000; Isaacman and Isaacman 1984; Lyons 2004). Also, some women have reported feeling personally empowered by performing traditionally female supportive roles that they felt were politically important (Cock 1991; Isaacman and Isaacman 1984; Kanogo, 1987). However, most women combatants have been censured because male comrades who engaged in human rights abuses against them (or those who were aware of such abuses) are in key government positions, the police, or the armed forces (Curnow 2000; Krog 2001; Lyons 2004; Shikola 1998). Most important, the testimonies of African women combatants who have been willing to talk make clear that violence was not integral to the empowerment they describe. Thus, Fanon overstated the role of violence in their psychological transformation and understated the overwhelming vulnerabilities they endured. For instance, Paulina Mateos, a former FRELIMO guerrilla commander, implies that her ability to survive the harsh elements of military camp life contributed to her sense of agency and dignity as a woman soldier:

> We suffered hunger and thirst and heat as the men did, and we learned to handle all kinds of arms ... sometimes we even surpassed the men ... so, I no longer feel that differences exist between men and myself since we fought side by side. We marched together, organized ambushes together, we suffered defeats together as well as the joys of victory. (Isaacman and Isaacman 1984: 161, 164, 165)

Ellen Musialela, who first became involved in Namibia's liberation struggle in 1964 when she was 14 years old, spent seven years as a nurse in the military wing and later was assigned to work in the political field after a debilitating snake bite. Her sense of pride has more to do with witnessing how she and other women coped with the difficulties that men and everyday military camp life presented:

> Some women have sacrificed their lives on the battlefield; some are very good at communications, reconnaissance and in the medical field. Of course, you also find that women in the camps are taking a very active role in our kindergartens, in our medical centres, as nurses, as teachers, and in other productive work ... Our women in the battlefield especially, are faced with a lot of problems ... I saw with my own eyes when I went to the battlefield in May, how women were forced to use grass during their periods and had to go without panties ... We feel proud that despite the traditional barriers between men and women, women have started to understand that we have to fight together to fight the system, because we are oppressed as women, and we are oppressed as blacks ... (1983: 85–6).

As one Tigrayan woman ex-combatant said:

> One of the things you learn from this long experience of struggle is that you're ready for anything. I never thought I would survive this long. I have seen so many battles, so many comrades have died ... You learn courage and that your life has meaning (Hammond 1990: 48).

Thus, despite its adverse effects, war can produce contradictory experiences for women that lead to some positive outcomes. Some women combatants' ability to survive the war leads them to (i) take advantage of literacy programs, (ii) find work with international and other relief aid organizations,

(iii) create their own self-help organizations, and (iv) and find employment in urban areas (UNRISD 2005). Paraphrasing Algerian-born feminist Marnia Lazreg's description of Algerian women fighters, it can be reasonably generalized to most African women combatants: 'First, women forged bonds with one another that transcended the usual episodic solidarity that characterized their relationships during peacetime. Second, they gained a sense of responsibility and purpose as well as another perspective on their lives. Third, confidence in themselves and a sense of partaking in history is evident. Fourth, they were exposed to the similarities between men and women, despite differences' (Lazreg 1994: 140). African feminist Patricia McFadden boldly adds, 'African [women] do not want to be pitied; they do not want to be studied and interrogated as victimized subjects whose agency is rarely acknowledged, let alone politically supported, at the global level. What African [women] have wanted for the past half-century since independence is the opportunity to craft their own futures and to define their own destinies...Cleaning up the mess of the past three hundred years of supremacist rule...cannot be an easy or pleasant task...[however] It is an opportunity that women are making the most of, a moment that is changing their lives forever' (McFadden 2005: 17).

Conclusion

Fanon could not have known how encouraging colonized people to redirect their 'counterviolent urges' would spin out of control after the wars of independence. He could not imagine political education in the midst of debt repayment and structural adjustment, the AIDS pandemic, the ongoing military activities of the former colonial powers, the economic interest of the global superpowers, the end of the Cold War, the conflicting interests of African governments, the plethora of private arms dealers in the midst of global militarization (de Waal 2002; Volman 1998; Zeleza, this volume, Introduction). His analysis, radically perceptive for its time, has limited application to the situations of African women, and in some respects African men, regarding the power of counter-revolutionary violence to restore human agency and dignity. Although he acknowledged the role of African women guerrilla fighters and their right to exist as autonomous human beings, he neglected other gendered psychopolitical factors that work against their recognition by African men as equal contributors to anti-colonial and postcolonial wars.

Fanon emphasized the racialized psychological effects of colonial subjugation on the colonized African, referring to the resultant inferiority complex as 'the epidermalization of inferiority'. I have argued, however, that the gendered psychological effects of the 'androcentricization of inferiority' among colonized men also occurred and require analysis. This psychological process created extremely distorted patriarchal aspects of men's colonized mentalities that involved the fusion of European and African male authority over African women through 'African customary law'. However, European men retained the ultimate power and authority that resulted in African men's ongoing resentments during the colonial period.

These resentments and African men's struggles regarding their own masculine identities resulted in the formation of revolutionary nationalist organizations that represented African men's efforts to be recognized not only as *Africans* but also as *men*. These patriarchal nationalist expressions became militarized during the anti-colonial war, further entrenching African men's androcentric colonized mentality. Military values like authoritarianism and the view that combat is 'men's work' created a sexual division of labor, hypermasculine attitudes and practices, and a form of blind compliance that worked against the equal recognition of women soldiers and their sense of agency. In addition, these factors increased women soldiers' susceptibility to human rights abuses – by the enemy and their fellow 'comrades' – that targeted their sexuality.

The contradictory values of democratic revolution and militarism reveal the degenerative rather than the transformative effects of violence, and women's first-hand accounts confirm these contradictions. After the war, the postwar censorship of women soldiers, the trauma that many experienced, and the pressure to resume traditional female roles leave only a select group of women feeling empowered by the war. Contrary to Fanon's belief, participation in revolutionary violence does not contribute to the mutual recognition of women; in fact, in some ways, it works against it.

Therefore, when any woman fights in a military force, we are forced to examine the complexities and interrelationships of gender, war and the aftermath of war. Merely becoming involved in military forces does not automatically liberate women or men from racially and sexually exploitive relationships. Furthermore, the equal right to engage in combat does not ensure that women soldiers will be equally valued or recognized as equals by men. In fact, women who choose to join military forces have to combat both the external enemy and the patriarchal attitudes and actions within the military force itself. Although engaging in war may sometimes be necessary, we need to understand the long-term psychological price of war and be prepared to deal with its gendered psychological repercussions on the soldier and society.

References

Adugna, Minale. 2001. *Women and Warfare in Ethiopia*. Gender Issues Report Series, No. 11. Addis Ababa: Organization for Social Science Research in Eastern and Southern Africa.
Arendt, Hannah. 1970. *On Violence*. New York: Hartcourt, Brace and World.
Arthur, Marie Jose. 1998. 'Mozambique: Women in the Armed Struggle.' In Patricia McFadden ed., *Gender in Southern Africa: A Gendered Perspective*, Harare: SAPES.
Banda, Fareda. 2005. *Women, Law, and Human Rights: An African Perspective*. Portland, OR: Hart.
Becker, Heike. 1995. *Namibian Women's Movement 1980–1992: From Anti-Colonial Resistance to Reconstruction*. Frankfurt-am-Main: IKO-Verlag für Interkulterelle Kommunikation.
Bennet, Olivia, Jo Bexley, and Kitty Warnock, eds. 1995. *Arms to Fight, Arms to Protect: Women Speak Out About Conflict*. London: Panos.
Black Radical Congress. 1998. 'Principles of Unity.' http://www.blackradicalcongress.org/unity.html.
Bourdillon, Michael. 1975. 'Is 'Customary Law' Customary?', *Native Affairs Department Annual* 11(2): 142–7.
Bulhan, Hussein. 1985. *Frantz Fanon and the Psychology of Oppression*. New York: Plenum.
Campbell, Horace. 2003. *Reclaiming Zimbabwe: The Exhaustion of the Patriarchal Model of Liberation*. Trenton, NJ: Africa World Press.

Chanock, Martin. 1989. 'Neither Customary nor Legal: African Customary Law in an Era of Family Law Reform.' *International Journal of Law and Family* 3: 72–88.

Cock, Jacklyn. 1991. *Colonels and Cadres: War and Gender in South Africa.* Cape Town: Oxford University Press.

Cock, Jacklin. 1994. *The Forgotten People: The Need for a Soldiers' Charter.* Cape Town: Institute for Democracy in South Africa.

Cockburn, Cynthia. 2001. 'The Gendered Dynamics of Armed Conflict and Political Violence.' In Caroline Moser and Fiona C. Clark, eds, *Victims, Perpetrators or Actors? Gender, Armed Conflict and Political Violence,* 13–29, London: Zed Books, 13–29.

Curnow, Robyn. 2000. 'Thandi Modise, a Woman at War', *AGENDA: Empowering Women for Gender Equity* 43: 36–40.

De Pauw, Linda Grant. 1998. *Battle Cries and Lullabies: Women in War from Prehistory to the Present.* Tulsa, OK: University of Oklahoma Press.

de Waal, Alex. 2002. 'The Political Cultures of Militarism,' in *Demilitarizing the Mind: African Agendas for Peace and Security,* Trenton, NJ: Africa World Press, 73–92.

El Saadawi, Nawal. 2004. 'War Against Women and Women Against War: Waging War on the Mind'. Paper presented at the World Social Forum, Mumbai. 6 January. http://www.nawalsaadawi.net/articlenawal/MumbaiNawalPaper.DOC.

Enloe, Cynthia H. 1983. 'The Military Needs Camp Followers' in her *Does Khaki Become You? The Militarisation of Women's Lives,* London: Pluto Press, 1–17.

Enloe, Cynthia H. 2004a. 'When Feminists Look at Masculinity and the Men Who Wage War: A Conversation between Cynthia Enloe and Carol Cohn', In *The Curious Feminist: Searching for Women in a New Age of Empire,* Berkeley, CA: University of California Press, 237–67.

Enloe, Cynthia H. 2004b. 'Demilitarization – Or More of the Same? Feminist Questions to Ask in the Postwar Moment.' In her *The Curious Feminist: Searching for Women in a New Age of Empire.* Berkeley, CA: University of California Press, 217–32

Evans, Mark. 2005. *Just War Theory: A Reappraisal.* New York: Palgrave Macmillan.

Fanon, Frantz. 1967a. *A Dying Colonialism.* Trans. Haakon Chevalier. New York: Grove.

Fanon, Frantz. 1967b. *Black Skin, White Masks.* Trans. Chales Lam Markmann. New York: Grove.

Fanon, Frantz. 1967c. *Toward the African Revolution.* Trans. Haakon Chevalier. New York: Grove.

Fanon, Frantz. 1968. The *Wretched of the Earth.* Trans. Constance Farrington. New York: Grove.

Fischer, Ann, David Tokar, Marija Mergl, Glenn Good, Melanie Hill, and Sasha Blum. 2000. 'Assessing Women's Feminist Identity Development: Studies of Convergent, Discriminant, and Structural Validity.' *Psychology of Women Quarterly* 24: 15–29.

Gaba, Lewis. 1997. 'Give Us Our Piece of the Pie: Women Ex-Freedom Fighters Meet in Africa.' *AfricaNews,* 13 April. Human Rights Information Network. www.hartford-hwp.com/archives/30/151.html.

Gibson, Nigel C. ed. 1999. *Rethinking Fanon: The Continuing Dialogue.* Amherst NY: Humanity Books.

Goldblatt, Beth, and Sheila Meintjes. 1998. 'South African Women Demand the Truth', in Meredeth Turshen and Clotilde Twagiramariya, eds, *What Women Do in Wartime: Gender and Conflict in Africa,* London: Zed Books, 27–61.

Goldman, Nancy L. 1982. *Female Soldiers – Combatants or Noncombatants? Historical and Contemporary Perspectives.* Westport, CT: Greenwood.

Goldstein, Joshua S. 2001. *War and Gender: How Gender Shapes the War System and Vice Versa.* Cambridge: Cambridge University Press.

Gordan, Lewis, T. Duncan Sharpley-Whiting and Renée T. White, eds. 1999. *Fanon: A Critical Reader,* Blackwood, NJ: Blackwell.

Grossman, Dave. 1995. *On Killing: The Psychological Cost of Learning to Kill in War and Society.* Boston, MA: Little, Brown and Company.

Halim, Asma Abdel. 1998. 'Attack with a Friendly Weapon', in Meredeth Turshen and Clotilde Twagiramariya, eds., *What Women Do in Wartime: Gender and Conflict in Africa,* New York: Zed Books, 85–100.

Hammond, Jenny, with Nell Bruce. 1990. *Sweeter Than Honey: Ethiopian Women and Revolution, Testimony of Tigrayan Women.* Trenton, NJ: Red Sea Press.

Hegel, G. W. F. 1996. *The Phenomenology of the Mind,* London: Allen & Unwin.

Helie-Lucas, Marie-Aimée. 1988. 'The Role of Women during the Algerian Liberation Struggle and After: Nationalism as a Concept and as a Practice towards both the Power of the Army and the Militarization of the People', in Eva Isaksson, ed., *Women and the Military System,* New York: St Martin's Press, 171–89.

Honwana, Alcinda. 2000. 'Untold War Stories: Young Women and War in Mozambique'. http://web.uct.ac.za/org/agi/pubs/newsletters/vol6/war.htm.

Houten, Helen van. 1998. 'Somali Women in War and Peace', in *Somali Between Peace and War:*

Somali Women on the Eve of the 21st Century, Nairobi: UNIFEM, 44–65.

Isaacman, Allen and Barbara Isaacman. 1984. 'The Role of Women in the Liberation of Mozambique.' *Ufahamu* 13(2): 128–85.

Jackson, Jay, and Eliot Smith. 1999. 'Conceptualizing Social Identity: A New Framework and the Impact of Different Dimensions.' *Personality and Social Psychology Bulletin* 25: 120–35.

Jinadu, Adele, L. 1986. *Fanon: In Search of the African Revolution*. New York: Kegan Paul.

Kabira, Wanjiku M. and Elizabeth A. Nzioki, eds. 1993. *Celebrating Women's Resistance: A Case Study of Women's Groups Movement in Kenya*. Nairobi: African Women's Perspective.

Kanogo, Tabitha. 1987. 'Kikuyu Women and the Politics of Protest: Mau Mau', in Sharon MacDonald, Pat Holden, and Shirley Ardener. eds, *Images of Women in Peace and War: Cross-Cultural and Historical Perspectives*, London: Macmillan, 78–99.

Kebede, Messay. 2001. 'The Rehabilitation of Violence and the Violence of Rehabilitation: Fanon and Colonialism.' *Journal of Black Studies* 31(5): 539–62.

Keitetsi, China. 2002. *Child Soldier: Fighting for My Life*. Cape Town: Jacana.

Kesby, Mike. 1996. 'Arenas for Control, Terrains of Gender Contestation: Guerrilla Struggle and Counter-Insurgency Warfare in Zimbabwe 1972–1980', *Journal of Southern African Studies* 22(4): 561–84.

Krog, Antjie. 2001. 'Locked into Loss and Silence: Testimonies of Gender and Violence at the South African Truth Commission. In *Victims, Perpetrators or Actors? Gender, Armed Conflict and Political Violence*, eds., Caroline Moser and Fiona Clark, 203–16. London: Zed.

Lazreg, Marnia. 1994. The *Eloquence of Silence: Algerian Women in Question*. New York: Routledge.

Lewis, Desiree. 2004. 'African Gender Research and Postcoloniality: Legacies and Challenges', in *African Gender Scholarship: Concepts, Methodologies and Paradigms*. Dakar: CODESRIA.

Longman, Timothy. 2006. 'Rwanda: Achieving Equality or Serving an Authoritarian State?', in Gretchen Bauer and Hannah Britton, eds, *Women in African Parliaments*, Boulder, CO: Lynne Rienner, 133–50.

Lyons, Tanya. 2004. *Guns and Guerrilla Girls: Women in the Zimbabwean Liberation Struggle*. Trenton, NJ: Africa World Press.

MacLean, Sandra. 2007. 'Fighting Locally, Connecting Globally: Inside & Outside Dimensions of African Conflict.' In *The Roots of African Conflicts: The Causes & Costs*, eds, Paul T. Zeleza and Alfred Nhema. Oxford: James Currey.

Maitse, Teboho, with Jen Marchbank. 2000. 'Revealing Silence: Voices from South Africa', in Susie Jacobs, Ruth Jacobson, and Jennifer Marchbank, eds, *States of Conflict: Gender, Violence and Resistance*, London: Zed Books,199–214.

Mama, Amina. 1996. 'Women's Studies and Studies of Women in Africa in the 1990s.' CODESRIA Working Paper Series, no. 5. Dakar, Senegal: Council for the Development of Social Science Research in Africa.

Mama, Amina. 1997. 'Sheroes and Villains: Conceptualizing Colonial and Contemporary Violence Against Women in Africa', in M. Jacqui Alexander and Chandra T. Mohanty. eds, *Feminist Genealogies, Colonial Legacies, Democratic Futures*, New York: Routledge, 46–62.

Mama, Amina. 2000. 'Transformation Thwarted: Gender-Based Violence in Africa's New Democracies.' http://www.uct.ac.za/org/agi/papers/.

Mama, Amina. 2001. 'Gender in Action: Militarism and War'. http://web.uct.ac.za/org/agi/papers/.

Mbilinyi, Marjorie. 1988. 'Runaway Wives in Colonial Tanganyika: Forced Labour and Forced Marriage in Rungwe District, 1919–1961', *International Journal of the Sociology of Law* 16(3): 11–25.

Mbilinyi, Marjorie. 1992. 'Research Methodologies in Gender Issues', in Ruth Meena, ed., *Gender in Southern Africa: Conceptual and Theoretical Issues*, Harare: SAPES, 31–70.

McFadden, Patricia. 1997. 'The Challenges and Prospects for the African Women's Movement in the 21st Century', *Women In Action* 1(1): 1–7.

McFadden, Patricia. 2000. 'Radically Speaking: The Significance of the Women's Movement for Southern Africa. http://www.wworld.org/programs/regions/africa/.

McFadden, Patricia. 2005. 'Becoming Postcolonial: African Women Changing the Meaning of Citizenship', *Meridians* 6(1): 1–22.

McKay, Susan, and Dyan Mazurana. 2004. *Where are the Girls? Girls in Fighting Forces in Northern Uganda, Sierra Leone and Mozambique: Their Lives During and After War*. Montreal: Rights & Democracy/International Center for Human Rights and Democratic Development.

Meena, Ruth. 1992. 'Gender Research/Studies in Southern Africa: An Overview', in *Gender in Southern Africa: Conceptual and Theoretical Issues*, Harare: SAPES, 1–30.

Mengisteab, Kidane, and Okbazghi Yohannes. 2005. *Anatomy of an African Tragedy: Political, Economic and Foreign Policy Crisis in Post-Independence Eritrea*. Trenton, NJ: Red Sea Press.

Mikell, Gwendolyn. 1997. *African Feminism: The Politics of Survival in Sub-Saharan Africa.* Philadelphia, PA: University of Pennsylvania Press.

Moser, Caroline and Fiona C. Clark. 2001. *Victims, Perpetrators or Actors? Gender, Armed Conflict and Political Violence.* London: Zed Books.

Mugambe, Beatrice. 2000. *Women's Roles in Armed Conflict and Their Marginalisation in the Governance of Post-Conflict Society: The Case of 'Luwero Triangle,' Uganda.* Gender Issues Report Series, No. 11. Addis Ababa: Organization for Social Science Research in Eastern and Southern Africa.

Musialela, Ellen. 1983. 'Women in Namibia: The Only Way to Free Ourselves', in Miranda Davies, ed., *Third World, Second Sex: Women's Struggles and National Liberation,* London: Zed Books, 83–95.

Nghe, N. 1963. 'Fanon et les problèmes de indépendence, *La Pensée,* 23–36.

Nnaemeka, Obioma. 2004. 'Neo-Feminism: Theorizing, Practicing, and Pruning Africa's Way.' *Signs* 29(2): 357–85.

Ochieng, Ruth Ojiambo. 2002. 'The Scars on Women's Minds and Bodies: Women's Role in Post Conflict Reconstruction.' Paper presented at the 19th International Peace Research Conference, Kyung Hee University, South Korea, 1 July. http://www.isis.or.ug/ papers.php.

Potgieter, Cheryl. 1997. 'From Apartheid to Mandela's Constitution: Black South African Lesbians in the Nineties', in Beverly Greene, ed., *Ethnic and Cultural Diversity Among Lesbians and Gay Men: Psychological Perspectives on Lesbian and Gay Issues,* (Vol. 3), Thousand Oaks, CA: Sage.

Salo, Elaine. 2001. 'Talking about Feminism in Africa with Amina Mama', *AGENDA: Empowering Women for Gender Equity* 50: 58–63.

Schmidt, Elizabeth. 1991. 'Patriarchy, Capitalism, and the Colonial State in Zimbabwe', *Signs* 16(4): 732–56.

Sellers, Robert, Stephanie Rowley, Tabbye Chavous, J. Shelton, J. Nicole and Mia Smith. 1997. 'Multidimensional Inventory of Black Identity: A Preliminary Investigation of Reliability and Construct Validity', *Journal of Applied and Social Psychology* 73: 805–15.

Sharpley-Whiting, T. Duncan. 1998. *Frantz Fanon: Conflicts and Feminisms.* Lantam, MD: Rowman and Littlefield.

Shikola, Teckla. 1998. 'We Left Our Shoes Behind', in Meredeth Turshen and Clotilde Twagiramariya, eds, *What Women Do in Wartime: Gender and Conflict in Africa,* New York: Zed Books, 138–49.

Singer, Peter Warren. 2004. *Corporate Warriors: The Rise of the Privatized Military Industry.* Ithaca, NY: Cornell University Press.

Tamale, Sylvia. 1999. *When Hens Begin to Crow: Gender and Parliamentary Politics in Uganda.* Boulder, CO: Westview Press.

Tamale, Sylvia. 2003. 'Out of the Closet: Unveiling Sexuality Discourses in Uganda.' http://www.feministafrica.org/fa%202/02-2003/sp-tamale.html.

Tamale, Sylvia. 2006. 'African Feminism: How Should We Change?', *Development* 49 (1): 38–41.

Thiam, Awa. 1995. 'Feminism and Revolution', in *Black Sisters, Speak Out: Black Women and Oppression in Black Africa,* Chicago, IL: Research Associates, 113–28.

Turshen, Meredeth and Clotilde Twagiramariya, eds, 1998. *What Women Do in Wartime: Gender and Conflict in Africa.* London: Zed Books.

United Nations Children's Fund [UNICEF]. 1997. *Cape Town Annotated Principles and Best Practices.* Proceedings of the Symposium on the Prevention of Recruitment of Children into the Armed Forces and Demobilization and Social Reintegration of Child Soldiers in Africa. Convention on the Rights of the Child. Cape Town, 30 April.

United Nations Research Institute for Social Development. 2005. 'Gender Equality: Striving for Justice in an Unequal World: Section 4: Gender, Armed Conflict and the Search for Peace'. Policy Report on Gender and Development: 10 Years After Beijing. http://www.unrisd.org/

Urdang, Stephanie. 1979. *Fighting Two Colonialisms: Women in Guinea-Bissau.* New York: Monthly Review.

Veale, Angela. 2005. 'Collective and Individual Identities: Experiences of Recruitment and Reintegration of Female Ex-Combatants of the Tigrean People's Liberation Army, Ethiopia', in *Invisible Stakeholders: Children and War in Africa,* ed. Angela McIntyre, Pretoria, South Africa: Institute for Security Studies, 105–126.

Volman, Daniel. 1998. 'The Militarization of Africa', in Meredeth Turshen and Clotilde Twagiramariya, eds, *What Women Do in Wartime: Gender and Conflict in Africa,* London: Zed Books, 150–162.

Walzer, Michael. 1992. *Just and Unjust Wars: A Moral Argument with Historical Illustrations.* New York: BasicBooks.

West, Lois, ed. 1997. *Feminist Nationalism.* New York: Routledge.

West, Harry. 2000. 'Girls with Guns: Narrating the Experience of War of FRELIMO's Female Detachment', *Anthropological Quarterly* 73(4): 180–94.

Wilson, Amrit. 1991. *Women and the Eritrean Revolution: The Challenge Road.* Trenton, NJ: Red Sea Press.

Notes

1   Powerful Western governments such as the United States, Britain, and other European superpowers are also deeply implicated in this market-driven global militarization (Cockburn 2001; Mama 2001; Volman 1998; see also MacLean, Chapter 6 this volume).

2   Fanon fought voluntarily against Nazi Germany for the French, however, he experienced racism during his military service and during his student days in France after the war. These experiences led him to become active in left-wing gatherings that challenged unjust French policies (Bulhan 1985). While working at the Algerian psychiatric hospital, he began to work secretly for the FLN. He eventually became an FLN spokesperson, editor of its major paper, and a doctor in FLN health centers, despite assassination attempts on his life, ongoing 'Arab prejudice against his color,' and 'African discomfort in the presence of his White [French] wife' (Bulhan 1985: 34).

3   Hussein Bulhan (1985), a clinical psychologist and biographer of Fanon, is the only scholar who has provided a thorough analysis of all of Fanon's psychological publications.

4   Male pronouns are used in both Hegel and Fanon's original writings.

5   Fanon loathed the racism of the United States; however, he reluctantly sought medical treatment there for leukemia. Shortly after his arrival he died at the age of 36 on 6 December 1961. On 3 July 1962, less than a year after his death, Algeria was declared an independent country (see Bulhan 1985 for additional details).

6   Some feminists believe that nationalism and feminism can be reconciled if progressive notions of gender and sexuality are included in the ideological policies (see West, 1997).

7   Such as the Eritrean People's Liberation Front and the Tigrayan People's Liberation Front, see Wilson 1991; the Popular Movement for the Liberation of Angola (MPLA), the Front for the Liberation of Mozambique (FRELIMO), and the African Party for the Liberation of Guinea-Bissau and Cape Verde (PAIGC), see Urdang 1979; Uganda's National Resistance Movement and the Rwandan Patriotic Front, see Longman 2006; and Namibia's, Zimbabwe's, and South Africa's military wings, see Cock 1991 and Lyons 2004).

8   Western feminists occasionally argue that African women should have refused to participate in liberation wars, given African men's patriarchal nationalist attitudes and practices; or that African women should have created separate feminist organizations as an alternative to the male-led revolutionary organizations. Algerian feminist Marnia Lazreg's response regarding Algerian women can be generalized to the situation of most African women during independence struggles, 'Looking at the past from the vantage point of the present is easier than reexperiencing it as it was lived. It is difficult to imagine a feminist movement, by which is meant a movement focused on the promotion of women's rights exclusively, emerging during the war. Who would have been its leaders? Who would have been its adversaries? French men? French women? Algerian men? All of these? Apart from a history of manipulation of women by colonial authorities that made any feminist activity suspect in the eyes of Algerians, native associations were only tolerated and often subjected to harassment, if not banned. An Algerian feminist association that would have inevitably questioned the active complicity of the colonial order in women's exclusion from high school education, training, health care, housing, jobs and so on would have found it difficult to survive' (1994: 139).

9   'Women's physical strength, while less than men's on average, has been adequate to many combat situations – from piloting to sniping to firing machine guns. One argument of those opposed to women in combat – that the women would be unable to drag wounded comrades from the battlefield under fire – is refuted by the record of women nurses' doing so. Women's supposedly lower levels of aggressiveness, and their nurturing nature have been no obstacle to their participation in combat' (Goldstein 2001: 127).

10 Some guerrilla armies prohibited sexual relationships between soldiers (however, officers were usually the exception), while other armies did not enforce disciplinary codes, given the protracted nature of the war and the inevitability of such liaisons. Some armies encouraged or forced soldiers to marry if a pregnancy occurred. Women were usually blamed for their pregnancies and any paternity issues that arose (Lyons 2004).

6

Fighting Locally,
Connecting Globally
Inside & Outside Dimensions of African Conflict

SANDRA J. MACLEAN

Regional relations, interests and transactions are well-documented features of recent civil wars in Africa. Partly because of these regional dimensions of conflict, many argue that Africa's regional organizations should play central roles in conflict resolutions. Efforts to promote a more influential role for regional organizations also reflect a growing attitude within Africa that African problems require African solutions. While this position is not new on the continent, it has taken on more resonance within Africa of late because of the inadequate and/or ineffective response of the international community in solving or averting some of the more horrific conflicts, such as in Rwanda. The view that Africans should solve African problems seems also to be gaining acceptance outside the continent as well. For instance, an editorial in the *Los Angeles Times* (17 August 2004) states, 'Africa gets little help from the outside world, as was clear in Rwanda when Hutus massacred Tutsis and is evident now in Sudan. [Therefore, as a solution, Africa] needs regional agreements to stop killers from crossing borders and requires armies with training and equipment to enforce the pacts.'

Few would disagree with these observations and prescriptions. Clearly, it is critical that resources be devoted to the (re)vitalization and building of effective peace-making/-keeping/-building capacity in African regional organizations. However, official regional organizations tend to focus most of their attention on formal initiatives at the state and/or inter-state level, although many of the factors that contribute to (at least by exacerbating and extending, if not by directly causing) conflict are linked by informal, often illegal transactions. Such transactions occur outside the boundaries of legitimate state practices or scrutiny, although in some cases with the support and cooperation of high-placed government officials. An important aspect of the regional dimensions of these transactions that tends often to be overlooked, and which is currently under-theorized, is the connectivity of the regional processes with other levels of interaction from the local through the global.

The objective of this paper is to explore the insertion of local and regional actors in transnational networks that contribute to African conflicts. The

166

analysis draws on insights from an emerging literature that seeks to elaborate an analytical framework for investigating the transnational linkages that feature in the political economy of conflict (Callaghy et al. 2001; MacGaffey and Bazenguissa-Ganga 2000; Lumpe 2000). Drawing on insights from this perspective, the main argument of the study is that conflict prevention and management need to be treated as processes involving local/national/regional/international/global complexes. It contends, also, that local and regional solutions for conflict should be supported and supplemented by actions at the international and global level. Among the international/global issues to be addressed are the national, regional and international relationships and commitments associated with NEPAD; emerging systems for governance of corporate social responsibility, especially in consideration of new increasingly global market demands for natural resources; and developing international norms based upon the notion of a 'responsibility to protect'.

Local-Regional-Global Connections in War

Africa is closely connected with the global political economy, even if not always in ways that contribute positively to African development and human security. Often the connections (through crime networks, illegal trade in natural resources or small arms trade) exacerbate and prolong, if not necessarily cause, war. As well, many legal connections, through foreign direct investment for example, are not always effectively conducted or sufficiently monitored to ensure that they promote human rights and/or development.

Several examples of the transnational connections involved in some of the covert areas of international commerce have been brought to light recently. For example, in his critical evaluation of global economic governance, William Tabb (2004: 377–8) provides details on off-shore banking sites that have been used by several of the world's kleptocratic rulers and former rulers to hide the proceeds of their rentier activities. His list of political leaders who have benefited from the relatively free movement of capital and the lack of transparency that exists in modern financial markets includes former leaders Ferdinand Marcos of the Philippines, Slobodan Milosevic of Yugoslavia, Jean-Claude Duvalier of Haiti, Benazir Bhutto of Pakistan as well as former African leaders Sani Abacha of Nigeria and Mobutu Sese Seko of Zaire. As an indication of the extent to which such practices have undermined prospects for development in the affected countries, Tabb (2004: 199) reports that ' ... decades into his kleptocratic rule Mobutu Sese Seko was allocating himself a salary in Zaire which exceeded government spending on education, health, and human services combined'.

Although the connection between underdevelopment and conflict cannot perhaps be proved empirically, it is reasonable to assume that the ability of leaders such as the late Mobutu Sese Seko to divert huge sums from developmental to personal purposes contributes appreciably to situations that foster civil war. The fact that the majority of modern civil wars have occurred in some of the world's poorest countries with extreme inequalities between elites and the general populace suggests a strong link (Nel 2003), and certainly there is a widely held belief among many academics and policy-makers that war and poverty, or more correctly, war and inequality are positively related. Ernie Regehr, conflict analyst and Director of Project Ploughshares, a Canadian-based NGO organized to promote peace and justice, was recently quoted as saying: '... it's not poverty itself that leads to war. It's economic injustice and imbalance. You have very low incidence of violence in poor countries where people at least think they're being treated fairly' (Todd 2004: C3). In those where treatment is perceived to be unfair, grievances tend to coalesce and escalate. Given this understanding, argues Regehr, it is possible to discern certain indications that a country is moving towards civil war. These signs include that:

• people do not have equal access to scarce natural resources;
• multiple ethnic groups carry legitimate grievances;
• the central government is weak;
• citizens have little confidence in their laws and institutions;
• people have easy access to weapons, particularly small arms, including rifles, grenades, mortar launchers and hand-held anti-aircraft missiles (ibid.).

Such conditions, ripe for the outbreak of conflict, existed prior to the civil wars that erupted in several of the postcolonial African states in recent years. In most if not all of them, the popular expressions of grievance and lack of confidence in the structures of government to which Regehr refers were responses to the increasing 'criminalisation of the state in Africa', the term used by Jean-François Bayart et al. (1999) to describe related processes of deepening patrimonialism and kleptocracy. Bayart et al. argue that 'criminal states,' exemplified by Mobuto-led Zaire (now the Democratic Republic of Congo), are identified by the use of violence by government elites to maintain control, the protection of a few key 'clients' or supporters that surround the elite core group, the use of the state's offices to conduct economic transactions (including, or especially, international ones) for personal gain, the development of criminal networks, and increasing reliance on these criminal activities to support the country's economy. Such practices are associated directly with a breakdown in governance, as over time, observes Morten Bøås (2004: 211), resentments related to 'social exclusion and marginality' converge out of common experiences 'rooted in corruption, violence (political and economic), and deep poverty.' The outcome is now tragically familiar as violent guerrilla insurgencies, composed often of large numbers of African youth, mount murderous campaigns against government forces, civilians and sometimes each other. While it is important to avoid over-generalizing – local situations vary and the particular form that the grievance takes (ethnic clashes, for instance) will be different for each – the set of factors identified by Regehr are common in the lead-up to most of Africa's recent wars.

Several scholars have offered explanations for the criminalization of the African state. Some have focused on the internal dimensions of African conflict; that is, the dynamics of political relations as a consequence of the historical construction of African social life in juxtaposition with governance systems and political economies that reconstruct traditional values and practices within modes of violent behaviour. Chabal and Daloz (1999), for example, argue that 'disorder is [a] political instrument' in Africa (1999: 144), and that violence as a vehicle for achieving political aims 'works' in accordance with aspects of African political culture, such as communal as opposed to individualist orientations and respect for 'ostentatious leadership' (Chabal and Daloz 1999: 166). While this essentially Afrocentric analysis is useful for understanding how specific social relations and political cultures respond to political and economic stimuli,[1] it tends to obscure by neglecting to pay attention to the role that external relations have played in the evolution of African social structures and governance models. Also, it pays insufficient attention to the relationship between recent African wars and globalization.

By contrast with Chabal and Daloz's more internally-focused analysis, scholars such as Christopher Clapham (1996; 2001) observe that Africa's connectedness in the international/global political economy has been a major factor in the development of patrimonial relationships in conflicted states. In particular, argues Clapham, the international norm of 'sovereignty' has been a useful device for rent-seeking leaders, who use the protection of offices sanctified by international law to make contacts for lucrative business transactions, and, more importantly, to avoid scrutiny when those transactions contravene legitimate business standards. Bayart (2000: 225), likewise, argues that it is through access to the trappings of statehood – control over security forces and financial resources, the ability to dispense patronage, to influence or prevent the emergence of strong electoral competition, and to provoke ethnic or agrarian agitation – that elites have been able to establish systems of exploitation.

Historically, leading African politicians have been adept in using 'strategies of extraversion', that is, positioning themselves in the interface between the national polity and the international political economy for purposes of regime maintenance and, in 'criminal state' cases, for personal accumulation (Bayart 2000, 2004). The Cold War period, in particular, offered ample opportunities for such practices given the interest of the superpowers in building their support in strategic African locations. With the end of the Cold War, the interest of external governmental actors in Africa waned, but new 'strategies of extraversion' came into play. Various features of globalization – market-led growth, technological innovations, improved communications, freer movements of capital, greater ease in transferring goods and people – opened up opportunities for private actors to move in to fill the vacuum left by the declining interest of governments. With this change, especially in those countries where inequalities are extreme and/or identity-based, and where the government is weak, conflict has usually not been far behind. Globalization effects – new technologies, expanding transportation networks, financial liberalization, and access to off-shore banking venues – have opened up or expanded opportunities in several areas, but especially in guns, minerals and drugs. And as William Reno (1997: 494) observes, the result is the development '... of new forms of political organization [that] undermine economic development, lead to overlapping jurisdictions, promote conflict among elites, and intentionally destroy bureaucracies'.

Mapping Transnational Networks

While there is an emerging literature on the transnational networks that contribute to African conflict, analysts working in the area acknowledge that it is difficult to obtain empirical information on the subject because of the covert nature of many of the activities. However, while the gathering of information and the construction of theory to explain the emergence of global networks, as with other features of globalization, are still at an early stage, there is a growing realization that global interconnections and networks are an important key to understanding African conflicts. Hence, there has been growing analytical interest in how African governments and insurgents have linked to outside actors and markets to wage civil wars and how war itself has then become functional – a venue for rent-seeking, again linked to the outside through transnational accumulation routes.

Within a political economy of conflict framework in which such issues are explored, several scholars, policy-makers, and researchers within various research institutes and think-tanks have begun to map the actual connections of the global networks, and where possible, to 'name names,' especially of individuals in high places (in government and business) who are involved. The earliest efforts to do this were by individuals – a Canadian consultant (Harker 2000) and an ambassador to the UN (Fowler 2000). These initiatives were followed soon thereafter by the UN Security Council (2001) which produced a detailed report on the exploitation of natural resources by warring factions in the DRC. Since then, there have been a number of attempts to expose the inside-outside dimensions of Africa's criminal, conflict-supportive networks. Geoffrey Wood's (2004) analysis of the 'criminal state' of Equatorial Guinea is a good example. Although Equatorial Guinea is not currently or recently involved in civil war, it has, as Wood (2004: 547) points out, 'a well-deserved reputation for gross human rights abuses and corruption'. Also noteworthy is the potential for conflict in the country, evidenced by an alleged coup attempt in March 2004.[2] According to Wood's analysis, several of Regehr's conditions for conflict are evident, and concentrated around a highly competitive struggle within the country to control the natural resources. What is apparent in the conditions fueling internal rivalries is the relationships with outside actors, especially oil companies that have recently become interested in this resource in Equatorial Guinea. A related and interesting observation by Wood is that government elites are involved in different, linked types of exploitative activities ('interlocking accumulation') involving tropical hardwood, toxic waste, pirate fishing, arms, aircrafts of convenience, drugs, oil, and money laundering (Wood: 2004: 553–65).

Analyses such as these suggest that there are ample opportunities of 'interlocking accumulation' in Africa in the global era, thus discrediting the view that Africa is outside or peripheral to the global economy. As Bayart

(2000: 267) succinctly puts it, 'more than ever, the discourse on Africa's marginality is a nonsense'. Indeed, it appears that there is a new 'scramble for Africa',[3] comparable in terms of the free-for-all resource extractions to the intensely competitive and exploitative activities of the colonial period. If, as in President Thabo Mbeki's (2003) words, 'Africa is still suffering the brutal consequences of the many years of the earlier globalization',[4] it is also suffering in the current period from new global forms of exploitation, located in transnational networks of accumulation, or to be more accurately descriptive, 'networks of plunder' (MacLean 2003).

While observations about current exploitative activities in Africa are hardly original, there is often little connection made in policy circles between the observations and practice when it comes to seeking ways either to prevent conflict or to reconstruct conditions of peace and development following conflict. Peace-making/-building initiatives continue to focus on the state directly, or on activities and actors within the conflicted state, rather than on the networks of plunder. Moreover, even when these networks are taken into consideration, they tend to be treated as aberrant constructions that are ephemeral and/or epiphenomenal to state processes; that is, the result of poor governance practices. The implication is that, with reformed governments, such networks would disappear. However, this approach ignores that networks – for promoting socially constructive objectives as well as for purposes of plunder – are a major factor that distinguishes the era of globalization from the order it is replacing. As Diane Stone (2002: 131) argues: 'Networks can ... be viewed as a mode of governance whereby the patterns of linkages and interaction as a whole should be taken as the unit of analysis, rather than simply analyzing actors within networks.' If networks are, indeed, a (the?) predominant new mode of social organization in the global era, our analyses and practices need to shift to accommodate these changes.

Yet, although we need to consider the centrality of the new network politics, the state continues also to be one of the important central actors. Not only does it loom large in the processes of political degeneration and corruption, but the reformation of states is critical for any meaningful reconstructions for peace and development. Therefore, whether seeking to discover the sources and fueling agents of African conflict or to investigate the possibilities for reconciliation and reconstruction, it is important to be aware of the modern state of Africa as a construction created by the interactive process of domestic and external forces, and to acknowledge that it is currently being de/reconstructed within the turbulence of a dynamic global political economy.

The term 'transboundary formations' that was used by Kassimir and Latham (2001: 276) to describe transborder relationships that 'produce and sustain forms of order and authority' provides an important lens for understanding the inside-outside forces of state-(re)building. Many such formations are being constructed as 'networks of plunder', as outlined above. However, not all transboundary formations are exploitative or pernicious; several are being established in the process of seeking remedies to prevent conflict and the conditions that contribute to it. It is equally important, therefore, to map the development of these more positive transnational networks. In short, remedies for poor governance cannot be adequately analyzed without taking into account new forms of global governance that are emerging to supplement or, in some cases, challenge the strategies of national governments.

Peace-making & Reconstruction in a Networked World

While national leaders in Africa (and elsewhere) rarely make public reference to global governance, globalization is certainly a significant factor in their policy calculations. Indeed, the New Partnership for African Development (NEPAD), the latest development plan for Africa (AU 2001), was formulated expressly to provide strategies to counter the negative effects of globalization in Africa and to build capacity for taking advantage of opportunities that globalization might provide for the continent. NEPAD is an important and impressive initiative, both for its realistic assessment of Africa's position in the global political economy and its visionary projections for a more optimistic future for the continent. It is also noteworthy for its comprehensiveness, in that it provides detailed overviews of, and prescriptions for, dealing with conflict prevention and resolution as well as problems and opportunities regarding governance and technical capacity in conflict-related issues of poverty/inequality, weak states, poor governance, and small arms.[5]

Notwithstanding its commendable and ambitious objectives, however, the possibility of NEPAD's success is questionable, perhaps doubtful. In its favor, it is a powerful statement of political will by the leaders of some of Africa's strongest states, and, at the very least, it is a positive force for promoting norms of good governance, human rights, and corporate responsibility. Its most serious short-coming, however, is its top-down origins; its grand vision lacks organic roots. As many civil society representatives have pointed out, NEPAD has been presented in terms of the benefits it offers to African people, yet the African people themselves had little to do with its genesis. Because it lacks solid social embeddedness, a number of critics have questioned whether African leaders will have the resolve or ability to tackle the governance issues that are outlined in NEPAD. Ian Taylor (2004) has expressed this concern, arguing that NEPAD ignores the reality of African statehood, that is, the role that patronage played in its construction and continues to play in regime maintenance in many African countries. In his words: 'we are expected to believe that the very same African elites who benefit from the neo-patrimonial state will now commit a form of class suicide. The possibility seems improbable' (Taylor 2004: 31).

'Africa's people must be the engineers of their own liberation,' argues Taylor (2004: 32), and in this, '... the international community's role should be to support this self-liberation, not legitimize the illegitimates'. Many other critics of NEPAD would agree with at least the first part of Taylor's statement, although some are more skeptical about the role that outsiders should (or are willing to) play. For instance, some believe that a meaningful partnership between African and Northern countries is unlikely, given both the history of dependence and the present inequalities in power and wealth

(Mulikita 2004; Kagwanja 2004). Others regard NEPAD's support for liberal democracy and a neo-liberal economic formula as problematic. They argue that this is a Western development model that discounts African culture and experiences, and that effective government for Africa needs to reflect precolonial African traditions and identities (Owusu-Ampomah 2004).

Each of these positions is compelling to some extent. If my analysis of the factors leading to the descent into conflict at the beginning of this paper is accurate, for instance, then strict attention should be paid to Taylor's concerns. Also, notwithstanding recent promises made by the G-8 nations, Africans' skepticism about donor partners' commitment has been justifiably fueled by low levels of foreign direct investment in Africa to date, the lack of attention paid by the dominant powers to the trade concerns of developing (including African) countries, and especially the insufficient response by the international community to recent African crises. Finally, surely, the 'crisis of alienation' to which Owusu-Ampomah (2004: 31) refers can only be addressed by constructing institutional systems that reflect the interests and identities of the people they serve.

Yet, although these concerns have some validity, they are limited in that they rehash old arguments that seek to establish blame for Africa's problems on *either* domestic *or* external actors and conditions. These opposing positions have been expressed repeatedly over the years, perhaps most clearly and forcefully in the early 1980s when they were set out in alternative visions for African development, presented in the Organization of African Unity's Lagos Plan of Action (1980) and the World Bank's Berg Report (1981) (Olukoshi 2002). Analyses that reproduce this long-standing, unresolved (unsolvable?) debate are not particularly helpful. Furthermore, and more importantly, they obscure the interconnectedness that characterizes political and economic relations now more than ever. In short, analysts seeking causal factors for African conflicts need to try to understand the nature and extent of global (economic, political and social) networking arrangements. Likewise, searches for potential solutions must begin to draw on the possibilities that exist in the emergence of new global governance structures.

This position does not negate the central role of Africans in determining their own futures, nor does it undermine the argument that African cultures and traditions are important for establishing relevant governance structures. Indeed, most observers, regardless of whether they are critical or supportive of NEPAD, accept that the key to an African Renaissance rests with Africans. Furthermore, most accept that success will only be achieved if African civil society is engaged and supportive of the initiatives. Yet, strong civil societies exist in juxtaposition with strong states, so bottom-up and top-down forces and ideas need to find some level of accommodation to construct a new 'social contract' for reform. At the present time, state forms (worldwide, not only in Africa) are being buffeted and recreated by globalization forces. Likewise, it is difficult, if not impossible, to segregate domestic civil societies completely from the rapidly proliferating global civil society. Given that, to attempt to find accommodation between state and society in local polities without considering and engaging global pressures and relations is to miss much of the present-day economic, political and social dynamic.

Moreover, analyses that privilege culture and tradition have taken on greater resonance in the current era of identity-politics; global forces are not only responsible for highlighting identity issues, they also contribute to changes in culture and identity. The danger in looking to tradition to solve the problems of today, is in the tendency to disregard fluidity and evolution. Cultures change and, especially in the complex global society, people are taking on multi-faceted identities. Therefore, while there may be value in examining traditional African democracies to discover governance structures that may be more compatible with present-day African social relations, it would be a mistake to discount that cultures and identities are not static, and that rapid change is a characteristic feature of the global world. It is important to take into consideration that different generations and different groups of Africans – say, urban youth or those who comprise the vast, expanding African diaspora – may have interests and views that are far removed from those that conditioned, or were formed by, precolonial traditions. Nation-states alone can no longer be counted on to provide effective governance for development and democracy; today's networked world requires new global governance arrangements.

Possibilities in Global Governance

The current discourse on global governance discusses new trends and exposes venues and interstices that offer possibilities for dealing with the new security issues of the global network world (Held and McGrew 2003; Ougaard and Higgott 2002). Global governance may be defined as sets of rules and conditioned patterns of behavior in which authority is exercised to achieve certain objectives. It is 'global' to the extent that it is concerned with issues of a global nature, and to the degree that it involves authoritative transnational actors. Global governance is usually considered also to comprise both state and non-state actors who interact over different levels of polity. Finally, a feature that is not necessarily definitive of, but frequently associated with, global governance is fluidity in the membership of the governance actors, especially involving members from non-state sectors.

Several emerging forms of global governance have particular relevance for dealing with conflict and security issues in Africa. Interrelated trends that define these new forms of governance include the proliferating knowledge network, the mixed-actor coalitions engaged in the advancement of global norms, and the institutionalization of new global security mechanisms. Although these trends are at an early stage, they are sufficiently developed to begin to reveal their emerging shapes and directions.

Mapping Global Networks

Manuel Castells' (1996, 1997, 1998) three volumes on 'the information society' were seminal in showing how the proliferation of information technology is changing the nature of political and social behavior in the present global age. Yet, for many in developing countries, the change associated with the information society may be increasing marginalization. Indeed, the information explosion has both highlighted and exacerbated North-South inequalities, and as the NEPAD documents point out, the so-called 'digital divide' requires significantly increased support from donor nations to build up information technology (IT) if these inequalities are to be reduced. Yet, although access to technology is limited and uneven in Africa, knowledge networks are a feature of the new information society that has spread over the entire globe and their relevance in Africa is established and growing (Mbabazi et al. 2002).

Within this new information society, Diane Stone (2002) has identified three different types of transnational networks currently operating: (i) knowledge networks that create, exchange and disseminate information transnationally; (ii) global policy networks, often mixed (state and non-state) actors working together to provide a public good, such as health care; and (iii) transnational advocacy coalitions that tend to operate in conjunction with new social movements for social or political change.

All three types exist in Africa. In recent years, there has been a virtual explosion of knowledge networks and there is now a rich array of academic centers, research institutes and think-tanks on the continent, often linked with similar knowledge institutions both inside and outside Africa. They are also frequently linked with government and international organizations (Mbabazi et al. 2002). Their most important functions are identifying, elaborating, and publicizing multiple facets of various problems. Certainly, as mentioned above, important information regarding the actors and actions involved in the criminal networks related to African conflict has been made available through the investigative work of members in an increasingly interactive knowledge network composed of a number of types of actors, ranging from academics and researchers to consultants and reporters. Various research institutes and think-tanks have become established as credible sources of information. They have also become authoritative members of the knowledge network because they produce rich, detailed analytical studies of specific issues and/or interrelated issues.[6] Both because of the electronic availability of this information and through intellectual connections with other similar institutions as well as with academics, governments, and international organizations, it is usual for the information to be widely and quickly disseminated. Hence, comprehensive bodies of research material on interrelated conflict topics are now readily available to researchers and policy-makers in as well as outside Africa.

Among the global policy networks, which are the second type identified by Stone, some of the more prominent in Africa are those operating around health issues such as HIV/AIDS, tuberculosis and malaria. However, security/conflict-related networks are also well established. The international small arms network has been one of the most active, especially in South(ern) Africa which has been a leader in suggesting and operationalizing certain innovations for dealing with this issue (MacLean 2002a, 2002b). In addition, the Kimberley Process on conflict diamonds, which snowballed into a major transnational effort over a very short period of time, can be situated in the global policy network category. Such networks have been instrumental in spreading information and advocacy trans-nationally, thus moving issues forward quickly to gain support for change in policy and/or social structures to improve conditions in a particular area. Another function that many of these networks perform, which is often overlooked, is to demonstrate the interconnectivity of issues involved in human (in)security. For instance, the connections between health and conflict (including HIV/AIDS and militaries) and in some cases, the treat-ment of security concerns as health issues (small arms, for example), have been an important contribution to understanding the multiple dimensions and connections of (in)security.

The third type of network, transnational advocacy coalitions, tends to operate in conjunction with new social movements for social or political change and/or overlap with the other two types of networks. However, these networks are distinguished by their members' commitment to encouraging social change. This type of coalition is most important for the development of new international norms. Among the more important coalitions for dealing with the economic sources of African conflict are those that encourage corporate social responsibility. Granted, the majority of codes of conduct for corporate behavior developed to date have been voluntary, leading to criticisms regarding the limits of their effectiveness.[7] Yet, the rapid, massive proliferation of such coalitions is impressive and hopeful, and an indication in itself of the strength of this movement. The impact is also demonstrated in the rate and extent to which the norm of social responsibility is being taken up by international organizations, demonstrated by the commitment of the OECD to extend the norm, and the initiation of the UN Global Compact to bring together relevant players to support responsible corporate activities.

Global networks for corporate social responsibility complement and, in some instances, interact directly with other networks that are concerned to halt the proliferation of small arms and to stop the illegal trade in these weapons and in conflict diamonds, drugs, and various natural resources that fuels war in Africa. Together, they form a complex network in the emerging global governance for peace, development and human security. Separately, and interactively, they help in constructing a new set of norms for a global order. In some cases they build on, but they may also challenge, traditional norms, including the long-established norm of sovereignty. States continue to be a central, if not the only, actor within the governance nexus, yet it is increasingly being made explicit that statehood carries with it responsibilities to citizens that must be upheld. As the 2001 report of the International Commission on Intervention and State Sovereignty (ICISS 2001: xi) asserts:

a) state sovereignty implies responsibility, and the primary responsibility for the protection of its people lies with the state itself;

b) where a population is suffering serious harm, as a result of internal war, insurgency, repression or state failure, and the state in question is unwilling or unable to halt or avert it, the principle of non-intervention yields to the international responsibility to protect.

A normative framework based upon a 'responsibility to protect' questions the primacy of sovereignty as the organizing principle of international relations. Sovereignty becomes secondary to human security, or in other words, human security becomes the answer to the question, 'What/who is sovereignty for?'

The establishment of the International Criminal Court (ICC) in 1998 and its entrance into force in 2002 have highlighted progression in the institutionalization of a new normative framework that privileges human security. The court has already intervened in the case of an African conflict by indicting Charles Taylor, former President of Liberia, for war crimes committed by Liberian-backed rebel groups in Sierra Leone's civil war. There have also been discussions about the possibility of using the ICC offices to bring President Robert Mugabe of Zimbabwe to justice for the crimes against humanity that many believe have been perpetrated by his regime.

The establishment of the ICC, the development of new norms that challenge the primacy of sovereignty and, perhaps especially, the emergence of new knowledge, policy and advocacy networks to deal with issues of security and conflict are indicative of a rapidly advancing system of global governance. Certainly, as with all social constructions, these are permeated by politics and power relations, and particularly in the South, many have been critical of Northern dominance, especially with regard to the ICC. Also, many are skeptical about the ability of enlightened or critical actors to avoid being subsumed by stronger state actors. Such cynicism may be justified; however, as Michael Pugh (2002: 227) has argued in response to those who worry that NGOs will tend to be co-opted into state projects, 'radical cosmopolitanism [which seems to describe the processes being addressed here] seeks expressions of solidarity with "alterities" (alternatives that practice tolerance) that are suppressed by policy-holders. ... NGOs and other non-state actors may be co-opted into statism.... But they also represent a potential for crossing frontiers to empower alterities and develop global society.'

Seeking solutions to reduce conflict in Africa involves precisely this – the search for potentials for crossing frontiers in order to empower alterities. The most important frontier to cross is the conceptual one that would free us from frameworks constrained by reified, dichotomous constructions of state versus international community, North versus South, us versus them. Empowering alterities would involve considering the possibilities that are emerging through the new global governance networks to deal with conflict and its root causes.

Conclusion

In a globalized world, conflict is often instigated or fueled by venal trans-national networks of corruption, crime and violence. Most, if not all, of the recent civil wars of Africa have been at least prolonged or exacerbated by the exploitative activities of such networks. While these cannot be understood outside the context of social relations within African countries and communities, neither can they be understood outside the context of the global political economy. Therefore, to seek solutions that focus only on the redemption of malfunctioning states is to ignore a major aspect of the problem.

This chapter has argued for analyses that examine the problem of African conflict within a framework that recognizes: a) the integration of the political and economic; b) the connection between development and security; and c) the interplay between the domestic and the international/global. Also, this framework explores the possibility that globalization involves the reconstruction of social relations towards an increasing array of interconnecting networks. While the venal networks described above represent the 'dark side' of globalization, other more positive networks are emerging. These networks either support or partly constitute the construction of new forms of global governance. While these emerging forms are not unproblematic, they may represent possibilities for creating norms and rules for a more humane order. At the very least, they appear to be the most promising of the options currently available.

References

African Union (AU). 2001. *The New Partnership for Africa's Development*. Abuja: African Union.

Bayart, Jean-François. 2000. 'Africa in the World: a history of extraversion', *African Affairs* 99 (395): 217–67.

Bayart, Jean-François. 2004. 'Commentary: towards a new start for Africa and Europe', *African Affairs* 103(412). July: 453–8.

Bayart, Jean-François. Stephen Ellis and Beatrice Hibou. 1999. *The Criminalisation of the State in Africa*. Oxford: James Currey.

BMO Financial Group. 2004. 'Commodity Price Index Hits New Record in October', *Commodity Price Report*. November. [Online] Available at: http://www.bmo.com/economic/commod/mcpr.pdf [accessed 20 November 2004].

Bøås, Morten. 2004. 'Africa's Young Guerillas: rebels with a cause?', *Current History*. May: 211–14.

Callaghy, Thomas, Ronald Kassimir and Robert Latham, eds, 2001. *Intervention and Transnationalism in Africa: Global-local networks of power*. Cambridge: Cambridge University Press.

Castells, Manuel. 1996, 1997, 1998. *The Information Age*. 3 Volumes. Oxford: Blackwell.

Chabal, Patrick. 2002. 'The Quest for Good Government and Development in Africa: is NEPAD the answer?' *International Affairs* 78 (3): 447–62.

Chabal, Patrick and Jean-Pascal Daloz. 1999. *Africa Works: Disorder as a political instrument*. Oxford: James Currey.

Clapham, Christopher. 1996. *Africa & the International System: The politics of state survival*. Cambridge: Cambridge University Press.

Clapham, Christopher. 2001. 'Rethinking African States', *African Security Review* 10 (3). [Online] Available at http://www.iss.ca.za/Pubs/ASR/10No3/Clapham.html.

Etzioni, Amitai. 2004. 'A Self-restrained Approach to Nation-building by Foreign Powers', *International Affairs* 80 (1): 1–17.

Fleisher, Michael L. 2002. '"War Is Good For Thieving!': the symbiosis of crime and warfare among the Kuria of Tanzania', *Africa* 72 (1): 131–9.

Fowler Report. 2000. *Report of Sanctions Committee on Violation of Security Council Sanctions against UNITA*, Robert Fowler, Chair. New York: United Nations.

Harker Report. 2000. 'Report to the Minister of Foreign Affairs on "Human Security in the Sudan: report of a Canadian assessment mission"' . Ottawa: DFAIT, January.

Held, David and Anthony G. McGrew, eds. 2002. *Governing Globalization: Power, authority and global governance*. Cambridge: Polity Press.

ICISS. 2001. *The Responsibility to Protect. Report of the International Commission on Intervention and State Sovereignty*. Ottawa: International Development Research Centre (December).

Kagwanja, Peter Mwangi. 2004. Book Review of *Fanon's Warning: a civil society reader on the New Partnership for African Development*, ed. Patrick Bond, *African Affairs* 103 (412): 493–4.

Kassimir, Ronald and Robert Latham. 2001. 'Towards a New Research Agenda', in T. Callaghy et al., eds, *Intervention and Transnationalism in Africa*, Cambridge: Cambridge University Press, 267–78.

Latham, Robert. 2001. 'Identifying the Contours of Transboundary Political Life', in T. Callaghy et al., eds, *Intervention and Transnationalism in Africa*, Cambridge: Cambridge University Press, 69-92.

Los Angeles Times. 2004. 'Editorial: Africa Must Stop Massacres'. 17 August. B12.

Lumpe, Lora, ed. 2000. *Running Guns: The global market in small arms*. London: Zed Books.

MacGaffey, Janet and Rémy Bazenguissa-Ganga. 2000. *Congo-Paris: Transnational traders on the margins of the law*. Oxford: James Currey and Bloomington, IN: Indiana University Press in association with the International African Institute.

MacLean, Sandra J. 2002a. 'Mugabe at War: the political economy of conflict in Zimbabwe', *Third World Quarterly* 23 (3): 513–28.

MacLean, Sandra J. 2002b. 'Small Arms and Human Security in Central Africa: national, regional and transnational dimensions of the problem', in D. Mortimer, ed., *Canadian International Security Policy: Reflections for a new era: selected proceedings of the International Security Research Outreach Program-York Centre for International and Security Studies Symposium*, Toronto: Centre for International Security Studies, 79–102.

MacLean, Sandra J. 2003. 'New Regionalisms and Conflict in the Democratic Republic of the Congo: networks for plunder and for peace in Southern and Central Africa', in F. Söderbaum and A. Grant, eds, *New Regionalisms in Africa*, Aldershot: Ashgate, 110–24.

MacLean, Sandra J. and Timothy M. Shaw. 2001. 'Canada and the New 'Global' Strategic Alliances: prospects for human security at the start of the 21st century', *Canadian Foreign Policy* 8 (3): 17–36.

Mbabazi, Pamela, Sandra J. MacLean and Timothy M. Shaw. 2002. 'Towards a Political Economy of Conflict and Reconstruction in Africa: Challenges for Policy Communities and Coalitions', *Global Networks: A Journal of Transnational Affairs* 2 (1): 31–47.

Mbeki, Thabo. 2003. 'Planned Speech to the University of Toronto', November. [Online] Available at http://www.utoronto.ca/president/mbeki.htm.

Mulikita, Njunga-Michael. 2004. 'NEPAD: a viable recovery blueprint for Africa?' *New Agenda: South African Journal of Social and Economic Policy* 13 (First Quarter): 46–8.

Nel, Philip. 2003. 'Income Inequality, Economic Growth, and Political Instability in Sub-Saharan Africa', *The Journal of Modern African Studies* 41 (4): 611–39.

Olukoshi, Adebayo. 2002. 'Governing the African Political Space for Sustainable Development: a reflection on NEPAD', Paper prepared for presentation at the African Forum for Envisioning Africa, CODESRIA, 26–29 April, Nairobi. [Online] Available at: http://www.worldbank.org/wbi/governance/parliament/nepad/lib1/session1c.pdf.

Ougaard, Morten and Richard Higgott, eds. 2002. *Towards a Global Polity*. London: Routledge.

Owusu-Ampomah, Kwame. 2004. 'Africa in the 21st Century: prospects for the transformation', *New Agenda: South African Journal of Social and Economic Policy* 13 (First Quarter): 28–33.

Pugh, Michael. 2002. 'Maintaining Peace and Security', in David Held and Anthony G. McGrew, eds, *Governing Globalization: Power, authority and global governance*, Cambridge: Polity Press, 209–33.

Reno, William. 1997. 'War, Markets, and the Reconfiguration of West Africa's Weak States', *Comparative Politics* 29 (4): 493–510.

Reno, William. 2001. 'How Sovereignty Matters: international markets and the political economy of local politics in weak states', in T. Callaghy et al., eds, *Intervention and Transnationalism in Africa*, Cambridge: Cambridge University Press, 197–215.

Stone, Diane. 2002. 'Knowledge Networks and Policy Expertise in the Global Polity', in M. Ougaard and R. Higgott, eds, *Towards a Global Polity*, London: Routledge, 125–44.

Tabb, William, K. 2004. *Economic Governance in the Age of Globalization*. New York: Columbia University Press.

Taylor, Ian. 2004. 'NEPAD Ignores the Fundamental Politics of Africa', *Contemporary Review* 285. July: 29–32.

Todd, Douglas. 2004. 'The Peace Revolution', *The Vancouver Sun*. 6 November: C1&C3-4.

United Nations Global Compact. [Online] Available at http://www.globalcompact.or/.

United Nations Security Council. 2001. *Report of the Panel of Experts on the Illegal Exploitation of Natural Resources and Other Forms of Wealth of the Democratic Republic of the Congo*, S/2001/357. New York: United Nations, 12 April.

Wood, Geoffrey. 2004. 'Business and Politics in a Criminal State: the case of Equatorial Guinea', *African Affairs* 103 (413): 547–67.

Notes

1 See the interesting analysis, for instance, by Michael L. Fleisher (2002), of which the opening phrase of the title is borrowed from a member of a cattle-raiding group in Tanzania: 'War is good for thieving',

2 The alleged coup was brought to light when a group of alleged mercenaries were arrested in Zimbabwe after the aircraft in which they were passengers landed at Harare airport. This incident and the subsequent trials of the alleged mercenaries received widespread attention in the press. Wood's (2004: 551–3) article provides an excellent summary of the details of the incident.

3 This new scramble for Africa is no doubt related to a recent increase in global commodity prices (BMO Financial Group 2004), the latter caused in part by the voracious demand unleashed by the economic liberation of the Chinese economy.

4 This is an excerpt from a speech that was to have been given at the University of Toronto, Canada, on 5 November 2003. Mbeki's visit to the university was cancelled and the speech was not delivered, but the planned speech is published at http://www.utoronto. ca/president/mbeki.htm.

5 See http://www.nepad.org/documents/4.pdf

6 See, for instance, the websites of African institutions such as the African Centre for the Cooperative Resolution of Disputes (ACCORD) www.accord.org.za; the Centre for Conflict Resolution (CCR) www.ccrweb.ccr.uct.ac.za; the Institute for Global Dialogue (IGD) www.igd.org.za; and the Institute for Security Studies www.iss.co.za. For organizations outside Africa that deal with African and/or conflict issues, see the website of Global Witness on conflict diamonds http://www.globalwitness.org/ or of the Canadian organization, Partnership Africa Canada www.partnershipafriccanada.org.

7 For examples of the range of coalitions, see the Consumer International Website http://wwwconsumersinternational.org/wcrd/sectwo/partI.html

7

Legislative Responses to Terrorism
& the Protection of Human Rights
A Survey of Selective African Practice
CEPHAS LUMINA

Overview

One of the consequences of the devastating 11 September 2001 (11 September) attacks in the United States has been renewed global concern with international terrorism.[1] Since that date, the US government has embarked on the so-called 'War on Terror'. This has involved attacks on Afghanistan and Iraq, resulting not only in the overthrow of the regimes in these countries but also in massive violations of the rights of individuals considered terrorists by the Bush Administration and the deaths of thousands of innocent civilians. The appalling treatment to which terrorist suspects have been subjected has led to concerns about the impact or implications of the war on terror on human rights.

In the aftermath of 11 September, governments around the world rushed to enact 'anti-terrorism' legislation. Among others, Australia,[2] Britain,[3] Canada,[4] India,[5] and the United States[6] have all passed anti-terrorism legislation. Furthermore, a number of countries in Africa,[7] where anti-terror legislation is not a new phenomenon (see Alexander and Nanes, 1986) and other parts of the developing world have either introduced or have been constrained to introduce anti-terrorist legislation by the US and its ally, the UK – as part of their 'either you are with us or you are against us' global anti-terrorism campaign (Mulama 2004). Others have resurrected draconian colonial anti-terrorism legislative measures. Almost invariably, these laws have substantially impinged upon or have serious implications for civil rights and democratic rights and freedoms,[8] particularly those of criminal suspects, political oppositions, migrants, refugees and asylum seekers, and for the fundamental principles of humanity.[9]

This chapter attempts to provide an overview of the range, and human rights implications, of anti-terrorism legislative measures adopted in selected African countries since 11 September. It also considers these legislative measures in the light of the fundamental principles of humanity as reflected in the Turku Declaration. It is argued that each state should have, in cooperation with others and in accordance with the dictates of international law, the liberty to adopt counter-terrorism legislation that not

181

only is consonant with its local circumstances but also helps it meet its obligations under international law, including the primary obligation to protect the rights of all people without discrimination of any kind. Most importantly, there is a need for the world to deal with the problem of terrorism in a holistic manner that ensures that, in their quest to deal effectively with the terrorist threat, states do not erode the rights of all those subject to their jurisdiction.

The chapter does not purport to provide an exhaustive treatment of the legislative practice in all 53 African countries in regard to countering terrorism. Rather, it offers an overview of legislative measures adopted post-11 September in selected African countries: Mauritius, Morocco, South Africa and Uganda. These countries have been selected as case studies for three main reasons: (i) they represent a diversity of legal systems and regions; (ii) each has a constitution that guarantees human rights; and (iii) each is a party to one or more of the various international and regional conventions relating to terrorism. It should be noted, however, that reference will be made where appropriate to the situation in other African countries. The human rights concerns explored in the paper include the effects of anti-terrorism legislation on refugees and minorities, on access to legal representation, on infringement of privacy, and on limitations to political rights and freedoms.

It should be noted from the outset that there is no universally accepted definition of terrorism. Terrorism is a controversial and elusive concept which evokes strong and contradictory responses. As the saying goes: 'One man's terrorist is another's patriot'.[10] For this reason, this paper does not attempt to define the term. Rather, it adopts the simple working definition that terrorism is the use of violence for political goals.

Terrorism: The International Legal Framework

Although there are a number of anti-terrorism treaties preceding 11 September (ranging from the 1963 Convention on Offences and certain Other Acts Committed on Board Aircraft to the International Convention for the Suppression of the Financing of Terrorism of 1999), the first significant action by the United Nations in relation to terrorism was taken in 1972 following the massacres at Lod Airport in Israel and at the Olympic Games in Munich. In the 1980s, both the General Assembly and the Security Council unanimously adopted a number of important resolutions condemning terrorism.

There are currently twelve universal conventions on specific aspects of terrorism: hijacking of aircraft;[11] the sabotage of aircraft;[12] attacks on 'internationally protected persons,' that is, heads of state and heads of government, foreign ministers, diplomats, etc;[13] the taking of hostages;[14] terrorist bombings;[15] and the financing of terrorist activities.[16] To these may be added the various international conventions on international humanitarian law,[17] which are designed, *inter alia*, to proscribe the use of terrorism during armed conflict. International humanitarian law prohibits terrorist activities in armed conflict by criminalizing (i) attacks against other than military targets; (ii) the use of force disproportionate to that needed to attain the military objective; and (iii) the use of force that does not discriminate between the target of the attack and persons who are not the object of such attack. It also prohibits the unnecessary use of force under any circumstances.

Since 11 September 2001, the UN Security Council has adopted several binding resolutions aimed at restricting terrorism and minimizing the ability of terrorists to mobilize support. On 28 September 2001, the Security Council adopted Resolution 1373. This Resolution criminalizes the provision of funds and services to terrorists and freezes the financial assets of people who commit terrorist acts. As with most other international instruments on terrorism, the Resolution does not define 'terrorism'. It further obliges UN member states to take measures to implement the Resolution.[18] Resolution 1373 also establishes a Counter-Terrorism Committee (UNCTC) to monitor its implementation.[19] It is notable that, although there are a number of international and regional treaties that aim to combat terrorism,[20] there is no single universal convention on the entire phenomenon of terrorism.

Post-11 September counter-terrorism initiatives at the universal level have not been limited to the Security Council. The General Assembly has established an Ad Hoc Committee on terrorism working primarily on developing a draft comprehensive anti-terrorism convention designed to fill the void left by the 12 sectoral treaties.

A number of conventions on terrorism have also been adopted at the regional level. These include the Arab Convention on the Suppression of Terrorism, 1998; the European Convention on the Suppression of Terrorism, 1977; the Organization of American States (OAS) Convention to Prevent and Punish Acts of Terrorism Taking the Form of Crimes against Persons and Related Extortion that are of International Significance, 1971; the Organization of African Unity (OAU) Convention on the Prevention and Combating of Terrorism, 1999; and the Protocol to the AU Convention on the Prevention and Combating of Terrorism, 2004. Other anti-terrorism initiatives in Africa include the African Union's (AU) September 2002 counter-terrorism conference in Algiers, the establishment of the African Centre for the Study and Research on Terrorism, the AU Declaration on the Prevention and Combating of Terrorism in Africa adopted at Algiers in October 2004,[21] and support for UN Security Council Resolution 1373 which, *inter alia*, reaffirms that the suppression of acts of international terrorism (including state-sponsored terrorism) is an essential contribution to maintaining international peace and security. Many states have also concluded bilateral agreements to deal with the problem of terrorism. These measures largely deal with the rendition of fugitive offenders.

It is notable that the international legal framework for dealing with terrorism has been criticizd for its perceived shortcomings. According to Cassese (1989: 11), there are three main limitations to international anti-terrorism measures: (i) inadequate ratifications; (ii) the lack of effective enforcement mechanisms in the event of violation; and (iii) the lack of specification that terrorist crimes are not 'political offences' and as such not exempt from extradition.

Legislative Responses to Terrorism in Africa:
A Survey of Selected Practice

Overview

As a starting point, it is worth noting, that at the national level, anti-terrorism legislation is not a new phenomenon in Africa. In many African countries, the colonial governments maintained all kinds of legislation to deal with what they considered terrorist activities but which the African people fighting for liberation and for their rights considered a just fight. Almost invariably, these activities were criminalized through penal codes for each colony based on some draconian law drafted in the far away colonial capitals of Brussels, Lisbon, London and Paris.

In South Africa, a plethora of laws enacted by the apartheid regimes prior to the democratic changes of 1993 ensured that the legitimate activities of the African National Congress (ANC) and its partners in the fight for freedom were curtailed and penalized through a range of criminal sanctions – from restrictions on movement to imprisonment and the death penalty. Under cover of the anti-terrorist legislation (e.g. Suppression of Communism Act 44 of 1950, Terrorism Act 83 of 1967, and Internal Security Act 74 of 1982), apartheid state security agents routinely and with impunity abrogated the human rights of suspected freedom fighters (branded 'terrorists'),[22] as well as members of their families, through arbitrary arrests, imprisonment without trial, torture and extra-judicial executions. One only has to browse through the report of the Truth and Reconciliation Commission (2003) to learn the ghastly details.

Another matter of note is that a number of African countries are parties to the international conventions and protocols relating to terrorism (South Africa is a party to nine of these) as well as to the AU Convention on Terrorism. These instruments enjoin states to take measures, including legislative measures, to combat terrorism. Thus, the AU Convention enjoins the states parties to adopt 'any legitimate measures aimed at preventing and combating terrorist acts in accordance with the provisions of (the) Convention and their respective national legislation'.[23] However, the Convention cautions that: 'Nothing in this Convention shall be interpreted as derogating from the general principles of international law, in particular the principles of international humanitarian law, as well as the African Charter on Human and Peoples' Rights' (Article 22). Furthermore, UN Security Council Resolution 1373 not only condemns the 11 September attacks in the US but also allows states to take the necessary steps to prevent the commission of terrorist attacks, including stopping the recruitment of members of terrorist groups, and adopting measures to prevent the financing, planning, facilitation and commission of terrorist acts.

Clearly, therefore, international law permits states to take national legislative measures to combat terrorism, but such measures must not offend against international law. However, the fact that most new anti-terrorism laws in Africa have been proposed or introduced under pressure from the USA[24] and the UK[25] makes it improbable that such legislation would reflect local concerns, including the protection of (usually, constitutionally guaranteed) human rights. As Makau Mutua (2003), the Chairman of the Kenya Human Rights Commission, has said with regard to his country's unpopular Suppression of Terrorism Bill of 2003: 'It [the bill] was not drafted by Kenyans or based on Kenya's needs. It originated in the United Kingdom. It is also a fact that both the UK and the US are intimidating and coercing Kenya into enacting this foreign and unnecessary law.'

It is a well-established principle that a state cannot legitimately invoke its domestic law to justify a failure to comply with its international treaty obligations and customary international law.[26] It is also important to note that a number of African states have not considered it necessary to enact any specific new counter-terrorism legislation. These states assert that their existing criminal laws already cover the specific conduct referred to as 'terrorist'.[27] Within the Southern African Development Community (SADC), only two (South Africa and Mauritius) of the 13 member states have enacted specific anti-terrorism legislation. Given the limitations of space, it is not possible to present more than an overview of the legislative responses in selected countries. Consequently, what follows is a survey of the anti-terrorism legislative measures adopted in Mauritius, Morocco, South Africa and Uganda.

Mauritius

The Republic of Mauritius is a party to three of the 12 UN conventions on terrorism; namely, the Convention for the Suppression of Terrorist Bombings, the Convention against Transnational Organised Crime, and the Convention on the Prevention and Punishment of Crimes against Internationally Protected Persons, including Diplomatic Agents. It is also a party to the AU Convention on the Prevention and Combating of Terrorism.

Post-11 September anti-terrorism legislation in Mauritius was first introduced by that country's government in January 2002 and controversially passed by Parliament despite a walkout by opposition parliamentarians. There are several key pieces of Mauritian legislation which aim to counter terrorism: the Prevention of Terrorism Act 2002, the Financial Intelligence and Anti-Money Laundering Act 2002, the Prevention of Corruption Act 2002, the Prevention of Terrorism (Special Measures) Regulations 2003 (as amended), the Financial Intelligence and Anti-Money Laundering Regulations 2003, the Anti-Money Laundering (Miscellaneous Provisions) Act 2003, and the Convention for the Suppression of Financing of Terrorism Act 2003.

The most controversial of these laws is the Prevention of Terrorism Act, which was adopted in circumstances that saw four presidents change office in one month because of their refusal to sign the Bill into law. It has been argued that the enactment of this Act was essentially a response to 'severe pressure that was threatening the country's economy' (Thomashausen 2003). Section 3 of the Prevention of Terrorism Act defines an 'act of terrorism' as 'an act which may seriously damage a country or an international organization; and is intended or can reasonably be regarded as having been intended to seriously intimidate a population' so as to unduly compel a government or an international organisation to perform or abstain from performing any act. The section further specifies activities which may constitute terrorism, including attacks upon a person's life that may cause death, kidnapping, seizure of aircraft, ships or other means of public transport, the manufacture, possession, acquisition or supply of weapons (including nuclear and biochemical weapons), and interference with public utilities the effect of which is to endanger life. The legislation also allows the police to detain 'terrorism' suspects without access to legal counsel for 36 hours and gives the government the right to extradite them or deny them asylum and to return them to countries where they might face human rights risks.

Under s10(6) (b) of the Prevention of Terrorism Act, the Minister responsible for national security may prohibit the entry into Mauritius of suspected international terrorists or terrorist groups. In terms of s25, the Minister may, for the purposes of the prevention or detection of offences, or the prosecution of offences under the Prevention of Terrorism Act 2002, give directions to service providers for the retention of communication data.[28] Furthermore, the police may obtain a court order authorizing a communication service provider to intercept, withhold or disclose to the police information or communications. Needless to say, civil society groups, opposition parties, and Amnesty International have expressed concern that most of the provisions of the Act are too broad and do not meet the international standards of fairness. In particular, Amnesty International has expressed concern that the term 'acts of terrorism' could be broadly interpreted to undermine fundamental human rights (Amnesty International 2003).

The Prevention of Terrorism (Special Measures) Regulations 2003, which came into effect on 25 January 2003, give effect to Part II, s10 (6) of the Prevention of Terrorism Act 2002, providing for the freezing of assets and funds of suspected international terrorists and terrorist groups. In terms of Regulation 3, the Central Bank or the Financial Services Commission may give directives to any financial institution under its regulatory control to freeze any account, property or funds held on behalf of any listed terrorist. It is an offence for a national or any person within Mauritius to give funds or economic resources directly or indirectly to listed individuals or entities.

The Financial Intelligence and Anti-Money Laundering Regulations provide for the verification of the 'true identity of all customers and other persons' with whom banks, financial institutions and cash dealers conduct business. The Anti-Money Laundering (Miscellaneous Provisions) Act 2003, which amends the Financial Intelligence and Anti-Money Laundering Act 2002 and establishes a National Committee for Anti-Money Laundering and Combating of the Financing of Terrorism, gives wide powers to the Central Bank and the Financial Services Commission to issue codes and guidelines on anti-money laundering. It also provides for derogation from the banks' duty of confidentiality to enable them to report suspicious transactions.

The Convention for the Suppression of Financing of Terrorism Act was enacted in 2003 to give effect to the International Convention for the

Suppression of the Financing of Terrorism 1999. The Act makes it an offence for any person to finance acts of terrorism and gives powers to courts to order forfeiture of funds intended to be used for or in connection with terrorist acts.

Morocco

The Kingdom of Morocco is a party to several UN conventions on terrorism. In the post-11 September period, it has ratified a further four of these conventions.[29] Following the Casablanca suicide bombings of 16 May 2003 that killed 45 people, the government of Morocco passed the Anti-Terror Act 03.03. This revises the Penal Code and Criminal Procedure Codes by adding new provisions and amending others. The Act contains a broad definition of acts of terrorism: any act done intentionally in relation to an individual or collective activity with the objective of causing serious disruption of public order by intimidation, terror or violence can be classified as an act of terrorism. The legislation lists specific acts including theft of goods, extortion, and the promulgation and dissemination of propaganda or advertisement in support of the mentioned acts. The Act also increases penalties which include the death penalty.[30] The permissible length of detention without judicial order for offences that are deemed to constitute acts of terrorism has been extended to twelve days, without right of appeal, and suspects may be denied access to counsel for up to ten days.

The Act allows for monitoring of telecommunications conversations and contacts. In its third report to the UNCTC, Morocco indicated that it plans to require persons working in the professions in addition to banking and financial institutions, to submit reports on suspicious transactions.[31]

South Africa

South Africa is a party to nine of the twelve anti-terrorism conventions of the UN and is also a party to the AU Convention on Terrorism, all of which, as stated above, enjoin the states parties thereto to take measures to give effect to the conventions. The country has also fallen victim to terrorism, including attacks on Johannesburg and Cape Town. It is therefore hardly surprising that the government has been keen to strengthen its legal arsenal against the crime.

In 2000, the South African Law Commission released a discussion paper (Discussion Paper No. 92) on a review of terrorism legislation (broad legislation inherited from the apartheid era) and draft legislation on terrorism. This attracted widespread condemnation and vehement public opposition because of the apprehension that it was an attempt to infringe fundamental rights and freedoms in South Africa, thereby forcing the government to withdraw the draft legislation. However, in the aftermath of the 11 September 2001 attacks in the United States, the South African government revived this legislation. The Anti-Terrorism Bill was tabled before the Parliamentary Portfolio Committee on Safety and Security in March 2003.

The Bill, which was designed to remedy the perceived shortcomings in the existing legislation (including the inability to curb urban terrorism) had wide-ranging implications for human rights and principles of humanity; its security measures seemed to contravene no fewer than 11 constitutional rights. The Bill was criticized on a number of grounds. One issue was the broad definition of what constitutes a 'terrorist act'. For example, the Bill defined any activity that might result in the 'disruption of essential public services' as a 'terrorist' act. Such wide and vague definition had the potential for abuse through, for example, characterization of legitimate strikes by public sector workers, demands for land, and civil disobedience campaigns as 'terrorism'. In effect, one could be guilty of a terrorist act when striking or participating in a public demonstration! The Bill also made provision for wide-ranging police powers to search vehicles and persons and provided for various offences, including providing support to or membership of a terrorist organisation, hijacking an aircraft, hostage taking and nuclear terrorism.

The controversy generated by the Bill needs to be viewed in the light of South Africa's past record of human rights violations against detainees and freedom fighters, using various security laws. Any legislation which may curtail human rights is politically sensitive in South Africa, because the former apartheid governments used similar laws to ban liberation movements and to persecute their leaders and activists, including members of the party now in power, the ANC. Another point of note obviating the need for anti-terrorist legislation is the fact that South Africa already has at least 33 pieces of legislation which can adequately deal with terrorism.

Sustained criticism of the Bill by various sectors of South African society forced the government to withdraw it and make some changes to it. The anti-terrorism legislation was reintroduced into Parliament as the Protection of Constitutional Democracy against Terrorist and Related Activities Bill of 2003 (Anti-Terrorism Bill), which the National Assembly passed unanimously on 12 November 2004. It received Presidential assent on 4 February 2005 and entered into force as the Protection of Constitutional Democracy against Terrorist and Related Activities Act 33 of 2004 on 11 February 2005.

The rationale for the enactment of the new anti-terrorism Act is the necessity to comply with international instruments (in particular Security Council Resolution 1373). According to the Parliamentary Select Committee, the offence of terrorism in s. 54 of the Internal Security Act (which the new Act repeals) was too narrow and only provided for terrorism against the South African government – a situation that was contrary to global trends in international terrorism, which can target any government.[32] Local legislation was also said to lack provision for specific offences, which 'must be created in terms of international conventions'. In short, the claim was that local laws 'do not meet all the international requirements related to terrorism and related activities'. The purpose of the Act is:

> To provide for measures to prevent and combat terrorist and related activities; to provide for an offence of terrorism and other offences associated or connected with terrorist activities; to provide for Convention offences; to provide for a mechanism to comply with United Nations Security Council Resolutions, which are binding on member states, in respect of terrorist and related activities; to provide for measures to prevent and combat the financing of terrorist and related activities; to provide for investigative measures in respect of terrorist and related activities; and to provide for matters connected therewith.

Thus, the new anti-terrorism Act as passed creates the offence of terrorism and prescribes a punishment of life imprisonment for the commission of a terrorist act, and makes it illegal to belong to designated terrorist groups,[33] Section 1 of the Act defines terrorist activity and terrorist-related acts but does not define 'terrorism'.

It also provides for 'convention offences' based on the twelve UN anti-terrorism conventions and the AU Convention, which include the financing of terrorism, hijacking aircraft or ships, hostage taking, causing harm to 'internationally protected persons' and committing hoaxes involving biochemical agents. Other offences relate to harboring and concealment of suspects and failure to report terrorist suspects to the authorities (ss. 11 and 12).

In terms of penalties, the Act provides for life imprisonment or a multi-million rand fine to be imposed on convicted terrorists (s. 18). In addition to any such punishment, the courts are empowered to make orders for the forfeiture of property reasonably believed to have been used in the commission of an offence or in connection with the commission of an offence (s. 19). The Act also provides for the making of court orders for the payment of wasted expenses incurred due to hoaxes.

It is notable that the Act provides for some safeguards. Thus, for instance, no investigative proceedings and no prosecution can be instituted without the written authority of the National Director of Public Prosecutions (NDPP) (s. 22). There is also a requirement that the NDPP promptly communicate the outcome of any prosecution to, *inter alia*, the UN Secretary General. The question is how effective these safeguards are likely to be. This is an assessment that can only be properly made once the Act is fully operational as law and a challenge to it arises.

Uganda

The Ugandan Anti-Terrorism Act of 2002 which entered into force in June 2002 is aimed at suppressing acts of terrorism, both locally and internationally. It provides for the punishment of persons who plan, instigate, support, finance or execute acts of terrorism; the prescription of terrorist organizations and the punishment of persons who are members of, or who publicly profess to be members of, or who convene or associate with or facilitate the activities, of terrorist organizations. The Act also makes provision for the investigation of acts of terrorism and the surveillance of terrorist suspects. Law enforcement officials have powers to monitor bank accounts, e-mails, telephone calls and other electronic communications of suspects. Employers are obliged to report absent employees where they suspect them of involvement in terrorist activities.

Unlike most other anti-terror laws, the Act defines terrorism. Section 7 of the Act provides that 'terrorism' is any act which involves serious violence against a person or serious damage to property, endangers a person's life (but not just the life of the person committing the act), or creates a serious risk to the health or safety of the public. Any such acts must be 'designed to influence the Government or to intimidate the public or a section of the public,' and must be in pursuance of a 'political, religious, social or economic aim' indiscriminately without due regard to the safety of others or their property. The section lists acts which constitute terrorism. The offence of terrorism carries a mandatory death sentence if the terrorist act directly results in the death of any person.

Section 8 of the Act provides for other terrorists offences including aiding, abetting, financing, harboring or rendering support to any person, with the knowledge or belief that such support will be used for or in connection with the preparation or commission or instigation of acts of terrorism. Conviction on any these offences carries the death penalty. The Act does not provide for any appeal procedure to challenge prescription as a terrorist organization.

The Human Rights Implications of Anti-Terrorism Laws

Having provided an overview of legislative responses to terrorism in selected African countries, it is appropriate now to consider the human rights implications of these anti-terrorism legislative measures.

The Primacy of International Human Rights Law

All acts of terror – whether by a state or groups of individuals – seriously impair the enjoyment of human rights by persons in the places targeted. The most visibly infringed right is the right to life. Thousands of people all over the world have lost their lives as a consequence of terrorist acts. The 11 September attacks in the US are but one instance. Terrorism has a long history, with a variety of perpetrators: the Red Brigade in Italy and Bader Meinhof in the Federal Republic of Germany in the 1970s; the US Central Intelligence Agency-sponsored terrorist activities against regimes that the US Administration did not favour; and the Israeli terror campaigns against Palestinians and *vice versa*, to name but a few. Africa has also had its fair share of 'terrorist' attacks – notably in Algeria, the 1998 bomb attacks on the US embassies in Kenya and Tanzania which killed hundreds, and the October 2002 Soweto bombings alleged to have been carried out by members of the right-wing Afrikaner Boeremag organization in South Africa.

All of the foregoing terrorist acts have resulted in loss of life and therefore in the curtailment of the right to life. However, it must be recognized that government efforts to curb terrorist activities have also culminated in the abridgement of many rights and freedoms, not only of the 'terrorist' suspects but also of innocent civilians. Some of the rights and freedoms infringed upon in the quest to curb terrorism include the rights to life, liberty, human dignity, expression, association and fair trial. Often, state measures to curb terrorism offend against the principles of humanity.

States have the primary responsibility for protecting the security of all persons under their jurisdiction. However, since 11 September, many states have adopted draconian new 'anti-terrorism measures', including new legislation, which are in breach of their international obligations and pose a serious threat to human rights.[34] The pressure on states to respond to the international terrorist threat has resulted in some states adopting legislative and administrative measures which effectively abridge or threaten to abridge human rights.[35] These include prolonged detention of suspects, curtailing the right of access to legal representation, removing the right of appeal, seizure of property and placing limits on freedom of expression. According to Amnesty International (2004: 5), these national legislative responses to terrorism are 'eroding human rights principles, standards and values'. In its report for 2004, Amnesty International (2004: 5-7) stated that countries have continued to flout international human rights standards in the name of the 'war on terror'. This has resulted in thousands of women and men suffering unlawful detention, unfair trial and torture – often solely because of their ethnic or religious background.

In recognition of the challenges to human rights posed by legislative responses to terrorism, on 25 October 2001 member states of the Commonwealth adopted a Statement on Terrorism in which they committed themselves to implementing UN Security Council Resolution 1373, 'in keeping with the fundamental values of the association including democracy, human rights, the rule of law, freedom of belief, freedom of political opinion, justice and equality'.[36] Significantly, the UN Security Council – the author of the resolution pursuant to which many of the states adopting ant-terrorism legislation purport to be acting – has recently reaffirmed 'the imperative to combat terrorism in all its forms and manifestations by all means, in accordance with the Charter of the United Nations and international law'.[37] It has also reminded states that 'they must ensure that any measures taken to combat terrorism comply with all their obligations under international law, and should adopt such measures in accordance with international law, in particular international human rights, refugee, and humanitarian law'.

Both the UN General Assembly and the Commission on Human Rights have adopted resolutions focusing on the need to protect human rights and fundamental freedoms while countering terrorism. The General Assembly resolution adopted on 18 December 2002 affirmed that states must ensure that any measure taken to combat terrorism complies with their obligations under international law, in particular, international human rights, refugee and humanitarian law.[38] The resolution also asks the High Commissioner for Human Rights to take a number of actions including examining the question of the protection of human rights while countering terrorism.

There are a number of controversial issues raised by anti-terrorist legislation. Significantly, the vague definitions of 'terrorism' in most anti-terrorism legislation leave the concept open to abuse. Such vague definition has led, for example in the US, to laws stereotyping people of Arabic and/or Eastern descent as well as organizations considered to be 'left-wing'. The definitional problem is perhaps best illustrated by the comments of the Chairman of the Kenyan Human Rights Commission on the Kenyan Suppression of Terrorism Bill of 2003: 'The Bill defines terrorism in such broad and vague terms that it cannot withstand the scrutiny of logic. Terrorism is such an innocuous bogeyman that it can be used as an open-ended excuse to deny suspects a broad range of constitutional guarantees' (Mutua 2003). Similar concerns formed part of the severe criticisms directed against the first post-11 September anti-terrorism legislation in South Africa.

While it is not intended to provide an exhaustive treatment of the human rights issues raised by anti-terrorism legislation, an overview of selected human rights may be instructive.

Refugees and Asylum Seekers

Some governments have used anti-terrorism legislation to suppress not only political oppositions but also minority groups. Some have used this legislation to evade their international obligations towards asylum seekers and refugees (Human Rights Watch. (2003). For example, Tanzania's Prevention of Terrorism Act 2002 gives immigration officers the power to arrest without warrant any person suspected of being a terrorist or of having been involved in international terrorist activities. The minister responsible for immigration is empowered to refuse asylum to any person.

In similar vein, the Mauritian Prevention of Terrorism Act of 2002 gives the government the right to extradite terrorist suspects or to deny such persons asylum and to return them to countries where they are at risk of persecution. Given the proliferation of conflicts in Africa and the attendant flow of displaced persons, such powers are too extensive and offend against the well-established international legal principle of non-refoulement.

Detention, Torture and the Right to a Fair Trial

Two of the most important rights of a criminal suspect are the right to be informed of the reason for their detention and the right to seek legal advice. Anti-terrorist legislation often curtails these under the pretext that more detention time is required for the law enforcement officials to complete their investigations. Where it is permitted, the right to counsel is limited to consultation with 'approved' legal practitioners. Under the Prevention of Terrorism (Special Measures) Regulations 2003 (Mauritius), a terrorist suspect can be detained for up to 36 hours without access to anyone other than a police officer or medical officer on request.[39]

In its report for 2004, Amnesty International stated that, in 2003, torture continued to be widespread in Algeria, particularly in cases which the government described as 'terrorist activities'.[40] According to Human Rights Watch, a number of people detained in a facility controlled by the Joint Anti-Terrorism Task Force in Uganda were tortured (Human Rights Watch 2003).

In his statement to the Third Committee of the UN General Assembly, Theo Van Boven, the Special Rapporteur on Torture, spoke of reported circumventions of the prohibition on torture in the name of countering terrorism. These attempts included the legal arguments of necessity and self-defence; attempts to narrow the scope of the definition of torture and arguments that some harsh methods should not be considered as torture but merely as cruel, inhuman or degrading treatment or punishment; acts of torture and ill-treatments perpetrated against terrorist suspects by private contractors; and the indefinite detention of suspects (including children) without determination of their legal status and without access to legal representation. As the Special Rapporteur has rightly stated, the definition of torture contained in the Convention against Torture cannot be altered by events (such as terrorism) or in accordance with the will or interest of states. It should be noted that the prohibition against torture is now firmly established as a rule of customary international law and, arguably, has the character of *jus cogens*.[41]

Freedom of Association, Expression and Assembly

These are basic civil rights which are crucial to any functioning democracy. However, they are also rights which have increasingly been curtailed or are under threat from anti-terrorism legislation as governments move to ban public demonstrations in the name of state security. Anti-terrorism legislation threatens to undermine democracy not only in Africa but across the world. Such legislation can easily be used to suppress or undermine democratic opposition.

To illustrate, the Zimbabwean Public Order and Security Act of 2002 makes it an offence to publish statements that promote public disorder or undermine public confidence in the law enforcement officials, or to insult the office of the president. The Ugandan government has been criticized for using the Anti-Terrorism Act of 2002 to 'repress political dissent and strictly limit freedom of expression' (Kagari 2003; also see Committee to Protect Journalists 2002). In September 2002, Ugandan radio stations were warned against giving publicity to an exiled political leader whom the government had labelled a 'terrorist' and threatened with prosecution under the Act, the terms of which make it an offence to give publicity to terrorists.

The Right to Privacy

The constitutions of all three countries surveyed guarantee the right to privacy.[42] However, their legislation confers powers on law enforcement agencies that potentially threaten this right. Some of the anti-terrorist legislative measures give the police extensive powers to combat terrorism, including the use of electronic surveillance to identify terrorists.[43] As stated above, the Ugandan Anti-Terrorism Act gives law enforcement officials extensive powers to monitor bank accounts, e-mails, telephone calls and other electronic communications of suspects. The potential for abuse under these provisions is considerable. Thus, it has been argued, for instance, that the phrase '... articles of a kind which could be used in connection with terrorism ...' in the Ugandan Anti-Terrorism Act is so 'vague that it could be used to search for almost any object' (Bossa and Mulindwa 2004: 7).

Other Human Rights Concerns

According to the UN Special Rapporteur on Religious Intolerance, anti-terrorist measures in a number of states have unduly limited freedom of religion or belief, in violation of international human rights standards.[44] Responses to terrorism have also led to new forms of racial discrimination and a growing 'acceptability' of the traditional forms of racism where certain cultural or religious groups are viewed as terrorist risks.[45] This has spawned new forms of racism that render it more difficult to combat racial discrimination and xenophobia.

Some of the anti-terrorism legislation surveyed *prima facie* poses a threat to the rights of the child. For example, while the Uganda anti-terrorist law imposes the sentence of death for the offence of terrorism, it does not expressly stipulate that it does not apply to children who might be involved in such activities. In view of the low age of criminal responsibility in Uganda, this lacuna is a serious concern (Bossa and Mulindwa 2004). There are also concerns about the lack of procedural safeguards concerning the extradition or the surrender of suspects.[46]

It should be noted that all of the countries surveyed have constitutional guarantees of human rights in their constitutions. Consequently, it will be interesting to see how the anti-terrorism legislative measures that have implications for human rights will be reconciled with the constitutional guarantees of human rights. Suffice it to say, these constitutions are proclaimed to be the 'supreme law' of the countries concerned and that any law inconsistent with the constitution is void to the extent of the inconsistency.[47]

Terrorism and the Principles of Humanity

The Turku Declaration on Minimum Humanitarian Standards affirms non-derogable minimum standards of humanity, which are applicable in all circumstances. It provides, *inter alia*, that all persons (including those whose liberty has been restricted) are 'entitled to respect for their person, honour and convictions, freedom of thought, conscience and religious practices' (Art. 3). It also prohibits a number of practices including outrages upon personal dignity.

On the face of them and with particular regard to the safeguards built therein, most of the anti-terror laws in Africa surveyed above respect these fundamental principles of humanity.[48] However, as indicated earlier, many of these laws have been roundly condemned as a threat to the rights enshrined in the countries' constitutions and in international human rights treaties.

While it is recognized that all countries have the responsibility and obligation under international law to give effect to the relevant UN and regional conventions and resolutions relating to terrorism, individual citizens have the right to be treated in accordance with the fundamental principles of humanity. In their current form, most of the African anti-terrorism laws are likely to erode not only the human rights of the people but also the fundamental principles of humanity.

Conclusion

The legislative responses to terrorism in Africa, in common with other anti-terrorist legislation elsewhere in the world, have the potential to impact negatively on human rights and freedoms such as the rights to freedom of expression, association, security of the person, religion, belief, opinion, assembly and demonstration, and to offend against the fundamental principles of humanity as defined in the Turku Declaration. As Amnesty International (2003: 7) stated in May 2003: 'The "War on Terror", far from making the world a safer place has made it more dangerous by curtailing human rights, undermining the rule of international law and shielding governments from scrutiny. It has deepened divisions among people of different faiths and origins...' The fact that many governments have been forced to introduce 'anti-terrorism' legislation by powerful states such as the US and the UK in their prosecution of the so-called 'war against terror', without due regard to their local circumstances, not only enhances the likelihood that these countries have not given much thought to the implications of such legislation for human rights, but also increases the risk of abuse by these states.

For these reasons, it is important that every state, in cooperation with others and in accordance with the dictates of international law, should have the freedom to adopt anti-terrorist legislation that not only suits it but also helps it meet its obligations under international law, including the obligation to protect the rights of all people irrespective of race, ethnic origin, political opinions, etc. Most importantly, there is a need for the world to deal with the problem of terrorism in a holistic manner that ensures that, in their quest to deal with the terrorist threat, states do not erode the rights of all persons subject to their jurisdiction. As the Policy Working Group on the United Nations and Terrorism (United Nations 2002: 5) stated in its 2002 Report:

> Terrorism is, in most cases, essentially a political act. It is meant to inflict dramatic and deadly injury on civilians and to create an atmosphere of fear, generally for a political or ideological (whether secular or religious) purpose. Terrorism is a criminal act, but it is more than mere criminality. To overcome the problem of terrorism it is necessary to understand its political nature as well as its basic criminality and psychology.

In sum, national legislative efforts to curb international terrorism should take full account of human rights and the fundamental principles of humanity.

References

Alexander, Y. and A.S. Nanes, eds. 1986. *Legislative Responses to Terrorism*. Dordrecht: Martinus Nijhoff Publishers.

Amnesty International 2003. *Amnesty International Report 2003*. London: Amnesty International Publications.

Amnesty International 2004. *Amnesty International Report 2004*. London: Amnesty International Publications.

Bossa, S.B. and T. Mulindwa. 2004. 'The Anti-Terrorism Act, 2002 (Uganda): Human Rights Concerns and Implications.' Paper prepared for Terrorism and Human Rights Network of the International Commission of Jurists, 15 September. [Online] Available at http://www.icj.org/news.php3?id_article=3517&lang=en

Cassese, A. 1989. *Terrorism, Politics and Law: The Achille Lauro Affair*. Cambridge: Polity Press.

Committee to Protect Journalists (CPJ). 2002. 'Attacks on the Press in 2002'. [Online] Available at http://www.cpj.org/attacks02/africa02/uganda.html.

Elagab, O.Y. 1999. *International Law Documents Relating to Terrorism*. London: Cavendish Publishing.

Han, H.H. 1993. *Terrorism and Political Violence: Limits and Possibilities of Legal Control*. New York: Oceana Publications.

Human Rights Watch. 2001. 'Opportunism in the Face of Tragedy: Repression in the name of anti-terrorism.' [Online] Available at http://www.hrw.org/campaigns/september11/opportunismwatch.htm

Human Rights Watch. 2003. *World Report 2003: Uganda*. [Online] Available at http://www.hrw.org/wr2k3/africa13.html.

Kagari, Michelle. 2003. 'Anti terror Bill an affront to human rights', *Daily Nation* 18 November. [Online] Available at http://www.nationaudio.com/News/DailyNation/

18112003/Comment/Comment181120036.html.

Mulama, Joyce. 2004. 'East Africa: The Church Slams Anti-Terror Bills'. [Online] Available at http://www.lewrockwell.com/ips/mulama.html

Mutua, Makau. 2003. 'Perverse Legislation: Kenyans must reject anti-terrorism Bill', *Daily Nation*, 2 July 2003. [Online] Available at http://www.nationaudio.com/News/DailyNation/02072003/Comment/Comment020720034.html

Pettit, Dominique. 2003. 'Two Islamic fundamentalists sentenced to death for preparing terrorist acts, murdering official, stealing weapons.' 7 November 2003. [Online] Available at http://www.freedomfiles.org/war/morocco.htm

Thomashausen, A. 2003. 'A Comparative Law Assessment of the Proposed South African Anti-Terrorism Legislation'. [Online] Available on the Parliamentary Monitoring Group website at: http://www.pmg.org.za/docs/appendices/030624thomas.htm

Truth and Reconciliation Commission of South Africa. 2003. *Truth and Reconciliation Commission of South Africa Report*. Cape Town: Truth and Reconciliation Commission. [Online] Available at: http://www.info.gov.za/otherdocs/2003/trc/rep.pdf

United Nations. 2002. *Report of the Policy Working Group on the United Nations and Terrorism*. Annex to UN Doc A/57/273 S/2002/875. [Online] Available at http://www.un.org/terrorism/a57273.htm

Notes

1 Terrorism is not a new phenomenon. For a historical background, see Cassese (1989); Han (1993); and Elagab (1999).

2 Australia's raft of anti-terrorism laws includes the Security Legislation Amendment (Terrorism) Act 2002 [No. 2], Suppression of the Financing of Terrorism Act 2002, Criminal Code Amendment (Suppression of Terrorist Bombings) Act 2002, Telecommunications Interception Legislation Amendment Act 2002, and Border Security Legislation Amendment Act 2002.

3 Anti-Terrorism, Crime and Security Act 2001. New legislation, the Prevention of Terrorism Act 2005, has been enacted to replace the Part 4 powers in the Anti-Terrorism, Crime and Security Act with a new scheme of Control Orders.

4 Anti-Terrorism Act 2001.

5 Prevention of Terrorism Act 2002. This Act has since been repealed by the Prevention of Terrorism (Repeal) Ordinance 2004 promulgated by the President of India on 21 September 2004.

6 PATRIOT Act 2001 and Homeland Security Act 2002.

7 African countries that have introduced or are in the process of introducing anti-terrorism legislation include Algeria, Egypt, The Gambia, Kenya, Mauritius, Morocco, Namibia, South Africa, Swaziland, Tanzania and Uganda.

8 In October 2001, Amnesty International (2001) raised the concerns that: 'In the name of fighting "international terrorism", governments have rushed to introduce draconian measures that threaten the human rights of their own citizens, immigrants and refugees ... Governments have a duty to ensure the safety of their citizens, but measures taken must not undermine fundamental human rights'. See 'The backlash – human rights at risk throughout the world'. [Online] Available at http://web.amnesty.org/ library/index/engACT300272001?OpenDocument

9 See *Declaration of Minimum Humanitarian Standards*, adopted by an expert meeting convened by the Institute for Human Rights, Abo Akademi University, Turku/Abo, Finland, 30 November–2 December 1990, reprinted in 'Report of the Sub-Commission on the Prevention of Discrimination and Protection of Minorities in its Forty-Sixth Session', Commission on Human Rights, Fifty-First Session, Provisional Agenda Item 19, at 4, UN Doc.E/CN.4/1995/116 (1995).

10 Illustratively, in 1985, the Angolan representative at the UN General Assembly stated that 'acts of terrorism cannot be compared under any pretext with the acts of those who are fighting colonial and racist oppression, and for their freedom and independence' (Cassese 1989: 7).

11 Convention for the Suppression of Unlawful Seizure of Aircraft, signed at The Hague on 16 December 1970.

12 Convention for the Suppression of Unlawful Acts against the Safety of Civil Aviation, signed at Montreal on 23 September 1971.

13 Convention on the Prevention and Punishment of Crimes against Internationally Protected Persons, including Diplomatic Agents, adopted by the General Assembly of the United Nations on 14 December 1973.

14 International Convention against the Taking of Hostages, adopted by the General Assembly of the United Nations on 17 December 1979.

15 International Convention for the Suppression of Terrorist Bombings, adopted by the General Assembly of the United Nations on 15 December 1997.

16 International Convention for the Suppression of the Financing of Terrorism, adopted by the General Assembly of the United Nations on 9 December 1999.

17 The four Geneva Conventions of 1949 and their Additional Protocols of 1977.

18 In February 2002, the Commonwealth Secretariat's Expert Working Group on Legislative and Administrative Measures to Combat Terrorism produced a report which offers a model framework for implementing UN Security Council Resolution 1373 of 28 September 2001.

19 See para. 6 of the Resolution. The CTC has instituted a periodic reporting system which requires states to submit reports on measures undertaken at national level to meet the commitments in the Resolution.

20 A listing of these conventions is available at http://untreaty.un.org/English/ Terrorism.asp.

21 Declaration of the Second High-Level Intergovernmental Meeting on the Prevention and Combating of Terrorism in Africa, 13-14 October 2004, Algiers. Mtg/HLIG/Conv.Terror/ Decl. (II) Rev.2.

22 For example, one of the world's most respected statesmen, Nelson Mandela, was for long considered a terrorist not only by the apartheid regime but by countries such as the US as well.

23 Article 4. See also Article 5 which requires the states parties to cooperate in preventing and combating terrorism 'in conformity with national legislation and procedures of each state' and Article 6, which recognizes the jurisdiction of each state party over certain 'terrorist acts'.

24 For example, in June 2003, the US ambassador to Kenya publicly criticised Kenya's anti-terrorism efforts claiming that there had not been a single arrest since the 1998 car bomb attack on the US embassy in Nairobi.

25 It is noteworthy that the unpopular Kenyan Suppression of Terrorism Bill was a precondition for the lifting of the flight ban which the UK government imposed earlier on all UK flights to Kenya allegedly on the grounds that they could be targets of a terrorist attack. The ban was lifted in June 2003 only after the publication by the Kenyan government of the anti-terrorism bill. The draft legislation proposed life imprisonment for anyone committing terrorist acts and a 10-year jail term for anyone suspected to be in possession of weapons of mass destruction. Eighteen opposition MPs refused to support the bill, which, they said, was draconian, unconstitutional and infringed fundamental civil rights.

26 See *The Lotus* (1927) PCIJ Rep Ser A, No. 10.

27 For instance, in response to the UN Counter-Terrorism Committee on 19 June 2002, the Government of Zambia stated that it had a number of provisions under its Penal Code (Cap. 87 of the Laws of Zambia) that could be used to fight against terrorism in accordance with Security Council Resolution 1373.

28 See also the Anti-Terrorism, Crime and Security Act 2001 (UK).

29 The Protocol for the Suppression of Unlawful Acts of Violence at Airports Serving International Civil Aviation, 1971; the Convention on the Prevention and Punishment of Crimes Against Internationally Protected Persons, Including Diplomatic Agents, 1973; the Convention for the Suppression of Unlawful Acts against the Safety of Maritime Navigation, 1988; and the Convention on the Suppression of Unlawful Acts against the Safety of Fixed Platforms Located on the Continental Shelf, 1988. Morocco ratified all of these conventions on 13 November 2001.

30 As of November 2003, 16 people had been sentenced to death under Morocco's anti-terrorism law. See Pettit (2003).

31 Third Report of the Kingdom of Morocco to the Counter-Terrorism Committee established pursuant to UN Security Council Resolution 1373 (2001). UN Doc S/2003/1173, para. 1.3.

32 See Minutes of the Security and Constitutional Affairs Committee, 29 January 2004, available at http://www.pmg.org.za/docs/2004/viewminute.php?id=3834.

33 This seems to be a common provision in counter-terrorism legislation. See, for example, the Anti-Terrorism Act of Canada and the Anti-Terrorism Act 2002 of Uganda.

34 The United Nations has recognized the threat to human rights posed by anti-terrorism measures through, *inter alia*, the appointment of an Independent Expert on Protection of Human Rights while Countering Terrorism.

35 See also the Berlin Declaration adopted by the International Commission of Jurists (ICJ) on 28 August 2004.

36 See 'Report of the Commonwealth Committee on Terrorism (CCT): Commonwealth Plan of Action'. Available at http://www.thecommonwealth.org.org/

37 See UN Security Council Resolution 1566 (2004), S/Res/1566 (2004), adopted by the Security Council at its 5053rd meeting on 8 October 2004.

38 General Assembly Resolution A/Res/57/219 of 18 December 2002. See also E/CN.4/Res/2003/68 adopted by the Commission on Human Rights at its 59th session on 25 April 2003.

39 The Anti-Terrorism (Amendment) Ordinance 2002 allows for detention without trial for up to 12 months!

40 See http://web.amnesty.org/web/web.nsf/print/2004-dza-summary-eng.

41 Rules or principles of international law having a higher status and from which no derogation is permitted.

42 Constitution of Mauritius 1968, s.9; Constitution of South Africa 1996, s 14; Constitution of Uganda 1995, s. 27.

43 Such provisions are not unique to African anti-terrorism legislation. For example, the Canadian Anti-Terrorism Act also gives the police extensive powers of surveillance. Under the Anti-Terrorism, Crime and Security Act 2001 of the United Kingdom, the Home Secretary has powers to issue a code of conduct for the retention of communications data by communications service providers for national security reasons.

44 Statement by Asma Jahangir, Special Rapporteur on Freedom of Religion or Belief, to the Third Committee of the UN General Assembly, 3 November 2004. See GA/SHC/3798. Available at: http://www.un.org/News/Press/docs/2004/gashc3798.doc.htm

45 Statement of the Special Rapporteur on Mercenaries to the Third Committee of the UN General Assembly, 3 November 2004. See GA/SHC/3798. Available at: http://www.un.org/News/Press/docs/2004/gashc3798.doc.htm

46 For example, questions have been raised about the extradition, without appropriate legal safeguards, of terrorist suspects by Pakistan to the United States.

47 For example, s. 2 of the Constitution of Mauritius 1968 proclaims: 'This Constitution is the supreme law of Mauritius and if any other law is inconsistent with this Constitution, that other law shall, to the extent of the inconsistency, be void.' See also Constitution of South Africa 1996, s. 2; and Constitution of Uganda, 1995, ss. 2(1) and (2).

48 For example, a special interpretation clause requires the definition of 'terrorist act' to be interpreted in accordance with international humanitarian law. Persons detained in terms of the legislation are also entitled to consult with a legal and medical practitioner, and to be visited by a partner and chosen religious counsellor.

8

Conflicts & Implications for Poverty & Food Security Policies in Africa

FONDO SIKOD

Conflict can be viewed as an ongoing process of variable intensity involving multiple interactions over time in which people not only have differing and sometimes incompatible views of facts, goals, methods or values, but sense interference from one another in the achievement of valued outcomes. Conflicts can be adaptive or maladaptive, functional/constructive or dysfunctional. Indeed, human and societal progress over the ages, for example, has been driven by conflict. But the liquidation of entire peoples and cultures has also been driven by conflict. The outcome of a given conflict, therefore, depends on how it is managed by contending forces. Lack of social reciprocity and/or tolerance for differences of opinion increases the risk of violence and war.

Why do people get involved in conflicts? Economists usually base their analysis of conflict on a rational-choice model. If expected gains from violent conflict exceed the costs, then individuals will choose to take up arms or at least support the insurrection (Moradi 2004). It may sound somewhat perverse, but it is assumed that those who provoke conflicts are rational, and do go through a mental process whereby they determine the expected gains and costs of starting a conflict. The types of conflicts we have experienced in Africa (and elsewhere) appear to have been carefully thought out, with the potential for success and failure weighted. Nevertheless, *ex-post* observation and analysis have shown how uncertain the outcomes of conflicts can be.

Violent conflicts cause immense humanitarian burdens and impair development prospects in the long run by the destruction of physical and human capital. When violent conflicts break out, they are rarely a short-term affair and a final resolution is difficult to achieve. The last three decades have seen many regions of Africa involved in war and internal or external conflict, from the seven or so countries directly involved in the Democratic Republic of Congo (DRC) to the Sierra Leone crisis and the war in Ethiopia/Eritrea and the various other civil wars. No less than 29 sub-Saharan African states have been at war since 1980. There have been over 9.5 million refugees and hundreds of thousands of people have been slaughtered. Political corruption, lack of respect for the rule of law, and

Table 8.1 Comparison of agricultural indicators between Africa and other developing regions and income categories

	Africa	Sub-Saharan Africa	Near East and North Africa	South Asia	East Asia and Pacific	Latin America and Caribbean	Middle income countries	High income countries	World
Proportion of arable land irrigated	7.0	3.8	28.7	39.3	31.9	11.6	19.9	11.9	20.0
Added value per worker ($/ year)	416	285	1 859	412	461	3 028	335	17 956	645
Per capita cereal production (kg/year)	147	128	128	224	336	259	339	746	349
Cereal yield (kg/ha)	1 225	986	1 963	2 308	4 278	2 795	2 390	4 002	2 067
Livestock productivity (kg/ha)	164	128	147	121	150	198	191	248	193
Fertilizer use (kg/ha)	22	9	69	109	241	85	111	125	100

Source: NEPAD (2003)

human rights violations are all common reasons given for some of the causes of Africa's problems. Although not the only reasons, some often overlooked root causes also include the artificial boundaries created by colonial rulers, and dysfunctional situations where the leadership lies with the former colonial master, to which the population might be opposed.

It would appear that Africa, especially sub-Saharan Africa, is prone to civil conflicts (Elbadawi and Sambanis 2000), and is a breeding place for rebel groups. This apparent propensity for violence is a root cause of the poverty and stagnation or retrogression the economies of the sub-region face. Nearly half the population of sub-Saharan Africa lives below the international poverty line, a higher percentage than in any other region. Sub-Saharan Africa has the highest prevalence of undernourishment and has shown little progress in reducing this in the last 30 years (Clover 2003).

Undernourishment is a key manifestation of poverty and, as poverty worsens, food becomes more important than ever. It deepens other aspects of poverty by reducing the capacity for work and resistance to disease, and by affecting children's mental development and educational achievements. While the average daily calorie intake in Africa is just over 2500, it is below 2000 in Somalia, Ethiopia and Sudan. This is very low, compared with over 3,600 calories per day on average in America, 3,500 in Central Europe, and 3,400 in the former Soviet Union. Even in Albania, the poorest country in Europe, the daily caloric intake is 40–75 per cent higher than in countries in the Horn of Africa (USDA, 2000).

Food security can be defined as the ability of countries, regions or households to meet their required levels of food consumption at all times. Production and imports constitute a nation's sources of food supplies. Although the agricultural sector provides the bulk of food in Africa, the overall food security situation in the continent has not been encouraging. According to recent FAO estimates, while the total number of people around the world suffering from severe malnutrition has been declining gradually over the past 20 years, Africa, particularly the sub-Saharan region, has been a notable exception from this worldwide trend, as can be seen in Table 8.1. Rather, there has been an increase in malnutrition over the same period, with the number of malnourished increasing from about 100 million to more than 200 million.

This paper looks at the implication of conflicts for poverty and food security in Africa. The choice of the sector is particularly important to Africa. It is the mainstay of most African economies, providing food, employment and revenues from foreign exchange to finance other sectors of the economy. Moradi (2004) used regression analysis to look at nutrition and agriculture as a determinant of civil wars in Africa, where conflicts have tended to be protracted and with very uncertain outcomes in terms of the desired objectives of the protagonists. The certain outcomes have been poverty and starvation. Through a mostly descriptive approach, the paper tries to show that conflict is a cause of food insecurity in Africa. Poverty, already a curse of the continent, is exacerbated by conflicts. The paper is divided into five parts: part one looks at some issues on the causes of conflicts in Africa; part two examines conflict as a cause of food insecurity; part three analyses the interaction between conflict, agriculture and poverty; part four focuses on food aid, conflict and food security; and the final part is the conclusion, with some recommendations for the way ahead.

Some Issues on the Causes of Conflicts in Africa

Many Africans see European colonial policies in Africa as a major root cause of conflicts. These include historical legacies such as the Berlin Conference of 1885, the scramble to divide Africa among European powers (without regard for ethnic realities), and the subsequent establishment of colonial commercial and political structures designed primarily to extract resources. Against this background, Africa became one of several locations in the world where superpower rivalries were played out during the Cold War. In the setting of a central strategic stalemate in Europe, Cold War antagonists tried to outflank one another in Africa, Asia and South America, using local players as pawns. As if this was not enough, the end of the Cold War was associated with a rebound phenomenon, in which long suppressed rivalries resurfaced at a time of declining international focus and attention, but nevertheless fueled by surplus weapons from Cold War stocks. Other external factors include economic motives on the part of arms merchants, foreign state and non-state actors (like multinational corporations). But all of Africa's problems cannot be blamed on external factors. Internal factors that promote conflict include the nature of power on the continent, a winner-takes-all mentality, zero-sum political games, centralization and personalization of power through manipulation of the constitution, lack of accountability, lack of transparency, lack of the rule of law, lack of peaceful transitional mechanisms, and absence of human rights, all of which are set against poverty, low levels of education and a background of deep-rooted ethnic and religious mindsets. And then we must not forget co-factors like conflict-creating environmental problems such as water and land shortages and environmental degradation.

The OAU identified certain contributing factors to 26 conflicts affecting over 60 per cent of the population of Africa between 1963 and 1998 as ethnicity in Rwanda and Burundi, power-sharing in the DRC 1998, Sudan 1983, São Tomé/Principe 1994 and Comoros 1995, inter-clan and other factional rivalries in Somalia, Liberia and Guinea Bissau, mercenaries in the DRC 1964, Guinea 1970 and Benin 1977, human rights violations under Idi Amin in Uganda from 1970 to 1979, and Cold War geopolitics in Chad 1977–80 and Mozambique 1975–92. In the post-Cold War era, however, we can identify the following classification of African conflicts:

a) Ethnic competition for control of the state: for example, Nigeria
b) Regional or secessionist rebellions: for example, Sudan, Senegal and Nigeria
c) Liberation conflicts: for example, Angola and Western Sahara
d) Fundamentalist religious opposition to secular authority: for example, Algeria
e) Warfare arising from state degeneration or state collapse: for example, Somalia, Sierra Leone, Congo-DRC (Ivory Coast is on its way to joining this group)
f) Border disputes: for example, Ethiopia-Eritrea and Cameroon-Nigeria
g) Protracted conflict within politicized militaries: for example, Congo-DRC and Sierra Leone
h) Ideological conflicts: for example, Mozambique and Angola
i) Farmer–pastoralist land conflicts for user rights: for example, the North-west Province of Cameroon.

Conflict types can be major or minor, superficial or deep-rooted, short-term or long-term, and they can overlap. A country like Nigeria, for example, has a variety of low-grade conflicts that result in chronic blood letting without it actually being in an openly declared state of war. It keeps the country off-balance.

Some African leaders have been in power for decades, and continue to manipulate the constitution to remain in power. In these countries, the leadership maintains itself by bribing the elites, the military and the media to continue to sing its praise. The citizenry has lost faith in the system, and is no longer able to hold the leadership accountable, but feels helpless. The *de facto* opposition in such situations becomes the military or a rebel group. In the late 1960s and 1970s, Africa witnessed a flurry of coups because of the lack of freedom and opportunity for people to express themselves and to change the leadership through the ballot box. While such conflicts, which are usually very bloody, have lessened, they have not completely stopped. In Sierra Leone, the 1996 democratically elected government was overthrown by the military in 1997. In its 2001 report, the African Development Bank analyzed 180 leadership transitions in Africa between 1960 and 1999. Fifty-six per cent of leaders left office via coup, war or invasion. Only 7 per cent left office by losing an election. Just over 9 per cent left office by natural death, accident, or assassination. Another 9 per cent left only because they were tired and chose to retire.

Once conflict becomes violent, it takes on a different level of dys-functionality. Collier and Hoeffler (2002b) have identified damage to and destruction of physical and human capital, reduction of long-term savings, diversion of capital externally (capital flight), economic disruptions and distortion of state expenditures (defense versus social spending) as among the economic effects of armed conflicts. Weapons are deadly and death is irreversible. Conflicts are also expensive, often resulting in the diversion of precious resources away from social needs. For example, according to SIPRI, world and regional military expenditure estimates from 1991 to 2000, Africa recorded an increase of 20 per cent while the rest of the world (combined) decreased military spending by 11 per cent. Public expenditures per capita can be even more revealing. In 1990, for example, the ratio of military to health spending was 16:1 in Ethiopia, 10:1 in Chad, 25:1 in Sudan, 4.5:1 in Mozambique and 14.25:1 in Angola (Ntangsi 2004).

Conflicts destroy both people and property. They also destroy the capacity to produce. Conflicts destroy the dignity of people. A fact of conflict that is often under-appreciated is that civilians are much more likely to die than soldiers, and children constitute over two-thirds of civilian deaths. Indeed, civilian deaths as a percentage of all deaths in war reached almost 90 per cent in the 1990s, compared with about 15 per cent in the First World War.

Conflict causes mass movements of people to uncertain regions. Who is endangered, and by what, is rarely as simple as the clarion call to arms in a crisis suggests. Armed conflict, more than any other force, has transformed the lives of millions of children and women. Children and their families are not just getting caught in the crossfire. Many are being targeted. Nothing is spared, held sacred or protected. It has become the singular characteristic of armed conflict in our time that children suffer most.

Africa has become an attractive and profitable dumping ground for nations and arms manufacturers eager to get rid of weapon stocks made superfluous by the end of the Cold War or by technological developments.

The Rebel Group Choice of Location: Cross-Sectional Determinants of Civil Wars

Whenever violent civil conflicts breakout, the group opposing the govern-ment forces is usually referred to as the rebels. An interesting issue about conflicts is whether regional characteristics affect the risk of civil war starting in a particular area of a country. At first glance, the very definition of guerrilla warfare seems to rule out a meaningful localization of rebel groups. If rebels are the weaker party and lack the numbers, equipment and training of a conventional army, the only survival strategy is to pursue a 'hit and run' tactic attacking small government units, damaging important infrastructure, and withdrawing thereafter at great speed (Moradi 2004). Frequently moving the bases is also an essential part of a successful and permanent resistance.

Mozambique's RENAMO is an example of following a strategy of guerrilla warfare. Its actions began in 1979 with tentative attacks along the North-western border provinces, but gained international attention only from 1982 when they started seriously to disrupt Mozambique's economy and infra-structure by cutting railway and power lines, destroying main roads and bridges, and sabotaging oil storage depots. The base of the RENAMO rebels shifted several times and eventually expanded to nearly all provinces of the country. In some cases, the rebels were operating from abroad without hurry-ing to control a large area in the interior. The Namibian SWAPO, for example, fought the de-colonization war from Southern Angola. Similarly, in both Rwandan civil wars of 1990 and 1994 the Tutsi rebels were based in neigh-boring Uganda. The fact that rebels choose an extraterritorial base stresses the importance of having a relatively safe sanctuary to which to retreat.

This pattern is not unique. Where the rebel groups' aim is to secede from the national territory, their operational center is usually confined mainly to the area that they intend to 'liberate'. In the Nigerian civil war 1967–70 the provincial government of the Eastern region exercised its pre-existent administrative power and the war turned out to be a quite conventional one. Despite characteristics of guerrilla warfare by other secessionist rebels, like the SPLA in Southern Sudan or the Eritrean EPLF, they waged the war mainly from within the country.

We can also identify outbreaks in many revolutionary wars, in which the rebels seek to overthrow the central government while leaving the national boundaries unchanged. Angola's war of de-colonization, for example, started with violent uprisings in 1961, which were organized by the rebels of the MPLA and UPA (Moradi 2004). While the former attacked police stations and prisons in the capital Luanda, the latter raised violence in the provinces of Lunda, Cuanza Norte, and Malanje and set up a front in the Northern provinces of Uige and Zaire (Henderson 1979). The civil war in Chad shows great similarities. In 1965 a broad but unorganized insur-rection took place mainly in Chad's districts of Guera, Ouaddai and Salamat. The civil war then started one year later, as the rebel group of northerners FROLINAT was organized in the northern B.E.T. region (Azam and Morrison 1999). These examples highlight the complex geography of civil wars.

Conflict as a Cause of Food Insecurity & Poverty in Africa

Food Security

As noted earlier, food security can be defined as the ability of a country, region or household to meet the required levels of food consumption at all times. Availability, access and affordability are all elements of food security. These are complex issues that encompass a wide range of interrelated economic, social and political factors, internal and external, which challenge Africa's ability to address food security.

A country will be faced with growing food insecurity when food supplies are nutritionally inadequate and/or fail to keep pace with population growth. In a simplified way, we can express this idea in the following form:

Per capita food   Total Consumption
Requirement   –   Population   = Food Gap,

Where total consumption is equal to production plus imports, production depends on labor, land, fertilizer, irrigation, etc., and imports depend on net foreign credit and grants, exports and food import prices. The key factors affecting food security are therefore agricultural productivity, foreign-exchange availability, and population growth (see Shapouri and Rosen 1998). How has Africa fared in terms of food security?

Agricultural Production
In comparative terms, Africa is the only region in the world where the average food production per person has been declining over the last 40 years, putting large segments of the population at risk of food insecurity and malnutrition. FAO reports that, for the continent as a whole, annual per capita production of cereals has fluctuated between 140 and 175 kg during the 1990s – far below the global average of 358 kg. Production growth in cereals for sub-Saharan Africa over the past 30 years was around 2.5 per cent per annum, and is expected to stay roughly at this level for the next 30 years. Meanwhile, agricultural production soared worldwide during the second half of the twentieth century through the improved biological potential of food-crop management techniques (wheat yield quadrupled in Mexico and rice production tripled over a 20-year period in South Asia). In Africa spending on agricultural research stagnated over the same period in comparison with other developing countries, leading analysts to believe that declines in research and productivity are inextricably linked (NEPAD 2003).

Although there has been some progress recorded in the volume of production, trade, value added and diversification, per capita output has recorded serious declines in both food and non-food production. During the 1960–1965 period, per capita output declined by 0.9 and 1.1 per cent for agricultural and food production respectively. These negative per capita values persisted throughout the period 1960–98. However, in a handful of countries, including Cameroon in the Centre, Ivory Coast in the West, Mauritius in the Southern region, Egypt and Morocco in the North and Malawi in the East, per capita agricultural and food production indexes recorded slight improvements during this period. In sharp contrast, large countries such as Kenya, Tanzania, Sudan, Congo (DRC), Ethiopia and Nigeria recorded substantial declines (Ntangsi 2004) The regional trends can be seen in Table 8.2.

Food Imports

There has been no particular trend in the growth rate in food imports. On a regional basis, as can be seen in Table 8.3, agricultural and food imports growth was highest for countries in the Southern African region, recording

Table 8.2   Annual average growth rate (in %) of agricultural and food output

Region	Total Agricultural Production						Food Production					
	1960–1965	1975–1980	1980–1985	1985–1990	1990–1998	1960–1998	1960–1965	1975–1980	1980–1985	1985–1990	1990–1998	1960–1998
Volume of production												
Central Africa	1.5	1.7	1.2	1.9	1.6	1.6	1.4	1.9	1.0	1.8	1.6	1.5
East Africa	1.0	0.6	1.6	2.5	2.1	1.6	1.2	0.7	1.1	2.3	1.7	1.4
North Africa	1.2	1.0	3.2	2.0	2.7	2.1	2.0	0.9	3.2	2.1	3.8	2.4
Southern Africa	0.8	–0.9	–0.8	2.7	–1.1	0.1	0.3	–0.6	–0.5	3.0	–1.6	0.1
West Africa	1.3	0.5	1.4	2.1	2.8	1.6	1.5	0.9	1.9	1.5	1.4	1.4
All of Africa	1.2	0.6	1.3	2.2	1.6	1.4	1.3	0.8	1.3	2.1	1.4	1.4
Per capita production												
Central Africa	–0.5	–1.0	–1.6	–1.4	–0.8	–1.1	–0.9	–1.1	–2.0	–1.2	–1.5	–1.3
East Africa	–0.7	–0.8	–1.4	–1.0	–0.6	–0.9	–1.2	–2.5	–2.2	–0.9	–1.5	–1.7
North Africa	–1.0	–0.4	–0.2	–1.2	–0.4	–0.6	–0.7	–2.0	0.2	–0.6	–0.3	–0.7
Southern Africa	–1.2	–2.4	–2.0	0.0	–0.6	–1.2	–2.0	–3.6	–3.9	–0.1	–4.6	–2.8
West Africa	–1.1	–2.0	–1.3	–1.1	–0.5	–1.2	–0.9	–2.2	–1.6	–1.1	0.5	–1.1
All of Africa	–0.9	–1.3	–1.3	–0.9	–0.6	–1.0	–1.1	–2.3	–1.9	–0.8	–0.5	–1.5

Source: Ntangsi (2004)

a rate of above 10 per cent between 1960 and 1998. In contrast, the Central African region experienced the least growth of about 3.3 per cent during the same period. The West African region recorded a remarkable drop from about 19 per cent during the period 1975–80 to less than 1 per cent during the 1990–8 period. To finance these imports over the period, countries had to set aside between 10 and 40 per cent of their export earnings. This can be a major constraint to a country without adequate foreign earnings, or one whose foreign earnings have been diverted to other uses. Ethiopia's response has been hampered by global economics; the sharp fall in coffee prices has cut incomes for many farmers, and the country is still labouring under a heavy debt burden. Donors have been uneasy about donating millions to a government that seemed to prioritize spending on war rather than on health and education.

Food production and imports constitute the regular source of food supply

Table 8.3   Growth rate of agricultural and food imports, 1960–98 (%)

Region	1960-65	1975-80	1980-85	1985-90	1990-98	1960-98
Central Africa	4.2	5.9	6.9	1.2	-1.8	3.3
East Africa	5.8	10.3	1.7	0.7	4.9	4.7
North Africa	9.2	11.5	3.9	3.4	2.0	6.0
Southern Africa	10.8	12.8	18.9	4.2	6.6	10.7
West Africa	17.2	18.9	8.3	1.0	0.8	9.2
All of Africa	9.4	11.9	7.9	2.1	2.5	6.8

Source: Adapted by author from Ntangsi (2004)

Table 8.4 Food insecurity in 2004

Highly food insecure[c]	*Nationally food secure*[a]	*Moderately food insecure*[b]
Burundi, Eritrea, Rwanda, Somalia, Angola, Cape Verde, Chad, Liberia, Sierra Leone	Benin, Ivory Coast, Guinea-Bissau, Nigeria	Cameroon, CAR DRC, Ethiopia, Kenya, Sudan, Uganda, Tanzania Lesotho, Madagascar, Malawi, Mozambique, Zambia, Zimbabwe Burkina Faso, Guinea, Mali, Mauritania, Senegal, Togo

a Adequate food but unequal distribution; b Meet 75 per cent or more of requirement; c Meet less than 75 per cent of requirement.
Source: Adapted by author from Shapouri and Rosen (1998)

for any people. According to Shapouri and Rosen (1998), food imports into sub-Saharan Africa will have to climb to nearly 13 per cent by the year 2008, to cover the food gap because the production and imports are not currently enough. The patterns of food security and insecurity across sub-Saharan Africa are outlined in Table 8.4.

Conflict & the Food Supply System

Conflict influences the food supply system through several channels, as outlined in Figure 8.1. Conflct has an impact on the following aspects of food production, distribution and consumption:

(i)   Human capital. In Africa, most of the labor (over 60 per cent) is in the agricultural sector, even if this sector contributes only about one-third of GDP. Conflict mostly takes away those of working age to serve as soldiers. Where there are not enough young people, children are conscripted. Besides those who serve as soldiers, many people are usually killed in the fighting. African rebels have often shown inhumanity that is hard to imagine. A gruesome case in point is that of Sierra Leone, where rebels often asked whether their innocent victims wanted 'a short sleeve or a long sleeve', that is, whether they preferred their arms chopped off (short sleeve) or their hand chopped off (long sleeve). Those who are not killed or maimed are often forced to flee their homes, villages or even countries, to become refugees somewhere else, with an uncertain future. Land being the most important resource in Africa, it is very unlikely that a refugee would be given/sold farmland. And yet, for the land to be productive requires investment. Where there is conflict, it is difficult for children to attend school normally. This has an impact on human capital formation, and the future of the nation to grow economically.

(ii)   Physical capital. This is the destruction of land, housing, equipment, etc. Mozambique and Angola are countries suffering the effect of landmines. No matter how fertile the land may be, the presence of land mines makes it impossible to cultivate the land. The government or the rebels may burn the land (grass, forests, etc.) For example, in the early 1980s in Ethiopia, the government's scorched earth policies destroyed hundreds of thousands of acres of food-producing land. Other physical capital may include markets, where people go to sell and buy food.

(iii) The environment. This is closely tied to physical capital. Mining the land, burning/scorching the land or forests, using chemicals destroy the environment and make it difficult to produce food.

(iv)   Social cohesion, institutional weakening, corruption and a dysfunctional judicial system. Conflicts usually lead to loss of family or village members, split families, and cause mental disorientation and a lack of the will to live. This destruction of the psyche can perpetuate conflict as it may lead to a desire to retaliate. Any such frame of mind may discourage production.

One of the most immediate effects of armed conflict is the disruption of food supplies. Farmers, who are often women and older children, become fearful of working on plots of land too far from their homes. They reduce the area under cultivation, and their water sources and systems of irrigation and flood control may also be destroyed. Restrictions on movement limit access to such necessities as seed and fertilizers and stop farmers from taking their produce to the market. Most households in developing countries, including many farm households, rely on market purchases to meet their food needs. Economic disarray heightens unemployment, reducing people's ability to buy food.

War and political upheaval are therefore major contributing factors to famine, the impact being felt at both household and national levels. At best, agricultural production is interrupted, but in protracted conflicts such as in Angola, production is devastated. Other direct economic outcomes include price changes for basic commodities, closure of markets, destitution and displacement, disruption of trade and aid flows. Evidence of environmental degradation and competition for natural resources can be found in many of the internal and even trans-boundary conflicts that contribute to many complex emergencies. Conflicts are also more likely to divert scarce resources into military budgets (to feed armies and purchase weapons) away from critical development needs, thus resulting in collapsed infrastructure.

Famine may not only be a by-product of war, it may also be an instrument of war. There are many cases in Africa of political interference; certain groups may be more vulnerable because of deliberate indifference or even victimization on the part of the government, coupled with the lack of political power of these groups. Evidence abounds in both Angola and Sudan of wide-scale starvation because of lack of access by aid organizations to those in need, and also of deliberate victimization by the government. In Angola civilian populations, which were the target of both parties to the conflict, were under constant patterns of attack and reprisal for the three years prior to the ending of the war, displaced by force or

Figure 8.1. Impact of violent conflict on economic growth and the food production system

	Physical Capital	Destruction (Stock) Destruction	Accumulation (influx) Uncertainty causing falling investment Capital flight Increased unproductive spending
	Human Capital	Deaths Debilitation	Brain drain Diminishing education indicators (e.g. desertion rates)
	Environment	Destruction	Depletion
Economic Growth, Food production	Total productivity of factors		Diminishing social cohesion Increased transaction costs caused by transportation Diversion of productive spending to military spending Institutional weakening Corruption Dysfunctional judicial system and processes

Source: Adapted by author from UNDP (2004)

threat of force, and their villages and homes often burned down as well as systematically plundered, preventing them from growing or harvesting crops and depriving them of basic resources. Most food crises in the Horn of Africa during the 1980s and 1990s were characterized by government hostility to the afflicted population, or by bad relationships between the national government and the international community.

Where there is no outright war, conflicts have made it impossible for farmers to achieve anything like their full production potential. Conflicts that affect the food production system have not always been at the macro level. There are many countries like Cameroon that may not experience outright conflicts, but that have problems in the food production system resulting from farmer-grazer conflicts for limited land. Grazing is carried out extensively, and land is limited in some areas, leading to conflicts.

Although the continent has vast amounts of productive land with good soils that many other parts of the world do not possess, conflicts have made it impossible for people to settle and cultivate the land to produce food that can be consumed by the local populations, and exported to earn foreign earnings to pay for other goods they cannot produce. To increase the productivity of land and labor will require generating and disseminating new technologies. To do this requires a stable environment. It is not possible to think in terms of productivity in an environment where people are always on the run, or where they are refugees and not sure of what will be happening to them next.

Conflict, Agriculture & Poverty

In sub-Saharan Africa, a large percentage of the population depend on agriculture for their livelihood, about 85 per cent of the population in 1950 and still 70 per cent in 1990. The situation has improved little today (Moradi 2004). Any crisis in the agricultural sector would directly influence their livelihood utility. Additionally, SSA is so poor that the hungriest 25 per cent of the people in these countries live from a daily food supply per capita of less than 2000 calories. Since individual availability of calories varies, many people in these countries have an even lower energy intake.

There is no doubt that there is a direct link between conflict, poverty and food insecurity. The regular food crisis Africa has been facing stems from poverty, and one root-cause of poverty is conflict. Even mineral- or resource-rich countries become very poor in times of conflict because a) rebels usually target such locations either for destruction or control; b) resources are diverted from other uses into supporting the conflict. During conflicts, farmers cannot cultivate large plots to allow them to harvest and sell some of the produce for fear of looting or being victimized if they move too far from their homes. Under such conditions, the farmers tend to be caught in the subsistence trap, and poverty becomes their lot. Farmers are also usually dispersed, and lack any political power. They are thus among the vulnerable groups in times of conflict.

Drought and conflict often interact so closely that they are inextricable as causal mechanisms. Virtually every country that has suffered famine in the past 20 years has suffered a war at the same time; this is particularly true of famines in the 1990s. While Africa has experienced many droughts, they were generally managed with reasonable efficiency. It has been the combination of war and drought that has caused large-scale suffering and deaths. Of the 25 countries in Africa that were facing food emergencies in 2003, ten were experiencing civil strife and four were emerging from conflicts.

Conflict, Food Aid & Food Security

Because of ongoing conflicts, the United Nations set up a special emergency office in 1992 for countries in the Horn of Africa to appeal for food aid. An estimated 1.8 to 2 million tons of food were required to meet the needs of nearly 20 million people affected by drought and civil strife in the Horn.

In 1991, Sudan's annual cereal requirements were estimated at 3.5 million tons for 26 million people. After a below-average harvest in 1990, a food gap of 1 million tons was estimated for the country for 1991, and donors provided over 600,000 tons of emergency food. Although the shipments prevented mass starvation, difficulties in transporting food to the region of Dar Fur in Western Sudan led to extensive starvation in 1991. One observer characterized the situation there as a 'silent famine', as people in the villages died waiting for food that was promised but never arrived in time. The growth of food aid for Africa as a whole can be seen in Table 8.5.

Table 8.5 Growth rate of food aid into Africa, 1960–98

Region	1960-65	1975-80	1980-85	1985-90	1990-98	1960-98
Central Africa	22.1	29.5	3.6	-2.5	2.1	11.0
East Africa	25.5	52.4	9.7	22.3	34.6	28.9
North Africa	12.0	10.4	0.6	16.6	-16.3	4.7
Southern Africa	35.0	33.5	29.7	-14.1	50.8	30.0
West Africa	4.5	3.9	19.0	-8.2	2.0	4.2
All of Africa	19.8	25.9	12.5	2.8	14.7	15.2

Source: Adapted by author from Ntangsi (2004)

These two examples raise two fundamental issues about food aid: a) it is a source to complement the food supply system of a nation, b) it cannot be considered a reliable source, and therefore a nation's food security cannot be based on food aid. The World Food Programme (WFP) and the Millennium Project Task Force raise the pertinent issue that access to food, and not a decline in food production, is the main cause of the current food crisis in Africa. In many African countries market systems are non-existent. After a bumper crop, prices collapse and the farmers have no incentive to increase production. In a bad year food prices soar and become unaffordable to the majority of people. Poor or non-existent transport infrastructure further hampers farmers' ability to provide communities with food. As an example, in 1987 a WFP report stated that Somalia had produced a surplus of food that year, yet Private Voluntary Organisations (PVOs) were continuing to distribute free food. Inevitably, indigenous food-distribution networks withered and disappeared. The country's economy adapted to foreign aid, not to production. Allegations have also been made that much of the food aid from NGOs and PVOs is distributed in areas where there are no food shortages, as these are the areas with adequate infrastructure to facilitate delivery. This has a devastating effect on local markets, and can become a source of conflict. Also, there is likely to be an influx of population from food-deficit areas, putting stress on the social facilities.

Once food-distribution systems are set in place they become very difficult to dismantle, and even when the crisis is over communities continue to receive food aid, which further weakens local production abilities. In the mid-1990s, of the world total of 32 million victims of disasters receiving relief assistance from the WFP, 21.5 million were living in Africa. Also, whilst WFP and FAO conduct assessments and make recommendations on whether there are possibilities for local or regional food purchases, WFP depends on voluntary contributions for its relief activities and has no say as to the origin of the food. By its own admission, it imports food at times when it would be much cheaper to buy it locally or regionally. Purchasing food in the region or even locally would act as an incentive to local production and would serve to stabilize food prices.

The effects of decreased productivity and increased food aid are also visible in the trade statistics for Africa. Africa's share of international agricultural trade has fallen from 8 per cent in 1965 to less than 3 per cent in 2000. For 30 years, its agricultural imports have been increasing faster than its agricultural exports, making the region a net agricultural importer since 1980. WFP statistics show that part of these 'imports' is food aid, with the continent receiving 2.8 million tons in food aid in 2000. In a perverted way, then, food aid that is supposed to help Africa is also a cause of conflicts and poverty.

There has also been a marked decrease in development assistance due to so-called donor fatigue. Official Development Assistance (ODA) flows were down 25 per cent in the four years 1996–2000. Another factor that influences this trend has been the increase in donor support for relief activities as opposed to long-term development. It is estimated that 70 per cent of donor funds are currently being channeled to relief aid. As already illustrated, providing relief to the exclusion of development exacerbates the food crisis in the long term. The increased focus on relief has created a widening gap in the transition from relief activities to development initiatives and has the potential of further threatening development and food security on the continent (NEPAD, 2003).

Conclusion

Agricultural production in Africa will remain the most important element for addressing food security and poverty in the continent, since most of the poor and the food-insecure are rural people. Essentially, food security has to do with physical supply and economic access. These two aspects constitute supply and demand, and are the two main factors that affect food security. Supply-side factors are concerned with food availability, which involves the natural resource endowments of a society, the available technology and its dissemination (for food production, storage and preservation), prices, market opportunities, and the ability to augment own production with external supplies (imports). Demand-side factors, on the other hand, determine the degree of access to available food. These include household incomes, assets, prices, demographic factors such as numbers, age, composition of households and gender, and socio-cultural factors like health, educational level, cultural norms and food consumption habits. Food security can therefore be regarded as an income problem. In Africa, food security and agricultural development are two sides of the same coin. Both concepts center on increasing agricultural productivity and the incomes of a large majority of the population that remains poor and derives its income from agriculture and related activities. To do this requires a stable environment and leadership with vision. The above discussions show that, because of conflicts, Africa may still be a long way from having a stable environment that would allow for increasing agricultural productivity and the incomes of the population.

The study concludes that, while much attention has been given to the impact of greed for resources as a motivation for civil wars, a more important cause of conflicts has been the failure of African governments to implement effective policies in favour of a secure and sufficient food supply for their people. There is need for significant change towards the democratization of society, allowing for autonomous expression of the various social forces and creating the basis for a real civil society. There is need for cooperation and unity, without which any national and popular attempt will remain extremely limited and vulnerable. The implication of this finding is that Africa is continuing to face the risk of civil wars that are in part triggered by poor food supply.

References

Anderson, David M. 1993. 'Cow Power: Livestock and the Pastoralist in Africa.' *African Affairs* #92: 121–34.

Azam, Jean-Paul and Christian Morrisson. 1999. *Conflict and Growth in Africa, Vol.1: The Sahel.* Paris: OECD.

Baye, F. M., Fondo Sikod and Samuel Fambon. 2001. 'Evolution of Poverty in Rural Cameroon in the Era of Globalization', *Nigerian Journal of Economic and Social Studies* 43 (2): pp 299–321.

Clover, Jenny. 2003. 'Food Security in Sub-Saharan Africa', *African Security Review* 12 (1): 29–38.

Collier, Paul and Anke Hoeffler. 2002a. *Greed and Grievance in Civil War*, Working Paper No. 2355, Washington, DC: World Bank,

Collier, Paul and Anke Hoeffler. 2002b. 'On the Incidence of Civil War in Africa', *Journal of Conflict Resolution* 46 (1): 13–28.

D'Silva, B. 1992. 'Civil war and Food crisis in the Horn of Africa – Sudan, Ethioia, and Somalia.' Agricultural Outlook. Washington, DC: US Department of Agriculture.

Easterly, W. and R. Levine. 1997. 'Africa's Growth Tragedy: Policies and Ethnic Divisions', *Quarterly Journal of Economics* 112 (4): 1203–50.

Elbadawi, I. and N. Sambanis. 2000. 'Why Are There So Many Civil Wars in Africa? Understanding and Preventing Violent Conflict', *Journal of African Economies* 9 (3): 244–69.

Esman and Herring, eds. 2001. *Carrots, Sticks, and Ethnic Conflict; Rethinking Development Assistance.* Ann Arbor: University of Michigan Press.

Glantz, Michael H., ed. 1987. *Drought and Hunger in Africa.* Cambridge: Cambridge University Press.

Goudi, Andrew and Bilin Neypati. 1999. *Conflict and Growth in Africa, Vol.3: Southern Africa.* Paris: OECD.

Henderson, Lawrence 1979. *Angola: Five Centuries of Conflict.* Ithaca, NY: Cornell University Press.

Klugman, Jeni, Bilin Neypati and Frances Stewart. 1999. *Conflict and Growth in Africa, Vol.2: Kenya, Tanzania and Uganda.* Paris: OECD.

Moradi, Alexander. 2004. 'Have Gun, Give Food: Agriculture, Nutrition, and Civil Wars in Sub-Saharan Africa'. Paper presented at the United Nations University – World Institute of Development Economics Research (UNU-WIDER) Conference on 'Making Peace Work', Helsinki, 4-5 June.

NEPAD Newsletter. 2003. 'The Food Crisis in Africa.' Midrand, South Africa, May. NEPAD Secretariat.

Ntangsi, Max Memfih. 2004. 'Agricultural Performance and Food Security in Africa'. Unpublished paper, presented to the staff of the Department of Economics, University of Buea.

Robbins, Richard H. and Stacey Rosen. 1998. Global Problems and the Culture of Capitalism. Boston: Allyn and Bacon.

Shah, Anup. 2003. Conflicts in Africa. http://www.globalissues.org/Geopolitics/Africa.asp.

Shapouri, S. and Stacey Rosen. 1998. 'Food Security Assessment: Why Countries Are At Risk'. *Agriculture Information Bulletin* No. 754. Washington DC: USDA, Trade Economics Division.

USDA. 2000. *The U.S. Response to Ethiopia's Food Crisis.* Foreign Agricultural Service Backgrounder. Washington, DC: USDA.

UNDP. 2004. *Human Development Report.* New York: United Nations.

9

Two Africas? Two Ugandas?
An African 'Democratic Developmental State'? or another 'Failed State'?

TIMOTHY M. SHAW & PAMELA K. MBABAZI

> For all practical purposes, the conflict in the region has split Uganda into two countries – the one, the southern Uganda of economic development and growth, and the other, stretching north of Lake Kyoga, a theatre of war for the past two decades (Ajulu 2004: 274).

> ... neither Africa's post-colonial history nor the actual practice engaged in by successful 'developmental states' rules out the possibility of African 'developmental states' capable of playing a more dynamic role than hitherto (Mkandawire 2001: 289).

Since 1990, Uganda has transcended an unenviable two-decade history of decline and trauma to reconstruction (Hansen and Twaddle 1998; Museveni 1997). When it achieved independence in 1962 Uganda was one of the most promising countries in Africa. However, twenty years of political strife, economic mismanagement, and armed conflicts left it devastated, with much of its physical and social infrastructure destroyed. Uganda's long string of tragedies is legendary. Ten leaders have ruled the country in the four decades since independence, including Idi Amin's 8-year reign of terror where an estimated 500,000 people died. It was not until 1986, when Yoweri Museveni gained power, that relative stability was achieved and it became possible to attempt to rebuild the economy. Museveni introduced a non-party system of democracy with the National Resistance Movement, with presidential elections held in 1996 and 2001 under a new multi-party constitutional dispensation. There were further elections in 2006.

During the last decade (1992-2002), Uganda has managed to maintain an impressive annual growth rate of 6.4 per cent, largely due to improvements in the policy environment and the restoration of peace in much but not all of the country, making it possible to rehabilitate facilities and increase capacity utilization, particularly in the south. Economic growth has also been a result of the increased flow of capital and technology from the private sector involving both local and foreign investors, following the economic liberalization of the 1990s (Bigsten and Kayizzi-Mugerwa 2001; Collier 1994; Deininger and Okidi 2002; Hansen and Twaddle 1998; Holmgren et al. 2000).

214

Despite the many advances on the political and economic scene and major developments in various parts of the country, there is still significant instability in some areas. The north of the country (in particular, Gulu, Kitgum and Pader Districts) has not benefited from the good macro-economic performance (ECA 2003; UNDP 2000, 2002, 2003a). In fact, poverty levels in northern Uganda have risen since the start of the new century.[1] This is especially so in the rural areas and amongst children. By contrast, the towns of Arua, Gulu, Lira, etc. have grown considerably as fearful communities left the increasingly unsafe countryside. The rebel Lord's Resistance Army (LRA) has been fighting a guerrilla-style war against the Ugandan government in the north since the late 1980s (Van Acker 2004). The fear of rebel attacks has forced an estimated 1.2 million internally displaced people (IDPs) to remain in protected camps in northern Uganda, with restricted access to health services, sanitation and food (IRIN 2003). This armed conflict has led to gross violations of human rights against civilians, destroyed infrastructure, adversely disrupted social-service delivery systems, paralyzed economic activity and caused social disintegration, thus retarding economic and human development in the north. Despite efforts by government and other actors to meet the needs of these affected areas, significant gaps remain in the provision of protection and delivery of social services to vulnerable groups.[2] Efforts to create peace and foster reconciliation in the region have not been successful either; rather, insecurity continues to spread terror and hinder development and relief activities (Van Acker 2004).

Four decades after formal independence, then, the Ugandan case illustrates the familiar pattern of a few winners and many losers (Ehrhart and Ayoo 2000; Kappel et al. 2004), yet some gains are more widely distributed than others; for example, cell-phones and UHT (Ultra Heated Treated) milk versus the traumas of HIV/AIDS, IDPs, street children/soldiers and orphans, etc. Meanwhile, fresh produce and foreign-exchange transfers from diasporas – themselves a relatively 'new' phenomenon around Uganda: a function initially of population dispersal because of Amin-era terror – come to balance traditional 'colonial' commodities as sources of export revenue, augmented by invisible, informal, often illegal, income from the Congo (Vlassenroot and Raeymaekers 2004; Prunier 2004). In short, the pattern of human development/rights/security in Uganda is uneven, as most analyses indicate, including the invaluable series of five *Human Development Reports* (HDRs) for Uganda. Meanwhile, what are the implications for comparative analyses/policies/practices arising from this novel African case of two states within one country (Shaw 2004a; 2004b)?

Today's Uganda(s) may thus constitute a challenging case of a divided society with profound implications for comparative analysis, policy and practice in Africa and elsewhere (Crook 2001; Nhema 2004; Osaghae 2001). This chapter juxtaposes analysis of Uganda as an 'African democratic developmental state' in the 'south', following a harrowing quarter-century of 'independence', with that as a 'divided society' in the 'north'. But both conceptual frameworks and existential relationships are interconnected in reality, albeit in complex ways; both also entail organic regional dimensions/relations in East Africa/Great Lakes Region/Horn. The two Ugandas always co-existed in tenuous ways, but in the new century the division has become wider with profound implications for prospects of development and democracy, human rights and human security in both parts. The chapter constitutes an experimental attempt to understand and interrelate both of today's Ugandas in the hope that this case study will throw light on the co-existence of conflict and growth elsewhere on the continent and inform state and non-state policies reflective of the 'responsibility to protect' (Field 2004; ICISS 2001; Nhema 2004).

The study draws, then, on a *variety of interrelated yet all too isolated disciplines and debates* – from political science/economy and international relations to African, development and security studies – to which we return at the end in a later section (Shaw 2004c). It seeks to juxtapose generic concepts like 'civil society' and 'governance' with cases drawn from Africa(s), especially Uganda(s); interestingly, in almost all instances, development and conflict genres exist in splendid isolation. So, in terms of extant literatures, there would appear to be at least two 'Ugandas'. While we concentrate here on the Great Lakes Region, this study reflects dichotomous analyses and debates from Sub-Saharan Africa as a whole (Villalon and Huxtable 1998). In particular, we juxtapose notions drawn from the overlapping Highly Indebted Poor Countries (HIPC), African developmental state and New Partnership for Africa's Development (NEPAD) genres. We also bring in notions of human development/security, given their salience in the contemporary continent (Hampson et al. 2001; UNDP 1994, 1999), plus the notion of 'responsibility to protect' (ICISS 2001). And we reflect in particular on the elusiveness of peace-building and prospects for reconstruction in today's Uganda – the roles of non-governmental organizations (NGOs) and think-tanks – given our respective continuing positions as Visiting Professor and Dean in the burgeoning Faculty of Development Studies, with its new building, at the new Mbarara University of Science and Technology (MUST) in Western Uganda.

Uganda in 2004: Conflict versus Development?

Definitions of, and relations among, states, economies and civil societies are everywhere in flux, given globalization, regionalism, migration, neo-liberalism, etc. (Maiguashca 2003). Yet, as indicated below, contemporary texts on government, international relations and/or political science seem rarely to appreciate this (Lemke 2003; Shaw 2004c). Likewise, the post-bipolar 'world community' now consists of some 200 mainly poor, small, weak countries, but most orthodox studies of 'foreign policy' fail to recognize their tenuousness or vulnerability, unlike the state of analysis in the less ominous/global 'world' of the 1960s (Khadiagala and Lyons 2001, World Bank 2002). Today, only a minority of 'critical' analysts focus on the 'other' side of globalizations: 'resistance' as well as global 'governance' (Maiguashca 2003: 5), involving, for instance, regional and global networks of informal/illegal trade in people and products, mafias/militias, drugs and guns, etc. (www.forcedmigration.org). Yet the formal governmental regimes of over half the members of the United Nations and the

World Bank exert at best a tenuous control over their territories, economies and civil societies (Fearon and Laitin 2004; Lemke 2003; Shaw 2004c). Gérard Prunier (2004) and Vlassenroot and Raeymaekers (2004) have recently provided detailed, informed histories of the complex economic, ethnic and strategic regional dimensions of Uganda's wars which stretch deep into Congo, Rwanda, Sudan, etc.: 'new regionalisms' (Soderbaum and Shaw 2003) indeed.

Uganda has undergone a profound policy reform process financed by international donors through 'foreign aid'.[3] As a result of sustained inflows of foreign direct investment (FDI) as well as development assistance, it has enjoyed sustained economic growth of 6 per cent p.a.. This has mainly been evidenced by expansion in construction, manufacturing – textiles and AGOA (African Growth and Opportunity Act) sugar and UHT milk, etc. – electricity, communications,[4] water, education and poverty reduction, to mention but a few. At a broader level, fiscal discipline has ensured macro-economic stability while liberalization, deregulation, and privatization have created a relatively successful new nation, at least in the south. There has, for instance, been increased access to safe water from 49 per cent (1998) to 57 per cent (2000). HIV prevalence has also declined from about 30 per cent in the late 1980s to 6.5 per cent in 2001, and the percentage of the population with access to health facilities had risen to 49 per cent by 2001 (UNDP 2002). Furthermore, the number of women in parliament rose from 18.6 per cent in 1996 to 26 per cent by 2002. However, the most profound legacy of Museveni's regime is in education. Primary school enrolment increased from 920,000 pupils in 1997 to 7.2 million in 2002, as a result of universal primary education (UPE). At Makerere University, still one of the most prestigious higher institutions in the country and region, impressive improvements have also been registered. Whereas Makerere's total student population in 1986 was less than 5,000 students (all government-sponsored), in 2000 the total student enrolment stood at over 25, 000 (more than a 450 per cent increase in 15 years), now consisting of a few government- and many private-sponsored students (Kwesiga 2000; Musisi and Muwanga 2003). Alongside this 'economic success story', however, lies the precarious situation in northern Uganda, one consequence of a series of incomplete 'transitions' since independence itself (Dicklitch 2000).

Northern Uganda has for a long time experienced conflict without any end in sight (Van Acker 2004). There is the brutal and relentless war between the Uganda government forces and the rebel Lord's Resistance Army, which has been going on since 1986. In addition, Karamojong cattle rustlers have for over four decades been carrying out raids, terrorizing their neighboring districts in the northern and eastern parts of the country. These conflicts have led to gross violations of human rights, mainly against women and children, and have destroyed infrastructure, paralyzed economic activity, led to social and cultural breakdown, and disrupted the economic and human development of the north, which, as a result, remains the poorest part of the country, with 63 per cent of the population, especially children and rural communities, estimated to be living below the poverty line in 2003 (Uganda Bureau of Statistics 2003). Moreover, attempts to bring peace to the region have so far failed, which has made it difficult to carry out reconstruction work and thus to restore pre-war conditions and levels of service delivery. Education, in particular, has been severely affected, due to the destruction of school buildings, looting of books and burning of supplies, and the targeted killings and abduction of teachers and children by the LRA. In terms of access to water and sanitation too, the forceful displacement of people into the camps has resulted in over-crowding and lack of basic supplies, and this has led to health problems among resident populations. The nutrition and health conditions of the conflict areas are also very poor, especially when compared with the rest of the country. For example, the infant mortality rates in 2003 were 290, 274 and 274 per 1,000 births for Gulu, Kitgum and Pader, respectively, whereas the national average was 8 per cent.[5]

In terms of developmentalism, the Museveni regime has been deter-minedly pro-market, whereas in terms of responding to persistent violence it has been resolutely coercive: no negotiations or amnesty until the LRA lays down its arms even where child abductees and soldiers are concerned. Uganda's no- (or one-?!) party regime of the National Resistance Movement (NRM) changes the context of both developmentalism and conflict. In the former, the catalytic government role is relatively unencumbered by opposi-tion other than that of some members of parliament, some elements in the media, and some institutions in civil society. And in the latter, similarly, the response of the government is relatively unhindered other than by national and global human rights groups, some regional pressures from the north, especially religious leaders in civil society in the early twenty-first century, plus some global concern, including diasporas and international non-governmental organizations (INGOs), especially those which are 'faith-based' (Van Acker 2004).

The reluctance of the Museveni regime to consider talking peace con-trasts with its own accession to power as a liberation army from the bush. Its own extensive, inclusive coalition on seizing power in the mid-1980s (Hansen and Twaddle 1998; see also ICISS 2001 Volume II: 61–63 on Tanzania's support for the overthrow of Amin in 1979: early 'responsibility to protect'?) can be contrasted with its exclusion of northern demands and opponents as the LRA violence continued into the new century and spread towards the south and east. Why would the Museveni regime deny its own experience with peace-building over the previous decade and a half? And does such reluctance in response to the impoverishment and alienation of the north compromise its embryonic status as a democratic developmental state? Furthermore, if the Ugandan state is itself still unwilling to open peace talks at the official, formal intergovernmental Track One level, then less formal, more non-governmental Tracks Two/Three may become imperatives, with any preliminary understandings then brought back to the official milieu. In short, a series of incomplete transitions, including ambiguous decolonization, have complicated transitions to successor regimes, including those at the end of the twentieth century and start of the twenty-first (Griffiths and Katalikawe 2003; Kyango-Nsubunga 2004).

Given the resilience of violence in the north, then, can we really characterize Uganda as a 'developmental state' (Bigsten and Kayizzi-

Mugerwa 2001; Holmgren et al 2000)? But, likewise, given the character of conflict in the north, can we really characterize this as a 'civil war' (Van Acker 2004)? And can the two halves of the territory exist the one without the other, especially if we recognize the broader regional dimensions of the conflicts in the Great Lakes Region/Horn (Prunier 2004; Vlassenroot and Raeymaekers 2004) ranging from the IGAD (Inter-Governmental Authority on Development) mid-2004 Naivasha talks re southern Sudan and the late 2004 international conference on the Great Lakes Region as a follow-up to the Sun City agreement on a roadmap for Congo, treated below? Both of these sets of confidence-building measures involve state and non-state 'Friends'. Moreover, given the particularly horrific character of the LRA attacks – child abductees/soldiers, mass rapes and use of drugs/girls as incentives – public relations/diplomacy dimensions are quite problematic: 'new security' features. Furthermore, can any Poverty Reduction Strategy Papers (PRSP) under the HIPC initiative take such violence into account in terms of moderating and reversing alienation through Confidence Building Measure (CBM)-type negotiation (Gariyo 2001, 2002)? And are HIPC and NEPAD compatible, leading to an original framework for an innovative form of local to continental African developmental governance (Parpart and Shaw 2002)? In short, might domestic inflexibility negatively impact on prospects of regional and continental human development/security?

We now turn to the global-local dimensions of Uganda as an emerging but fraught (Human Rights Watch 2003a, 2003b) democratic developmental state, before going on to an analysis of its current HIPC governance and continuing conflict (Shaw 2004b). Certainly there are limitations to democratization in Uganda, in both state and non-state sectors (Furley 2000; Mugaju and Olaka-Onyango 2000). Conversely, it is more developmental as well as democratic than ever, notwithstanding violence in the north.

Global

Just as states are highly heterogeneous, so likewise are non-state actors. The two non-state 'corners' of the 'governance' 'triangle' (Commonwealth Foundation 1999: 16) include global corporations and local micro-enterprises, along with informal and illegal as well as formal and legal enterprises. Thus it is imperative to recognize that 'global capitalisms' are in fact heterogeneous rather than homogeneous: relationships around the governance triangle vary.

Similarly, NGOs vary from familiar global INGOs to very local grassroots organizations (Commonwealth Foundation 1999; Desai 2002). In particular, NGOs can be distinguished in terms of whether they are primarily engaged in policy advocacy as think-tanks or in service delivery as sub-contractors, although most do both in varying proportions. Major INGOs have become increasingly engaged with international agencies in the UN and IFI nexuses in terms of both advocacy and subcontracting (Nelson 2002). And such legal arrangements are matched by illegal transnational networks amongst mafias, militias, and private armies (Avant 2004; Howe 1998; International Alert 2000; Shearer 1998a, 1998b). Indeed, the former – INGOs and the UN – have been instrumental in throwing considerable light on the latter, non-state security formations. As Fearon and Laitin (2004: 13) indicate, with the end of the Cold War, 'new' security concerns have proliferated and become dominant even if not all international relations (IR) scholars are yet prepared to admit this.

'Global civil society' is very heterogeneous (Glasius et al. 2002), with global social movements coming to play increasingly salient yet quite incompatible roles. On the one hand, many contemporary INGOs have been the sources which identify and popularize new global issues, such as ecology, genetic engineering, gender, global warming, the International Criminal Court, landmines, ozone depletion, small arms, etc. and now 'blood diamonds' (Smillie et al. 2000). These have led to major global coalitions such as the International Campaign to Ban Landmines (ICBL) which resulted in the 'Ottawa Process' (Hubert 2000; Tomlin et al. 1998), now replicated in the 'Kimberley Process' to outlaw 'conflict diamonds' (Smillie et al. 2000). But they have also advanced 'anti-globalization' sentiments as reflected in the 'Battle of Seattle' against the Multilateral Agreement on Investment (MAI) and subsequent alternative summits and counter-demonstrations at major global and regional summits (www.attac.org, www.nologo.org), notwithstanding the disruption or diversion of 11 September (Glasius et al. 2002).

In turn, as indicated in a subsequent section, major global corporations increasingly seek to insulate themselves from popular pressures/boycotts through a variety of strategies: from association with the UN Global Compact to corporate codes of conduct, ethical as well as fair trade initiatives, strategic alliances with certain international organizations (IOs) or NGOs, etc. (Shaw and van der Westhuizen 2004). Thus many of the multinational corporations which feature in Naomi Klein's (2000) *No Logo* in terms of being targets of anti-corporate campaigns – e.g. McDonalds, Nestlé, Nike, Shell, Coca-Cola, etc. – are most active in the UN Global Compact (www.unglobalcompact.org; Parpart and Shaw 2002)! The Coca-Cola company in Uganda has been involved in a variety of community development projects including building schools and health centres, arguably due to such pressure. Meanwhile, given its HIPC and anti-terrorist credentials, Uganda is becoming a major beneficiary of the US African Growth and Opportunity Act (AGOA) with some US$6 million investment in the early 2000s leading to the revival of the Jinja textile industry, the establishment of the Tri-Star apparel factory,[6] and a rapid rise in exports of cotton and processed coffee (for the first time ever ex-Uganda) in 2003: from US$32,000 in 2002 to $1.5 million in 2003.

One novel aspect of South-North trade in the new global political economy is 'supply chains' (Mbabazi 2005) which link local producers to global markets in novel ways in a variety of sectors, including 'new' horticulture, etc., in a distinctive form of 'partnership' (Nadvi 2004). Typically these link producers of fresh flowers (Asea and Kaija 2000), fruit and vegetables, fish, etc. to major supermarket chains, using information technology for communication and airfreight/containers for transportation. These, in turn, are open to pressure from advocacy groups with regard to ecology, gender, labor, etc., leading to Ethical Trade Initiatives and the Extractive Industries Transparency Initiative as well as Fair Trade, conditionalities over gender, housing and labor practices, etc., as is apparent in thumb-print sketches of the sources of specialized coffee beans in Aroma, Costa, Second Cup, Starbucks: 'chain governance'.[7]

Continental

The first few examples of developmental states were authoritarian. The new ones will have to be democratic, and it is encouraging that the two most cited examples of such 'democratic developmental states' are both African – Botswana and Mauritius (Mkandawire 2001: 310).

Inter- and non-state relations in Africa were changing at the turn of the century (Khadiagala and Lyons 2001) because of globalization/neo-liberalism extra-continentally but also because of new threats/leaders intra-continentally, now advocated in terms of an 'African Renaissance' – ranging from the African Union and the African Economic Community to the New Partnership for Africa's Development with its ambitious and controversial African Peer Review Mechanism, and resonance within the G8 community about an Africa Action Plan (MacLean et al., 2002), reinforced by the bilateral Blair (see below) 'initiative' for the continent, with the former animating a comprehensive Commission for Africa in the run-up to the UK's chairing of both the G8 and the EU in 2005. These may inform and legitimize regional peace-keeping responses – 'responsibility to protect' – to resilient regional conflicts. And they might even facilitate, perhaps unintentionally, non-state definitions of 'new' regionalisms such as ecology, ethnicity, brands, religions, sports, etc. (Parpart and Shaw 2002). They may also extend legitimacy to new African developmental states and their related NEPAD ideology (Taylor and Nel 2002).

Similarly, given its recent espousal of 'human security', countries like Canada (as indicated below, now Co-Chair of the Friends of the GLR) commit more resources to the continent than 'national interest' alone would justify, in part because of notions of 'human security' and in part given concerned diasporas. As Chris Brown (2001: 194) suggested, at the turn of the century: 'As a continent where human security is manifestly at risk, Africa came to figure more prominently in Canada's foreign policy during 2000 than a narrow examination of national interests might suggest.' Furthermore, in follow-up to the April Sun City agreement, the GLR was to receive further attention in the run-up to the planned November 2004 international conference in Tanzania, which was preceded by national consultations in the seven participating countries, including Uganda, where a civil society consultation was facilitated in August 2004. This ongoing initiative, intended to advance and reinforce the national process of preparing for elections in Congo in 2006, was supported by the 28 state and 10 inter-state 'Group of Friends of the Great Lakes Region' which is co-chaired by Canada and the Netherlands, which are already connected in the Human Security Network. But the protracted history of complex conflicts in Congo and incomplete transitions throughout the region should give pause for thought (Vlassenroot and Raeymaekers 2004) about the obstacles to be overcome. Likewise, even if Dar Fur constitutes a further setback for regional peace, the conclusion of IGAD's Naivasha talks gives cause for hope that the southern Sudan dimension of Uganda's conflict might finally be in transition away from decades of conflict (Prunier 2004). Hopefully some of the lessons learned by the Uganda Debt Network (UDN) et al. from the HIPC/PRSP (Gariyo 2001, 2002) can be adapted to the war in the north, given the 'responsibility to protect' (ICISS 2001) (see below): a second wind for Tracks Two and Three?

National

Patterns of 'governance' in Africa – increasingly inseparable from the notion of a democratic developmental state – are in flux at all levels, local to continental, and in all sectors – from state and corporate to NGOs; i.e. the three 'corners' of the governance 'triangle'. Contemporary notions of governance have a variety of conceptual, ideological, institutional, political and theoretical sources and correlates (Quadir et al. 2001). Governance on the African continent like other continents varies over time and between regions (Reinikka and Collier 2001; Shaw and Nyang'oro 2000). And it reveals similarities and dissimilarities with the other continents: in the way democracy in Uganda as elsewhere brings tensions amongst state and non-state actors (Furley 2000). As elsewhere, notions of comparative politics/ development have evolved profoundly over the past decade as the mix of 'globalizations' and 'liberalizations' has impacted in cumulative ways. The focus on the state has been superseded by the recognition of diverse and changeable patterns of governance reflected in concepts like public-private partnerships, networks, coalitions, etc. (Mbabazi et al. 2002).

The debate continues over whether 'globalization' does offer some opportunities for some African states, civil societies and companies at all levels, with the more optimistic 'liberals' insisting that it does, despite all the negative evidence and press during the past two decades (Reinikka and Collier 2001). Coinciding with some promising developments, then, are moves away from orthodox structural adjustment programs (SAPs) and conditionalities towards poverty-reduction programs through the HIPC initiative. To qualify, African regimes have had to meet SAP, then HIPC, terms and design acceptable poverty-reduction strategies in association with civil society.

In the case of Uganda, one of the relatively few currently successful HIPC cases, in the late 1990s the Uganda Debt Network (UDN) acted as an intermediary between government and private sector, on the one hand, and civil society, on the other, at both design and implementation stages, moving from being policy advocate to being policy agent or subcontractor, achieving the status of an 'authoritative epistemic community' (Callaghy 2002). As UNCTAD (2003: 148) indicated in a 'box' (No. 7) on the Uganda case, the latter's Poverty Eradication Action Plan (PEAP) was founded on four pillars: (i) creating a framework for economic growth and transformation; (ii) ensuring good governance and security; (iii) directly increasing the ability of the poor to raise their incomes; and (v) directly increasing the quality of life of the poor. Thus Uganda is something of a model in terms of designing a Policy Framework Paper (PFP) and then maintaining momentum through Poverty Reduction Strategy Papers (PRSPs) in collaboration with a wide network of ministries, international organizations and NGOs, both local and global.

If SAPs generated considerable skepticism, even defeatism, on the continent, then their *de facto* successor, offering a distinctive form of globalization – negotiated debt relief for Heavily Indebted Poor Countries (HIPC) (Anena 2001; Gariyo 2001, 2002) – is leading to a novel form of governance. As Callaghy (2002: 138,142) suggests:

> all HIPC debt relief is now to be tied directly to poverty reduction. This is to be ensured by the creation of Poverty Reduction Strategy Papers (PRSPs) put together by debtor countries *in consultation with civil society groups ... If seriously implemented*, this new process could be an important change in international governance on debt, aid and development more generally and may have major implications for the unfolding of democratization processes in Africa and elsewhere.

The UDN continued to grow and increase its capabilities. By 2000 it had more than sixty members as well as strong ties to the Uganda Joint Christian Council and business, student and labor organizations. It was becoming very active in coordinating civil society participation in the PRSP process, which it was doing with the help of Northern NGOs. Lastly, it had improved its own organizational capabilities and was running its own independent website.

In the process of so negotiating and facilitating HIPC governance, the UDN has itself been somewhat transformed not only in status, but also in practice – not just advocacy but also delivery – raising issues about cooptation, etc. (Nelson 2002). Given the influential role which the donors play in today's Uganda, there may be a danger in their tending to divide NGOs into delivery or advocacy types when both varieties are needed to make governance more efficacious and accountable (Lister and Nyamugasira 2003). Moreover, there may be a danger in privileging civil society excessively to the detriment of formal, multi-party politics: civil society, especially when legitimated or reinforced by global donors/media, can 'squeeze out' other democratic processes like elections.

The distinctively 'Ugandan' debate about Movement versus multi-party politics (Furley 2000; Mugaju and Olaka-Onyango 2000) is not separable from the parallel discourse about occasional formal elections versus continuous civil society activity/advocacy, let alone continued advocacy of some form of 'federalism', notwithstanding its chequered history in the country. These, combined with the fraught issue of a third term for President Museveni, have led to a problematic period in mid-decade: can Uganda finally transcend a set of complete transitions? Certainly, redevelopment has not been evenly distributed across the country, as indicated in the following section. Museveni gets most support for his handling of the political debate from the west and least from the north. In short, there are profound limits to 'democracy' even in today's Uganda (Furley 2000). Notwithstanding the violence in the north, can these shortcomings be excused or disregarded in relation to 'developmental' success; i.e. the trade-off between economic and political 'liberalizations'?

Finally, to conclude this section, Kevin Dunn (2001: 46, 49) has chided orthodox analysts about their increasingly outdated and inappropriate analytical approaches which reveal a lack of nuanced understanding of the distinctive patterns of dynamic, mixed-actor governance on the continent, especially in 'divided' territories like Uganda:

> Just a few of the labels attached to the African state over the past decade or so include 'failed', 'lame', 'fictive', 'weak', 'collapsing', 'quasi', 'invented', and 'imposed', 'shadow', 'overdeveloped', and 'centralized', 'swollen', 'soft', 'extractive' and 'parasitic', 'premodern', and 'post-state.' What needs to be recognized is that the African state is not failing as much as is our understanding of the state.

Local

Finally, then, given decentralization and urbanization, the local level of governance – city and community – is of growing importance for human development/security. It reveals similar patterns of partnership to the other levels; i.e. increasing roles of non-state actors in terms of service delivery, confidence-building, etc. as well as in conflict amelioration (Crook 2001) with dramatic contrasts between north and south as already indicated and advanced further below when Gulu is contrasted with Mbarara. As we see in the case of HIV/AIDS,[8] subcontracting to local NGOs for AIDS awareness and care such as hospices, etc. (and also local NGOs for education) has become commonplace and is increasingly replicated in conflict zones.

Furthermore, during the past decade there has been cumulative positive growth in Western Uganda, albeit from a very weak base following the Amin/Obote II regimes. This has advanced both human development and human security, the former defined by the UNDP (1994: 13) as expanding human capabilities and choices whilst minimizing vulnerabilities, and the latter (ibid.: 24) as 'freedom from fear and freedom from want': human security is not a concern with weapons, it is a concern with 'human life and dignity' (ibid.: 22). We turn now to an overview of human development/security in two very different districts/parts of Uganda: Mbarara and Gulu.

Mbarara District, which is one of 45 districts located in the south-western region of the country, has enjoyed an annual growth rate of about 6.5 per cent per annum over the recent past.[9] By most developmental parameters, it compares very favourably with other districts in the country. For example, the maternal mortality rate is 506 per 100,000 live births, the infant mortality rate 120 per 1000 live births, the antenatal care attendance rate at least 50 per cent, delivery by trained staff 14 per cent, rural safe water coverage is 29 per cent (1999), the number of households with latrines is 72 per cent (1999) while the percentage of population within 5 km of a health unit is 56 per cent. Although the major economic activity in the district is farming, the district also has a number of small-scale industries in the private sector, including: milk cooling plants, a nail and iron bars factory, hotels and bars, bakeries, carpentries and garages which offer minimal job opportunities to the local population. There is also a soda factory for Coke products and a well-established state university.[10] In terms of infrastructure, the district seems to be doing well too, with 21 sub-counties having access to electricity which only 6 sub-counties lack. With regard to education, the adult literacy rate is relatively high at 52.6

per cent (as compared with the national average of 50 per cent), and school enrolment for UPE children stands at 271,611. However, if we look at the situation in Gulu District in northern Uganda, we get a very different picture.

The ongoing war has turned *Gulu District*, once a highly productive area as the major source of cotton for the textile industry at home and abroad, into one of the poorest in the country. Today, little of the money in Gulu town itself is generated locally. Reflective of the 'political economy of conflict' perspective (Collier 1994, Reno 2002), it comes from the army, the NGO community, the central government, donors and the extensive Acholi diaspora, which is said to fund much of the construction in the town. The escalation of the conflict since June 2003 has meant that hundreds of thousands of people have poured into camps after fleeing direct attacks by the rebel LRA and regular fighting between the warring parties.[11] The largest IDP camps in the north are located in Gulu District. The displacements and the volatile security situation have severely impeded the access of the majority of the IDPs to farmland and hence reduced significantly the general food security situation. This has further exacerbated the appalling humanitarian conditions in the camps. The contrasts between Mbarara and Gulu districts both symbolize and reinforce the division of the country into two.

Furthermore, nutrition surveys indicate that malnutrition is more prevalent among displaced children than among the under-age population at large, although throughout the country rural children are poorer than urban. Malnutrition rates increase significantly when the WFP reduces rations to the camps because of shortages of food deliveries (WFP, 2003). A large number of public health units have been closed down, health workers have moved to safer areas, and expectant mothers are not attended to adequately. Diseases like malaria and acute respiratory infections are widespread, claiming the lives of many people in both the district and the north in general (ibid.). In the congested camps, particularly in Gulu, each person receives an average of three litres of safe water as opposed to the recommended 20 litres. This congestion, coupled with an acute shortage of latrines – there is one latrine for every 145 people in some camps – has made the sanitation problems in them even more severe. Undoubtedly, poor health among the displaced population has been aggravated by the congested camps and the breakdown of social structures;[12] fertile breeding ground for alienation, sympathy for the 'rebels', etc.

There are also difficulties in introducing free primary education due to the problems of displacement. Few, if any, of the school infrastructures were designed to cope with the influx of displaced pupils. Also, because of the displacements of teachers, students and schools, funds allocated under the UPE scheme fail to reach their destination. The result is a recurrent lack of school materials, an acute shortage of teachers, and an increase in pupil:classroom ratio, which increased from 112:1 in the mid-1990s to approximately 234:1 in 2003 in some schools in Gulu District (WFP 2003). On the whole, then, conflict and displacement in Gulu have undermined progress, and society and economy there continue to regress.

The glaring contrasts between Mbarara and Gulu Districts at the local level reinforce the division of the country into two distinct, divergent parts at the national level, with serious regional dimensions and reverberations (Prunier 2004; Vlassenroot and Raeymaekers 2004). Such highly uneven development poses profound challenges for policy as well as analysis: can human development/security be advanced and sustained in the south if it is so elusive in the north (Van Acker 2004)? Does the 'responsibility to protect' in the north limit the prospects of a 'democratic developmental state' in the south? And are the two parts of Uganda really so separate or interrelated, even interdependent? We now turn to some consequences in terms of liberalization and privatization before pursuing a case study of northern Uganda.

Civil Society, the State & the Economy in Contemporary Uganda: Beyond Liberalization & Privatization

At the start of the twenty-first century, as noted above, NGOs are now engaged in service delivery[13] and/or policy advocacy from the local to the global levels (Desai 2002; Lister and Nyamugasa 2003; Nelson 2002), leading to 'partnerships' of multiple types which impact on the state, whether it seeks such links or not. 'NGOs create alliances and networks to place pressure on the state' (Desai 2002: 497).

However, one side of the governance 'triangle' (Commonwealth Foundation 1999) – that between the state and civil society – is focused on democratization or 'political liberalization'. In contrast, the other side – that between the state and the private sector – is preoccupied with 'economic liberalization' or privatization. In such a fluid context, the roles of 'think-tanks' as well as NGOs (e.g. the spectrum in Uganda from the Private Sector Foundation and the Economic Policy Research Centre (see more below) to the Centre for Basic Research (CBR) and the UDN versus 'old,' more established 'academic' research institutions like the Makerere Institute for Social Research (MISR) at Makerere University) are in flux, as indicated in the broad-based (winning?) coalition supporting the PRSP process (UNCTAD 2003). Symbolically, a new project of the Netherlands Institute of International Relations' Conflict Research Unit on 'Democratic Transition in Post-Conflict Societies: building local institutions,' which has Uganda as one of its eight case studies, has been collaborating with the CBR (Barya et al. 2004).

HIV/AIDS has also led to innovative civil society-state/corporate partnerships in Uganda as well as elsewhere on the continent, as noted above. NGOs and private companies have been active in financing hospices for the dying, prevention campaigns, orphanages for children without parents etc., and multinational corporations are increasingly active in terms of infected workers. Hospice Uganda has received sizeable donations from local corporate bodies such as Mobile Telephone Network (MTN), Standard Chartered Bank (U) and Roko Construction, among others. The stand-off between civil society and the state over HIV/AIDS in South Africa is not replicated in Uganda (www.tac.org.za), as the Museveni regime has been in the vanguard of straightforward communication/education, leading to the regional Great Lakes Initiative for AIDS. No wonder Uganda's 'ABC' AIDS prevention policies – Abstinence, Being faithful to your partner and using a Condom – have become something of a model all over the world including the United States,[14] as indicated by Museveni's appearance at the World AIDS conference in Bangkok in July 2004.

'African capitalism' (Shaw and van der Westhuizen 2004) in contemporary Uganda is quite distinctive and different from that elsewhere, even if not all analysis appreciates this. It includes not only traditional and contemporary 'colonial' commodities and supply chains but also informal (and illegal?) and formal regional exchanges. It therefore now includes fruit, horticultural and vegetable global exports as well as coffee and tea, and in the region it includes electricity, Coca Cola, Mukwano soap products, UHT milk (Mbabazi 2005), etc. Uganda's earnings from fish exports, for instance, had risen from US$18.6 million in 1999 to approximately US$90m by 2002 (Uganda Government 2003).

Today's Uganda also includes the burgeoning remittance economy of foreign exchange being sent home for either subsistence or investment by diasporas in Britain, Canada, South Africa, etc,. typically via Western Union or MoneyGram.[15] And in addition to serving as an entrepot for Central African resources, it also serves as a conduit for informal coltan, diamonds and gold out and guns and other basic needs in. The mix of legal and illegal is problematic and controversial, with the UN contributing to both data and debates. Yet, clearly, the Ugandan economy as a whole, as well as a few individuals in particular, have at times gained from the Congolese conflict/ expeditionary force (Vlassenroot and Raeymaekers 2004).

In addition, the termination of apartheid has enabled South African capital, franchises, links, technologies, etc. to enter Uganda as elsewhere in Africa, thus competing with local (African and Asian), British/European and Asian capital: Century Bottlers' Coca Cola franchise, MTN cell-phones, MNet cable and satellite TV, Nandos and Steer fast food franchises, Woolworths upmarket shopping (two branches in the 'new' Kampala), Shoprite supermarket also with two branches, Metro Cash-and-Carry wholesaling, South African Breweries(SAB)/Miller and a new Game superstore recently opened in Lugogo at the start of the Jinja Road.

Such alternatives lead to new opportunities and to 'new regionalisms', beyond the established inter-state East African Community (EAC), now augmented by the East African Legislature, and on to new security provisions, and Great Lakes Region and Lake Victoria basin to flexible non-state forms of regionalisms defined by ecologies, ethnicities, infrastructures, technologies, viruses, etc. The division of the country is both impacted by and also affects the range of its formal and informal regional relations (Prunier 2004; Vlassenroot and Raeymaekers 2004), especially when the informal or new dimensions are included: does the 'border' between the two 'Africas' pass through the middle of Uganda?

We now turn to look more specifically at the less positive, more distressing, case of northern Uganda, with its own 'new regionalisms' dimensions and dynamics.

The Case of Northern Uganda

In northern Uganda, living conditions remain critical, especially for the rural and youthful poor. Conditions are characterized by widespread poverty and food insecurity (see Table 9.1). The two-decade-long LRA rebellion led by Joseph Kony continues to pose one of the big challenges to the country's economic, social and political development (Van Acker 2004), symbolizing and exacerbating the alienation of some/many in Acholiland, in particular. The rebellion has caused untold suffering to innocent civilians through indiscriminate killings, rapes, abductions of children, who are forcefully conscripted into rebel ranks, and massive displacement of people. There are currently over 1.6 million internally displaced persons in northern Uganda (see Fig. 9.1). Many people have been displaced, hundreds killed and over 10,000 children abducted (Boas 2004; FEWS NET/Uganda, May 2004).

The traditional 'geographic' or 'ecological' region of northern Uganda covers the districts of Gulu, Kitgum and Pader. However, the 'political' definition of northern Uganda now includes all those districts that have suffered under armed conflicts, and therefore embraces ten more districts: Apach and Lira in Lango sub-region; Moyo and Adjumani in Madi sub-region; Arua, Yumbe and Nebbi in West Nile sub-region; and Kotido, Moroto and Nakapiripirit in Karamoja sub-region (Nannyonjo 2004). It also includes the five districts in Teso sub-region (Katakwi, Kaberamaido, Soroti, Kumi, and Pallisa), which have also been affected by the war in many respects. Thus, northern Uganda can be taken to include 18 districts, though it is essentially Gulu, Kitgum and Pader in Acholi, Lira and Apach in Lango, Kotido, Moroto and Nakapiripirit in Karamoja that have been most affected and devastated by the long-standing armed conflict (see map).

People in the region are mainly confined to IDP camps and currently depend on the food aid provided by the international community and local NGOs. The main victims of the LRA have been the Acholi people from the districts of Gulu, Kitgum and Pader, though, as noted above, neighboring districts have also borne the brunt of the war. More than one million Acholi have moved into protected camps. As a result, there has not been much cultivation and hunger is widespread. Having suffered for so many years, Acholi leaders are desperate for peace and have been at the forefront of efforts to open up a dialogue with the rebels (Refugee Law Project 2004) even if the Museveni regime remains sceptical and ambivalent, asserting that the LRA is almost defeated so reconstruction and reconciliation, including treatment for traumas on both/all sides, can commence. In August 2004, an ICC delegation arrived to pursue the Ugandan regime's complaint concerning the LRA's human rights abuses. Figure 9.1 is a map of northern Uganda showing the main districts affected by the war.

The conflict in northern Uganda has led to gross human right violations, and retarded economic activity and social development; northern Uganda therefore now lags behind the rest of the country in terms of human development as well as human security. As a result, the Human

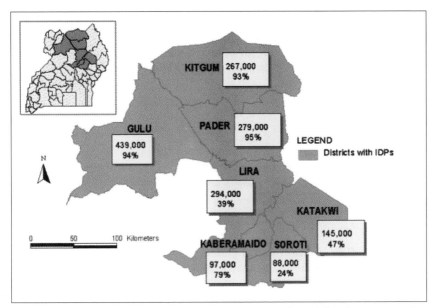

Figure 9.1 The northern Uganda districts most affected by the LRA with IDP members

Source: World Food Programme Uganda and Uganda Bureau of Statistics

Development Index (HDI) for northern Uganda in 2001 was 0.350, which is much lower than the national average of 0.449 and that for other regions such as central (0.552) and western (0.45). It is the northern region districts of Moroto, Nakapiripirit and Kotido, which recorded the lowest levels of human progress at 0.184, 0.184 and 0.195, respectively, when compared with other regions in the country (UNDP 2002: 126). The northern region, reflective of the more rural, youthful characteristics of the poor, in 2002/3 had the highest incidence of poverty at 63 per cent, compared with national averages of 39.0 per cent and 22.3 per cent, 46.0 per cent and 32.9 per cent for the central, east and western regions, respectively (Table 9.1).[16] According to Justine Nannyonjo (2004), insecurity is the major cause of poverty in most of the districts in northern Uganda and hence a primary reason for acquiescence in or support for the LRA (Boas 2004; Prunier 2004).

The reasons for the LRA rebellion in northern Uganda have never been clear, since it lacks an articulate political leadership to express its grievances, though amongst its causes are historic regional alienation and desertion by demobilized soldiers from previous regimes. It is also an indication of incomplete transitions between earlier regimes, especially the takeover by Museveni's NRM (see Kyango-Nsubunga 2004). As noted above, the war has turned much of the north, once known as the bread-basket of Uganda, into one of the poorest regions in the country. Since the outbreak of the war, an estimated three-quarters of the population have fled the hinterland into IDP camps near towns in fear of rebel attacks. The

Table 9.1 Poverty and Human Development Statistics for Uganda 2002/3

Location	Population Share[a]	Human Development Index	Poverty Indicator PO[b] Headcount	Mean Consumption per Adult Equivalent (CPAE
National	100.0	0.44	38.8	35,736
Central	29.6	0.55	22.3	52,747
East	27.4	0.44	46.0	28,483
West	24.7	0.45	32.9	33,818
North	18.2	0.34	63.0	21,615

a) Excludes Pader District in the north.
b) PO is defined as the percentage of individuals estimated to be living in households with real private consumption per adult equivalent below the poverty line for their region.
Sources: Uganda Bureau of Statistics (2003) and UNDP (2002)

number of IDPs in northern Uganda more than doubled from about 650,000 in July 2002 to 1.4 million as of December 2003.[17] But if the mix of hard line in the Sudan and generosity to returnees works, then the number of IDPs may begin to decline.

The LRA is headed in part by members of the previous national army that was defeated by the Museveni-led National Resistance Army in 1988 (see next section) (Prunier 2004; Van Acker 2004). Although the LRA's wider political agenda is unclear, its immediate objectives seem to be the overthrow of the current government and the dismantling of the IDP camps. The LRA reportedly consists of more than 80 per cent abducted children, many of whom have been converted in the most brutal ways to become extremely violent fighters. The rebels force them to kill and watch beatings, rape and the slaughtering of friends and relatives (Gersony 1997; Pain 1997). Disobedience is likely to result in their falling victim to the same fate. Since the beginning of the conflict in 1986, a total of more than 20,000 children have been abducted. Some 4,500 were reportedly fighting for the LRA as of July 2003 (Human Rights Watch 2003b: 21).

There has been little evident will on either side – government or the rebels – to end the conflict peacefully. The government appears to be encouraged in its strategy of pursuing a 'military solution' by considerable assistance from the United States, which is provided in exchange for Ugandan support for the fight against international terrorism (Office of the Prime Minister, November 2003; UNOCHA 2004). Despite some attempts in the new century, mostly involving some international – inter- or non-state – pressure, to open dialogue with the LRA for a negotiated peace, the Ugandan government has consistently chosen to confront the problem in the north by military means. Any attempt at kick-starting a peace process is further complicated by an apparent lack of will on the part of the rebels to engage in serious talks, as well as mutual mistrust on both sides (HURIPEC 2003: 121; IRIN 2003). Confidence-building measures would be required, probably initially at the more informal non-state level of Tracks Two and Three. But the core of the NRM regime around Museveni has its roots in a guerrilla war and so prefers fighting to talking. Following the repeated failures to settle the conflict locally and nationally, domestic and international NGOs like Acholi Peace Forum, Kacoke Medit, and ABETO, among others, have called for urgent international mediation (HURIPEC 2003: 144–5). But so far they have failed to assemble broad winning coalitions of non- as well as inter-state actors, such as those mobilized for the Ottawa and Kimberley Processes around landmines and conflict diamonds, respectively.

The impact of the LRA has undoubtedly been horrific. The failure by the NRM government to end the war in the north through either negotiations and/or force has translated into frustration and resentment towards it, as revealed by the limited support that Museveni received in the region during the most recent elections in 2001 and 2006, as indicated below. Symptomatically, most of the members of the Parliamentary Advocacy Forum (PAFO) – a pressure group in Parliament against the 'third term project' of President Museveni, now part of the (new) Forum for Democratic Change coalition – are representatives from the north: another indicator of a divided country. In turn, as the Naivasha talks yield some positive outcomes, violence in Dar Fur intensifies; the LRA as well as the UPDF has a military strategy (see next section).

The recruitment and deployment of local militias also pose a potential threat to Uganda's future stability. Following the LRA's attacks in 2003/4 further south and east in Soroti and Teso, and the UPDF's apparent inability to cope with these incursions, three groups of local militias, based on previously demobilized soldiers – namely the Arrow Boys, the Amuka Boys and the Rhino Boys – were formed with government support to mobilize the local population against rebels in these areas (Refugee Law Project 2004). Although this rapid deployment of local militias appears to have been instrumental in halting the spread of the LRA to other parts of eastern Uganda, there is a potential risk of precipitating ethnic clashes as three different ethnic groups – namely, Acholi, Langi and Iteso – are now well-armed yet there remain historic tensions amongst them. The ways in which this militarization of society in northern and eastern Uganda has played into an ethnicization of popular perceptions is becoming increasingly evident.

Governance in Contemporary Uganda: Beyond Peace-Building to Human Development/ Security?

For Uganda, the future looks too ghastly to contemplate (Ajulu 2001).

As noted above, the 2001 and 2006 elections not only confirmed the traditional divide between the south and the north but, perhaps even more critically, opened another internal divide within the NRM. These are very sensitive issues which will require delicate handling if Uganda is to avoid a return to the lawlessness of the 1970s and 1980s, more especially now with the recent yet problematic transition of the country to multi-party politics under the 'third' term of President Museveni from 2006. The wild card in this situation remains the ability of Museveni to control his army after its misdemeanours in the DRC, corruption around procurement and 'ghost' soldiers (Tangri and Mwenda 2001, 2003) and military control of southern Sudan (Prunier 2004; Vlassenroot and Raeymaekers 2004). In short, approaching the end of the first decade of the new century, Uganda is confronting multiple, interrelated legacies of incomplete transitions, dating back to before independence. So the sustainability of such an 'African renaissance' is problematic, unless a judicious balance is maintained among patterns of governance at all levels. In particular, the notion of 'national development' is problematic, as recognized already when the 'gap' between, say, Kitgum and Kabale or Mbarara and Gulu is rather wide (Baker 2001; UNDP 2000), as indicated in the continued tensions and violence spreading over two decades and now involving over 20,000 child abductions and well over a million internally displaced people, increasingly guarded by army-backed (ethnic?) militias (Ehrhart and Ayoo 2000; UNDP 2000).

It should be mentioned here that, despite apparently agreeing in mid-April 2004 to negotiate, and the formal cessation of hostilities in August 2006, the NRM government is still ambivalent about entering into any meaningful and sustained dialogue, let alone talks with the LRA, seemingly maintaining its earlier positions,[18] irrespective of the advocacy from a Coalition for Human Rights and Justice Initiatives for Northern Uganda and related religious and development groups. Instead it appears to be seeking to augment its image as a staunch ally of the US 'war on terrorism'. However, under pressure from some Northern donors as well as civil society concentrated in the north of the country, President Museveni did agree to an internationally brokered peace process in mid-2004 and formal cessation in August 2006; small steps towards some form of 'responsibility to protect' (ICISS 2001) or international administration/trusteeship (Berdal and Caplan 2004; Fearon and Laitin 2004)?

Conclusion

The official, optimistic scenario presented by Uganda in the early twenty-first century in terms of African or HIPC governance – an African demo-cratic development state (Bigsten and Kayizzi-Mugerwa 2001; Holmgren et al 2000) – is that of a continuous negotiation among corporations, donors, NGOs/networks, the World Bank, states and partnerships involving new capital/franchises/technologies and commodity/supply chains, etc.; in other words a view reflective of today's 'south' (Shaw 2004b). In contrast, the critical, pessimistic preview suggests arbitrary decision-making, exponential corruption, state violence, etc., as reflected in growing concerns regarding accountability, transparency, etc. and is articulated by a range of concerned INGOs like Amnesty International, ICG, Panos, SCF, World Vision etc; i.e. another view reflective of the 'north' (David and Wallace 2000; Shaw 2003). If such a division is present – two Ugandas, reflective of two Africas – can one 'national' polity and policy ever be representative and effective? Given Uganda's comeback in the 1990s and setbacks in the new century, are there lessons to be learned for local to global decision-makers (Shaw 2003)?

Here, we look briefly into possible lessons for established disciplines such as political science, international relations and political economy, as well as for interdisciplinary fields such as African/Development/Security Studies (Abrahamsen 2000; Duffield 2001; Haynes 2003; Lemke 2003; Payne 1999; Shaw 2004c). As suggested earlier some of these exist in splendid isolation from each other. In terms of orthodox cannons, case studies like contemporary Uganda suggest the imperative of going beyond the state and the formal economy and examining myriad links between these and the non-state/-formal: real triangular forms of mixed actor governance from local to regional, not just national or global, levels. And in terms of more recent interdisciplinary perspectives, there is a need to reflect on new issues/relations around developing countries and communities, so questions of traditional and 'new' security cannot be separated from the GLR etc. (Lemke 2003; Osaghae 2001; Prunier 2004; Vlassenroot and Raeymaekers 2004). Indeed, Uganda in the twenty-first century (Van Acker 2004), as in the nineteenth and twentieth, suggests the imperative of situating 'external' challenges and opportunities in the context of state-society relations – what we now know as 'globalization' (Dunn and Shaw 2001). The place of new, poor, small, weak states in a globalizing, let alone turbulent, world is crucial for analysts and citizens alike, especially if such states tend to be divided like Uganda (Lemke 2003; Shaw 2004a).

As Callaghy (2002: 144) concludes in his suggestive study of 'HIPC governance' in Uganda, somewhat parallel to the continent's centrality in anti-landmine and -blood diamond, Ottawa and Kimberley Processes, respectively, coalitions:

> Africa has been central to the evolution of the international regime on public debt, although not its primary driving force. New actors and processes have been unleashed in response to Africa's plight that might significantly alter the way the larger development regime functions. In the long run, the most significant changes may well not be HIPC itself, but rather the new processes and transboundary formations that it helped to unleash.

But maybe HIPC governance overlooks spatial (e.g. the north) and sectoral (e.g. security, especially the army) limitations of its approach, which the World Bank (2002) has begun to try to rectify through its LICUS initiative and the OECD (2004) through renewed advocacy of security sector reform. Yet might some of the HIPC/PRSP learning process – how to animate and maintain heterogeneous coalitions (Gariyo 2001, 2002) – be transferred to confidence-building measures around the north? For conflict to be contained and development enhanced in the new century, the two halves of Uganda need to be reintegrated. Such a task is very challenging, and can only be contemplated if the complexities of contemporary conflicts and developmentalism are recognized, including their integral regional dimensions. The division of Uganda undermines the possibility and potential of another democratic development state on the continent. Hence the imperative of a conceptual and political leap beyond established and unhelpful assumptions and formulations, for both theory and policy.

References

Abrahamsen, Rita. 2000. *Disciplining Democracy: Development discourse and good governance in Africa.* London: Zed Books.

Ajulu, Rok. 2001. 'Uganda's Flawed Presidential Election Bodes Ill for the Future', *Global Dialogue* 6 (2): 20–22.

Ajulu, Rok. 2004. 'African Security: can regional organisations play a role?' in Shannon Field, ed., *Peace in Africa: Towards a collaborative security regime,* Johannesburg: Institute for Global Dialogue, 265–82.

Akinrade, Sola and Amadu Seray, eds, 1999. *Africa in the Post-Cold War International System.* London: Cassel Academic.

Anena, Catherine. 2001. *Participation of Civil Society in Policy-Related Advocacy for Poverty Reduction in Uganda: An Experience from the Uganda Debt Network.* Kampala: UDN, October.

Asea, Patrick K and Darlison Kaija. 2000. *Impact of the Flower Industry in Uganda.* ILO Sectoral Activities Programme. Working Paper No. 148, Geneva: ILO, January.

Avant, Deborah. 2004. 'The Privatization of Security and Change in the Control of Force.' *International Studies Perspectives,* 5 (2): 153–7.

Baker, Wairama G. 2001. *Uganda: The marginalization of minorities.* London: Minority Rights Group International.

Barya, John-Jean et al. 2004. *The Limits of 'No-Party' Politics: the role of international assistance in Uganda's democratisation process.* Working Paper 28. The Hague: NIIR/Clingendael, August.

Berdal, Mats and Richard Caplan, eds. 2004. 'Special Issue on the Politics of International Administration'. *Global Governance,* 10 (1): 1–137.

Bigsten, Arne and Steve Kayizzi-Mugerwa. 2001. *Is Uganda an Emerging Economy? A Report of the OECD Project 'Emerging Africa'.* Research Report 118. Uppsala: Nordic Africa Institute.

Boas, Morten. 2004. 'Africa's Young Guerrillas: rebels without a cause?', *Current History* 103 (May): 211–14.

Brown, Chris. 2001. 'Africa in Canadian Foreign Policy 2000: The Human Security Agenda.' in Fen Hampson, Norman Hillmer and Maureen Molot, eds, *The Axworthy Legacy,* Montreal: McGill-Queens University Press, 192–212.

Callaghy, Thomas M. 2002. 'Networks and Governance in Africa: innovation in the debt regime', in Thomas Callaghy, Ronald Kassimir and Robert Latham, eds, *Intervention and Transnationalism in Africa: Global-local networks of power,* New York: Cambridge University Press, 115–48.

Collier, Paul. 1994. 'Economic Aspects of the Ugandan Transition to Peace', in J.P.D. Azam et al., eds, *Some Economic Consequences of the Transition from Civil War to Peace,* Oxford: CSAE, Oxford University.

Commonwealth Foundation. 1999. *Citizens and Governance: Civil Society in the New Millennium.* London: Commonwealth Foundation.

Crook, Richard C. 2001. *Strengthening Democratic Governance in Conflict-Torn Societies: Civic organizations, democratic effectiveness and political conflict.* Brighton: International Development Studies Working Paper 129, Brighton: Institute of Development Studies at the University of Sussex, May.

David, Lewis and Tina Wallace, eds. 2000. *New Roles and Relevance: Development NGOs and the Challenge of Change.* West Hartford, CT: Kumarian.

Deininger, Klaus and John Okidi. 2002. 'Growth and Poverty Reduction in Uganda, 1992–2000: panel data evidence.' Research Series No.28. Kampala: EPRC, March.

Desai, Vandana. 2002. 'Role of NGOs', in Vandana Desai and Robert Porter. eds, *The Companion to Development Studies,* London: Arnold, 495–99.

Dicklitch, Susan. 2000. 'The Incomplete Democratic Transition in Uganda', in Remonda Bensabat-Kleinberg and Janine Astrid Clark, eds, *Economic Liberalization, Democratization and Civil Society in the Developing World,* Basingstoke: Palgrave, 109–28.

Duffield, Mark. 2001. *Global Governance and the New Wars: The merging of development and security.* London: Zed Books.

Dunn, Kevin C. 2001. 'MadLib No.32: the (*blank*) African state: rethinking the sovereign state in international relations theory', in Kevin C Dunn and Timothy M Shaw, eds, *Africa's Challenge to International Relations Theory,* Basingstoke: Palgrave, 46–63.

Dunn, Kevin, C. and Timothy M. Shaw, eds, 2001. *Africa's Challenge to International Relations Theory,* Basingstoke: Palgrave.

ECA. 2003. 'Uganda: a tale of two economies', in *Economic Report on Africa 2003: Accelerating the pace of development.* Addis Ababa: ECA, 65–98.

Ehrhart, Charles and Sandra Josephine Ayoo. 2000. *Conflict, Insecurity and Poverty in Uganda: Learning from the poor.* UPPAP Briefing Paper No.4. Kampala: MFPED and Oxfam UK.

Fearon, James D and David D Laitin. 2004. 'Neotrusteeship and the Problem of Weak States', *International Security* 289 (4): 5–43.

Field, Shannon, ed. 2004. *Peace in Africa: Towards a collaborative security regime.* Johannesburg: IGD.

Furley, Oliver. 2000. 'Democratization in Uganda', *Commonwealth and Comparative Politics* 38 (3): 79–102.

Gariyo, Zie. 2001. 'The Poverty Reduction Strategy Program (PRSP) Process in Uganda', Kampala, October.[Online] Available at www.udn.org.

Gariyo, Zie. 2002. 'Civil Society and Global Finance in Africa: the PRSP process in Uganda', in Jan Aart Scholte with Albrecht Schnabel, eds, *Civil Society and Global Finance*, London: Routledge for UNU and Centre for Studies in Globalization and Regionalization (CSGR), 51–63.

Gersony, R. 1997. *The Anguish of Northern Uganda: Results of a field-based assessment of the civil strife in Northern Uganda.* Kampala: USAID.

Glasius, Marlies, Mary Kaldor and Helmut Anheier, eds. 2002. *Global Civil Society 2003.* Oxford: Oxford University Press.

Griffiths, Aaron and James Katalikawe. 2003. 'The Reformulation of Uganda Democracy', in Sunil Bastian and Robin Luckham, eds, *Can Democracy be Designed? The politics of institutional choice in conflict-torn societies*, London: Zed Books, 93–119.

Hampson, Fen Osler, Norman Hillmer and Maureen Appel Molot, eds. 2001. *The Axworthy Legacy.* Toronto: Oxford University Press.

Hansen, Holger Bernt and Michael Twaddle, eds. 1998. *Developing Uganda.* Oxford: James Currey.

Haynes, Jeff. 2003. 'Tracing Connections between Comparative Politics and Globalization',' *Third World Quarterly* 24 (6): 1029–47.

Holmgren, Torgny, Louis Kasekende et al. 2000. 'Uganda', in Shantayanan Devarajan, David Dollar and Torgny Holmgren, eds, *Aid and Reform in Africa: Lessons from ten case studies*, Washington, DC: World Bank.

Howe, H M. 1998. 'Private Security Forces and African Stability: the case of Executive Outcomes', *Journal of Modern African Studies* 36 (2): 307–31.

Hubert, Don. 2000. *The Landmine Ban: A case study in humanitarian advocacy.* Occasional Paper No.42. Providence, RI: Watson Institute.

Human Rights Watch. 2003a. *Stolen Child: Abduction and Recruitment in Northern Uganda.* Vol. 15, No.7 (A): 1–31.

Human Rights Watch. 2003b. *Abducted and Abused: Renewed conflict in Northern Uganda.* Vol. 15, No.12 (A): 1–77.

HURIPEC (Human Rights and Peace Centre). 2003. *The Hidden War, The Forgotten People.* Kampala: Faculty of Law, Makerere University.

ICISS. 2001. *The Responsibility to Protect: Report of the International Commission on Intervention and State Sovereignty.* Two vols. Ottawa: International Development Research Centre (IDRC), December.

International Alert. 2000. 'The Privatization of Security and Peacebuilding: a framework for action.' [Online] Available at www.international-alert.org.

IRIN. 2003. 'Report.' April and July. Humanitarian News and Analysis from the UN Office of Co-ordination of Humanitarian Affairs at www.irinnews.org.

Kappel, Robert et al. 2004. *The Missing Links: Uganda's economic reforms and pro-poor growth.* Leipzig: University of Leipzig for GTZ, February.

Khadiagala, Gilbert M. and Terrence Lyons, eds. 2001. *African Foreign Policies: Power and process.* Boulder, CO: Lynne Rienner for SAIS.

Klein, Naomi. 2000. *No Logo: Taking aim at the brand bullies.* London: Flamingo.

Kwesiga, Joy. 2000. *Women's Access to Higher Education in Africa: Uganda's Experience.* Kampala: Fountain Press.

Kyango-Nsubunga, John. 2004. 'Uganda: the politics of "consolidation" under Museveni's regime, 1996–2003', in Taisier M. Ali and Robert O. Matthews, eds, *Durable Peace: Challenges for peacebuilding in Africa*, Toronto: University of Toronto Press, 86–112.

Lemke, Douglas. 2003. 'Review Article: African lessons for international relations research.' *World Politics* 56 (2): 114–38.

Lister, Sarah and Warren Nyamugasira. 2003. 'Design Contradiction in the "New Architecture of Aid"? Reflections from Uganda on the roles of civil society organisations', *Development Policy Review* 21 (1): 93–106.

MacLean, Sandra J., H. John Harker and Timothy M. Shaw, eds. 2002. *Advancing Human Security and Development in Africa: reflections on NEPAD.* Halifax, Nova Scotia: Centre for Foreign Policy Studies.

Maiguashca, Bice. 2003. 'Introduction: Governance and Resistance in World Politics', *Review of International Studies* 29 (Special issue): 1–22.

Mbabazi, Pamela. 2005. *Supply Chains and Liberalisation of the Milk Industry in Uganda.* Kampala: Fountain Publishers.

Mbabazi, Pamela K., Sandra J. MacLean and Timothy M Shaw. 2002. 'Governance for Reconstruction in Africa: challenges for policy communities/coalitions', *Global Networks* 2 (1): 31–47.
Mkandawire, Thandika. 2001. 'Thinking about Developmental States in Africa', *Cambridge Journal of Economics* 25: 289–313.
Mugaju, Justus and J Olaka-Onyango, eds. 2000. *No-Party Democracy in Uganda: Myths and Realities*. Kampala: Fountain Press.
Museveni, Yoweri K. 1997. *Sowing the Mustard Seed: The struggle for freedom and democracy in Uganda*. Basingstoke: Macmillan.
Musisi, Nakanyike B and Nansozi K Muwanga. 2003. *Makerere University in Transition 1993–2000*. Oxford: James Currey.
Nadvi, Khalid. 2004. 'Globalization and Poverty: How can global value chain research inform the policy debate?' *IDS Bulletin* 35(1), January: 20–30.
Nannyonjo, Justine. 2004. 'Conflicts, Poverty and Human Development in Northern Uganda'. Paper presented at EGDI/WIDER Conference on Making Peace Work, Helsinki, June.
Nelson, Paul. 2002. 'The World Bank and NGOs', in Vandana Desai and Robert Porter, eds, *The Companion to Development Studies*. London: Arnold, 499–504.
Nhema, Alfred G., ed. 2004. *The Quest for Peace in Africa: Transformations, democracy and public policy*. Utrecht: International Books in association with OSSREA.
OECD. 2004. 'Security System Reform and Governance: Policy and good practice.' DAC Guidelines and Reference Series, Paris: OECD.
Office of the Prime Minister. 2003. 'IDP Numbers – For Soroti Cabinet Meeting.' Government of Uganda, 11 November.
Osaghae, Eghose E. 2001. 'The Role and Function of Research in Divided Societies: the case of Africa', in Marie Smyth and Gillian Robinson, eds, *Researching Violently Divided Societies: Ethical and methodological issues*. London: Pluto for UNU Press, 12–33.
Pain, Dennis. 1997. *'The Bending of Spears': Producing consensus for peace and development in Northern Uganda*. London: London International Alert with Kacoke Madit, December.
Parpart, Jane L and Timothy M Shaw. 2002. 'African Development Debates and Prospects at the turn of the Century', in Patrick J. McGowan and Philip Nel, eds, *Power, Wealth and Global Equity: An international relations textbook for Africa*, eds. 2nd edn. Cape Town: Oxford University Press, 296–307.
Payne, Anthony. 1999. 'Reframing the Global Politics of Development', *Journal of International Relations and Development* 2 (4): 369–79.
Prunier, Gérard. 2004. 'Rebel Movements and Proxy Warfare: Uganda, Sudan and the Congo (1986-99).' *African Affairs* 103 (412): 359–83.
Quadir, Fahimul, Sandra J. MacLean and Timothy M. Shaw. 2001. 'Pluralisms and the Changing Global Political Economy: Ethnicities in crises of governance in Asia and Africa', in Fahimul Quadir et al., eds, *Crises of Governance in Asia and Africa*, Aldershot: Ashgate, 3–30.
Refugee Law Project. 2004. *Behind the Violence: Causes, Consequences and the Search for Solutions to the War in Northern Uganda*. Refugee Law Project Working Paper Number 11, February.
Reinikka, Ritva and Paul Collier, eds. 2001. *Uganda's Recovery: The role of farms, firms and government*. Washington, DC: World Bank.
Reno, William. 2002. 'Uganda's Politics of War and Debt Relief', *Review of International Political Economy* 9 (3): 415–35.
Shaw, Timothy M. 2003. 'Human Development, Security and the Prospects for African Governance in the Twenty-first Century: lessons from/for Uganda and the Great Lakes Region', in Bruce Morrison, ed., *Transnational Democracy in Critical and Comparative Perspective: Democracy's range reconsidered*, Aldershot: Ashgate, 107–18.
Shaw, Timothy M. 2004a. 'Africa', in Mary Hawkesworth and Maurice Kogan, eds, *Routledge Encyclopedia of Government and Politics*, 2nd edn. London: Routledge, 1184–97.
Shaw, Timothy M. 2004b. 'Uganda as an African 'Developmental State'? Prospects for human development/security at the turn of the century', in Graham Harrison, ed., *Global Encounters: International political economy, development and globalization*. Basingstoke: Palgrave Macmillan, 63–73.
Shaw, Timothy M. 2004c. 'International Development Studies in the Era of Globalization … and Unilateralism.' *Canadian Journal of Development Studies* 25 (1):17–24.
Shaw, Timothy M. 2005. 'From Terrorism to Human Development/Security in Africa? Progressing beyond anarchy and conflicts for resources and survival?' in Christopher Ankersen, ed., *Global Terrorism after 9/11*, Cambridge: Polity.
Shaw, Timothy M. and Janis van der Westhuizen. 2004. 'Trade and Africa: transforming fringe into franchise', in Brian Hocking and Steven McGuire, eds, *Trade Politics*, 2nd edn. London: Routledge, 90–102.
Shaw, Timothy M. and Julius E Nyang'oro. 2000. 'African Renaissance in the New Millennium? From anarchy to emerging markets?', in Richard Stubbs and Geoffrey R. D. Underhill. eds, *Political Economy and the Changing Global Order*, 2nd edn. Toronto: Oxford

University Press, 275–84.
Shearer, David. 1998a. *Private Armies and Military Intervention*. IISS Adelphi Paper 316. London: International Institute for Strategic Studies.
Shearer, David. 1998b. 'Outsourcing War.' *Foreign Policy* 112 (Fall): 68–81.
Smillie, Ian, Lansana Gberie and Ralph Hazelton. 2000. *The Heart of the Matter: Sierra Leone, diamonds and human security*. Ottawa: Partnership Africa Canada.
Soderbaum, Fredrik and Timothy M. Shaw, eds. 2003. *Theories of New Regionalism: A Palgrave Reader*. Basingstoke: Palgrave Macmillan.
Tangri, Roger and Andrew M. Mwenda. 2001. 'Corruption and Cronyism in Uganda's Privatization in the 1990s', *African Affairs* 100 (398): 117–33.
Tangri, Roger and Andrew M. Mwenda. 2003. 'Military Corruption and Ugandan Politics Since the Late 1990s', *Review of African Political Economy* 98: 539–52.
Taylor, Ian and Philip Nel. 2002. 'New Africa, Globalisation and the Confines of Elite Reformism: "Getting the rhetoric right", getting the strategy wrong', *Third World Quarterly* 23 (1): 163–80.
Thomas, Caroline. 2000. *Global Governance, Development and Human Security*. London: Pluto.
Tomlin, Brian et al., eds. 1998. *To Walk without Fear: The global movement to ban landmines*. Toronto: Oxford University Press.
Uganda Bureau of Statistics. 2003. *Uganda National Household Survey 2002/2003*. Report on the Socio-Economic Survey. Entebbe: Uganda Bureau of Statistics.
Uganda Government. 2003. 'Background to the Budget.' Entebbe: Government Printer, June.
UNCTAD. 2003. *Investment and Technology Policies for Competitiveness: Review of Successful Country Experiences*. Technology for Development Series, Geneva: UNCTAD/ITE/IPC.
UNDP. 1994. *Human Development Report 1994*. New York: Oxford University Press.
UNDP. 1999. *Human Development Report 1999*. New York: Oxford University Press.
UNDP. 2000. *Uganda Human Development Report 2000*. Kampala: UNDP.
UNDP. 2002. *Uganda Human Development Report 2002*. Kampala: UNDP.
UNDP. 2003a. *Uganda Human Development Report 2003*. Kampala: UNDP.
UNDP. 2003b. 'Uganda Mid-Year Review'. New York and Geneva. Internet, May.
UNOCHA (UN Office for the Coordination of Humanitarian Affairs). 2004. *Humanitarian Update* Vol. VI, Issue I.
Van Acker, Frank. 2004. 'Uganda and the Lord's Resistance Army: The new order no one ordered', *African Affairs* 103 (412): 335–57.
Villalon, Leonardo A and Philip A Huxtable, eds. 1998. *The African State at a Critical Juncture: Between disintegration and reconfiguration*. Boulder, CO: Lynne Rienner.
Vlassenroot, Koen and Timothy Raeymaekers. 2004. 'The Politics of Rebellion and Intervention in Ituri: The emergence of a new political complex?' *African Affairs* 103 (412): 385–412.
World Bank. 2000. *Country Assistance Strategy: Uganda*. Washington, DC: World Bank.
World Bank. 2002. *World Bank Group Work in Low-Income Countries Under Stress (LICUS): A task force report*. Washington, DC: World Bank, September.
World Food Programme. 2003. *Uganda: Projected 2003 Needs*. Kampala: World Food Programme.
World Food Programme. 2004. 'Emergency Report No. 20'. [Online] Available at http://www.who.int/disasters/country.cfm
World Food Programme (WFP) (14 May 2003). 'Emergency Report No. 20 of 2003'.

Notes

1 Existing household survey data in Uganda on income and poverty trends show that a third of the chronically poor and a disproportionate number of households moving into poverty are in northern Uganda where the security situation has not permitted growth in incomes (Uganda Government 2003).

2 In the *New Vision* of 27 Jan. 2004 in the Women's Vision section, an article, 'A dog's life for mothers in Gulu Protected Camp', highlighted the appalling conditions in the camps: 'the maternal mortality rate is 700 out of 100,000 deliveries (yet national figure is 500), the infant mortality ratio is 172:1,000 (yet the national figure is 88) and Pabbo camp, with a population of 60,000 people and an average of 3200 births per year, has only one midwife.'

3 Aid grew from US\$ 228m. in 1986 to US\$ 905m. in 2000, which has had implications for the increased debt, despite HIPC. Thus, in spite of being forgiven over US\$ 1 billion since 1999, Uganda's debt burden has continued to grow at a rate of US\$ 108m a year, and today stands at US\$ 3.9billion.

4 For example, there has been a growth from 50,000 telephone lines in 1995 to over half a million mobile phone subscribers courtesy of Celtel, MTN and UTL.

5   United Nations, *Uganda Mid-year Review* (May 2003). New York and Geneva, p. 4.
6   The Tri-Star factory, based in Bugolobi, a few kilometres from the heart of Uganda's capital city, Kampala, is headed by a Sri Lankan businessman, Veluppilai Kananathan. About 3000 women have so far been recruited and trained on the job in various areas of specialization such as hemming skirts, stitching pockets or attaching buttons.
7   One of us has produced a doctoral thesis – the first in the Faculty of Development Studies at MUST, on internal supply chains around a national sector: milk (Mbabazi 2005).
8   (I)NGOs, national and local NGOs, faith-based groups and community-based organizations (CBOs), and households have played a crucial role in Uganda's HIV/AIDS efforts. Community-level responses have been essential in a variety of initiatives, including home-based care, support for orphans and vulnerable children, and HIV/AIDS prevention and mitigation, much of this work being carried out through community-based and religious organizations. By 1997, there were at least 1,020 NGOs and CBOs involved in HIV/AIDS work in Uganda (World Bank 2000). In September 2003, Dr Alex Coutinho, Executive Director of TASO, noted that there were 2,500 NGOs working on HIV/AIDS in Uganda. Civil society was providing 90 per cent of post-test counseling and care. Seventy per cent of Ugandans on Anti-Retroviral Drug Treatments (ART) were receiving treatment services from the Joint Clinical Research Center. NGOs and CBOs were also providing nutritional supplementation to 35,000 persons living with HIV/AIDS (PLWHA). One of the key players in the response to the HIV/AIDS epidemic in Uganda has been TASO, established in 1986, which provides care and support to approximately 60,000 AIDS patients and their families, as well as over 1,000 orphans. TASO was the first indigenous AIDS organization in Africa and now serves as a global role model. With seven centers across Uganda, it continues to play a major role in AIDS care, education, and support. Among its many projects, it is working with the World Food Program to provide food aid support to families affected by HIV/AIDS. Other key organizations include the Uganda Network of AIDS Service Organizations, the National Forum of PLWHA Networks, the National Guidance and Empowerment Network of PLWHA, the AIDS Information Center, Hospice Uganda, the National Community of Women Living with HIV/AIDS, the Uganda Youth Anti-AIDS Association, and Uganda Women's Effort to Save Orphans (see http://www.unaso.or.ug/members.php).
9   Some critics have contended that this development is largely a result of state patronage, considering that the NRM ruling elite to a large extent originate from Mbarara District.
10 See http://www.ugandadish.ord/mbarara.doc (accessed May-2004)
11 See: http www.db.idpproject.org/sites/idpsurvey.nsf/wviewsingleEnv/ugandaprofile+summary (Accessed May 2004)
12 See Human Rights Watch 2003b (http://www.Human Rights Watch.org/reports/2003/uganda0703/).
13 Even in northern Uganda, it is the NGOs that are largely responsible for providing assistance, such as health care and food, to internally displaced persons and trying to maintain the infrastructure.
14 See the website http://www.unesco.org/hiv/IATT_Education/AIDS-Ed_3-5-03_Murphy. ppt.
15 The second largest recent source of foreign exchange in Uganda for the last two years has been remittances from Ugandans living abroad, a condition that has set the government thinking of ways in which to send/encourage more Ugandans to go aboard for 'Kyeyo' (manual/odd jobs).
16 The data are based on the statistical definition of northern Uganda as consisting of 13 districts only.
17 See: http www.db.idpproject.org/sites/idpsurvey.nsf/wviewsingleEnv/ugandaprofile+summary (Accessed May 2004)
18 The NRM government has on many occasions undermined any steps towards a non-military solution to the war in northern Uganda, seeming to insist on solving the problem through military means with an apparent lack of commitment to non-military solutions. Apart from the infamous move by the top big-wigs in government giving a seven-day ultimatum to the LRA in February 1994 – at a time when the then Minister for Pacification of the north was said to be on the verge of brokering a negotiated settlement – there has been a repeated call by the army to fight its way to victory. Furthermore, in early 2000 President Museveni signed a blanket Amnesty passed by the Ugandan Parliament, but at the same time he claimed that he did not believe in it – 'We should apply the law of Moses; an eye for an eye and a tooth for a tooth to bring discipline in society' he instead suggested. (*New Vision*, 21 January 2000).

Index